Newsweek

Periscope Almanac 2009

Year in Review through the Lens of Periscope

KAPLAN) PUBLISHING

This publication is designed to provide accurate and authoritative information in regard to the subject matter covered. It is sold with the understanding that the publisher is not engaged in rendering legal, accounting, or other professional service. If legal advice or other expert assistance is required, the services of a competent professional should be sought.

© 2008 Newsweek, Inc.

Published by Kaplan Publishing, a division of Kaplan, Inc.
1 Liberty Plaza, 24th Floor
New York, NY 10006

All rights reserved. The text of this publication, or any part thereof, may not be reproduced in any manner whatsoever without written permission from the publisher.

Printed in the United States of America

10 9 8 7 6 5 4 3 2 1

ISBN-13: 978-1-4277-9831-2

Kaplan Publishing books are available at special quantity discounts to use for sales promotions, employee premiums, or educational purposes. Please email our Special Sales Department to order or for more information at kaplanpublishing@kaplan.com, or write to Kaplan Publishing, 1 Liberty Plaza, 24th Floor, New York, NY 10006.

Table of Contents

Letter from the Editor v

Campaign 2008 1

National Affairs 97

International Affairs 155

The Economy 195

War 215

Culture and the Arts 241

China and the Olympics 351

Society and Living 363

Appendix: Best of 2008 431

    2008 Presidential Primary Time Line 432

    2008 Beijing Summer Olympics Medals 447

    2008 Nobel Laureates 450

    2008 Pulitzer Prizes 451

    2008 Academy Awards 453

    2008's Top Movies 458

    2008 Tony Awards 459

LETTER FROM THE EDITOR

Wow.

The old Chinese saying goes, "May you live in interesting times." It was meant as a curse, but sometimes it feels like a blessing. In 2008, like no other year in recent memory, it was a little of both. And let's all agree on this much: 2008 was really, *really* interesting. Two American wars, one in slow decline, the other in sharp escalation. A crippling financial crisis—unparalleled since the Great Depression of the 1930s—that spread, like a swift, airborne virus, around the world, leaving capsized economies in its wake. The brutal tragedy of the deadly Sichuan earthquake in China, followed in a matter of months by communal redemption: a mesmerizing Olympic Games of unique beauty and historic athletic achievement.

And of course, a presidential campaign for the ages, culminating on November 4 with a result that was at once astonishing and, owing to the unanimity of the pre-election polls, strangely inevitable. When Barack Obama, just 47 years old and with less than a single term as a U.S. senator under his belt, was finally chosen to be the 44th President of the United States of America, there was the vaguest hint of an anti-climax. The element of surprise, even with something as unlikely and previously unthinkable as the election of an African-American president, was all but gone by the time it actually came to pass. Let's face it: in the final days and hours, there was doubt, but there was never any serious doubt. All that remained was for the votes to be counted and—at least for his 70 million supporters—for the party to begin.

From *Newsweek*'s 16th floor headquarters in midtown Manhattan, we could hear it for hours into the early morning while we closed our special Presidential Election issue: from the sidewalks and streets down below, a non-stop chorus of ecstatic cheers and cathartic shrieks, yellow cabs blaring their horns in rhythmic syncopation. Harlem in particular, the capital of black America, was in a state of total delirium, with men and women in their 70s, 80s, and 90s weeping over a day they never imagined they'd live to see. And around the globe, citizens and newspapers celebrated a revived and redeemed image of a nation that, over the last eight years, many had come to view with dismay and skepticism. Once again, America's capacity to surprise and inspire had electrified the world.

The world needed some good news. On almost all other fronts, it was an anxious, unsettling year. Before Obama began his run to the presidency with a victory in the Iowa caucus on January 3, the major story on the international stage was the reverberations from the horrific assassination of former Pakistani prime minister Benazir Bhutto just before the new year. That set the grim tone for a year in which Islamofascism seemed to gain strength in Bhutto's homeland and in neighboring Afghanistan at precisely the moment when the economic might of the West began to crack and crumble. Despite a global war on terror that is now in its sixth year, Al Qaeda is, by all accounts, stronger than it has ever been since 9/11. The countries arrayed against the forces of Islamist terror, meanwhile, are weary and distracted by problems closer to home. This is the predicament that Obama will inherit when he takes control of the country in January.

It is a challenge that will only be magnified by America's economic duress. When the sub-prime lending crisis dominated the news in the year's early months, it was, for too many

Americans, like a fight raging down the block: close enough to see and hear, but too far away to feel threatened oneself. Then, for the next few months, the ills of the economy receded back to being a private anxiety: a crucial election issue, for sure, but one that still wasn't burning white hot. Then came September: banks began folding by the day; the stock markets plummeted; hard earned dollars vanished from retirement accounts in a blink; and millions of Americans were living in homes that were suddenly worth less than the mortgage they still had left to pay.

The U.S. economy went from being *an* issue in the presidential election to the *only* issue. Indeed, while there were many reasons for John McCain's defeat in November, most pundits believe his point of no return came in the third week of September, on the day that Lehman Brothers collapsed. The Republican presidential nominee told an audience in Jacksonville, Florida, that "the fundamentals of the economy are strong." Within 10 days, McCain had reversed course, calling the economic crisis so dire that he needed to suspend his campaign and, perhaps, the first presidential debate. But his flailing performance—he was right the second time, but too late—sealed his fate. Americans of all stripes had caught on much faster than he did, and in politics, you can't afford to be too slow with voters. They wanted answers, and McCain didn't have any. Or, at the least, he didn't have them quick enough.

The plight of the economy came in a year when Americans finally confronted the reality that, in the 21st century, the power of the purse might reside elsewhere. The ubiquity of China in the news—the violent suppression of protests in Tibet, the Sichuan earthquake, the Beijing Olympics—underscored its growing role on the world stage. A newly aggressive Russia, flush with petro-dollars and content with Vladimir Putin's bellicose foreign policy, seemed to embark on a new post-Cold War strategy to contest American hegemony: if not openly hostile, then actively a thorn in the side. The rest of the world, which had spent the past eight years so angry with America, was beginning to imagine a post-American age.

And yet, this was not an imagined future that filled the international community with joy—it came with reluctance and anxiety. How else to explain the outpouring of joy and relief across the world when America elected Barack Obama? This was not a good year, not at all—but it sure was interesting. And it ended with a single stroke that gave billions of people more hope than they've felt in a generation.

Devin Gordon
Senior Editor, "Periscope"

Campaign 2008

YEAR IN REVIEW

"This whole thing," said former president Bill Clinton at the start of the primary season back in January, "is the biggest fairy tale I have ever seen." For much of America, that's what it must have felt like on the morning of November 5, when everyone woke up to the news that the country had elected the first African-American president in U.S. history. Did it actually happen? Was it all a dream? But it was real—and perhaps most remarkable of all, it wasn't even close.

The other question so many of us wondered about that morning: is it really over? In the middle of it, the 2008 presidential campaign was, by turns, inspiring, exhilarating, infuriating, offensive, and absurd—but it was also the Greatest Show on Earth for ten relentless months. And lest we forget, as we reflect on matters as trivial as flag pins and Joe the Plumber, it was the greatest civic moment in this nation's history. Approximately 120 million people—many of whom waited patiently in lines for hours—had cast their vote in an epochal election.

For the victor, Barack Obama, the 47-year-old U.S. senator from Illinois, it began with a single word: Iowa. Entering the primary campaign as a virtual afterthought to Sen. Hillary Clinton (who was running essentially as an experienced incumbent), Obama knew that his only chance was a statement victory—a signal to the country that "the skinny kid with a funny name" was for real. With rapturous speeches, he won by nine points. Clinton finished third. In the aftermath, Clinton's husband uttered that now-famous line about the Obama fairy tale, setting a pattern: Obama's opponents always underestimated him, and never hid their scorn toward someone who had not waited his turn. First Clinton, then Sen. John McCain, both of whom realized too late that they were in the fight of their lives.

In the general election, the pundits and the public expected skin color to be a defining and decisive issue. But if anything, it may have been a net-positive for Obama. It propelled African-American voters to the polls in historic numbers, and earned him victories in historically red Southern states such as Virginia. The Reverend Jeremiah Wright, whose fiery sermons threatened to derail his former parishioner's campaign in March, barely rated an appearance by the fall. Not that Obama didn't take some body blows. It's amazing, in retrospect, that so many Americans voted for an unpatriotic, terrorist-loving, Marxist, elitist, Muslim celebrity with a middle name picked, he joked, "by someone who obviously didn't think I would ever run for president." To hear his opponents tell it, Obama was apparently the riskiest man alive.

But in the end, it was Obama's tranquility—his grace, his preternatural calm—that convinced a majority of Americans that he was the right person to lead a nation in peril. Although it seemed to be a masterstroke at the time, McCain's running mate choice of Alaska governor Sarah Palin ended up badly damaging voters' image of him as a steady leader. The choice, in some ways, turned this presidential election into a referendum on Palin's capacity to lead the country—and too many Americans found her wanting. In a peculiar irony, the junior senator—and not the war veteran and lion of the Senate—came to be seen by the majority of the country as the steady leader we so desperately need. And it wasn't even close.

WEEK OF JANUARY 7

FIRST PERSON

The 1,440-Minute Cycle

As "Stumper," NEWSWEEK's *blogger covering the 2008 election, Andrew Romano is obsessed—understandably—with watching the press watch the campaign. His take on the "media primary":*

Is there a dirtier phrase in politics than "the media"? Some days it's hard to see why you hate us—"you" being liberals, conservatives, candidates and all other carbon-based life forms. There's as much good journalism getting done now as, say, 40 years ago. But other days, I get it. Take Nov. 20, 2007. At 9 a.m., Barack Obama launched a comprehensive education plan at a Manchester, N.H., high school; an hour later he told students that he "got into drinking," "experimented with drugs" and "wasted a lot of time" as a teenager. Obama had already written about his wayward youth. But the press perked up. "That's going to be the story of the day," said one reporter. By noon, OBAMA ON PAST SUBSTANCE ABUSE was atop the Drudge Report. Education, to say the least, was not.

This is the first presidential election to move at the speed of the Internet. After years of dismissing bloggers as peanut galleryists in pajamas, every major media outlet is requiring reporters to provide a daily play-by-play at its in-house blog. (Me? Guilty as charged.) Meaning we're now stuck with a 1,440-minute news cycle. In theory, that's dandy (no hiding); in practice, it totally skews the signal-to-noise ratio. While the demand for campaign news has exploded, the supply hasn't. (Did more really "happen" in 2007 than 2003, or 1983, or 1923?) To fill the void, reporters resort to the tiny blips, slips and digits that constitute the "horse race." And candidates, des-

> **To fill the void, reporters resort to the tiny blips, slips and digits that constitute the "horse race."**

perate for attention, provide the grist.

No wonder you're mad. Three weeks after Obama's appearance in Manchester, Carolyn Washburn, editor of The Des Moines Register, launched her newspaper's Republican debate by saying, "We're going to focus on issues Iowans say they still want to know more about." When the roster didn't include Iraq or immigration, the pundits pounced. "The worst debate in Western history," said Charles Krauthammer. And yet Washburn delivered: taxes, education, global warming and trade. There were no snowmen, no slapfests. The 1,440/7 media emerged empty-handed. Iowans emerged informed. Who did a better job? We report. You decide.

RACE

Lost in the Obama Era

Jesse Jackson can still get a crowd going—when he can find one. He appeared at a Los Angeles restaurant this fall, primed to discuss school dropout rates and home foreclosures. But only eight people showed up, mostly reporters. It's no longer Reverend Jackson's day in the sun, or any other black leader's whose

> **So where does that leave the leaders to whom black America has long turned in times of crisis— Jackson, and the Revs. Andrew Young and Al Sharpton?**

name isn't Barack Obama. So where does that leave the leaders to whom black America has long turned in times of crisis—Jackson, and the Revs. Andrew Young and Al Sharpton? At times they can seem like jealous, cranky old men, as in December when Young suggested Bill Clinton was "every bit as black as Barack." Or when Jackson said Obama was "acting white" by skipping a giant rally for the Jena Six.

But it's not just jealousy. They are also frustrated by mainstream voters' eager

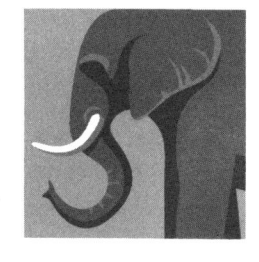

JANUARY | Campaign 2008-5

embrace of an African-American raised without a traditional African-American experience—who's not, in other words, an "angry black man." Reared in Hawaii by white grandparents, Obama didn't have a family history of segregation and Jim Crow laws. And sources close to all three reverends say the men are hurt that Obama hasn't sought their advice, even privately. (Still, Jackson has endorsed Obama.) The leaders appreciate Obama's dilemma. They know he'd lose many white voters if he reached out to leaders known primarily for advocating black issues. Obama's refrain is that there is just one America. It may be what America wants to hear—but the three lions of the old school couldn't disagree more.

—ALLISON SAMUELS

WEEK OF JANUARY 14

ANALOGY CHECK

This Stage Isn't Big Enough for Two Seabiscuits

History repeats itself, but not without a few wrinkles. We make the comparisons—and then we pick them apart.

THE COMPARISON

Bathed in Iowa's afterglow, Republican Mike Huckabee and Democrat John Edwards both seized on the same hackneyed metaphor for their candidacy: each man says he's Seabiscuit, the underdog racehorse that upset Triple Crown winner War Admiral in 1938.

WHY IT WORKS

It better suits Huckabee, who came from nowhere to win, while Edwards is still stuck in the "behind" portion of his "come-from-behind" story. But like Seabiscuit, both men are populist competitors. Also, the 1938 horse race occurred in ... November. Hmm.

WHY IT DOESN'T

Seabiscuit was on the track with only one other Thoroughbred; both Huckabee and Edwards are in crowded fields, with no incumbent—no War Admiral. But where it really breaks down is on the simplest level: Seabiscuit was a horse. —Devin Gordon

WEEK OF JANUARY 28

POLITICS

Leading Democrats to Bill Clinton: Pipe Down

Prominent Democrats are upset with the aggressive role that Bill Clinton is playing in the 2008 campaign, a role they believe is inappropriate for a former president and the titular head of the Democratic Party. In recent weeks, Sen. Edward Kennedy and Rep. Rahm Emanuel, both currently neutral in the Democratic contest, have told their old friend heatedly on the phone that he needs to change his tone and stop attacking Sen. Barack Obama, according to two sources familiar with the conversations who asked for anonymity because of their sensitive nature. Clinton, Kennedy and Emanuel all declined to comment.

On balance, aides to both Bill and Hillary still see Bill as a huge net plus in fund-raising, attracting large crowds and providing a megaphone to raise doubts about Obama—even if some of those doubts are distortions. But there's concern that in hatcheting the Illinois senator and losing his temper with the news media (last week he thrashed a San Francisco TV reporter for asking about a lawsuit filed by Clinton-backing teachers union members to limit the number of Nevada caucuses), Clinton is drawing down his political capital and harming his role as a global statesman. "This is excruciating," says a member of the Clintons' circle, who asked for anonymity. "But the stakes couldn't be higher. It's worth it to tarnish himself a bit now to win the presidency."

During a December taping with PBS's Charlie Rose, a frustrated Clinton called Obama "a roll of the dice," as aides tried to end the interview. Then, in New Hampshire, he argued angrily that the story of Obama's principled position on the Iraq War was a "fairy tale," a charge few reporters bought. Rep. James Clyburn of South Carolina, the top-ranking African-American in Congress and officially neutral, found Clinton's tone insulting and said so publicly.

When the former president called Kennedy, the Massachusetts Democrat gave Clinton an ear-

> "In the event of an unexpected drop in poll numbers, this plane will be diverted to New Hampshire."
> —Sen. Hillary Clinton, January 2008
>
> *Perspectives*

ful, telling him that he bore some blame for the injection of race into the contest. In any event, both Hillary and Obama made peace on the race issue at the Las Vegas debate. The Clinton camp now fears that Kennedy is leaning toward Obama, according to the Clinton source, though Kennedy's office says he is making no endorsement "at this time."

Clinton aides admit the boss sometimes goes off script. Obama officials say this itself should be a campaign issue. Greg Craig, who coordinated Clinton's impeachment defense in 1998 and is now a senior Obama adviser, argues that "recent events raise the question: if Hillary's campaign can't control Bill, whether Hillary's White House could."

There is little precedent for a former president's engaging in intra-party attacks. In 1960, Harry Truman criticized the idea of a Roman Catholic president and tried briefly to stop John F. Kennedy's nomination. "I urge you to be patient," he told JFK publicly. But in 2000, former president George Bush declined to attack his son's GOP primary opponent, John McCain.

Clinton is undeterred by the criticism and will likely keep hammering Obama if he thinks it helps Hillary. "History will judge the impact on the Clinton legacy, not daily or weekly political reporters," says Matt McKenna, Bill Clinton's press secretary. —JONATHAN ALTER

CAMPAIGN '08

A Troll Through the Muck

For more than a month, former Arkansas governor Mike Huckabee has tried to distance himself from a secretive political group, financed by several of his campaign donors, that has been bombarding voters with "robo-calls" attacking his Republican campaign rivals. The automated calls—up to one million have been made in South Carolina alone—allege that John McCain wants to conduct research on "unborn babies" and that Mitt Romney set up "sanctuary cities for illegal aliens." "I wish they would stop," Huckabee said to reporters when asked about the calls last week.

While publicly decrying the attacks, however, Huckabee has done nothing else to stop them. In fact, Patrick Davis, executive director of Common Sense Issues, the group behind the calls, told NEWSWEEK that he's had no contact at all with the Huckabee campaign.

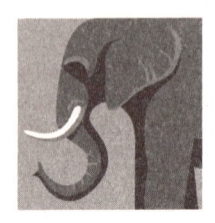

Davis said his group is "helping to define the issues" and that it may launch a new wave of robo-calls during the run-up to contests in Florida and key Super Tuesday states. Huckabee spokeswoman Alice Stewart says federal election laws bar the campaign from telling Davis directly to stop. "It's a violation to coordinate with them," she said. Not so, said Kenneth Gross, a top federal election lawyer who is unaffiliated with any campaign. "Telling somebody not to do something does not constitute coordination," he said. "I don't see why they couldn't send a missive that says, 'We don't want these calls to continue'."

Common Sense Issues' campaign isn't the only attack under scrutiny. An Oregon pollster who organized a pro-McCain phone survey has been subpoenaed by the New Hampshire attorney general's office, which wants to know who ordered the survey. According to a script obtained by an Oregon TV station, the pollsters asked voters whether their views would be affected if they knew Romney "got the Mormon Church" to help him avoid the Vietnam War; by contrast, the poll noted that McCain's son, a Marine, is serving in Iraq. (Operators are instructed to pronounce it "eye-rack.") The pollster, Bob Moore, told NEWSWEEK that he plans to fight the subpoena and keep his client secret. He insists his phone poll was a legitimate exercise in "message testing."

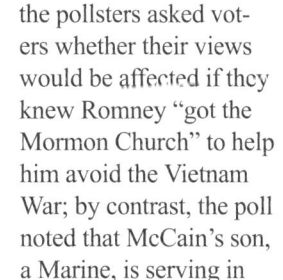

—MARK HOSENBALL *and* MICHAEL ISIKOFF

THE DIGNITY INDEX

I Lost by Less Than That—I Demand a Recount!

A weekly mathematical survey of bad behavior that measures, on a scale of 1 to 100, just how low a person can go.

He received just 2 percent of the New Hampshire primary vote, but Democrat **Dennis Kucinich** is paying $27,000 for a recount. Because, gosh darn it, he is **sure** he got 3 percent. Score: **17**

BET boss **Bob Johnson's** cheap flick at Obama's teenage misdeeds was low, but his claim that he was alluding to Obama's "community organizing" was worse. It also made no sense. Score: **68**

Elections are ugly everywhere, but **South Carolina**, with its smears, push polls and Confederate flags, turns "ugly" into an art. Score: **92**

WEEK OF FEBRUARY 11

CAMPAIGN 2008

Barack + GOP = 'Obamacans'

Susan Eisenhower is more than just another disappointed Republican. She is also Ike's granddaughter and a dedicated member of the party who has urged her fellow Republicans in the past to stick with the GOP. But now Eisenhower, who runs an international consulting firm, is endorsing Barack Obama. She has no plans to officially leave the Republican Party. But in Eisenhower's view, Obama is the only candidate who can build a national consensus on the issues most important to her—energy, global warming, an aging population and America's standing in the world. "Barack Obama will really be in a singular position to attract moderate Republicans," she told NEWSWEEK. "I wanted to do what many people did for my grandfather in 1952. He was hugely aided in his quest for the presidency by Democrats for Eisenhower. There's a long and fine tradition of crossover voters."

Eisenhower is one of a small but symbolically powerful group of what Obama recently called "Obamacans"—disaffected Republicans who have drifted away from their party just as Eisenhower Democrats did and, more recently, Reagan Democrats in the 1980s. They include lifelong Republican Tricia Moseley, a former staffer for the late senator Strom Thurmond, the onetime segregationist from South Carolina. Now a high-school teacher, Moseley says she was attracted to Obama's positions on education and the economy.

Former GOP congressman Joe Scarborough, who anchors MSNBC's "Morning Joe," says many conservative friends—including Bush officials and evangelical Christians—sent him enthusiastic e-mails after seeing Obama's post-election speeches in Iowa, New Hampshire and South Carolina. "He doesn't attack Republicans, he doesn't attack whites and he never seems to draw these dividing lines that Bill Clinton [does]," Scarborough told NEWSWEEK.

Plenty of Republicans are immune to the Obama swoon, of course. The Republican National Committee has emphasized a recent analysis suggesting that

> **Even small numbers of Obamacans can help reinforce the candidate's unity message.**

Obama had the most liberal voting record in the Senate last year. But even small numbers of Obamacans can help reinforce the candidate's unity message and bolster his "electability" argument. In Iowa, the campaign identified more than 700 registered Republicans who committed to caucusing for Obama (although staffers say they don't yet know how many showed up to vote). And in the Super Tuesday state of Colorado, campaign staffers say they found more than 500 erstwhile Republicans who were willing to switch their party registration. Even if Republicans don't convert in more significant numbers, the friendly outreach may blunt the ferocity of GOP attacks. One senior aide to John McCain has already said he's reluctant to attack Obama: last year McCain's adman Mark McKinnon wrote an internal memo promising not to tape ads against the Illinois Democrat if he were the nominee.

—RICHARD WOLFFE

ELECTION QUIZ

Which of Us Just Ran for President?

Once upon a time, as many as 18 people were competing in the race for the White House. Now, heading into Super Tuesday, the field is down to a small handful of front runners. But before we turn to the survivors, let's take a fond look back at the also-rans with a game of "Did I Run or Not?" Four of the men shown below ran for president; four of them did not—and one of those four is currently in jail. Can you guess who's who?

1. Jim Gilmore
Fmr. Gov., Va.
2. Ted Stevens
Sen., Alaska
3. Duncan Hunter
Rep., Calif.
4. Lindsey Graham
Sen., S.C.
5. Evan Bayh
Sen., Ind.
6. Bob Ney
Fmr. Rep., Ohio
7. Mike Gravel
Fmr. Sen., Alaska
8. Tom Tancredo
Rep., Colo.

Answers: those who ran—1. Gilmore, 3. Hunter, 7. Gravel, 8. Tancredo. those who didn't run—2. Stevens, 4. Graham, 5. Bayh, 6. Ney (currently serving a 30-month prison term for his conduct in the Jack Abramoff lobbying scandal).

WEEK OF FEBRUARY 18

CAMPAIGN FINANCE

Accounting 101: The Clintons

Hillary and Bill Clinton are not nearly as wealthy as, say, Mitt Romney, but her recent $5 million emergency loan to her own presidential campaign has made one thing clear: the Clintons are doing just fine, thanks. Other matters related to the loan are less clear. For starters, where did Hillary Clinton find the cash? Her aides were reluctant to provide details. In e-mail responses to NEWSWEEK, campaign spokesman Howard Wolfson wrote that she "didn't borrow any money" and noted that she "has made considerably more than" $5 million from her 2003 memoir, "Living History." The loan itself, Wolfson wrote, "came from Senator Clinton's [50 percent] share" of joint resources with her husband.

Clinton, unlike rival Barack Obama, has not released her tax returns. But disclosure forms that Clinton filed with the Senate provide some clues to her family finances. They show Bill Clinton has earned tens of millions of dollars in recent years giving speeches at rates of up to $450,000 apiece. During one week in 2006, the former president collected $1.7 million for talks in Europe and South Africa. (He also collected speaking fees from Citigroup, Goldman Sachs, the Mortgage Bankers Association and other big firms.) The documents are more circumspect about other Clinton financial interests, including his annual income as a "partner" in billionaire pal Ron Burkle's businesses and from Vinod Gupta's InfoUSA. Both payouts are listed as "over $1,000"—a description that is legally adequate but not very enlightening. Clinton spokespeople recently said the former president is preparing to sever his dealings with Burkle and Gupta "should Senator Clinton become the Democratic nominee," in order to avoid any conflicts. But Gupta, whose firm has paid Bill at least $3.3 million since 2003, told NEWSWEEK that he is still paying fees to him; Burkle's spokesman could not be reached for comment.

When the Clintons left the White House, they were drowning in legal bills. But by last year, they had sufficient cash flow to

> **Bill Clinton has earned tens of millions of dollars in recent years giving speeches at rates of up to $450,000 apiece.**

pay off the mortgage on their home in Washington, D.C. According to local property records, they took out a 30-year, $1.995 million mortgage in 2001 but paid it off in full last November. (The Clintons also own a home in Chappaqua, N.Y., but there is no record of a similar mortgage payoff.) Election-law experts say that it is legal for candidates to make unlimited loans—or outright donations—to their own campaigns, as long as they do not seek public campaign subsidies. Candidates can even charge their campaigns interest, as John Kerry did in 2004. But a Clinton campaign adviser, who

---

CAMPAIGN 2008: EDUCATION

Time to Put the Candidates to the Test

In this primary season, one major issue has been all but missing in action: education. Most experts agree that No Child Left Behind, President Bush's plan for closing the achievement gap between rich and poor kids, is a noble effort. But it has serious downsides. It punishes struggling schools, turns classes into test-prep factories and has caused some states to lower, not raise, standards. How will the next president fix it? NEWSWEEK asked two experts, the Education Sector's Thomas Toch and Jeanne Allen, chief of the Center for Education Reform, to evaluate each candidate's plan. Then we assigned grades. —PEG TYRE

THE STANCE

Clinton: She has Bill bashing NCLB on the campaign trail but also pushed for more federal money to help schools give higher-quality tests. Would track every student in every grade. Wants more money for early-childhood education.

Obama: Wants the federal government to measure skills such as conducting research, defending ideas and solving problems. Wants schools to use test data to help shape lessons. Favors performance pay for teachers.

Huckabee: Wants to give states more power to decide the benchmarks for NCLB; eliminate test-prep factories by ensuring all kids get music, arts education, and give parents the option of transferring kids out of failing schools.

McCain: Likes NCLB but wants to change the tone: support, not confront, failing schools. He'd revamp Head Start and improve rates of high-school graduation, too. Supports the spread of charter schools and vouchers.

continued

asked not to be identified discussing internal matters, said that fundraisers have been told that Hillary's loan is interest-free. Wolfson wrote that the campaign had signed a promissory note for the loan and that Clinton could forgive the debt if she wishes, though the campaign adviser said "she expects to get paid back when this is over."

—MARK HOSENBALL and MICHAEL ISIKOFF

DELEGATES

They Make Me Feel Super

You've probably never heard of Debra Kozikowski, but Hillary Clinton and Barack Obama sure have. Since Super Tuesday, heavyweights from both campaigns have been wooing Kozikowski, a Massachusetts Democratic Party official. Obama enlisted her governor, Deval Patrick, to deliver a plea on the candidate's behalf, while Clinton asked party elder Harold Ickes to speak with her. Why the star treatment? Kozikowski is a "superdelegate," one of 796 politicians and party loyalists who get a vote for the nomination. This year their votes could make all the difference. In most presidential elections, one candidate racks up enough delegates in primaries and caucuses to capture the 2,025 needed to cinch the nomination; the superdelegates are mostly symbolic. But so far the primaries have yet to produce a clear winner—and as a result, those 796 "supers" suddenly have a lot more friends. (The Republican Party does not have superdelegates.)

Louisiana superdelegate Claude (Buddy) Leach told NEWSWEEK he

---

THE REALITY CHECK

B− Allen say she's currying favor with the largely Democratic teacher's unions, who hate the rigid NCLB, while still backing accountability. Toch says look for her to warm up to the idea of performance pay if she's the nominee.

B+ Well intentioned, but Allen warns that the skills he likes are hard to test statewide. Toch applauds efforts to test kids on thinking, not regurgitation. Performance pay, he warns, is easy to talk about but hard to execute.

D+ States set benchmarks now, says Toch, and they range from laudable to laughable. (Arkansas: the pits.) Allen says locals are often the worst culprits in bad schooling. A national barometer ensures states educate all kids.

B+ Allen applauds his stance on school choice but frets that supporting schools means coddling school boards and unions. Ensuring more kids graduate from high school is a good idea, says Toch, but how exactly do you do that?

received at least 10 calls from the campaigns last week. Some of the callers, he says, were also happy to discuss Leach's other great passion besides politics: duck hunting. "I'm flattered that they'd call someone as unimportant as I am," Leach says. His wife isn't. "My phone has become her nemesis." It's against party rules to promise anything in exchange for votes, so the schmoozing has been more subtle: *If you come with us, we'll remember it later.* Leach and Kozikowski say they're still mulling their pick, though Kozikowski has been more wowed by Obama's efforts. She loved talking with her friend Governor Patrick, but wasn't so sure about Hillary's choice of old-timer Ickes. "He doesn't meet my definition of star quality," she says. "I'm holding out for Jack Nicholson."

> Those 796 "supers" suddenly have a lot more friends.

—ELEANOR CLIFT *and* SARAH ELKINS

WEEK OF FEBRUARY 25

THE DIGNITY INDEX

Chris Matthews Can't Fight This Feeling Anymore

A weekly mathematical survey of dubious behavior that measures, on a scale of 1 to 100, just how low a person can go

Looking to the fall, **Barack Obama** gives John McCain a backhanded compliment by citing McCain's "half century" of service. We get it, Barack: he's old. Not cool. Score: **7**

MSNBC host **Chris Matthews** says a recent Obama speech sent "a thrill up my leg." Not sure what that means, except that his Oba-man crush is getting out of control. Score: **23**

After the Roger Clemens hearing he pressed for turns into a mudslinging fiasco, Rep. **Henry Waxman** says he "regret[s]" holding it in the first place. Ladies and gentlemen: Congress! Score: **59**

ANALOGY CHECK

We're Gonna Party Like It's 1984

History repeats itself, but not without a few wrinkles. We make the comparisons, then pick them apart.

THE COMPARISON

Pundits have noted parallels between the Hillary Clinton-Barack Obama contest and another razor-tight Democratic battle: 1984's Walter Mondale-Gary Hart matchup. Clinton, like Mondale, entered the race as the well-oiled establishment choice, while the younger, looser Obama echoes Hart's call for a new generation of leadership.

WHY IT WORKS

In both, the inspiring upstart shocks the party by capturing more states. (Hart won 28 to Mondale's 24; at press time, Obama leads Clinton, 20 to 12.) Still, neither 2008 candidate is likely to win the 2,025 pledged delegates needed to clinch the nod, meaning the climax may also mirror 1984; with superdelegates deciding the outcome.

WHY IT DOESN'T

Superdelegates and big-state wins put Mondale 623 ahead of Hart before the June primaries: hardly a nail-biter. Then 40 more supers put Mondale over the top. But if Obama's lead (about 130) holds, supers will face a tougher choice: the insider who (barely) lost the delegate battle versus the upstart who (barely) won. —ANDREW ROMANO

WEEK OF MARCH 10

CAMPAIGN 2008

Attack Ads On the Way

A new series of TV commercials featuring sinister photos of Osama bin Laden may signal what's to come this fall: a wave of secretly financed political attack ads. The spots, by a group called Defense of Democracies, which was just created by former Republican National Committee spokesman Cliff May, target 15 House Democrats for their failure to support a White House-backed electronic-spying bill. May told NEWSWEEK he plans to spend $2 million on the ads, but declined to identify who is financing the effort, saying he set up the group as a tax-exempt nonprofit—known in the federal tax code as a "501(c)(4)"—thereby permitting it to engage in political advocacy without disclosing donors.

The ads spotlight what some experts say is a gaping loophole in the campaign-finance laws. On Dec. 26, 2007, the Federal Election Commission quietly issued new rules in the wake of a Supreme Court decision last June that give more latitude for 501(c)(4) groups to run political "electioneering" ads without disclosing contributors. That helped blow open the floodgates. In 2004, the chief conduit for such ads were so-called 527 groups, among them the Swift Boat Veterans for Truth. But 527s had to identify donors. Now, said one GOP consultant who asked not to be identified talking strategy, "everybody

> "They targeted [former Alabama governor] Don Siegelman because they could not beat him fair and square."
> —*Former AZ attorney general Grant Woods, March 2008*
> *Perspectives*

ANALOGY CHECK

Win (the Next) One for the Huckster

History repeats itself, but not without a few wrinkles. We make the connections, then pick them apart.

THE COMPARISON

Mike Huckabee's insistence on staying in the primary race against John McCain, despite calls from his own party to quit, resembles Ronald Reagan's doomed GOP bid in 1976. Reagan fought Gerald Ford all the way to the convention, where he lost on a close first-ballot vote. He won the White House four years later. Could Huck do it, too?

WHY IT WORKS

In both cases, a two-term governor (Arkansas for Huck, California for Reagan) known for his rhetorical gifts runs to the right of a moderate, party-backed candidate. Longtime Reagan strategist Ed Rollins is now Huckabee's campaign chair and is advising him to use Reagan's '76 strategy as a blueprint for another run in 2012.

WHY IT DOESN'T

A flurry of late primary wins got Reagan to within 100 delegates of Ford; Huck trails McCain by some 600 and seems unlikely to close the gap. Plus, Huck's support comes largely from religious conservatives. If he runs again, it's doubtful that he could rally the kind of broad coalition that Reagan built in 1980. —MATTHEW PHILIPS

is doing 501(c)(4)s because you don't have to disclose anything."

The rush to take advantage is underway. A consortium of liberal groups led by former Clinton chief of staff John Podesta announced plans last week for a $20 million campaign attacking John McCain for his Iraq War support. The ads are part of a $200 million "independent" effort that will aim to "define" McCain on a host of fronts, including his "temperament," said one participant who asked not to be identified discussing the consortium's plans. Freedom's Watch, a conservative 501(c)(4) whose board includes Las Vegas casino billionaire Sheldon Adelson, is planning to spend up to $250 million attacking the eventual Democratic presidential nominee for being soft on Iraq. Meanwhile,

> "[Obama] cured my leprosy!"
> —Comedian Jon Stewart, March 2008
> Perspectives

veteran "oppo" researcher Dave Bossie says his longstanding Citizens United 501(c)(4) has begun work on a $10 million effort that will include a feature film about Barack Obama. Among the issues "on the table," Bossie told NEWSWEEK, are Obama's ties to indicted developer Tony Rezko and former Weather Underground radical William Ayers. (Innocuous in both cases, Obama says.) "What we are trying to do is educate and inform voters," Bossie says. They might never find out, though, who's paying for their education.

—MICHAEL ISIKOFF

BY THE NUMBERS

Promises, Promises

Presidential candidates vow daily to enact (pricey) legislation that will usher in an era of peace, prosperity and guilt-free eating. And while their most earnest vows often come a cropper after the transition from campaigning to governing (remember President Clinton's stimulus package and universal-health-care plan?), it's worth looking at the costs of such pledges. President George W. Bush, who promised a massive tax cut, pursued it with single-mindedness once in office. NEWSWEEK crunches the numbers on the top candidates' top priorities:

—DANIEL GROSS *and* DANIEL STONE

Barack Obama: Obamanomics is a lot like Rubinomics, which the Clintonites favored in the '90s. It would boost taxes on high earners (by letting Bush income-tax cuts expire) to fund targeted tax cuts for the middle class and new spending on health care; redeploy funding from Iraq to the war on domestic woe, and possibly lift the cap on the payroll tax to shore up Social Security.

Health Care*
$240 billion

Obama would let individuals and small companies buy health-care benefits similar to the ones that members of Congress get. (He'd mandate coverage for children.) Families that couldn't afford rates would be eligible for subsidies, while others would be covered by expanding Medicaid and SCHIP programs.

Education
$75 billion

He's pitching a refundable $4,000 tax credit on tuition and promising to raise Pell Grants to keep up with inflation. He's pledged $10 billion a year for a Zero-to-Five early-education plan (aiming for universal access to preschool); 40,000 scholarships for teachers, and grants for dropout-prevention programs.

Energy
$60 billion

Obama's pledged $150 billion over 10 years to transition into the next generation of energy. He'll double funding for research on clean energy, create a Green Jobs Corps and set up a five-year, $50 billion federal Clean Technologies Venture Capital Fund. He'll offset costs by auctioning off rights to emit carbon.

Hillary Clinton: Clinton would let the Bush tax cuts expire in 2010, and (like Obama) she'd end the loophole that lets hedge-fund managers pay lower tax rates than their secretaries. She plans to use the proceeds to beat down the deficit and pursue her signature issues: universal-health-care coverage, education reform, new savings programs, greener energy and housing aid.

Health Care
$400 billion

Clinton wants to extend health care to every American. She'd use tax credits to limit premiums to a fixed percentage of family income and expand rolls of Medicaid and the SCHIP children's coverage program. Expanding the pool of the insured should bring savings.

---

*All figures are first-term, four-year expenditures. sources: Congressional Budget Office, Joint Committee on Taxation, the Washington Post, McCain for President, Department of Veterans Affairs, Democratic National Committee, Hillary Clinton for President, Public Citizen, U.S. Public Interest Research Group, Obama for America, Republican National Committee, New York Times, Center on Budget and Policy Priorities

But costs will likely exceed $100 billion/year.

Education
$88 billion

For K-12, Clinton will leave behind No Child Left Behind, recruit thousands of new teachers and principals, aid at-risk youth and expand after-school programs. For college kids, she'd create a $3,500 college tax credit; increase Pell Grants and AmeriCorps scholarships, and invest in community colleges.

Energy
$58 billion

Clinton has a 10-year, $150 billion plan for the environment: create a $50 billion "strategic energy fund" (paid for in part by higher taxes for oil companies, which will invest in new sources of energy and technology), double funding for federal basic energy research and add $20 billion of Green Vehicle Bonds.

John McCain: After initially opposing the Bush tax cuts as a costly giveaway to the wealthy, McCain is now stumping to extend the rate reductions on income, capital gains, dividends and estates, which are largely set to expire in 2010. It's unclear how he will make up the lost revenue— $3.6 trillion over 10 years —while boosting defense spending and reining in the deficit.

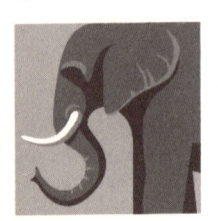

Defense
$550 billion

An ardent supporter of the surge, McCain has pledged to maintain U.S. presence in Iraq for 100 years if necessary. Victory has its price. Congressional Budget Office reports it costs some $10 billion per month for combat operations. Price tag for staying in Iraq at current troop levels through 2012: $550 billion.

Border security
$23.5 billion

McCain sponsored the Comprehensive Immigration Reform Act of 2006, whose reform of visa programs and immigration-control measures bears an $18.5 billion price tag through 2012. Additionally, he's pledged $5 billion in the next four yours for a high-tech fence along the U.S.-Mexico border.

Energy
$5 billion

He cosponsored the Climate Stewardship and Innovation Act of 2007, which would authorize $3.7 billion in federal subsidies for new nuclear power plants. He could revive an amendment that he sponsored to the Energy Policy Act of 2005; it would've given $1.5 billion to cap greenhouse gases at 2000 levels by 2010.

WEEK OF MARCH 17

CAMPAIGN 2008

In a Spat Over Secrecy, Two Rivals Go Their Separate Ways

After months of trying out various lines of attack against Barack Obama, Hillary Clinton seems to have found one that resonates with voters: raising doubts about whether Obama has the experience to be commander in chief. Obama has responded by hammering Clinton's penchant for secrecy. The Obama campaign criticizes Clinton for her refusal to disclose her tax returns, expedite the release of her White House records from the National Archives and share the names of donors to her husband's Presidential Library. Obama's charges got a boost last week when the Archives confirmed (in response to a USA Today Freedom of Information request) that it withheld 1,114 pages of White House documents on President Bill Clinton's controversial pardons of Marc Rich and others—including two felons who hired Hillary's brother Tony Rodham to get their pardon requests approved. The Clinton Library Foundation says the Archives made the decision. But an Archives spokeswoman says it did so based on a 2002 letter from Bill Clinton, who asked that documents involving confidential legal advice be "considered for withholding." "What the American people don't need is more George Bush secrecy in the White House," Obama campaign manager David Plouffe says.

Obama claims that his administration would be "open" and "transparent." To prove the point, his campaign released e-mails his Senate office exchanged with U.S. officials on behalf of a man imprisoned in Iraq. The intervention had the potential to cause trouble for Obama because the man, Aiham Al-Sammarae, was a business associate of Antoin (Tony) Rezko, the political fundraiser now on trial for corruption in Chicago. Obama has taken heat for his murky relationship with Rezko, a political fixer who had a part in Obama's purchase of a house. (Obama now calls that transaction "boneheaded" and says he has given Rezko-related campaign donations to charity.) Conservative bloggers have played up the

> "They're both not ready [for] that 3 a.m. call."
> —Susan Rice, a foreign-policy adviser to Sen. Obama, March 2008
> *Perspectives*

Al-Sammarae connection as a key to the Rezko story. Despite requests from NEWSWEEK, the Obama camp initially declined to release the e-mails. Late last week they did, and the e-mail exchange appears routine.

On Oct. 16, 2006, Obama's Senate office received a faxed plea from Al-Sammarae's son. A onetime Iraqi exile, Al-Sammarae returned to Iraq after Saddam's fall to serve as Iraq's Electricity minister but was sentenced to two years in prison for corruption. Al-Sammarae's son claimed in the fax that his father was railroaded for exposing Iraqi government incompetence, and feared his life was in danger in prison. (Neither Al-Sammarae nor his family responded to requests for comment.) Obama's office sent an inquiry to the U.S. consul in Iraq expressing the Al-Sammarae family's concern and requesting "an update on the status of this case." The consul responded with an e-mail explaining that the U.S. Embassy in Baghdad had monitored the case to ensure that Al-Sammarae was "being treated in a humane manner." Obama spokesman Bill Burton says the inquiry about Al-Sammarae "was based on a request from a constituent." Obama's office marked the file "no further action." Al-Sammarae escaped from prison and reportedly headed back to Chicago.

—MARK HOSENBALL *and* MICHAEL ISIKOFF

WEEK OF MARCH 24

CAMPAIGN 2008

A Delegate Loophole?

Citing wiggle room in an obscure, 26-year-old Democratic Party rule, Hillary Clinton's campaign is leaving the door open to the idea of attempting to persuade Barack Obama's pledged delegates to switch their votes at the last minute and back the New York senator—despite fears among some party officials that it could throw this summer's Denver convention into chaos.

The question of whether pledged delegates must stick to the candidate they were elected to vote for has prompted party chatter for weeks. Clinton herself drew notice last week during a NEWSWEEK interview when she said her delegate numbers aren't "bleak at all," even though by most counts she trails Obama by more than 100. "Even elected and caucus delegates are not required to stay with whomever they are pledged to," she added. Although her campaign quickly denied it was waging any effort to "flip" Obama's pledged delegates, Clinton's remarks weren't academic. After the 1980 battle between Jimmy Carter and Ted Kennedy, her chief strategist Harold Ickes noted, the party changed a rule that required pledged delegates to stick with their candidates no matter what. The current rule, adopted in 1982, states that pledged delegates "shall in all good conscience reflect the sentiments of those who elected them." A "good conscience" reason for a delegate to switch, Ickes told NEWSWEEK, would be if one candidate—such as, say, Clinton—was deemed more "electable." If delegates believe she has a better chance in November than Obama, Ickes said, "you bet" that would be a reason to change their vote. (He added, however, that the campaign is "focused" on winning over uncommitted superdelegates "at this point.")

Ickes's comments prompted a fierce comeback from Obama spokesman Bill Burton. "Despite repeated denials," he said, "the Clinton campaign finally admitted that they will go to any length to win." One party official, who asked for anonymity when discussing sensitive matters, said the strategy behind Clinton's invocation of the 1982 rule was clear: "They're trying to open up a window for some of the Obama people to change their minds." —MICHAEL ISIKOFF

> **"Even elected and caucus delegates are not required to stay with whomever they are pledged to," she added.**

WEEK OF MARCH 31

IRAQ

A Slip-Up, Then a Spin

An offhand assertion by Sen. John McCain last week has become a litmus test for one of the presidential campaign's biggest questions: who's really ready to be commander in chief? While in the Mideast, McCain asserted that it's "common knowledge ... that Al Qaeda is going back into Iran and receiving training and are coming back into Iraq from Iran."

After his friend and supporter, Sen. Joe Lieberman, whispered in his ear, McCain quickly corrected himself. "I'm sorry," he said, "the Iranians are training extremists, not Al Qaeda." Democrats pounced, saying McCain's comments show he doesn't even know the difference between Shiites in Iran and the Sunnis who run Al Qaeda. McCain's team shot back, calling the Dems naive about Iran. His supporters pointed to the 9/11 Commission finding that contacts likely occurred between Tehran and Al Qaeda. "This whole idea that Shiite Iran wouldn't aid Sunni extremists is laughable and would certainly be news to Hamas, the Al Aqsa Martyrs Brigade, Palestinian Islamic Jihad and the Taliban [all Sunni groups]," Randy Scheunemann, McCain's chief foreign-policy adviser, told NEWSWEEK.

Here's a reality check. While U.S. military and intelligence officials have occasionally suggested that Iran might be supporting Sunni militants, including Al Qaeda in Iraq, they have not publicly provided evidence of it. The two top U.S. commanders in Iraq, Gen. David Petraeus and his deputy, Gen. Ray Odierno, have not repeated such allegations. U.S. officials said last year they had indications that some Iranian munitions intended for Shiite militias might have ended up in Qaeda hands, but they said there was no hard evidence that this help was deliberate. Philip Zelikow, executive director of the 9/11 Commission and a former senior adviser (whose portfolio included Iran) to Secretary of State Condoleezza Rice, told NEWSWEEK that while there was evidence Iran had contacts with Al Qaeda before 9/11, "I don't recall anyone telling me of significant evidence linking Iran directly to Al Qaeda in Iraq." And McCain's comments? The facts, Zelikow said, "might have gotten embedded in his head in the wrong way." —MICHAEL HIRSH

CAMPAIGN 2008

Hillary: What's in a Name?

Preston Bynum still remembers Hillary Rodham. The former chief of staff for Arkansas Gov. Frank White, Bynum worked on White's campaign to oust a young Bill Clinton from the governor's mansion in 1980, an effort that succeeded in part because voters disapproved of Hillary's decision to keep her maiden name. "White was just very perceptive," Bynum told NEWSWEEK. "He would say, 'Can you believe they're married and she never took his name?' " Bynum said the flap underscored her exoticness in Arkansas. "She was still kind of a hippie," he recalled, adding that her style "just didn't sit well with people."

Soon enough, Hillary Rodham was Mrs. Bill Clinton. Governor White's widow, Gay, said she thinks Hillary's curtsy to Arkansas's old-fashioned mores helped Clinton defeat White in their 1982 rematch. "Right after my husband was elected, she pretty much became Hillary Clinton," White said. "It must have been received well." Webb Hubbell, Hillary Clinton's old friend from Little Rock's Rose Law Firm, said the furor "bothered her because she had her own identity. She had gone to law school, she had things going on that were her own."

The issue followed the Clintons to Washington. In a poll conducted just after Bill took office, 62 percent of respondents said the First Lady should be known as Hillary Clinton rather than Hillary Rodham Clinton. Later, a New York Times column asserted that "there have been . . . four wives of Bill Clinton": Hillary Rodham, Mrs. Bill Clinton, Hillary Clinton and, "rather suddenly about the time her husband became President," the full HRC.

Neel Lattimore, Clinton's deputy press secretary at the time, said that Hillary's inner circle was baffled by the obsession. Staff referred to her interchangeably as Hillary Rodham Clinton or Mrs. Clinton. Emphasizing that use of Rodham was "not some mandate from on high," Lattimore denies that the First Lady changed her name for political reasons. But the press never let it go. In 1999, Maureen Dowd wrote a satirical column addressed to "Ms. Rodham Clinton Rodham." Is it any wonder that in her Senate races and now in her presidential bid, Ms. Rodham Clinton Rodham has decided to keep it simple? The campaign goes with just Hillary, spokesman Jay Carson said, "because it reflects the warmth and familiarity people feel toward her."

> **Soon enough, Hillary Rodham was Mrs. Bill Clinton.**

—SUZANNE SMALLEY *and* MARTHA BRANT

WEEK OF APRIL 7

CAMPAIGN 2008

Keep Your Enemies Closer

Hillary Clinton is courting a Pennsylvania primary endorsement from an unlikely source: the Pittsburgh Tribune-Review, a newspaper owned by the Clintons' erstwhile archenemy, banking heir Richard Mellon Scaife. Once described by the Clinton White House as the "Wizard of Oz" behind what Senator Clinton called a "vast right-wing conspiracy" to smear the couple, Scaife published stories implying foul play in the death of Clinton aide Vince Foster, which investigators ruled a suicide.

But that was then. Now Hillary is running for president, and last week she gave a lengthy interview to the paper's editorial board and

---

ANALOGY CHECK

How About We Settle This in Private?

History repeats itself, but not without a few wrinkles. We make the connections, then we pick them apart.

THE COMPARISON

With the fate of the Clinton-Obama contest all but in the hands of the party's superdelegates, history buffs are reminded of another close election in which the outcome was decided by politicians: 1824, when Andrew Jackson won the popular vote but lost the election in the House after Henry Clay agreed to support John Quincy Adams.

WHY IT WORKS

Obama's failure to close out Clinton despite his popular vote cushion is similar to Jackson's predicament. If Clinton wins by way of superdelegates, Obama would likely echo Jackson's charge of a "corrupt bargain" in which the establishment silenced the people. And, as Jackson did, he could use it as a platform to run in four years.

WHY IT DOESN'T

The superdelegates will decide who gets to challenge John McCain, not who will be president, as the House did in 1824. Adams and Jackson were also both Democratic-Republicans, then the only major political party. Most significantly, the comparison only holds up if Clinton wins, and that appears unlikely at the moment. —MATTHEW PHILIPS

used the occasion to bash Barack Obama for his ties to the Rev. Jeremiah Wright. The Tribune-Review posted video excerpts of her remarks on its Web site along with a picture of her sitting next to Scaife. Scaife's lawyer and editorial-board member Yale Gutnick told NEWSWEEK that Clinton "made a deep and favorable impression" and that Scaife was "very impressed with what she had to say." The paper, he said, is waiting to see if Obama also appears in person before deciding whom to endorse.

Clinton's chat with Scaife is the latest twist in what looks like a concerted campaign to schmooze, if not neutralize, a man she once considered a deadly foe. Last summer Bill Clinton invited Scaife and Christopher Ruddy, author of Foster conspiracy stories, to lunch at his Harlem office. The result: Ruddy publicly praises him, and Scaife donated to a Clinton charity. Hillary Clinton's campaign spokesman Howard Wolfson said that the rapprochement with Scaife represents her willingness "to try to move beyond the fights of the '90s." —MARK HOSENBALL

ENOUGH ALREADY

No More Apologies

Everything wears out its welcome eventually. In this periodic feature, we say when.

Thank you, James Carville. Calling New Mexico governor Bill Richardson "Judas" because he decided to endorse Barack Obama rather than Hillary Clinton was tacky and

---

THE DIGNITY INDEX

A Former Bash Brother Trashes Yet Another

A weekly mathematical survey of dubious behavior that measures, on a scale of 1 to 100, just how low a person can go

GOP hopeful **John McCain** is selling tickets for seats on his Straight Talk Express. Cost: a $50 campaign donation. It's no Lincoln Bedroom, but the Coolidge Aisle Seat is lovely. Score: **6**

Another black eye for newspapers: the **Los Angeles Times** eats up a con man's tissue-thin lies for a story that pins a 1994 Tupac Shakur shooting on hip-hop mogul Puff Daddy. Score: **38**

In his new tell-even-more-all book, steroidal ex-slugger **Jose Canseco** fingers Alex Rodriguez as a juicer without facts or full explanation. Must be lonely in the gutter. Score: **73**

small—but at least the Ragin' Cajun didn't try to fudge the record or "take it back" like a 6-year-old in a playground. No, he stood by his big dumb words, faced the Orwellian flash mob and took his lumps. How . . . refreshing! Because you know what we're done with? The rejecting and the denouncing. The regretting and the apologizing. Enough. So thank you, James Carville, for bringing us a step closer to that future oasis of sanity where we all react how we ought to whenever someone says something stupid: we ignore it.

—DEVIN GORDON

WEEK OF APRIL 14

CAMPAIGN 2008

Peace and Bitterness

The Clintons are resisting the disclosure of a document that could help clarify the New York senator's claims that she was "instrumental" in Northern Ireland peacemaking. The document's unlikely author: Chelsea Clinton. As a Stanford University senior in 2001, the former First Daughter wrote a 150-page thesis on the subject. Her faculty adviser, Prof. Jack Rakove, has said that Chelsea spoke with her father "at some length" about the negotiations. But the Clinton camp has declined to make it public. Through Clinton aides, Chelsea has directed reporters to ask Stanford for the document. But Stanford says it doesn't have a copy in its library, and Rakove, who does have one, says that only Chelsea can give the green light. The thesis, says Clinton spokesman Philippe Reines, "was written to satisfy an academic requirement—not media curiosity."

Regardless of what Chelsea's thesis may reveal about her mother's role in the accord, some British officials remain sore at her father for one of his earliest decisions in the negotiating process. In 1994, Bill Clinton granted a U.S. visa to nationalist leader Gerry Adams at a time when the Provisional IRA, the clandestine affiliate of Adams's Sinn Fein movement, was still conducting a terrorist cam-

Major believes that Clinton's decision "set back the peace process," though Clinton was helpful later on.

paign. A source close to Britain's former prime minister Sir John Major, who asked for anonymity when discussing a sensitive matter, says Major believes that Clinton's decision "set back the peace process," though Clinton was helpful later on. Indeed, two years later, U.S. officials were red-faced when the IRA broke a truce and set off a massive bomb near London's Canary Wharf. Nancy Soderberg, a senior adviser on Ireland to Bill Clinton, said the State and Justice Departments and FBI all urged Clinton not to grant the visa because it would look like the U.S. was rewarding terrorism. But Soderberg, who initially opposed the visa, later concluded that it would hasten IRA involvement in the peace process—a judgment that she says history has vindicated.

Soderberg also said that Mrs. Clinton's involvement at the time with Ulster women's groups "really did support the peace process." Former Northern Ireland

---

ANALOGY CHECK

She's No Quitter, But What About Him?

History repeats itself, but not without a few wrinkles. We make the connections, then pick them apart.

THE COMPARISON

Despite increasing calls for her to drop out of the Democratic nomination race, Hillary Clinton insists that she's staying in because she's "never been a quitter." Her defiance brings to mind the protestations of Richard Nixon, who in his day leaned into such head winds—once successfully, and once to no avail.

WHY IT WORKS

During his veep run in 1952, facing illegal campaign donation charges, Nixon said in his "Checkers speech" that he would stay put, silencing calls for him to step aside. With her nomination hopes dimming, Clinton has similarly turned the pressure on her to quit into a display of her willingness to tough it out.

WHY IT DOESN'T

There's a big moral difference between weathering self-inflicted scandals and fighting back for the chance to win a still-unresolved election. Also, while Nixon did quit over Watergate in 1974—after saying for more than a year that he wouldn't—Clinton might never walk away. She could just lose. —MATTHEW PHILIPS

peace broker George Mitchell told NEWSWEEK that neither Hillary nor Bill sat at the peace table, as the discussions were limited to U.K. and Irish officials, and Northern Ireland politicians. But he reiterated Soderberg's view that Mrs. Clinton played a "helpful and supportive role" with Ulster women. She's still winning the Irish vote today: Clinton is slated to attend the Irish-American Presidential Forum in New York this week.

—MARK HOSENBALL, JOHN BARRY and DANIEL STONE

WEEK OF APRIL 21

THE DIGNITY INDEX

The Misspeller and the Misspeaker

A weekly mathematical survey of dubious behavior that measures, on a scale of 1 to 100, just how low a person can go.

In a new campaign ad, the presumptive Republican nominee spells his own name wrong. That's right: he's **Johm McCain,** and apparently he approved this message. Score: **8**

Democratic Party boss **Howard Dean** says his side won't bring up McCain's age (other than this once!) because Dems have "a higher ethical bar." How much higher? Score: **25**

After his wife "misspoke" about Bosnia, **Bill Clinton** "misspeaks" about her misspeaking, digging the hole deeper. Even she told him to let it go. Score: **58**

WEEK OF APRIL 28

POLITICS

Obama: Can't 'Swift Boat' Me

The Obama campaign is planning to expand its research and rapid-response team in order to repel attacks it anticipates over his ties to 1960s radical Bill Ayers, indicted developer Antoin Rezko and other figures from his past. David Axelrod, Obama's chief strategist, tells NEWSWEEK that the Illinois senator won't let himself be "Swift Boated" like John Kerry in 2004. "He's not going to sit there and sing 'Kumbaya' as the missiles

Campaign 2008-30 | APRIL

are raining in," Axelrod said. "I don't think people should mistake civility for a willingness to deal with the challenges to come." The move appears to be an acknowledgment that the Obama campaign may not have moved aggressively enough when questions about Ayers and Rezko first arose, and it comes amid fresh indications that conservative groups are preparing a wave of attack ads over the links.

Operatives such as David Bossie, whose Citizens United group made the Willie Horton ad that helped sink Michael Dukakis's 1988 presidential bid, are sharpening knives as expectations mount that Obama will be their target in the fall. Bossie says he is assembling material for TV spots about Obama's ties with Ayers, a Chicago professor and unrepentant former member of the Weather Underground, a group that bombed several government buildings to protest the Vietnam War. The Ayers issue bounced around right-wing media for months, but it received broad exposure at last week's debate on ABC, when Obama was asked a question about their relationship. Obama, who lives near Ayers in Chicago's Hyde Park, attended an event at Ayers's house when Obama ran for the state Senate in 1995—and served on the board of a nonprofit with him for several years. "Obama is aware of the acts Ayers committed when he was 8 years old and has called them 'detestable'," says spokesman Ben LaBolt, adding that Obama occasionally bumps into Ayers in his neighborhood "but has not seen him for months." At a recent dinner party, according to one guest who asked not to be identified discussing a private gathering, Ayers "ridiculed" the notion that Obama shared his left-wing views: "He thought the idea that there was a political connection between them was absurd." (Ayers declined to comment.)

Rezko's Chicago corruption trial, meanwhile, continues to raise questions for Obama. Last week a prosecution witness testified that Obama attended a 2004 party at Rezko's mansion for Nadhmi Auchi, an Iraqi tycoon who was later banned from the United States due to a fraud conviction in France. A spokeswoman for Illinois Lt. Gov. Pat Quinn told NEWSWEEK that the event was a sit-down dinner, at which Quinn made a brief speech welcoming Auchi to Chicago. According to court documents, Rezko later sought to enlist unnamed "Illi-

> "He's not going to sit there and sing 'Kumbaya' as the missiles are raining in," Axelrod said.

APRIL | **Campaign 2008-31**

nois government officials" for help lobbying the Feds to allow Auchi back into the country. A lawyer for Auchi says his client denies any wrongdoing in France and has no recollection of meeting Obama; the senator, who denies doing any favors for Auchi, "does not recall attending this event," says Obama spokesman LaBolt, nor does he "recall meeting Mr. Auchi at any other time."

—Mark Hosenball and Michael Isikoff

ABORTION

A Maverick, But He's No Moderate

John McCain boasts one of the most consistent pro-life voting records in the Senate, but he doesn't do much boasting about it. Even during the primaries—when touting his anti-abortion credentials could have scored with his conservative critics—he mostly avoided the subject. Why? "My record is clear," McCain said, when asked by reporters earlier this year. "I am a pro-life conservative."

But several pro-choice groups are nervous that his record isn't speaking loudly enough—that, on the contrary, it's been overshadowed by his reputation as a maverick who bucks the party line. Their fears are bolstered by a new Planned Parenthood survey, conducted in 16 likely battleground states, which shows that 23 percent of McCain's female, pro-choice supporters mistakenly believe he shares their views on abortion. An additional half of the respondents said they did not know enough to describe his position. "There's an enormous education gap," says Cecile Richards, president of Planned Parenthood, lamenting that most women "have no idea what John McCain's stance is."

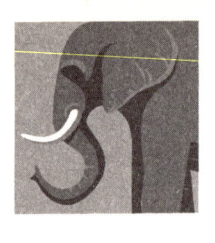

Pro-choice groups attribute that gap to voters who confuse McCain-the-maverick with McCain-the-moderate, based on his willingness to split from his party on certain issues. Abortion, though, isn't one of them. "The press describes him as a moderate maverick, so people take that to mean that he's pro-choice, or not as bad on choice," says Ted Miller, a spokesperson for NARAL Pro-Choice America. "But if you look at his voting record, he's nowhere near moderate." In an effort to correct such misimpressions, NARAL recently launched MeetTheRealMcCain.com and has begun buying up Google ads, like one that asks "Is McCain Pro-Choice?" and links to a NARAL site. "We can't take any knowledge for granted," says Miller, "so we're raising the questions." Planned Parenthood, meanwhile, is working on an "aggressive" educational campaign aimed at female voters in battleground states.

> **Half of the survey respondents said they did not know McCain's position on abortion.**

The National Right to Life Committee, a pro-life organization that recently endorsed McCain, says it welcomes the efforts of its rivals. "As more people learn of his desire to protect unborn children, that will help his campaign," says executive director David O'Steen. Finally, some common ground: the utility of informing voters about McCain's abortion record could be the one area where pro-life and pro-choice groups are in total agreement.

—SARAH KLIFF *and* HOLLY BAILEY

CAMPAIGN 2008

What Hillary's Got In Her Back Pocket

The e-mails come by the hundreds: prayers and Chinese proverbs, quotes and jokes, sent by Hillary Clinton's friends, intended to inspire and to buoy her through the tough times. The aphorisms are part of a collection Clinton has maintained all her life, starting in a scrapbook when she was a little girl, later as clippings in a binder she toted around as First Lady and, more recently, on her BlackBerry. On the eve of the Pennsylvania primary, Clinton offered NEWSWEEK's Karen Breslau an exclusive look at her collection, and she also opened up about issues of trustworthiness, getting emotional—and why she's staying in the race. Excerpts:

I hear your binder just went digital. Any examples of things people have sent to you that you'd like to share?

Here's one I love from Proverbs: "She sets about her work vigorously; her arms are strong for her task . . . She is clothed with dignity and strength; she can laugh at the days to come." [*Laughs*] I just thought that was so wonderful . . . Oh, of course, then everybody is constantly sending me the Churchill quote: [*Imitating a deep, gravelly voice*] "Never give in. Never give in. Never, never, never, never—in nothing great or small, large or petty, never give in, except to convictions of honor and good sense." I must have gotten a hundred copies of this one. It was so amazing, they came in a rush after I won Ohio and Texas and Senator Obama's supporters started saying I should get out.

You have any good jokes?

Here's a good one. Helen Clark, former prime minister of New Zealand: her opponents have observed that in the event of a nuclear war, the two things that will emerge from the rubble are the cockroaches and Helen Clark. [*Laughs*]

You've written about keeping a quote from Lee Atwater, the Republican consultant, saying on his deathbed that he wished he'd lived his life with more compassion. Any other unlikely candidates who've offered solace? Anything from Newt Gingrich saying "Keep your chin up, kid"?

Uh, no. But I have actually had a good relationship with him . . . [*Reading from BlackBerry*] "Dance as though no one is watching you, love as though you've never been hurt, sing as though no one can hear you." That's the only way I can sing! . . . Someone sent this to me after [someone posted a video of] me singing the national anthem on YouTube.

There has been tension reported in your campaign between "humanizing" you versus proving your mettle as commander in chief. Are you satisfied at this point with the fuel mixture or is it something you still are tinkering with?

I never saw that as a big contretemps. I'm the first woman with a serious chance to do this. We're making this up as we go. Nobody has any kind of formula or equation. We trigger expectations and reactions that are constantly causing us to re-evaluate what do people think and how do we best respond.

People say they admire your tenacity, but at some point it gets to the question: "But can she win? Look at the math." At what point does tenacity become denial?

But why don't people ask [Obama] the same question? Neither of us can win without superdelegates. Neither of us can

> "Why should I leave? I don't understand . . . Why don't people ask [Obama] the same question?"

possibly get to the nomination unless something totally unforeseen happens, without doing what we are doing now. Why should I leave? I don't understand that reasoning. I've won the states we have to win in the fall. I have a broader coalition that we have to build on in order to win in November. I believe my experience is much better suited to go toe-to-toe with John McCain. And it's up to voters, and to people who get selected as delegates, however that process occurs, to make that determination. But I'm not going to short-circuit the process.

We've seen in a number of polls recently the issue of trustworthiness, that you are consistently ranked lower than your rival. Our most recent NEWSWEEK Poll shows the same trend. And what do you do about it? It's not just Bosnia, it's broader.

If you have been subjected to incredible criticism, some of it justified—most of it not, in my opinion—for as long as I have, there is a lot of psychological research which is very clear that if someone says something negative about a person, even if it is disproved, there is a residue of perception that's left. I think it's a miracle that I'm doing as well as I am, that I'm in a close competition to be the Democratic nominee, that most people, if given the time, sort through all this stuff about me and they conclude that they can count on me to fight for them.

What do you carry with you from that experience when you grew emotional in New Hampshire? Have there been times where you find yourself going, "Oh, I'm doing too much policy, turn back to the heart"?

The idea that there is the me who cares about policy and then there's the "real me" just totally misunderstands me. I have worked my entire life to change and improve conditions for people. That's very important to me, because that's how I judge myself. I'm not asking someone to marry me. I'm asking them to vote for me . . . So, yes, I give the same speeches, talk about the same solutions over and over again, because I want someone to walk away from [a Clinton] event saying, "You know, I really liked that idea about taking the $55 billion away from special interests and I think she'll do it," instead of, "Aaaah, what a wonderful speech. And what does it mean? I don't know, but it sure made me feel good."

WEEK OF MAY 12

CAMPAIGN 2008

Something Wasn't Wright, So Oprah Left His Church

For any spiritually minded, up-wardly mobile African-American living in Chicago in the mid-1980s, the Trinity United Church of Christ was—and still is—the place to be. That's what drew Oprah Winfrey, a recent Chicago transplant, to the church in 1984. She was eager to bond with the movers and shakers in her new hometown's black community. But she also admired Trinity United's ambitious outreach work with the poor, and she took pride in upholding her Southern grandmother's legacy of involvement with traditional African-American houses of worship. Winfrey was a member of Trinity United from 1984 to 1986, and she continued to attend off and on into the early to the mid-1990s. But then she stopped. A major reason—but by no means the only reason—was the Rev. Jeremiah Wright.

According to two sources, Winfrey was never comfortable with the tone of Wright's more incendiary sermons, which she knew had the power to damage her standing as America's favorite daytime talk-show host. "Oprah is a businesswoman, first and foremost," said one longtime friend, who requested anonymity when discussing Winfrey's personal sentiments. "She's always been aware that her audience is very mainstream, and doing anything to offend them just wouldn't be smart. She's been around black churches all her life, so Reverend Wright's anger-filled message didn't surprise her. But it just wasn't what she was looking for in a church." Oprah's decision to distance herself came as a surprise to Wright, who told Christianity Today in 2002 that when he would "run into her socially . . . she would say, 'Here's my pastor!'" (Winfrey declined to comment. A Harpo Productions spokesperson would not confirm her reasons for leaving the church.)

> "Oprah is a businesswoman, first and foremost," said one longtime friend.

But Winfrey also had spiritual reasons for the parting. In conversations at the time with a former business associate, who also asked for anonymity, Winfrey cited her fatigue with organized religion and a desire to be involved with a more inclusive ministry. In time, she found one: her own. "There is the Church of Oprah now," said her longtime friend, with a laugh. "She has her own following."

Friends of Sen. Barack Obama, whose relationship with Wright has rocked his bid for the White House, insist that it would be unfair to compare Winfrey's decision to leave Trinity United with his own decision to stay. "[His] reasons for attending Trinity were totally different," said one campaign adviser, who declined to be named discussing the Illinois senator's sentiments. "Early on, he was in search of his identity as an African-American and, more importantly, as an African-American man. Reverend Wright and other male members of the church were instrumental in helping him understand the black experience in America. Winfrey wasn't going for that. She's secure in her blackness, so that didn't have a hold on her." And while Winfrey, who has endorsed Obama and campaigned on his behalf, had long understood the perils of a close association with Wright, friends say she was blindsided by the pastor's personal assault on Obama. "She felt that Wright would never do anything to hurt a man who looked up to him as a father figure," said her close friend. "She also never thought he'd intentionally hurt someone trying to make history and change the lives of so many people."

—ALLISON SAMUELS

OPINION

A Tax Holiday to Nowhere

Hillary Clinton has joined John McCain in proposing the most irresponsible policy idea of the year: suspending the federal gas tax this summer. Both of them know it's a terrible pander, and yet they're pushing it anyway for crass political advantage. The goal is to depict Barack Obama as an out-of-touch elitist, by any means necessary. I could highlight a long debate among economists on suspending the gas tax, but there is no debate. Not one respectable economist supports the idea, unless they are official members of the Clinton or McCain campaigns. For relief at the pump, try tax credits—but not this. Why is the gas pander so bad? Let's count the ways:

■ It's a direct transfer of money from motorists to oil companies. If the federal excise tax were lifted, oil companies would simply raise prices and pocket most of the difference. Clinton's proposal to recover the $8.5 million with a windfall profits tax on oil companies sounds nice but won't happen. Besides, she already committed that money to developing renewable energy.

■ It offers taxpayers only peanuts. The American Association of State Highway and Transportation Officials says the average savings to motorists would be $30. That measly number was somehow not included in Clinton's explanation of her support.

■ It sends more hard-earned money to the Middle East, which is terrible for our national security. Remember, 15 of the 19 terrorists on 9/11 came from Saudi Arabia. How did they get the terrorist training? Oil money.

■ It makes it more likely you'll have a car accident or waste even more time in traffic. The proceeds from the gas tax go for highway construction and upgrades. Because the tax was last raised 15 years ago, our infrastructure is a mess, with potholes and dangerous

> **Suspending the tax would result in a direct transfer of money from motorists to oil companies.**

crossings practically everywhere. Thousands of repair projects will be further delayed.

■ It will cost 300,000 construction jobs, according to Transportation. Which makes it kind of ironic when Clinton starts her rallies saying she wants "jobs, jobs, jobs."

—JONATHAN ALTER

WEEK OF MAY 19

CAMPAIGN 2008

Mac's Convention Quandary

After John McCain nailed down the Republican nomination in March, his campaign began wrestling with a sensitive personnel issue: who would manage this summer's GOP convention in St. Paul, Minn.? Thecampaign recently tapped Doug Goodyear for the job, a veteran operative and Arizonan who was chosen for his "management experience and expertise," according to McCain press secretary Jill Hazelbaker. But some allies worry that Goodyear's selection could fuel perceptions that McCain—who has portrayed himself as a crusader against special interests—is surrounded by lobbyists. Goodyear is CEO of DCI Group, a consulting firm that earned $3 million last year lobbying for ExxonMobil, General Motors and other clients.

Potentially more problematic: the firm was paid $348,000 in 2002 to represent Burma's military junta, which had been strongly condemned by the State Department for its human-rights record and remains in power today. Justice Department lobbying records show DCI pushed to "begin a dialogue of political reconciliation" with the regime. It also leda PR campaign to burnish the junta's image,

> **Who would manage this summer's GOP convention in St. Paul?**

drafting releases praising Burma's efforts to curb the drug trade-and denouncing "falsehoods"by the Bush administration that the regime engaged in rape and other abuses."It was our only foreign representation, it was for a short tenure, and it was six years ago," Goodyear told NEWSWEEK, adding the junta's record in the current cyclone crisis is "reprehensible."

Another issue: DCI has been a pioneer in running "independent" expenditure campaigns by so–called 527 groups, precisely the kind of operations that McCain, in his battle for campaign-finance reform, has denounced. In 2004, the DCI Group led a pro-Bush 527 called Progress for America, which was later fined (along with several other 527s on both sides of the political divide) for violating federal election laws. Goodyear, however, says that DCI is "not in the 527 business anymore."

Ironically, Goodyear was chosen for the post after the McCain campaign nixed another candidate, Paul Manafort, who runs a lobbying firm with McCain's campaign manager, Rick Davis. The prospect of choosing Manafort created anxiety in the campaign because of his long history of representing controversial foreign clients, including Philippine dictator Ferdinand Marcos. More recently, he served as chief political consultant to Viktor Yanukovich, the former Ukrainian prime minister who has been widely criticized for alleged corruption and for his close ties to Russia's Vladimir Putin—a potential embarrassment for McCain, who in 2007 called Putin a "totalitarian dictator." "The Ukrainian stuff was viewed as too much," says one McCain strategist, who asked not to be identified discussing the matter. Manafort did not return calls for comment.

—MICHAEL ISIKOFF

ELECTIONS

How Global Politics Got Starbucked

For Western democracies, the U.S. presidential race is more than a source of spectacle—it's a preview of a key American export: campaign tactics. "Elections have become as similar as Starbucks," writes London Times editor James Harding, whose stinging new book, "Alpha Dogs," traces the international campaign playbook back to the

---

THE DIGNITY INDEX

And on the Seventh Day, Rush Rested

A weekly mathematical survey of bad behavior that measures, on a scale of 1 to 100, just how low a person can go.

We wanted to give **Hillary Clinton** a pass this week, but her line about Obama's "weakening" sway with "white Americans" is the kind of polarizing dig that crippled her run. Score: **6**

Along with swinging the outcome in Indiana with his Operation Chaos, the all-powerful **Rush Limbaugh** also ripped a tree out of the ground with his bare hands and ate it. Score: **32**

Rep. **Vito Fossella** gets busted for DWI while en route to see his mistress and love child, then sobs on the House floor, then resigns. Otherwise, a good week. Score: **53**

Sawyer Miller Group, a U.S. firm launched in the 1970s that married Madison Avenue with Pennsylvania Avenue, selling candidates like consumer goods in an "electronic democracy." It was among the first political consultancies to wrap intellectual voter appeals in emotional clothes—and it was good at it, steering to victory four senators, six governors and overseas leaders including Czechoslovakia's Vaclav Havel and Israel's Shimon Peres before dissolving in the early 1990s. Today, Sawyer Miller has acolytes inside the campaigns of Hillary Clinton, Barack Obama and John McCain. And its techniques—nonstop polling, sloganeering, attack ads—have become worldwide staples.

Overseas, in fact, it's not uncommon for candidates to sing an American tune, word for word. Last year British Prime Minister Gordon Brown nipped a line from Al Gore's failed U.S. presidential run. "Sometimes people say I'm too serious," he joked, just as Gore did in 2000, before pledging to "[never] let you down." Similarly, Newt Gingrich's 1994 "Contract With America" became Silvio Berlusconi's 2001 "Contract With the Italian People." "The things that drive elections are the same in Nebraska as they are in Ghana," Sawyer Miller alum Mark McKinnon, architect of George W. Bush's ad campaigns in 2000 and 2004, tells Harding.

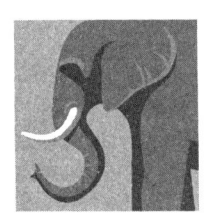

Harding is conflicted about this turn of events. Sound bites can oversimplify discourse—but that very simplicity helps engage voters, he notes, drawing political

> **"Alpha Dogs" reads like an episode of "Mad Men"... swaggering carpetbaggers fueled by idealism.**

debate out of smoke-filled back rooms. "We now live in a tactical age, not an ideological one," he tells NEWSWEEK. As a result, "managers, speechwriters, pollsters and get-out-the-vote specialists have more power than we'd like to admit." "Alpha Dogs" often reads like an episode of "Mad Men": a tale of swaggering carpetbaggers fueled by idealism and undone by greed. Working out of a discreet Manhattan office—located next door to the Copacabana nightclub and downstairs from Sammy Davis Jr.'s apartment—Sawyer Miller brought millions of new voters to the polls. Its tactics, though, have disillusioned just as many.

—TONY DOKOUPIL

WEEK OF MAY 26

CAMPAIGN 2008

McCain vs. Lobbyists

Stung by the news that two aides once lobbied for the Burmese junta, John McCain last week rolled out a sweeping new conflict-of-interest policy for his campaign, requiring all staffers to fill out questionnaires identifying past or current clients that "could be embarrassing for the senator." Aides say that McCain was furious over the Burma connection (which he learned from a NEWSWEEK story) and was "adamant" about banning campaign workers from serving as foreign agents or getting paid for lobbying work.

But the fallout may not be over. One top campaign official affected by the new policy is national

---

ANALOGY CHECK

Beware of the (Third) Party Crashers

History repeats itself, but not without a few wrinkles. We make the comparisons—then pick them apart.

THE COMPARISON

When former GOP congressman Bob Barr launched a Libertarian bid for the White House last week, politicos recalled another intervention by a third-party candidate with spoiler potential. In 2000, Ralph Nader seemed to nick enough Democratic votes to harm Al Gore's campaign. Could Barr do the same to Republican John McCain?

WHY IT WORKS

Nader's consumer-rights work and progressive platform attracted voters who saw Vice President Gore as a status quo Washington insider. Similarly, Barr's antiwar credentials and evangelical roots may siphon off Republicans who are dissatisfied with either McCain's patience in Iraq or his distance from the church.

WHY IT DOESN'T

Nader got nearly 3 million votes in 2000; Barr's Libertarian predecessor captured fewer than 400,000, so Barr has some galvanizing to do. And Nader was on the ballot in 43 states, while the Libertarian Party is currently on the ballot in only 28—and not in battlegrounds such as Pennsylvania, Virginia and Ohio.

—SCOTT SPJUT

finance co-chair Tom Loeffler, a former Texas congressman whose lobbying firm has collected nearly $15 million from Saudi Arabia since 2002 and millions more from other foreign and corporate interests, including a French aerospace firm seeking Pentagon contracts. Loeffler last month told a reporter "at no time have I discussed my clients with John McCain." But lobbying disclosure records reviewed by NEWSWEEK show that on May 17, 2006, Loeffler listed meeting McCain along with the Saudi ambassador to "discuss US-Kingdom of Saudi Arabia relations."

Another potential problem: Loeffler's firm started paying $15,000 a month last summer to one of its lobbyists, Susan Nelson, after she left to become McCain's full-time finance director, said a source familiar with the arrangement (who asked not to be identified talking about sensitive matters). Campaign officials were told the payments were "severance" for Nelson and that they ended by November. But in "February or March," Loeffler rehired Nelson as a consultant to "help him with his clients" while she continued on the McCain payroll, according to a campaign official who asked not to be identified talking about personnel matters. Federal election law prohibits any outside entity from subsidizing the income of campaign workers.

McCain's officials say they have been assured that Nelson did actual work for Loeffler's lobbying clients—and that the payments were proper. But after NEWSWEEK posed questions about the matter, they confirmed Loeffler's resignation and the termination of Nelson's consulting contract. (Loeffler and Nelson did not respond to requests for comment.) Also last week, energy adviser Eric Burgeson was ousted.

If other staffers are not in compliance with the new rules, "they will become so or they will leave the campaign," said McCain spokeswoman Jill Hazelbaker. She also accused the Obama campaign of an "absurd double standard" because it has not disclosed the names of all advisers who may have lobbying ties. Responded Obama spokesman Bill Burton: "Washington lobbyists don't give money to our campaign, and they're not going to run our White House."

—MICHAEL ISIKOFF

WEEK OF JUNE 2

CAMPAIGN 2008

Obama's Lobbyist Connection

When Illinois utility Commonwealth Edison wanted state lawmakers to back a hefty rate hike two years ago, it took a creative lobbying approach, concocting a new outfit that seemed devoted to the public interest: Consumers Organized for Reliable Electricity, or CORE. CORE ran TV ads warning of a "California-style energy crisis" if the rate increase wasn't approved—but without disclosing the commercials were funded by Commonwealth Edison. The ad campaign provoked a brief uproar when its ties to the utility, which is owned by Exelon Corp., became known. "It's corporate money trying to hoodwink the public," the state's Democratic Lt. Gov. Pat Quinn said. What got scant notice then—but may soon get more scrutiny—is that CORE was the brainchild of ASK Public Strategies, a consulting firm whose senior partner is David Axelrod, now chief strategist for Barack Obama.

Last week, Obama hit John McCain for hiring "some of the biggest lobbyists in Washington" to run his campaign; Obama's aides say their candidate, as a foe of "special interests," has refused to take money from lobbyists or employ them. Neither Axelrod nor his partners at ASK ever registered as lobbyists for Commonwealth Edison—and under Illinois's loose disclosure laws, they were not required to. "I've never lobbied anybody in my life," Axelrod tells NEWSWEEK. "I've never talked to any public official on behalf of a corporate client." (He also says "no one ever denied" that Edison was the "principal funder" of his firm's ad campaign.)

But the activities of ASK (located in the same office as Axelrod's political firm) illustrate the difficulties in defining exactly who a lobbyist is. In 2004, Cablevision hired ASK to set up a group similar to CORE to block a new stadium for the New York Jets in Manhattan. Unlike Illinois, New York disclosure laws do cover such work, and ASK's $1.1 million fee was listed as the "largest lobbying contract" of the year in the annual report of the state's lobbying commission. ASK last year proposed a similar "political campaign style approach" to help Illinois hospitals block a state proposal that would have forced them

Campaign 2008-44 | JUNE

to provide more medical care to the indigent. One part of its plan: create a "grassroots" group of medical experts "capable of contacting policymakers to advocate for our position," according to a copy of the proposal. (ASK didn't get the contract.) Public-interest watchdogs say these grassroots campaigns are state of the art in the lobbying world. "There's no way with a straight face to say that's not lobbying," says Ellen Miller, director of the Sunlight Foundation, which promotes government transparency.

Axelrod says there are still huge differences between him and top McCain advisers, including the fact that he doesn't work in D.C. But his corporate clients do have business in the capital. One of

> **Axelrod says there are still huge differences between him and top McCain advisers.**

them, Exelon, lobbied Obama two years ago on a nuclear bill; the firm's executives and employees have also been a top source of cash for Obama's campaign, contributing $236,211. Axelrod says he's never talked to Obama about Exelon matters. "I'm not going to public officials with bundles of money on behalf of a corporate client," Axelrod says.

—MICHAEL ISIKOFF

WEEK OF JUNE 9

CAMPAIGN 2008

More Headaches For McCain's Camp

For weeks now, John McCain's presidential campaign has faced awkward questions about the outside activities of several top advisers. Add one more name to the list: former Texas senator Phil Gramm, McCain's longtime friend and one of his five campaign co-chairs. (A sixth, former congressman Tom Loeffler, quit recently after NEWSWEEK reported on his lobbying work for Saudi Arabia.) According to McCain spokeswoman Jill Hazelbaker, the co-chair position affords Gramm "broad input into the structure, financing and conduct of the campaign." She added that Gramm, who has a doctorate in economics, is also "a valued voice on economic policy." Gramm is not a paid McCain adviser, but his day job—vice chairman of a U.S. division of Zurich-based financial giant UBS—could pose new tests for a candidate who has promised high ethics standards and ditched advisers who failed to meet them.

UBS has recently written off huge losses in subprime-mortgage-based securities, and last week liberal bloggers noted that Gramm was a registered UBS lobbyist on mortgage-securities issues until at least December 2007.

NEWSWEEK has learned that UBS is also currently the focus of congressional and Justice Department investigations into schemes that allegedly enabled wealthy Americans to evade income taxes by stashing their money in overseas havens, according to several law-enforcement and banking officials in both the United States and Europe, who all asked for anonymity when discussing ongoing investigations. In April, UBS withdrew Gramm's lobbying registration, but one of his former congressional aides, John Savercool, is still registered to lobby legislators for UBS on numerous issues, including a bill cosponsored by Sen. Barack Obama that would crack down on foreign tax havens. "UBS is treating these investigations with the utmost seriousness and has committed substantial resources to cooperate," a UBS spokesman told NEWSWEEK, adding that Gramm was deregistered as a lobbyist because he spends less than 20

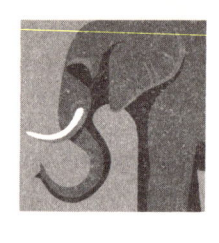

THE DIGNITY INDEX

Chapter 4: Why I Hate the Minneapolis Airport

A weekly mathematical survey of dubious behavior that measures, on a scale of 1 to 100, just how low a person can go

Bill Clinton claims his wife is "winning the general election" (wait, isn't that held on a single day in November?) but the media are "cover[ing] it up." Wow, we are so evil! Score: **13**

Longtime Index fave Sen. **Larry Craig** is now peddling a tell-all memoir in which he'll discuss the U.S. Senate, the state of politics in America and, oh yeah, what really happened in those stalls. Score: **46**

Obama backer and Chicago Rev. **Michael Pflegler** pours salt in Hillary's wounds, says she's upset because "there's a black man stealing my show." Classy. Score: **58**

percent of his time on such activity. Hazelbaker said the McCain campaign "will not comment on the details . . . of ongoing investigations and legal charges not yet proved in court."

McCain's campaign is already distancing itself from some of Gramm's other work for UBS: his involvement in attempts to sell financial products known as "death bonds," which BusinessWeek described last summer as one of "the most macabre investment scheme[s] ever devised by Wall Street." Not long after joining UBS, the Houston Chronicle reported, Gramm helped lobby Texas officials, including Gov. Rick Perry, to sign on to a UBS proposal in which revenue would be generated for a state teachers' retirement fund by selling bonds, whose proceeds would in turn be used to buy annuities and life-insurance policies on retired teachers. UBS would advance money to the retirement fund, then repay itself, compensate bondholders and pocket profits when insurance companies paid off on retirees who died. According to a banking-industry source, who asked for anonymity when discussing a sensitive matter, Gramm was involved in efforts to pitch similar UBS products to other financial institutions.

Gramm's office declined NEWSWEEK's request for comment. A source familiar with the bank's current business, who also asked for anonymity, said UBS no longer markets the kind of plan that Gramm was allegedly trying to sell to Texas. Hazelbaker said that McCain, who has been critical of the financial industry's performance in the subprime market, disapproves of death bonds and "supports increased accountability, transparency and capital backing in our financial markets as a solution to these problems." Death bonds, she continued, "move markets away [from]—not toward—these goals." —MARK HOSENBALL

FAST CHAT

For Paul, It Ain't Over Till It's Over

John McCain may be the presumptive nominee, but the Republican race isn't over—at least not to Ron Paul. The Texas congressman remains an official GOP candidate and has about $5 million in the bank, and a mighty band of fanatical followers. Will the fiercely antiwar conservative become a distraction for McCain at the Republican convention? Paul spoke with NEWSWEEK's Daniel Stone. Excerpts:

What kind of presence will you have at the convention?
We'll have a big rally there

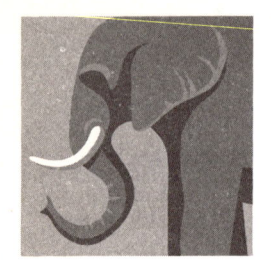

one of the days. Since they won't give us a spot, we'll make our own spot. We won't disrupt things—that doesn't achieve anything. But we'll have a presence and present views and try to . . . get in on the committees to vote on platforms. That's not disruptive.

What are your feelings toward [Libertarian nominee] Bob Barr?

We're pretty friendly. We're allies, he's a good friend. He has called me a couple times recently, so it's very cordial.

Even though he has been targeting your supporters?

I can't blame him. I'm sure that's his goal. [*Laughs*]

What's your relationship like with McCain?

It pretty much doesn't exist. He has his beliefs and I have mine, and they just don't come together very well.

The nomination is out of reach. How does this end for you?

It's always been about changing the party and changing the country. So I don't see things in conventional political terms. I'll continue to do what I started out to do: to change the direction of the party as well as the country.

What will happen to your campaign's leftover money?

It'll be used in an organization that has not yet been decided, to carry on exactly what we're doing in the campaign, to promote these views that everybody comes together on.

After the convention, will you endorse a candidate?

I'm not going to tell [my supporters] what to do. The support was really organized outside the campaign, so it'd be kind of odd to say, "Well, now that you've all come together, I'm going to tell you what you ought to do." They'll figure out what to do.

Most of your supporters are libertarian. Why are you still a Republican?

It affords me opportunities to talk about the Constitution. If I had not been in one of the major parties, I wouldn't have been in the debates. If I hadn't been in the debates, no one would have ever heard of me.

WEEK OF JUNE 16

CAMPAIGN 2008

His Jewish 'Problem': A Myth?

Barack Obama received a standing ovation when he proclaimed his unwavering support for Israel to the influential lobbying group AIPAC last week. In her own AIPAC speech, Hillary Clinton said she was sure "that Senator Obama will be a good friend to Israel." But Clinton's reassuring words didn't soothe the wounded feelings of some prominent Jewish Obama supporters, who charge that Clinton campaign operatives manufactured fear about Obama's ethnic background and doubt about his loyalty to Israel in an effort to turn Jewish primary voters against him.

Obama has long had a strong core of liberal Jewish supporters in Chicago; his national Jewish support grew as his campaign surged. But so did rumors that he had a "problem" with Jewish voters because of his family background (middle name: Hussein) and that some of his aides held pro-Palestinian views. David

THE DIGNITY INDEX

Virginia Is for (Redneck, Incestuous) Lovers

A weekly mathematical survey of dubious behavior that measures, on a scale of 1 to 100, just how low a person can go.

Cheers to the first daredevil who climbed the New York Times tower last Thursday. But the second guy, **Renaldo Clarke**? Get your own building, Captain Original. Score: **3**

Vice President **Dick Cheney** angers an entire state with an inbreeding joke about a pair of his distant cousins: "And we don't even live in West Virginia." Swing and a miss, Dick. Score: **28**

NBC journo **Andrea Mitchell** angers half a state by describing an Obama stop in western Virginia as a visit to "redneck" country. At least the veep was trying to be funny. Score: **35**

Geffen, the Hollywood mogul who once backed the Clintons but turned to Obama, told NEWSWEEK that her campaign bears some responsibility for "an awful lot of disinformation" that sowed doubts about the candidate's support of Israel among "older Jewish voters in Florida." New Jersey Rep. Robert Andrews, an Obama backer, says that two months ago a top Hillary campaign operative told him Obama would have a "hard time winning in November" because of his alleged Jewish problem and indicated Clinton's campaign was going to take advantage of those fears. Andrews says he found such talk "offensive," but he didn't know whether Hillary had sanctioned it. Asked for comment, the Clinton campaign referred NEWSWEEK to an article in the Newark (N.J.) Star-Ledger, in which spokesman Phil Singer called similar comments by Andrews "sad and divisive."

Obama has trailed Clinton among Jewish voters in polling matchups against John McCain (though both beat him soundly). But Obama has many high-profile Jewish fund-raisers, and aides claim his support among Jews will equal or surpass John Kerry's 75 percent in 2004. McCain has enlisted high-profile help of his own to help win Jewish votes: Connecticut Sen. Joseph Lieberman, a self-described "independent Democrat" who has criticized Obama's leadership qualities, has agreed to head up a booster group called Citizens for McCain. In a brief but animated Senate floor confrontation last week, according to a campaign aide who asked for anonymity when talking about private discussions, Obama told Lieberman he was surprised by Lieberman's personal attacks and his half-hearted denials of the false rumors that Obama is a Muslim. (The aide says Lieberman was "strangely muted" during the exchange; a Lieberman spokesman says the chat was "private and friendly.") McCain spokeswoman Jill Hazelbaker says Lieberman "played a key role in reaching out to the Jewish community in the primary . . . and you can expect that will continue."

—MARK HOSENBALL, JAKE SHERMAN *and* RICHARD WOLFFE

WEEK OF JUNE 23

CAMPAIGN 2008

A Bid for an Obama Cabinet

They both ran for the White House, though one got closer—much closer—than the other. They both sit on the Senate Foreign Relations Committee with their junior colleague Barack Obama. And if the Illinois senator is elected president in November, they both apparently would like to be his secretary of State. A source close to Massachusetts' John Kerry, who asked for anonymity when discussing the senator's political aspirations, says the Foreign Relations Committee's third-ranking Democrat (and 2004 presidential runner-up) is keen to be the nation's top diplomat. That also could well be the case for Connecticut Sen. Christopher Dodd, the committee's second-ranking Democrat (and 2008 presidential also-ran). The committee's chairman, Delaware Sen. Joseph Biden, is also frequently mentioned by Democratic insiders as a potential secretary of State—though, like Dodd, he might have his eyes on a bigger prize: the vice presidency. (Kerry does not appear to harbor veep aspirations.)

Kerry is a decorated Vietnam War veteran, but because his Senate experience is in foreign relations rather than military affairs, he's more intrigued by the State Department than the Pentagon, according to the source. (He also speaks fluent French.) Dodd, meanwhile, has recently been showcasing his expertise on Latin America: at an April conference at the U.S. Naval Academy, he laid out a blueprint for a "new relationship" between the United States and the region. Dodd's plan would include efforts to "dramatically improve" relations with Raúl Castro's Cuba by lifting a U.S. trade embargo and travel ban. While Dodd's office had no comment on his ambitions, an aide did confirm that Dodd is a fluent Span-

> **A source close to Kerry says the senator would like to be Secretary of State.**

ish speaker and noted that he chairs a subcommittee on Western Hemisphere affairs. Biden speaks no foreign languages but is regarded as one of the Democrats' foremost foreign-policy wise men. He has said he wouldn't turn down an offer to run as Obama's VP, and while his spokeswoman had no comment, another Biden adviser, who asked for anonymity, says that he likewise would not decline an offer to become secretary of State.

Of the three senators, Kerry endorsed Obama first. Biden and Dodd both abandoned their presidential bids after poor showings in the Iowa caucuses, but only Dodd has endorsed Obama. During the primaries, Biden said he would support the eventual nominee but remained neutral in the race between Obama and Hillary Clinton. How diplomatic.

—MARK HOSENBALL

POLITICS

Better Get a Better Vetter

When Barack Obama enlisted Washington insider Jim Johnson to vet potential running mates, the last thing his campaign expected was that Johnson himself

---

ENOUGH ALREADY

Pounded

Everything wears out its welcome eventually. In this periodic feature, we say when.

Now that Michelle and Barack Obama have introduced millions of Americans to the concept of the "pound"—also known as a "bump" or, to a hip few, "some dap"—it's time for the bad news: you can't do it ever again. The victory pound was a great moment of political theater, and the Obamas executed it with much more élan than, say, Mitt Romney's use of the word "bling" at a campaign stop on Martin Luther King Day. But politicians appropriate urban youth culture at their peril, and even if they pull it off, they kill it for the kids forever. So, please, we beg of you, whether you're black or white, young or old, if the first attempted pound of your life occurred in the last three weeks, you get one freebie and that's it. Otherwise you're the guy who was still saying "fo' shizzle" in 2007. And you don't wanna be that guy.

—DEVIN GORDON

would become an embarrassment. A former aide to Vice President Walter Mondale, Johnson has since had a lucrative business career that involved him, at least on the margins, in controversies over excessive executive pay and subprime loans. But according to a top Obama adviser, who asked for anonymity when discussing political deliberations, the campaign tried to turn a blind eye to potential Johnson controversies arising from his private business activities.

Johnson's veep-vetting credentials: he had done it for Mondale in 1984 and John Kerry in 2004 —though his 1984 effort did not go well. After Mondale chose Geraldine Ferraro, questions arose about her husband's business interest. But Obama's people were undaunted. "That was 24 years ago," the adviser said.

Johnson was supposed to share veep-vetting duties with Caroline Kennedy and ex-Clinton administration official Eric Holder, but his

---

ANALOGY CHECK

He's Running in the Opposite Direction

History repeats itself, but not without a few wrinkles. We make the connections—then we pick them apart.

THE COMPARISON

When Ronald Reagan won the Republican nomination in 1980, he ignored the advice of party poohbahs who wanted him to pacify the establishment by picking former president Gerald Ford as his running mate, going with George H.W. Bush instead. Likewise, Barack Obama is likely to resist pressure to make Hillary Clinton his veepstakes winner.

WHY IT WORKS

Ford and Clinton would have unified their parties, assuaging fears about the nominee's experience gap. But the chief appeal of Reagan's campaign was his promise to take his party in a new direction; ditto for Obama. Also, a factor for both men in their decisions: the threat of being eclipsed by an ex-president living at the Naval Observatory.

WHY IT DOESN'T

Unlike Hillary this year, Ford didn't run for president in 1980; his name was raised during the convention. (That didn't stop him from asking Reagan's veep-search team for the powers of a "co-presidency.") And while Hillary does have more experience in government than Obama, Ford actually sat in the Oval Office. —ADAM B. KUSHNER

own business activities suddenly became the focus of scrutiny. The Wall Street Journal raised questions about reduced-interest loans he received from Countrywide Financial, headed by a Johnson pal. Critics also began examining Johnson's role as a director of companies accused of doling out excessive executive pay—an issue Obama has worked on in the Senate. Earlier this year, Johnson was deposed in a lawsuit against him and other officers and directors of UnitedHealth, whose CEO departed in 2006 in a scandal over "backdated" stock options. Johnson was on the board of the company when it granted the options, though he later led an internal investigation into the alleged excesses (and left the board this month). The former CEO has reached a tentative settlement under which he would compensate the company more than $600 million. Brian Brooks, Johnson's lawyer, said there was "no evidence, or suggestion, of any wrongdoing" by Johnson at UnitedHealth and that he didn't seek discounts on any Countrywide loans. Johnson, he said, would not "comment on the private conversations he has had with Senator Obama and his campaign."

—M. H

WEEK OF JUNE 30

MILITARY

McCain's Boeing Battle Boomerangs

One of John McCain's most celebrated achievements in recent years was his crusade to block a Pentagon contract with Boeing for a new fleet of midair refueling tankers. Incensed over what he denounced as a taxpayer "rip-off," McCain launched a Senate probe that uncovered cozy relations between top Air Force officials and Boeing execs. A top Air Force officer and Boeing's CFO ended up in prison. Most significantly, the Air Force was forced to cancel the contract—saving taxpayers more than $6 billion, McCain asserted.

But last week, McCain's subsequent effort to redo the tanker deal was dealt a setback. Government auditors ruled that the Air Force made "significant errors" when it rebid the contract and awarded the $35 billion project to Boeing's chief rival, partners European Aeronautic Defense and

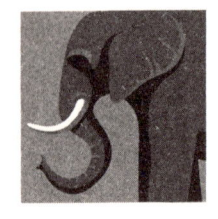

Space Co. (or EADS) and Northrop Grumman. It's likely the Air Force will have to redo the bid yet again, which analysts say will delay the replacement of the fleet's 1950s-era refueling tankers. The auditors' ruling has also cast light on an overlooked aspect of McCain's crusade: five of his campaign's top advisers and fund-raisers—including Tom Loeffler, who resigned last month as his finance co-chairman, and Susan Nelson, his finance director—were registered lobbyists for EADS.

Critics, including some at the Pentagon, cite in particular two tough letters McCain wrote to Deputy Secretary of Defense Gordon England in 2006 and

---

READY, SET ... PANDER!

We Feel Your Pain, But We Also Have a Plane to Catch

When disaster strikes in an election year, candidates are never far behind. How Obama and McCain handled their visits to the flooded heartland:

WHERE THEY WENT

Obama: Quincy, Ill., on June 13, two days into the crisis and four days before two of the area's three levees were overtopped.
McCain: Columbus Junction, Iowa (population: 1,900), on June 19, a week into the crisis, the same day President Bush visited the state.

WHAT THEY DID

Obama: Grabbed a shovel and filled about 20 sandbags held open by a local 10-year-old Boy Scout. Gave speech, prayed for victims.
McCain: Surveyed damage with the mayor and gave a gift to an Iowa National Guardsman getting married that day. Gave speech, stayed 30 miles from Bush.

HOW THEY DID

Obama: Bonus points for getting there fast, and for steering clear of Iowa at the request of the governor, who feared a visit would sap resources from the recovery effort.
McCain: If you arrive at a disaster on the same day as Bush, you got there a bit late. Also blew off the Iowa gov's request to stay away, but no harm, no foul.

VISIT TIME

McCain: 80 mins.
Obama: 75 mins.

—Matthew Philips *and* Sarah Ball

another to Robert Gates, just prior to his confirmation as Defense secretary. In the first letter, dated Sept. 8, 2006, McCain wrote of hearing from "third parties" that the Air Force was about to redo the tanker competition by factoring in European government subsidies to EADS—a condition that could have seriously hurt the EADS bid. McCain urged that the Pentagon drop the subsidy factor and posed a series of technical questions about the Air Force's process. "He was trying to jam us and bully us to make sure there was competition by giving EADS an advantage," said one senior Pentagon official, who asked for anonymity when discussing a politically sensitive matter. The assumption within the Pentagon, the official added, was that McCain's letters were drafted by EADS lobbyists. "There was no one else that would have had that level of detail," the official said. (A Loeffler associate noted that he and Nelson were retained by EADS after the letters were drafted.)

Chris Paul, who serves as McCain's top aide on the issue, wrote in an e-mail to NEWSWEEK that "the letters . . . were absolutely not provided, or drafted, by EADS or Northrop Grumman or . . . submitted on their behalf. Those letters

> "This shows how a sort of naive crusade for good government can actually backfire," said Loren Thompson.

THE DIGNITY INDEX

Are You Awake? No? Good, You're Fired.

A weekly mathematical survey of dubious behavior that measures, on a scale of 1 to 100, just how low a person can go.

At Tennessee's Bonnaroo Music and Arts Festival, hip-hop egotist **Kanye West** enrages fans by not starting his set until 4:25 a.m. Yes, 4:25 *in the morning.* Score: **12**

Yes, **Barack Obama** would've been nuts to accept public campaign financing and pass on a potential $500 million war chest . . . But a promise is a promise. And he broke his. Score: **27**

In a low moment for a franchise that's had plenty, the **New York Mets** fired Willie Randolph at 3 a.m. EDT, 3,000 miles from home, after a victory that night. All class. Score: **88**

arose from, and reflect, Senator McCain's longstanding interest in . . . full and open competition." The campaign would not allow Paul to answer follow-up questions about whether McCain had input from EADS lobbyists on the letters or about the identity of the "third parties." McCain said last week his "paramount concern" was "that the Air Force buy the most capable aerial refueling tankers at the most reasonable cost." But some defense analysts say the controversy over the Air Force rebid—and the higher costs that will result—have taken some of the shine off McCain's efforts. "This shows how a sort of naive crusade for good government can actually backfire," said Loren Thompson, of the Lexington Institute, a defense think tank. —MICHAEL ISIKOFF

WEEK OF JULY 7/JULY 14

BOOKS

No Storybook Ending Here

Once upon a time, there was a girl who wanted to fly among the planets and stars. She had blond locks, pink cheeks and (says this storyteller) blue, blue eyes. Her name was Hillary, and she tried to fly to the highest office in the land. The children's book is called "Hillary Rodham Clinton: Dreams Taking Flight," and author Kathleen Krull finished it in December—just as Clinton's dreams began plummeting back to Earth. But Krull kept the faith through Iowa, the Bosnia flap, the Bill blow-ups. "I really thought she was going to win," says Krull. As Hillary tried to resuscitate her campaign (which was not involved with the book), Krull revised her draft, still hoping. Even after Clinton conceded, Krull refused to change the book's last words: "Was the land ready? No matter—she was propelling her way into history."

It's hard to create a best seller out of a book about a failed presidential candidacy, so what's a publisher to do with a title that only a few months ago seemed like a sure bet? "We just have to roll with whatever the political climate is," says Simon & Schuster's Paul Crichton, who's been tasked with promoting the book. For Clinton, that means sharing the stage once again with you-know-who. Come convention season, "Dreams Taking Flight" will be displayed at Barnes & Noble alongside another S&S title, "Barack Obama: Son of Promise, Child of Hope." (The imprint will also release a picture book about John McCain, written by his daughter, former NEWSWEEK intern Meghan McCain.)

The Obama book has been updated with an additional page about his primary win, but Clinton's won't change—unless Obama offers her the veep spot, says Krull, something she's "optimistic" about. But if that doesn't pan out, all is not lost. Back when Bill Clin-

> "We just have to roll with whatever the political climate is," says Simon & Schuster's Paul Crichton.

ANALOGY CHECK

I'm Sorry, But There's Someone Else

History repeats itself, but not without a few wrinkles. We make the connections—then we pick them apart.

THE COMPARISON

Sen. Joe Lieberman, the self-styled "independent Democrat," has campaigned for his GOP friend John McCain and suggested he might speak at the rival convention. Both parties see shades of former Georgia senator Zell Miller, who backed President Bush in 2004 with a fiery convention speech lambasting Democrats on national security.

WHY IT WORKS

On the surface, it's a match. Both senators base their break with their party on irreconcilable differences over national security and the Iraq War. And both have chastised Democrats for abandoning the foreign-policy principles of past presidents from the party, with Lieberman invoking JFK and Miller pining for the days of Harry Truman.

WHY IT DOESN'T

Miller didn't have to govern after his turnaround; he wrote a memoir and retired from the Senate. Lieberman, though, still has four years left in his term. The courage of his convictions may ruin his career. If Obama wins, Lieberman could be stripped of his committee posts. If it's McCain, he could wind up with a cabinet job. —ADAM B. KUSHNER

ton was in the White House, Krull had written another children's book profiling the past presidents. Her illustrator drew Bill in running shorts, toting a saxophone. His wife's portrait looms above. And in the corner of the page, the Clintons' cat, Sox, hoists a sign: CHELSEA IN 2016. —APRIL YEE

FAST CHAT

Speak the Language

Hoping to sway voters in a crucial demographic, both John McCain and Barack Obama will speak in July at a conference for the nation's largest Latino advocacy group, the National Council of La Raza. Its CEO, Janet Murguia, discussed the courtship with NEWSWEEK's Jamie Reno:

Polls show Obama ahead among Latinos, but weak among those born outside the U.S. Why?

I believe it's simply because they don't know Obama yet. He has a very positive record of working with Latinos in his home state. Now that he's the [likely] nominee, Latinos will look more closely at him.

There has been talk about the so-called black-brown divide in this country—that lingering tensions between African-Americans and Hispanic Americans could cost Obama votes.

There are some real tensions, and we should not ignore them. But ultimately, Latinos, like everyone else, will look at issues they care about and vote accordingly.

Sen. Robert Menendez has said McCain "walked away" from the Latino community on immigration. Do you believe that?

McCain needs to clarify his position. Many Latinos viewed him as someone strongly in favor of reform, [but] eyebrows were raised as he backed away from that positioning. Still, many Latinos will find McCain appealing and will want to honor his military service. Our community is very patriotic.

WEEK OF AUGUST 11

CAMPAIGN 2008

Veepstakes: A New Name

The "shortlist" of options to be Barack Obama's running mate is longer than most media accounts have suggested. In addition to the familiar front runners—Delaware Sen. Joe Biden, Indiana Sen. Evan Bayh and Virginia Gov. Tim Kaine—there are at least two other veepstakes contenders: New Mexico Gov. Bill Richardson, who enraged Hillary Clinton supporters by endorsing Obama during the primaries, and a genuine dark horse, Texas Rep. Chet Edwards, whose district includes President George W. Bush's ranch in Crawford. Obama's campaign had hoped to announce his pick this week to grab the spotlight before the Beijing Olympics. But now a decision is unlikely to come until the week before the party convention, which begins in Denver on Aug. 25. According to party sources close to the selection process, who asked not to be identified discussing an internal matter, progress was slowed by Obama's overseas trip—and because his list is more fluid than generally thought. Edwards, 56, has been pushed by House Speaker Nancy Pelosi and other congressional Democrats who cite his work on veterans' affairs and nuclear nonproliferation, as well as his potential to attract Southern white blue-collar voters. Pelosi has called Edwards "one of the finest people I've ever served with." His stock rose further, one source said, after a meeting with Obama, though his low national profile remains a hurdle.

In fact, Obama aides have identified potential drawbacks to all the front runners. Biden brings foreign-policy expertise, but there are lingering concerns that his garrulous tendencies might knock the campaign off message. Bayh, who the sources say has been lobbying hard for the nod, brings solid centrist credentials. (An aide says Bayh is not "actively" pursuing the job.) But his wife serves on numerous corporate boards, and she also previously worked as a lawyer for drug giant Eli Lilly—an inconven-

> "He's the biggest celebrity in the world. But is he ready to lead?"
> —Campaign ad for John McCain, August 2008
>
> *Perspectives*

WEEK OF AUGUST 18/AUGUST 25

POLITICS

John McCain's Court Jester

All Steve Duprey wanted to do was make John McCain laugh. Riding on his campaign plane last June, the candidate was feeling low. The day before, he'd flubbed the delivery of a major speech in New Orleans and was being lampooned on the cable shows. So Duprey, McCain's close friend, informal adviser and faithful traveling buddy, got up from his seat and began handing out candy to campaign aides. Soon everyone aboard was cracking up: Duprey was decked out in a skimpy rainbow bikini—or, rather, a T shirt painted to look like one, front and, ahem, back. He'd picked up the shirt near Bourbon Street the night before, figuring the sight of a nearly bald 54-year-old guy dolled up like some kind of tragic "Baywatch" extra might just lift McCain's mood. He was right. McCain, perched in his usual spot up front, rolled his eyes and shook his head, a wide grin on his face.

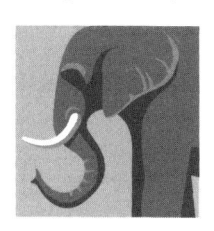

Duprey, a New Hampshire real-estate developer who's been in Republican politics for decades, never thought he'd spend a year traveling almost full time with the GOP nominee. A former New Hampshire state-party chairman, he began advising McCain back in 2006 and stuck close to his friend of two decades, even when his campaign nearly went belly up last year. Duprey ferried McCain around in his own Chevy Suburban, driving him to town halls and events all over New Hampshire. After McCain won the primary there, the senator and his aides invited Duprey to stay on for the ride. In the months since, he's evolved into the campaign's "chief morale officer," as he describes it. "I try to bring a little levity to the situation and make sure that, to the degree we can, we're enjoying this campaign."

No one is having more fun than Duprey himself. Known to campaign aides as the "Sultan of Swag," he travels with a huge stash of corny McCain-themed shirts, hats and jackets, which he designs and pays for out of pocket and gives away to aides and volunteers. Last month, he had the thrill of giving a prized TEAM KALEEFORNIA baseball cap to Gov. Arnold Schwarzenegger.

Years ago, Duprey was something of a maverick contender himself. In 1972, just after he turned 19, he ran for a seat in the New Hampshire State Legislature and won. At the time he was a college student working part-time as a bartender. He was the youngest elected lawmaker in the state's history, and worked on term papers from his seat during legislative debates. Duprey ultimately served two terms before heading to Cornell Law School. He worked for a while at a law firm, then got into building hotels and rehabbing old buildings in downtown Concord. A low moment came when Duprey's company was fined for mortgage fraud. (He says he did nothing wrong and was not personally charged.)

All along, Duprey stayed involved in Republican politics. He met McCain through Sen. Phil Gramm, who was campaigning in New Hampshire. Duprey says he and McCain spent a memorable evening making jokes at a snooty GOP party. "We both shared this sort of irreverent sense of humor at what was normally a stuffy social function," he recalls. In 1992 Duprey ran for Congress and lost, but was elected the following year as chairman of the New Hampshire GOP—a post he held for nearly a decade.

Though Duprey describes himself as "the guy who wears silly T shirts," he's clearly important to McCain. Aides say the candidate often turns to Duprey for an "average Joe" perspective on how the campaign is going. When McCain's day-to-day campaign manager Steve Schmidt recently brought on several former White House staffers to help run the show, McCain made it clear that Duprey was to remain at his side, no matter what. "He's become the indispensable man," says McCain.

> **Duprey figured the sight of a nearly bald 54-year-old guy dolled up like a "Baywatch" extra might lift McCain's mood.**

Lately, Duprey has started to expand his selection of McCain apparel. He now has a catalog of his offerings, which include buttons, McCain flip-flops—"sandals," he insists—a beach ball and McCain logo sunscreen. (A skin-cancer survivor, McCain often lectures his staff and reporters about protecting themselves from the sun.) Last week, McCain aide Mark Salter paraded through the press cabin with another Duprey product: a shirt with the word DUEL? on the front and TOWN HALL. HIGH NOON. ANYWHERE. on the back. It was a poke at Obama's comments a few days before that he was prepared to "duel" McCain on taxes. "I thought it was quite clever," says Duprey, who admits to spending a significant amount of time coming up with new designs and slogans. "What can I say? It's a sign of an underactive and overutilized mind." —HOLLY BAILEY

WEEK OF SEPTEMBER 1

GUNS

Silence on a 'Terror Gap'

Sen. John McCain portrays himself as a strong supporter of Second Amendment rights. But does that extend to gun rights for suspected terrorists? His campaign won't say where he stands on a bill to eliminate a gun-control loophole that even the Bush administration wants closed: a gap in federal law that inhibits the government from stopping people on terrorist watch lists from buying guns. The bill was inspired by an official audit covering a five-month period in 2004 which found that, because of the loophole, the Feds had to greenlight 35 out of 44 cases where a gun buyer was on a terrorist watch list. One group opposed to closing the loophole is the National Shooting Sports Foundation, a gun manufacturers' trade association. Until this spring, one of its congressional lobbyists was Randy Scheunemann, now a top McCain campaign adviser on foreign policy.

Last year the Justice Department, with White House approval, sent a bill to Congress that would close the loophole by giving the attorney general power to block gun sales to those who are identified via instant background checks as people on such watch lists. As a safeguard, the Bush bill would allow an alleged terrorist to go to court to challenge a gun ban. But the proposal has made little progress in the face of opposition from gun enthusiasts. Ted Novin, spokesman for the NSSF, says it opposes plugging what supporters of the bill call a "terror gap" because it denies "due process" to gun buyers. "Anyone can be put on this list," he says.

Registration documents filed by Scheunemann's company, Orion Strategies, list the terror-gap bill as one of its specific lobbying objectives, and the registrations listed Scheunemann as a lobbyist until he took a leave. McCain's campaign refused to answer questions about whether the senator supports or opposes the White House plan to close the loophole, and it also declined to say if Scheunemann had ever lobbied McCain on gun-control bills. "Randy Scheunemann is a foreign-policy adviser to Senator McCain, and he is on leave from Orion Strategies. We have no further comment," says Jill Hazelbaker, a campaign spokeswoman.

—Mark Hosenball

CAMPAIGN 2008

Solitude for McCain's Wordsmith

Like any writer, Mark Salter has his comfort zone. He often rises before dawn to draft his boss's speeches, drinking coffee and chain-smoking Marlboro cigarettes in the quiet before the day gets hectic. Recently, he retreated to his cottage off Penobscot Bay in Maine to work on the most important draft of his career: John McCain's Sept. 3 acceptance speech at the Republican National Convention. But even that wasn't without its distractions. Sitting on his deck with his laptop early one morning, Salter noticed a doe and two fawns tiptoeing nearby. "And that was it. I just stared," he said, joking that the speech may now include a Bambi reference or two.

Speechwriters often consult memorable addresses of the past for inspiration. Salter went back and read just one: George H.W. Bush's 1988 convention speech, written by Peggy Noonan, which is best known for the indelible line, "Read my lips: No new taxes." The speech was a huge hit and helped redefine Bush to voters. Down nearly 20 points in the polls in the summer, he went on to beat Michael Dukakis. Salter and aides are tight-lipped about what McCain will say, though the candidate will likely stick to themes he's already touted on the trail, including his military service and his time as a prisoner of war. McCain will also likely flash his willingness to buck his party, though its unclear how far he'll go to distance himself from President Bush, who is still popular with hardcore conservatives.

The pressure for McCain isn't just what he'll say, but also how he'll say it. The senator enjoys the combat of unscripted town halls but hates giving long, formal speeches, and it shows in his sometimes awkward delivery. McCain began practicing the speech last weekend at his cabin near Sedona, Ariz. Aides say it will likely run about 20 minutes—shorter than past acceptance speeches, which usually clock in at about 35 minutes. Already, McCain himself has been playing the expectations game. "Senator Obama will give a great speech at their convention . . . and I don't expect to match up with that," he recently told GOP donors at an event in Iowa. "But I think it's going to be substance that matters."

Salter consulted just one prior speech: George H.W. Bush's at the 1988 convention.

—HOLLY BAILEY

WEEK OF SEPTEMBER 8

IN THE BUBBLE

'Is She Attrac . . . Nevermind.' The Palin Pick at 34,000 Feet.

Charlotte, N.C. — I landed here at noon last Friday after leaving Denver and the Democratic convention on a 6:45 a.m. flight. This meant, unfortunately, that I didn't get to experience the unveiling of McCain's new running mate, Alaska Gov. Sarah Palin, in real time. (The news broke at 10:30.) But the awkward timing did afford me an interesting vantage point on the announcement, as all of the Democratic delegates, strategists and various and sundry other politicos on that Boeing A321 got the news simultaneously on their CrackBerrys, the moment we touched down.

I would describe the reaction as shock and awe. Everyone was taken totally by surprise—including me. At first, it's hard to see how asking someone with even less seasoning than Obama to stand a mere (septuagenarian's) heartbeat away from the Oval Office won't hinder the Republicans' ability to attack the Illinois senator for his alleged "inexperience." As thumbs twiddled over trackballs and Beltway types barked into their phones, I overheard a few telling reactions. A flight attendant said she was "pissed": "Does he think we're stupid enough to vote for a woman just because she's a woman?" A few rows back, a woman called a colleague to ask if Palin was "attractive." "Is she attractive?" she repeated when her interlocutor misheard. *"Is she attrac . . .* nevermind." The most revealing response came from a tall gentleman with reading glasses. "Whooooaaaa," he said into his phone. "Sarah who?"

But as I listened to my Democratic planemates discuss the new nominee, I became less and less sure that her inexperience would hurt McCain. Every time Team Obama calls Palin a rookie, it gives McCain yet another opportunity to question his rival's résumé. The pick presents Democrats with a knotty challenge: how do you argue that a fresh, groundbreaking Washington outsider is too inexperienced to be second fiddle while at the same time arguing that Obama—a fresh, groundbreaking Washington outsider himself—is ready to lead the free world? The truth is, no one votes against a ticket topped by someone as experienced as McCain solely because the No. 2 isn't an old Washington hand as well. But plenty of folks are willing to reject a No. 1. because of a skimpy résumé. Experience is an argument McCain *wants* to have—and Palin, oddly enough, helps him have it.

—ANDREW ROMANO

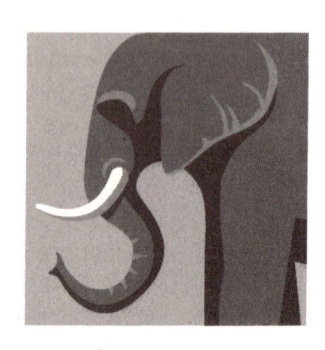

"I guess a small-town mayor is sort of like a 'community organizer,' except you have actual responsibilities."
—*Alaska Gov. Sarah Palin, September 2008*
Perspectives

ENOUGH ALREADY

Let's Quit Playing Games

From the pundits who brought you "thrown under the bus," "taking the gloves off" and sundry other sports analogies in electoral politics comes the latest irritating game in town: the "game changer." Back in March, Sen. Barack Obama's ties to the Rev. Jeremiah Wright were dubbed a primary-season game changer— until Obama's exculpatory speech on race changed the game right back again. Hillary's big win in Pennsylvania was a game changer (or maybe not), as was Obama's world tour (though it's unclear for whom, him or John McCain). Last week the game allegedly changed twice in 13 hours: first with Obama's convention speech, then the next day with McCain's veep selection of Alaska Gov. Sarah Palin.

By the time you read this, it'll probably have "changed" a few more times. And there's the rub: do we really believe that something as massive as a national presidential campaign fundamentally shifts more than once or twice per election? It's another byproduct of millisecond news cycles: if today's story *isn't* game-changing, we might as well change the channel. And we can't have that. So this week, as the media grade each GOP convention speaker (game changers all!), let's test-drive a new sports analogy: game over. —Sarah Ball

STRAIGHT TALK

Biden: Literally Serious That He's Not Joking

The only thing that matters more to Joe Biden than speaking his mind is letting you *know* that he's speaking his mind. He abuses words and phrases meant to emphasize his honesty. His favorite is "literally." During his debut in Springfield, Biden used it eight times, once promising that Obama would "literally,

---

CATCHPHRASE

The stats on Joe Biden's impromptu assurances of sincerity:

- **8** Number of times Biden used 'literally' in Springfield
- **3** Most repetitions of 'literally' in a row last Tuesday in Denver
- **7** Number of 'candid catchphrases' in that speech
- **12** Number of minutes he spoke

literally change the . . . world." Last Tuesday in Denver, he upped the ante. "Your children's futures," he said, are "literally, literally, literally at stake." Biden managed to pack six other candid catchphrases into his 12-minute remarks. His attack on McCain's tax cuts was "literally factual." (A twofer.) "I'm not making this up," he added. Praising Michelle Obama, he deployed an "I mean this sincerely"; health care got an "I'm serious" or two. Other lines were qualified with "I'm not joking" and "this is not hyperbole." And just in case anyone wasn't sold, Biden inserted two new alerts into Wednesday's VP speech: "this is the God's truth" and "I mean it." We're not joking.

INTERVIEW

Sebelius: What 'Hillary Holdouts'?

Denver—Remember the Hillary holdouts— a.k.a. the 48 percent of Clinton supporters who told NBC pollsters before the convention that they were undecided, unsatisfied with the options or backing John McCain? Well, at least one Obaman doesn't believe they're real. Her name? Kansas Gov. Kathleen Sebelius.

Asked last Wednesday whether the Hillary holdouts spell trouble for Obama, Sebelius told NEWSWEEK that the conversation was "oddly anti-feminist." That Hillary supporters "would honor her by voting for John McCain seems to me to be totally insane," she said. She even wondered whether people were lying to pollsters. "I'm not at all convinced that some of this isn't ongoing mischief being played by the other team," she said. Told

> **"Does he think we're stupid enough to vote for a woman just because she's a woman?"**
> — *Flight attendant, after the Palin pick.*
> Perspectives

that some delegates—Democrats—were still refusing to vote for Obama, Sebelius was incredulous. "They're seriously going to support John McCain?" she asked. *No, they're just not going to vote.* "Well, that's a very effective strategy," the governor snapped.

A true believer, she even thinks Obama can become the first Democrat since FDR in 1936 to win Kansas. Helping him, she says, will be an armada of women surrogates. "It was tricky in the primary to use a lot of women and not appear to be women against Hillary," she said. "But now we'll be out there against John McCain." For Obama, that's a good thing—just in case those Hillary holdouts do, you know, exist.

WEEK OF SEPTEMBER 15

CAMPAIGN 2008

Heaven Help Them Decide

Going back to Ronald Reagan, the Rev. Wilfredo De Jesús—the senior pastor of a 4,500-member Hispanic evangelical church in Chicago—has pulled the lever for Republicans in presidential elections. "I always voted on the issue of abortion and the sanctity of marriage," he says. This time, though, Sen. Barack Obama's message of faith and social justice, combined with strident GOP rhetoric on illegal immigration, has persuaded him to endorse the Democrat. That switch illustrates the extent to which the Latino evangelical vote is in play—a development that could prove decisive on Nov. 4. Though polls show Obama beating Sen. John McCain among Hispanics as a whole by roughly 30 points, Hispanic evangelicals are a tougher sell. In 2004, 63 percent of them voted for President Bush.

Comprising about one third of Hispanic voters overall, evangelicals are more affluent, more likely to be citizens and more likely to vote than non-evangelicals. (Hispanics make up 15 percent of the U.S. population.) They're difficult to categorize—conservative on social issues, but liberal on economic ones. Unlike white evangelicals, who are often wedge-issue driven, they "tend to look at a candidate in a more holistic fashion," weighing stances on matters as diverse as poverty and the death penalty, says Claremont McKenna College professor Gaston Espinosa. "Having said that, abortion and the same-sex marriage issue are very important." Neither candidate quite fits the bill. Though McCain is pro-life, he's fiscally conservative, and he backtracked on immigration reform during the primaries. Obama supports legalizing immigrants, but he's also pro-choice.

By most accounts, the Obama campaign has been more aggressive in wooing Latino evangelicals. It's reaching out regularly to pastors, organizing conference calls for them to question the candidate and sponsoring faith forums for voters. (The McCain campaign didn't respond to repeated requests to describe its activities.) "It's a really tough decision for me," says Richard Ramos, an evangelical who works at a faith-based non-profit and voted for Bush twice. This time? He's got two months to make up his mind.

—ARIAN CAMPO-FLORES
and JIM MOSCOU

'PALINSANITY'

Worldly! Rootsy! Experience Is in the Eye of the Beholder

The most amusing aspect of "Palinsanity"—the Republican response to Obamania—is watching both liberals and conservatives tie themselves in logical knots to justify their feelings about John McCain's running mate. Once upon a time (in August), the

> **Both sides are viewing Palin through the prism of their own cultural and political biases.**

GOP cautioned the country against fresh-faced stars who seduce worshipful crowds with savvy language. They argued that a brief, unconventional CV couldn't possibly prepare anyone for the presidency. Not anymore. Now they're calling Sarah Palin a "rock star." Meanwhile, the people who've spent the last 19 months claiming that words can move the masses and that experience isn't as important as judgment—i.e., Democrats—are complaining that the Mooseburger Queen of Wasilla is insubstantial and unprepared. Dizzy yet?

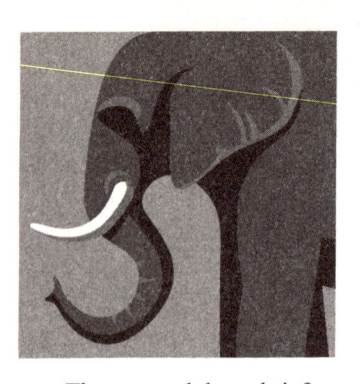

The problem is that both sides are viewing Palin through the prism of their own cultural and political biases. Before joining the campaign circus, both Obama and Palin served about a decade in local roles and about two years in statewide office. Where they differ is in *what kind of experience* they have—and how that experience resonates with the people already inclined to support them. Obama's résumé—Indonesia, memoirs, Harvard, legislature—conforms to a Democratic ideal of leadership: worldly, brainy, fluent, cooperative. Palin's résumé—frontier mom, unlikely mayor, reformist governor—fits a more Republican mold: familial, rootsy, self-sufficient, executive. *Obama's better than we could ever be,* Democrats declare. *Palin's one of us,* Republicans respond. But for either camp to claim that its candidate is the only one qualified for the White House—when neither crosses the traditional threshold of pre-presidential dues-paying—is self-serving. Here, experience is in the eye of the beholder.

Dems say Obama has proven his managerial mettle in part by helming a blockbuster campaign—and they're right. But remember: in a race for the presidency, you're required to spend years wooing voters and handling harsh questions from the press; in a race for the vice presidency, you're plopped down in Minnesota 60 days before the election. When he launched his bid, Obama was no more seasoned than Palin is now—so if his on-the-trail experience is allowed to count as a credential, Palin should get the chance to prove herself as well.

Of course, Palin couldn't possibly catch up to her rival in 60 short days—but then again, she's not seeking the highest office in the land. So 60 days will have to suffice. Here's hoping that during the next two months, America will ditch the double standards about

> **"I shot rabbits; she hunts moose. So there's no comparison there."**
> **—Veep finalist Mitt Romney, on Palin's superior blue-collar appeal.**
>
> *Perspectives*

"words" and "experience" and start asking Palin tough questions about where she wants to take the nation. In the end, Palin may sink. She may swim. But the important thing is making sure that on Nov. 4, voters have enough info to say for themselves whether she's ready to roll. It should be a wild ride.

Everybody Loves Palin!

$10,000,000

Amount raised by the McCain campaign in the two and a half days after Alaska Gov. Sarah Palin joined the GOP ticket	Amount raised by the Obama campaign in the 24 hours after Palin delivered her speech at the 2008 Republican convention

ENOUGH ALREADY

Meating of The Minds

In the Russell Crowe movie "Gladiator," there's a scene in which Maximus gets tossed onto the floor of the Colosseum into a swarm of hulking warriors and roaring tigers, and the crowd, smelling blood, leans forward in anticipation. Maximus, though, ends up carving everyone else to pieces. The crowd falls silent. *"Are you not entertained?"* he shouts.

Maybe I spent too much time watching conventions over the past two weeks, but I thought of that scene every time I heard a TV talking head toss out the fortnight's most unappetizing phrase: "red meat." As in, "Boy, Obama/Palin sure threw those folks some red meat." The term is yet another effort to turn nebbishy politics into primal bloodsport, and the implication is that we're all a bunch of mouth-breathers who think issues are for sissies—that insulting our opponent is part of the American fabric.

The result? Too many speeches with too much red meat, not enough meat and potatoes. Between now and Nov. 4, let's not talk about "red meat" again unless we're having it for dinner.

—DEVIN GORDON

POLITICS

The Wives, Center Stage

Though few people saw it because of Hurricane Gustav, the Republican convention in St. Paul began with podium appearances by the current First Lady and, if the GOP gets its way, the next First Lady. NEWSWEEK's Jon Meacham sat down with Laura Bush and Cindy McCain for a conversa-

---

CONVENTION CHOREOGRAPHY

All Together Now: 'She Hugs Them.'

How much of what happens at a political convention is scripted? All of it. Notice what the teleprompter said when Cindy McCain took the stage with her children in St. Paul. FYI, "give another humdrum speech" never appeared on the screen. Guess the parties allow their speakers to improvise that part.

tion in neighboring Minneapolis. Excerpts:

What advice would you give to Gov. Sarah Palin about dealing with the intersection of the personal and the political?

> "I have been looking forward to the chance to vote for a Republican woman, and now I'm going to get that chance."

BUSH: Well, we met with her this morning, but . . . we didn't dare give her any advice. We know she can take care of everything—she's very, very strong. But the one thing I said to both Cindy and Sarah is to say to the press [that] our kids are off limits, and that's just absolutely the way it is. They're not running, and it's just really not fair to have the press ask about family members.

Do you feel that was possible with your daughters?

BUSH: By and large, I think that they were left alone, and we appreciate [that] very much.

There seems to be an instant simpatico between the senator and the governor. Is that a fair way to put it?

MCCAIN: It is. She's very much like my husband in how she approaches things, her maverick attitude, her straight talk, her intelligence . . . And more importantly, she will really work well with him. Their attitudes are all about reform and prosperity, so she could not be a more perfect pick for him. I'm so glad he did it.

Did you expect to see a woman on the ticket?

BUSH: I was surprised, and I'm absolutely thrilled. I've been looking forward to the chance to vote for a Republican woman, and now I'm going to get it. [S]he just has a certain grit that I think Western women have and that I admire very much.

Mrs. McCain, with your two sons in the military, how do you cope with knowing they're possibly in harm's way and trying to support your husband as he makes these critical decisions?

MCCAIN: It's not about coping—both of my sons made a choice to do this. [But] I'm also a mother, so of course I worry, and I would worry if they crossed the street. But I'm so proud of them. They had every option in the world to do whatever they wanted and they chose this.

Mrs. Bush, being married to a commander in chief, do you discuss those subjects when he comes home?

BUSH: Of course we talk about it, and that is by far the most difficult decision the president ever makes—to send our troops into harm's way. On the other hand, do I think it was the right thing to do? Absolutely . . . It's very tough. But Americans can do things that are hard.

Did it help that his father had been in the same position?

BUSH: Umm, maybe, I mean, I don't know about that. I don't know if you can practice for that. We didn't expect that. . . [B]oth of us thought we would have a time of almost total domestic issues. The cold war was over, the Central European countries were liberated from the Soviet Union; that's just what we would thought it would be. But the one thing you know—and John McCain knows this—is that when you are running for this job you don't know what is going to happen, but you know that things are going to happen. You have to be prepared, and he is prepared.

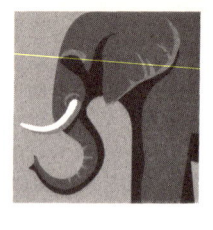

You both are married to men with formidable mothers. How did that influence them?

McCAIN: Oh, in my husband's case, she was clearly the strongest influence in his life, because his father was gone so much. She not only shaped his sturdiness . . . but also his values, the way he approaches things. I think a lot of his straight-talk attitude comes from his mother. I don't know if you ever met her, but she's a pistol, and I love her to death.

WEEK OF SEPTEMBER 22

CAMPAIGN 2008

A Police Chief, a Lawsuit And a Small-town Mayor

Eleven years before the current investigation into her dismissal of Alaska's top cop, Sarah Palin was embroiled in a similar dispute over another personnel issue: her firing of the police chief in her hometown of Wasilla. Palin's decision to terminate Irl Stambaugh, months after she was elected mayor in 1996, created a ruckus. It also led to a bitter and protracted lawsuit charging that she fired Stambaugh out of pique—in part because he'd crossed the interests of influential backers, including bar owners and gun enthusiasts who'd contributed significantly to Palin's campaign, according to court and state records reviewed by NEWSWEEK. Palin denied these allegations under oath, and ultimately prevailed, after a federal judge concluded that the mayor had the right to fire any department head she wanted. Palin "made the decision . . . because the people of Wasilla had elected her to reform Wasilla's government and he actively worked to frustrate those efforts," says Taylor Griffin, a spokesman for the McCain-Palin campaign.

But the dispute is now getting renewed scrutiny in light of a number of other controversial personnel moves by the GOP veep nominee, including her firing of the Wasilla librarian (she was later reinstated) and Alaska Public Safety Commissioner Walt Monegan, whose dismissal last summer prompted the investigation, dubbed "Troopergate," by Alaska's legislature. (Monegan alleged he was fired because he resisted pressure from Palin and aides to can a state trooper involved in a messy custody battle with Palin's sister. A state panel last week voted to subpoena 13 members of Palin's administration in the probe, as well as her husband.)

Stambaugh, a former Anchorage police captain who once supervised Monegan, was hired as Wasilla's first police chief in 1993 and created the town's small police force, says former Wasilla mayor John Stein. But weeks after Palin beat Stein in 1996, she expressed displeasure with the chief. One big issue, Stambaugh said, was that he and other police chiefs had opposed a state-legislature bill to permit concealed weapons in schools and bars, which Stambaugh called "craziness." But Palin, elected with backing from the National Rifle Association, which lobbied for the bill, told him she was "not happy" with his position, and that the NRA wanted him fired, says Stambaugh. Palin told him he "shouldn't have done that," Stambaugh told NEWSWEEK. (Palin denied in a deposition

> When she was mayor, Palin's policies made her a favorite among local bar owners and gun activists.

that the NRA contacted her about the weapons bill.)

An even bigger clash involved a proposed city ordinance backed by Stambaugh to close the town bars at 2 a.m. instead of 5. Stambaugh says he believed this would help curb late-night drunken driving at a time when, according to Stein, the former mayor, "people were driving out from Anchorage to the valley for more alcohol and crashing." But Palin, as a council member, had voted against the measure—making her the favored candidate among bar owners, one of whom held a fundraiser for her. Records obtained by NEWSWEEK show that Wasilla bar owners contributed $1,250 to her mayoral campaign—more than 10 percent of all the money she raised in 1996. Griffin did not respond to requests for comment on those contributions.

Stambaugh says it was only after clashing with Palin on these and another issue, involving efforts to restrain a "poker run" game enjoyed by snowmobile drivers where they play a hand at each bar, that he was fired. John Cramer, the city administrator hired by Palin, acknowledges that personal

---

APPLES AND ORANGES

Small-Town Folks, Making It Big

History repeats itself—but not without a few wrinkles. We make the connections, then pick them apart.

THE COMPARISON

Veep nominee Sarah Palin answers concerns about her inexperience by comparing herself to Harry Truman, who became president three months into his term, when FDR died. At the time, Truman didn't even know about the development of the atom bomb.

WHY IT WORKS

Both had non-elite upbringings and, as Palin says, "unlikely" paths to high office. In the reformer category, both were early supporters of pork projects (Truman's early political career was backed by the Pendergast machine) who later lambasted wastefulness and fraud.

WHY IT DOESN'T

Truman, a World War I vet, was selected more for his 10-year service in the Senate, where he voted on major national legislation and steered a war-preparedness committee, than his origins as a small-town Missouri haberdasher, as Palin has suggested.

—ADAM B. KUSHNER

and political antagonisms may have played a role. Stambaugh, who backed Stein openly in the 1996 race, showed the new mayor little deference. At one meeting of town officials, Cramer says he heard him tell Palin: "Little lady, if you think you have our respect, you don't. You have to earn it." (Stambaugh denies making the comment.) Stambaugh filed suit, alleging breach of contract and civil-rights violations. In the course of the lawsuit, Palin filed an affidavit complaining that Wasilla cops had done an unauthorized state police check on her and her husband—which appears to have foreshadowed her later uneasy relationship with law enforcement. (Earlier this year, Palin told aides she no longer wanted the standard detail of six troopers assigned to protect Alaskan governors.) A federal judge ultimately tossed the case, on legal grounds, and ordered Stambaugh to pay $22,000 of Palin's legal fees—proof, according to Griffin, that the case was "frivolous." Stambaugh says his dispute should be looked at in the context of others involving Palin. "It's not just me," he says. "It's Monegan, it's the librarian. The list goes on and on. She believes she can fire people for whatever reasons she wants." In Stambaugh's case, a judge ruled she could do just that.

—MICHAEL ISIKOFF
and MARK HOSENBALL

WEEK OF SEPTEMBER 29

ALASKA

Palin's Pipeline to Nowhere

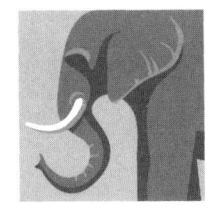

The principal achievement of Sarah Palin's term as Alaska's governor, a natural-gas pipeline project backed by $500 million in state tax money, might never be built unless Canadian authorities can strike a deal with some of the country's angry Indian tribes. Approximately half of the proposed pipeline would run through Canada; native tribes who live along its route complain they haven't been consulted about it and are threatening to sue unless they are compensated. Representatives of the Canadian tribes, known as First Nations, say Palin and other pipeline proponents are treating them with disrespect. The tribes' lawyers warn that the courts are on their side and say the Indians have the power to delay the pipeline for years—or even kill it entirely by filing endless lawsuits.

> "This is what I would call a commercial dance of the fireflies."

Palin's advisers say they considered these risks before they committed state funds to the project earlier this year. The state hired Canadian lawyers, who produced a lengthy report warning about possible lawsuits and cautioning that First Nations in Canada's Yukon Territory could be among the "most litigious." The report estimated that the Indians could delay the pipeline for up to seven years. But Jeffrey Rath, a lawyer for First Nations, says this timetable is "wildly optimistic." He notes that one of his clients, the 250-member Prophet River First Nation, litigated an unrelated land claim for 11 years before recently settling. Liz Logan, chief of a First Nations umbrella group in British Columbia, told NEWSWEEK that TransCanada, the company Palin's administration selected to pursue the project, has "very much downplayed the extent of the legal difficulties they face in Canada." One of Canada's top pipeline experts, Professor Andre Plourde of the University of Alberta, agrees that the seven-year timetable proposed by Palin's lawyers for sorting out First Nations claims is "optimistic indeed."

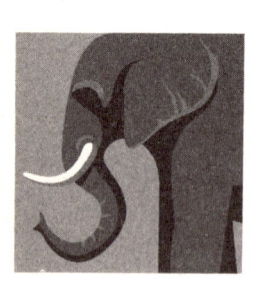

Kurt Gibson, one of Alaska's top officials overseeing the pipeline project, says it is "premature" in the process to start consulting with Canadian Indians. "This is what I would call a commercial dance of the fireflies," he says, meaning that the two sides are each jostling for economic advantage. But Robert C. Freedman, a lawyer for the Dene Tha' First Nation, says that if authorities keep putting off dealing with the natives, "it's going to be a pipeline to nowhere when it crosses into Canada." In an interview with NEWSWEEK, Patrick Galvin, Palin's revenue commissioner, conceded that "there are risks associated with this project . . . Nobody has said that this project is absolutely going to happen, guaranteed."

—MARK HOSENBALL

CAMPAIGN 2008

All the Candidates' Cars

When you have seven homes, that's a lot of garages to fill. After the fuss over the number of residences owned by the two presidential nominees, NEWSWEEK looked into the candidates' cars. And based on public vehicle-registration records, here's the score. John and Cindy McCain: 13. Barack and Michelle Obama: one.

One vehicle in the McCain fleet has caused a small flap. United Auto Workers president Ron Gettelfinger, an Obama backer, accused McCain this month of "flip-flopping" on who bought daughter Meghan's foreign-made Toyota Prius. McCain said last year that he bought it, but then told

After taking heat, Obama dumped his family's Chrysler 300C guzzler for a 2008 Ford hybrid.

a Detroit TV station on Sept. 7 that Meghan "bought it, I believe, herself." (The McCain campaign did not respond to multiple requests for comment.)

Obama's lone vehicle also is a green machine, a 2008 Ford Escape hybrid. He bought it last year to replace the family's Chrysler 300C,

> **"I think—I'll have my staff get to you."**
> —Sen. John McCain, asked by a reporter how many houses he and his wife own, September 2008.
> *Perspectives*

a Hemi-powered sedan. Obama ditched the 300C, once 50 Cent's preferred ride, after taking heat for driving a guzzler while haranguing Detroit about building more fuel-efficient cars.

McCain's personal ride, a 2004 Cadillac CTS, is no gas sipper, but it should make Detroit happy because it's made by General Motors. "I've bought American literally all my life and I'm proud," McCain said in the interview with Detroit's WXYZ-TV. But the rest of his fleet is not all-American. There's a 2005 Volkswagen convertible in the garage along with a 2001 Honda sedan. Otherwise, there's a 2007 half-ton Ford pickup truck, which might come in handy on the Sedona ranch; a vintage 1960 Willys Jeep; a 2008 Jeep Wrangler; a 2000 Lincoln; and a 2001 GMC SUV. The McCains also own three 2000 NEV Gem electric vehicles, which are bubble-shaped cars popular in retirement communities.

Only the Cadillac is registered in the candidate's name. Cindy McCain's name is on 11 vehicles, though not the one she actually drives. That car, a Lexus, is registered to her family's beer-distributor business and is outfitted with personalized plates that read MS BUD.

—KEITH NAUGHTON and HILARY SHENFELD

VOTING

A Redo of Flori-Duh

During the 2000 election, Palm Beach, Fla., resident Sandy Blank watched, horrified, as her county became a mess of butterfly ballots, hanging chads, erroneous votes for Pat Buchanan—and a national punch line. (The Onion rechristened the state "Flori-duh.") The voting disaster inspired civic activism: Blank become a Palm Beach poll worker. "I wanted to change things," she says. Instead, six weeks before the presidential election, the situation there is as messy as ever, and a botched primary in late August only underscored the threat of another calamity. In that primary, roughly 3,500 votes went missing; then, after an audit, there were *more* ballots than voters, which should be impossible. But this is Palm Beach. "It's a crisis of confidence," says Blank, reporting a paltry 3 percent turnout at her polling station.

Voting-technology experts say that Palm Beach represents a checklist of how not to run elections. The county—with an assist

> **Experts say that Palm Beach represents a checklist of how not to run elections.**

from the state government—responded to the 2000 election in precisely the wrong way: by repeatedly switching voting machines rather than settling on one type and training people on it. "Switching technology is the fun, shiny stuff, but it's pointless," says Thad Hall, author of "Electronic Elections." "You need to focus on the procedures." On Nov. 4, however, Palm Beach will use its third system in three presidential elections. Most systems have similar accuracy rates, and the touchscreens that Palm Beach used in 2004 worked fine—but those were scrapped because of a new state law requiring paper ballots. "It's a lot to ask us and the voters to keep switching," says Palm Beach County Commissioner Mary McCarty. That law prompted another potential gaffe: the ballot design that Palm Beach settled on for 2008. Design experts recommend simple, familiar "fill in the oval" ballots; Palm Beach is going with "complete the arrow" ballots, where voters draw a line to finish an arrow next to candidates' names. Research shows error rates with "arrow" ballots are about 33 percent higher than those with "oval" ballots.

Palm Beach officials are expecting at least 500,000 voters on Nov. 4 and are redoubling efforts to prepare, convening a special task force. The state is on their case, too: Florida Secretary of State Kurt S. Browning is planning on weekly conference calls with Palm Beach's election supervisor. Running a smooth election, says Browning, "is not rocket science." In Palm Beach, apparently, it's even harder.
—SARAH KLIFF

WEEK OF OCTOBER 6

CAMPAIGN 2008

A Freddie Mac Money Trail Catches Up With McCain

Few advisers in John McCain's inner circle inspire more loyalty from him than campaign manager Rick Davis. McCain and his wife, Cindy, credit the shrewd, and sometimes volatile, Republican insider with rescuing the campaign last year when it was out of money and on the verge of collapse. As a result, McCain has always defended him—even when faced with tough questions about the foreign lobbying clients of Davis's high-powered consulting firm. "Rick is a friend, and I trust him," McCain told NEWSWEEK last year.

Last week, though, McCain's trust in Davis was tested again amid disclosures that Freddie Mac, the troubled mortgage giant that was recently placed under federal conservatorship, paid his campaign manager's firm $15,000 a month between 2006 and August 2008. As the mortgage crisis has escalated, almost any association with Freddie Mac or Fannie Mae has become politically toxic. But the payments to Davis's firm, Davis Manafort, are especially problematic because he requested the consulting retainer in 2006—and then did barely any work for the fees, according to two sources familiar with the arrangement who asked not to be identified discussing Freddie Mac business. Aside from attending a few breakfasts and a political-action-committee meeting with Democratic strategist Paul Begala (another Freddie consultant), Davis did "zero" for the housing firm, one of the sources said. Freddie

---

APPLES AND ORANGES

Cracking the Highest Glass Ceiling

History repeats itself, but not without a few wrinkles. We make the connections, then pick them apart.

THE COMPARISON

Former lawyer Tzipi Livni is poised to become Israel's next prime minister, which would make her the first woman to hold the post since Golda Meir. But critics (including influential Labor Party head Ehud Barak) say she lacks the necessary experience to lead. Livni's camp is crying sexism—sound familiar, Sarah Palin?

WHY IT WORKS

Like Palin, Livni is considered a newcomer to national politics, and both women see themselves as maverick corruption busters (Livni has been called "Mrs. Clean"). Both are also attractive—a fact that has led certain commentators to unfairly dismiss them as "the prettiest girl in kindergarten" (Livni) and "a ditzy cheerleader" (Palin).

WHY IT DOESN'T

Livni has been in politics for less than a decade, but she's hardly green—she has been Israel's foreign minister since 2006 and has played a crucial role in negotiating with the Palestinians. That's a much heftier résumé than Palin, who has spent less than two years heading a state with one tenth the population of Israel. —KATIE BAKER

Mac also had no dealings with the lobbying firm beyond paying monthly invoices—but it agreed to the arrangement because of Davis's close relationship with McCain, the

> **The mortgage giant paid Davis Manafort a $15,000-per-month fee between 2006 and August 2008.**

source said, which led top executives to conclude "you couldn't say no."

The McCain campaign told reporters the fees were irrelevant because Davis "separated from his consulting firm . . . in 2006," according to the campaign's Web site, and he stopped drawing a salary from it. In fact, however, when Davis joined the campaign in January 2007, he asked that his $20,000-a-month salary be paid directly to Davis Manafort, two sources who asked not to be identified discussing internal campaign business told NEWSWEEK. Federal campaign records show the McCain campaign paid Davis Manafort $90,000 through July 2007, when a cash crunch prompted Davis and other top campaign officials to forgo their salaries and work as volunteers. Separately, another entity created and partly owned by Davis—an Internet firm called 3eDC, whose address was the same office building as Davis Manafort's—received payments from the McCain campaign for Web services, collecting $971,860 through March 2008.

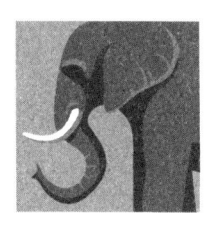

In an e-mail to NEWSWEEK, a senior McCain official said that when the campaign began last year, it signed a contract with Davis Manafort "in which we purchased *all* of [Davis's] time, and he agreed not to work for *any* other clients." The official also said that though Davis was an "investor" in 3eDC, Davis has received no salary from it. As to why Davis permitted the Freddie Mac payments to continue, the official referred NEWSWEEK to Davis Manafort, which did not respond to repeated phone calls. One senior McCain adviser said the entire flap could have been avoided if the campaign had resisted attacking Barack Obama for his ties to two former Fannie Mae executives, which prompted the media to take a second look at Davis. "It was stupid," the adviser said. "A serious miscalculation and an amateurish move." Still, this adviser said, McCain's faith in his campaign manager remains unswerving.

—MICHAEL ISIKOFF *and* HOLLY BAILEY

WEEK OF OCTOBER 13

CAMPAIGN 2008

Obama's 'Good Will' Hunting

The Obama campaign has shattered all fund-raising records, raking in $458 million so far, with about half the bounty coming from donors who contribute $200 or less. Aides say that's an illustration of a truly democratic campaign. To critics, though, it can be an invitation for fraud and illegal foreign cash because donors giving individual sums of $200 or less don't have to be publicly reported. Consider the cases of Obama donors "Doodad Pro" of Nunda, N.Y., who gave $17,130, and "Good Will" of Austin, Texas, who gave more than $11,000—both in excess of the $2,300-per-person federal limit. In two recent letters to the Obama campaign, Federal Election Commission auditors flagged those (and other) donors and informed the campaign that the sums had to be returned. Neither name had ever been publicly reported because both individuals made online donations in $10 and $25 increments. "Good Will" listed his employer as "Loving" and his occupation as "You," while supplying as his address 1015 Norwood Park Boulevard, which is shared by the Austin nonprofit Goodwill Industries. Suzanha Burmeister, marketing director for Goodwill, said the group had "no clue" who the donor was. She added, however, that the group had received five puzzling thank-you letters from the Obama campaign this year, prompting it to send the campaign an e-mail in September pointing out the apparent fraudulent use of its name.

"Doodad Pro" listed no occupation or employer; the contributor's listed address is shared by Lloyd and Lynn's Liquor Store in Nunda. "I have never heard of such an individual," says Diane Beardsley, who works at the store and is the

> **The unknown donor listed his employer as "Loving" and his occupation as "You."**

mother of one of the owners. "Nobody at this store has that much money to contribute." (She added that a Doodad's Boutique, located next door, had closed a year ago, before the donations were made.)

Obama spokesman Ben LaBolt said the campaign has no idea who the individuals are and has returned all the donations, using the credit-card numbers they gave to the campaign. (In a similar case earlier this year, the campaign returned $33,000 to two Palestinian brothers in the Gaza Strip who had bought T shirts in bulk from the campaign's online store. They had listed their address as "Ga.," which the campaign took to mean Georgia rather than Gaza.) "While no organization is completely protected from Internet fraud, we will continue to review our fund-raising procedures," LaBolt said. Some critics say the campaign hasn't done enough. This summer, watchdog groups asked both campaigns to share more information about its small donors. The McCain campaign agreed; the Obama campaign did not. "They could've done themselves a service" by heeding the suggestions, said Massie Ritsch of the Center for Responsive Politics. —MICHAEL ISIKOFF

PALIN

An Apparent Flip-Flop on Gay Rights

Watching the vice presidential debate, you might have gotten the impression that Sarah Palin supports civil rights for same-sex couples. During an exchange on the topic, both she and Joe Biden said they oppose gay marriage. But Biden added that he and Barack Obama favor granting gay couples many of the same benefits—hospital visitation rights, health benefits—that married couples enjoy. Palin was tougher to pin down. She clearly didn't want to appear intolerant, but neither did she want to seem to embrace gay rights. "[N]o one would ever propose, not in a McCain-Palin administration, to do anything to prohibit, say, visitations in a hospital or contracts being signed . . ." she said.

The folks in Alaska might have been surprised to hear that. In the

> **"If it took an amendment to our Constitution," Palin said in 2007, "I would go there."**

past, Palin has described her opposition to granting gay couples the benefits married couples receive. In an August 2007 interview with NEWSWEEK, Palin said she had upheld such benefits (angering fellow conservatives) but only because the state Supreme Court said it was unconstitutional to deny them:

NEWSWEEK: And do you have a position on that? Would you like to see it? Do you care?

PALIN: I would vote to further define the definition of marriage as it pertains to benefits even—yes, I would.

That is, not extend benefits to same-sex couples?

Correct. And if it took an amendment to our constitution, I would go there . . .

The Alaska governor was careful not to say anything like that during the debate. Biden, sensing an opportunity, tried to force Palin into clarifying her position. "I'm glad to hear the governor . . . thinks there should be no civil-rights distinction . . . between a committed gay couple and a committed heterosexual couple. If that's the case, we really don't have a difference."

Moderator Gwen Ifill threw it back to Palin: "Is that what you said?" Palin dodged the question: "Your question to him was whether he supported gay marriage and my answer is the same as his and is that I do not." A spokeswoman for the McCain campaign told newsweek that Palin opposes "all forms of discrimination against people with different lifestyles."

—KAREN BRESLAU

WEEK OF OCTOBER 20

ALASKA

Troopergate: Not Over Yet

A new Alaska legislative report finding that Gov. Sarah Palin abused her power and violated state ethics laws spells new trouble for the McCain campaign. Special counsel Steve Branchflower's report could lead to fines or legislative action to censure Palin. It also directly challenges the vice presidential candidate's credibility on key points related to the "Troopergate" controversy. Palin has said she fired Walt Monegan, Alaska's public-safety commissioner, last summer solely because of budget disputes and "insubordination" by Monegan. But Branchflower found that a likely "contributing" factor was Palin's desire to fire state trooper Mike Wooten, her ex-brother-in-law. While Palin had the right to fire Monegan, Branchflower found that she allowed her husband and top aides to put "impermissible pressure" on subordinates to "advance a personal agenda." The report also questioned Palin's public contention that her family "feared" Wooten, noting that shortly after she took office she ordered a sizable reduction in her personal protection detail.

McCain campaign spokeswoman Meg Stapleton dismissed the report as the product of "a partisan-led inquiry run by Obama supporters." But there could be more land mines ahead. Some weeks ago, the McCain team devised a plan to have Palin file an ethics complaint against herself with the State Personnel Board, arguing that it alone was capable of conducting a fair, nonpartisan inquiry into whether we went to the personnel board," said a McCain aide who asked not to be identified discussing strategy. While the McCain camp still insists Palin "has nothing to hide," it acknowledges a critical finding by Petumenos would be even harder to dismiss.

—Michael Isikoff

> **Palin has said she fired Walt Monegan, solely because of budget disputes and "insubordination"**

she fired Monegan because he refused to fire Wooten, who had been involved in a messy custody battle with her sister. Some Democrats ridiculed the move, noting that the personnel board answered to Palin. But the board ended up hiring an aggressive Anchorage trial lawyer, Timothy Petumenos, as an independent counsel. McCain aides were chagrined to discover that Petumenos was a Democrat who had contributed to Palin's 2006 opponent for governor, Tony Knowles. Palin is now scheduled to be questioned next week, and the counsel's report could be released soon after. "We took a gamble when

Nader in Florida: Remember Me?

Eight years ago Democrats had good reason to blame Ralph Nader for peeling off enough votes from Al Gore to cost him Florida and the presidency. But this year Democrats may have good reason to welcome the so-called Nader effect. According to recent CNN/Opinion Research polls, Barack Obama leads John McCain by four points in a two-way choice among likely Florida voters. That gap grows to eight points with Nader in the mix, along with other minor-party

> **Nader is now contesting 45 states**

candidates such as Libertarian Bob Barr.

Another sign the Nader effect may have reversed course is how the Democrats are dealing with him this time. In 2004, John Kerry met with Nader to try to dissuade him from running, and party lawyers contested his place on the ballot. This time, the Obama campaign has made no similar effort to obstruct Nader.

Who are the voters whom Nader siphons from McCain? Kevin Hill, an associate professor of political science at Florida International University, says Nader's populist rhetoric appeals to white working-class voters who lean conservative. "It's probably more of a protest than anything else," he says. McCain aides argue that Nader's poll ratings are too low to be significant. But at Nader's HQ, the lack of attention is welcome: instead of fighting ballot challenges, Nader is now contesting 45 states, and his campaign suggests he'll far exceed his dismal total of about 400,000 votes in 2004.

—RICHARD WOLFFE

CAMPAIGN 2008

In the Swing of It

They're called battleground states, but in truth, battles are raging in a few select regions. Each candidate's path to the White House depends on flipping a few key states that went the other way in 2004. newsweek spoke to election experts in each state to find out how they can do it.

McCain Target
Wisconsin

10 ELECTORAL VOTES
2004: 50% KERRY   49% BUSH

Bio: Virtually all white and fairly rural, Green Bay and the surrounding valley region has a healthy export economy, but the paper industry is getting shredded.

Outlook: Ten-point spread favored Bush in '04, so McCain, who's well behind in statewide polling, needs an even bigger margin for a shot at the state.

McCain Target
New Hampshire

4 ELECTORAL VOTES
2004: 50% KERRY   49% BUSH

Bio: Boston-area families head here for cheaper housing and to escape "Tax-achusetts." Moderate on social issues, and prefer free trade over fair trade.

Outlook: With half the state's vote, this region went for Bush in '04 by a slim margin. If McCain wins big with blue-collar Dems here, he could carry the state.

McCain Target
Pennsylvania

21 ELECTORAL VOTES
2004: 51% KERRY   48% BUSH

Bio: What used to be rolling Republican farmland is now home to strip malls, housing developments and affluent white—though still conservative—commuters.

Outlook: Since Bush's strong showing in '04, Dems have closed the registration gap. With Obama's statewide lead, McCain has to hold here to have a fighting chance.

Obama Target
Colorado

9 ELECTORAL VOTES
2004: 52% BUSH   47% KERRY

Bio: Republican heartland has purpled in recent years as blue-collar Latinos and influx of tech and telecom jobs have countered conservative farmers to the east.

Outlook: Obama's shot in Colorado rests in Arapahoe County's 300,000 voters, who went for Bush by 3 percent in '04. Other key counties: Jefferson, Adams, Douglas.

Obama Target
Viginia

13 ELECTORAL VOTES
2004: 54% BUSH   45% KERRY

Bio: Between flush Republican Va. Beach and bluecollar, military-heavy Norfolk/Newport News, Tidewater is politically diverse and economically stable.

Outlook: If blacks in Norfolk and Portsmouth give Obama 95 percent of their vote and he cuts the GOP margin in Va. Beach to 52 percent, he probably wins.

Obama Target
Ohio

20 ELECTORAL VOTES
2004: 51% BUSH   49% KERRY

Bio: With aging residents and a shrinking workforce, this Appalachian region has been hit hard by a crumbling coal industry and declining seasonal work.

Outlook: A bellwether despite small population, it skewed red in '04. After getting clocked by Clinton here in the primary, Obama has a lot of work to do in SE Ohio.

Obama Target
Florida

27 ELECTORAL VOTES
2004: 52% BUSH   47% KERRY

Bio: Home to almost half the state's population and a booming Central American community, the I-4 corridor in the past decade has had an influx of young, educated professionals, as well as retirees migrating from nearby Southern states.

Outlook: With McCain's hold on the Panhandle, Obama needs to swing central, purple counties like Pinellas, which Bush won by less than half a percent in 2004. If Obama can flip that, he has a shot at the state.

CAMPAIGN 2008

Florida GOP: Red With Dismay

Tom Slade, a former Florida GOP chair, was getting about five calls a day last week from fellow Republicans saying the same thing: "Do something." The source of their alarm was the seemingly perilous condition of Sen. John McCain's campaign in the state. After leading for months in Florida, recent polls show him trailing Sen. Barack Obama by about five points. Much of the reversal, no doubt, stems from the economic crisis. But part of the blame lies with the McCain team itself, according to numerous Florida Republicans. Slade says he's hearing complaints that the campaign isn't coordinating volunteers well and its state director, Arlene DiBenigno, is ineffective. Others say its voter-turnout operation is lagging. (A Florida spokesman for McCain declined to respond to these assertions.) "The campaign is kind of on the ropes," says one GOP strategist who requested anonymity to give a candid assessment. McCain "could lose Florida now, and if he does, it's game over."

Tension has reportedly been mounting between the campaign and state Republicans. Several weeks ago, Florida GOP chair Jim Greer convened a private meeting with both camps to discuss the darkening outlook. News of the gathering, which apparently grew tense, leaked to media. Greer denies any discord, telling NEWSWEEK the point was to "make sure that the ship was on its right course." But a McCain loyalist who was present and also requested anonymity says Greer was just looking out for himself— either by appearing to save the day or "forewarning of a crisis so he couldn't be blamed."

Then there's Republican Gov. Charlie Crist, whose enthusiasm for McCain, some say, has waned since he was passed over as a veep pick. He recently told reporters that "his foremost responsibility" is governing his state and that he was eager to help the Arizona senator "when I have time." Then about a week ago, he went to Disney World instead of a McCain rally. Crist tells NEWSWEEK that worries about his commitment are unfounded. "I couldn't be more enthusiastic," he says. "I love John McCain, and I'm doing all I can" to help him. Last

Friday, he joined the candidate at rallies in Miami and Melbourne. Unfortunately, another distraction emerged that day: one of McCain's top fundraisers in the state, Harry Sargeant III, was accused of overcharging the government for fuel deliveries in Iraq by his contracting company. (A lawyer for Sargeant has denied the allegations.)

Not all Florida Republicans are despairing, though. The GOP chairs of some counties along the critical Interstate 4 corridor, including Pinellas, home to St. Petersburg, say their troops are fired up and have all the resources they need. The recent flurry of complaints were "a little bit of preliminary finger-pointing," says Brian Ballard, McCain's Florida finance chair. "I think everybody now gets the point that we've got to work together."

—ARIAN CAMPO-FLORES

SECRET SERVICE

The Death-Threat Debate

During a heated moment in his final presidential debate with Sen. John McCain, Sen. Barack Obama noted the anger of some supporters at rallies for McCain's running mate, Alaska Gov. Sarah Palin. "All the public reports suggested," Obama said, that people shouted "things like 'terrorist' and 'kill him'." Making a death threat against a presidential candidate can be a crime. But even before Obama cited "reports" of the threats at the debate, the U.S. Secret Service had told media outlets, including NEWSWEEK, that it was unable to corroborate accounts of the "kill him" remarks—and according to

> **Secret Service concluded the male voice could have been saying 'tell him,' not 'kill him.'**

a law-enforcement official, who asked for anonymity when discussing a political matter, the Obama campaign knew as much. Now some officials are disgruntled that Obama gave added credence to the threat by mentioning it in front of 60 million viewers. At this point in the campaign, said one, candidates will "say anything to make a particular point."

During a warm-up speech for Palin at an Oct. 15 rally in Scranton, Pa., a journalist with the city's Times-Tribune paper, David Singleton, reported hearing someone say "kill him"; he told NEWSWEEK that the remark was made casually, rather than angrily, by a male voice. Singleton stands by his account, but he acknowledges that he was unable to identify who made the remark. Secret Service spokesman Eric Zahren says his agency examined videotape from that event and an earlier Palin event in Clearwater, Fla., at which a similar threat was supposedly made, and concluded that the voice could've been saying "tell him" or "tell them." But Washington Post reporter Dana Milbank, who was in Clearwater, said "the guy was a few feet in front of me . . . '[T]ell him' doesn't make any sense as a response to what Palin was saying." An Obama campaign spokesman told NEWSWEEK that "whether or not the [Secret Service] is investigating that particular comment is irrelevant. What is true is that the tone of the rhetoric at McCain-Palin campaign events has gotten out of hand."

—MARK HOSENBALL

ELECTIONS

Case of the Vanishing Male Voter

Hillary Clinton and Sarah Palin have helped draw unprecedented attention to female voters this year. But what will men do at the ballot box on Nov. 4? Many of them will just stay home, according to New York University professor Rogan Kersh, an expert on voting patterns. Over the past 40 years, the voting rate for both men and women has tumbled—but much more steeply for men. In 1964, a record 72 percent of voting-age males made their mark for president. By 2004, that figure had slipped to just 56 percent, or 16 million fewer men than if the rates had stayed level. That's a turnout gap roughly the size of Michigan and Indiana combined.

Some politicos say that the Democratic Party has suffered more from the male malaise, since its base of white working-class

Participation rates have tumbled for both sexes over the past 40 years—but more steeply for men.

men has eroded. But the shift cuts against the GOP, too. Strong female majorities and sluggish male turnout helped elect Bill Clinton to two terms. This election, the missing male vote could sink John McCain. His choice of Palin—whose favorability rating is four points higher among men than women, according to a Pew poll late last month—might not pay off. Meanwhile, Barack Obama is going where the boys are, buying ad space in videogames such as NBA Live and Grand Theft Auto. Whether or not it works, the question remains: why don't more men vote?

Isolation: Men are less likely than women to attend church, consume news, trust authority and believe that people are generally good, according to the University of Michigan's General Social Survey, a biannual tracking of attitudes and behaviors. "I'm basically an outsider," says Chris Cox, 32, a systems administrator from Omaha. Voting, he explains, is like choosing "between a douche bag and a turd sandwich."

Education: Higher education is the top predictor of voting, and increasingly men aren't as schooled as women. In recent decades, male enrollment has dropped below that of women at the undergraduate level.

Crime: Of the 5.3 million convicted felons barred from voting in this country, more than 80 percent are men. That number has steadily swelled since the 1980s, says UC-San Diego political scientist Samuel Popkin, who explains the male voting problem simply: "Men go to jail."

Culture: It's a guy thing—but mostly a single-guy thing. Married men are not only more likely to vote than their bachelor counterparts, but according to gender sociologist Michael Kimmel, they are frequently swayed by their wives about who gets their votes. Wise decision.

—Tony Dokoupil

FAST CHAT

Veterans Day: Grading the Pols

John McCain is the candidate most associated with military veterans, but a new report by the nonprofit Iraq and Afghanistan Veterans of America gives him a weak grade on his support for vet issues. Newsweek's Jesse Ellison talked to the group's executive director, Iraq War veteran Paul Rieckhoff.

Your methodology has been criticized.
Yes. Some folks say, 'You shouldn't have hit people who missed votes.' [But] it's part of your job as a senator. The bottom line is, you can't support veterans if you're not there to vote on the issues.

You gave Barack Obama a B and McCain a D. Why did Obama do so much better?
Our scorecard is heavily weighted on the GI bill. McCain was not a supporter. And he missed six of the nine key votes. Obama, although he got a B, is still below average. McCain missed more votes than Senator [Tim] Johnson, who was in a coma. They both missed more votes than Ted Kennedy, who had a brain tumor.

McCain, of course, is a veteran. It seems hard to believe that he would fare so badly.

People tend to blur the war and the warriors, the people and the policy. You don't have to be a veteran to support veteran's issues.

Some accuse your organization of being a partisan political group masquerading as a nonpartisan think tank.

Plenty of Republicans got A's. We put the formula in place and we put in the votes, and it spits out a grade. People want to say, 'You gave McCain a grade.' Well, this is what McCain earned.

But you did release the report just weeks before the election.

We released it now to inject it into the national political discussion. If you look back on the first debate, the only discussion of veteran's issues was this wristband conversation they had. "I've got a wristband." "No, I've got a wristband." That's not the level of dialogue we need.

WEEK OF NOVEMBER 3

MCCAIN CAMPAIGN

Not the Change They Wanted

The disclosure that the Republican National Committee spent more than $150,000 on clothing and accessories for vice presidential candidate Sarah Palin and her family set off recriminations among GOP officials—and, more important, party donors. It wasn't just the volume of the purchases—which included new dresses for Palin, suits for husband Todd and outfits for her children—it was the use of swanky stores like Neiman Marcus. One top party fundraiser told NEWSWEEK that, ever since the story broke on Politico.com, he was bombarded with calls from Republican donors who were "furious" that their contributions were used for such purposes. "This has damaged everybody's credibility," griped the fundraiser (who asked not to be identified talking about party business). Among those upset was Saul Anuzis, the Michigan Republican Party chairman, still smarting over McCain's decision to pull out of his state. "I have no idea how you spend $150,000 on clothes," he says. Lobbyist Andrea McWilliams, a GOP fundraiser in Texas, said the flap undercut the party's message. Palin's "transformation from low couture to haute couture isn't the kind of change that voters had in mind," she said.

The decision to greenlight the

purchases was made after Palin arrived in Minneapolis for the Republican Party convention. Campaign aides quickly concluded that she lacked the necessary wardrobe for two months of intensive national campaigning. "She didn't have the fancy pantsuits that Hillary Clinton has," explained one staffer (who, like most others interviewed for this account, declined to be identified speaking about the episode). The problem was figuring out how to pay for new dresswear: the 2002 McCain-Feingold law, co-authored by the GOP candidate, tightened the rules to ban using campaign funds for personal clothing. While Jeff Larson, a veteran GOP consultant who headed the party's "host" committee, provided his credit card for the Palin family shopping spree, he was directed to send the bills over to the Republican National Committee (which was not covered by the clothing ban in McCain-Feingold). RNC officials were not happy about it. "We were explicitly directed by the campaign to pay these costs," said one senior RNC official who also requested anonymity. After at first declining to comment, a McCain spokeswoman said the clothes would be donated to charity after the campaign was over.

Palin said she was getting a bum rap. "If people knew how frugal we are," she said. She told Fox News that her "favorite" store is an Anchorage consignment shop called Out of the Closet. Still, some of the disgruntled party donors said her claim of frugality was hard to square with the details in campaign spending reports, such as the $75,062 one-day tab at the Neiman Marcus in Minneapolis, and $4,902 spent at Atelier New York (a high-end men's store). One veteran GOP consultant (who also requested anonymity) said the real puzzle among his peers is why Larson didn't find a way to disguise the expenses, at least until after the election. Larson declined to comment.

—MICHAEL ISIKOFF *and* SUZANNE SMALLEY

> **Some GOP donors say they are "furious" about this use of their party's funds.**

National Affairs

YEAR IN REVIEW

Historically, the second term of a U.S. presidency is pocked by scandal, controversy and investigation—the sins of the first term coming to public light—and the final year of the Bush administration was, unsurprisingly, no exception. The administration's conduct of the war, especially in matters of criminal detention and torture, fell under increased scrutiny. New Attorney General Michael Mukasey ordered an investigation into the destruction of CIA videotapes showing the use of enhanced interrogation techniques, including waterboarding, on suspected terrorists. Revelations that such behavior was discussed and countenanced by the highest levels of the administration, including the president and the vice president, helped undermine the last vestiges of George W. Bush's legitimacy with the American public. (And Mukasey himself only became the nation's top lawyer after his predecessor, Alberto Gonzalez, resigned amid charges that he had overseen a purge of several top federal prosecutors for purely partisan reasons.)

Scandals of a more salacious kind also dominated the headlines in 2008, making up for what they lacked in import with a surfeit of illicit melodramatic flair. And for a change, most of the sex scandals this past year claimed the political careers of Democrats, not Republicans. The year began with the stunning fall of New York Governor Eliot Spitzer, whose crusading, anti-corruption reputation evaporated in a blink with the revelation that he'd run up a large tab with an exclusive prostitution ring. He resigned from office just two days after the story broke. The city of Detroit's talented young mayor, Kwame Kilpatrick, wound up in jail after he tried to cover up, with lies and firings, a long-running affair with his chief of staff. A series of steamy text messages did him in. And then, this summer, came the political and personal fall of former Democratic presidential candidate John Edwards, who went in a matter of weeks from Barack Obama's short list of potential running mates to a shamed political has-been. Edwards was forced to admit that he had cheated on his wife Elizabeth while she was stricken with terminal cancer. A bizarre, late-night confrontation with reporters from the National Enquirer at the Beverly Hilton hotel, where Edwards had arranged to meet his former mistress and her infant child (not his, he still insists) precipitated the story's explosion into the mainstream. At the time, Edwards held no political office and was no longer a presidential candidate, but for a country weary of news about war and presidential campaigns, the story was practically catnip.

It took a brutal and terrifying hurricane season to restore a sense of moral seriousness to the nation's news consumption. After dodging the bullet of Hurricane Gustav, which took dead aim at New Orleans and had the region bracing for a repeat of Katrina, the Gulf Coast near Houston was slammed just weeks later by Hurricane Ike, crippling much of the Texas coastline and wreaking havoc with the American South's natural gas supply. In the days that followed, several major cities suffered through gas pump shortages that recalled the long lines and hot tempers of the late 1970s.

WEEK OF JANUARY 7

FAST CHAT

Classified Disinformation

Veteran national Archives official J. William Leonard learned the hard way the perils of questioning Vice President Dick Cheney. Leonard challenged the Office of the Vice President's claims to be exempt from federal rules governing classified information, prompting a counterstrike by Cheney's top aide, David Addington, who tried to wipe out Leonard's job. (Addington did not respond to requests for comment.) Now Leonard is quitting as director of the archives' Information Security Oversight Office, the unit that monitors the handling of government secrets. In a conversation with NEWSWEEK's Michael Isikoff, he says that the fight with Cheney's office was a "contributing" factor in his decision to retire. (For more, visit Newsweek.com.)

Explain how all this happened.
Up until 2002, OVP was just like any other agency. Then they stopped reporting to us. At first, I took that to mean "We're too busy." Then we routinely attempted to do a review of the OVP and it was articulated back to me that they weren't really subject to

FIRST PERSON

An Airport Bathroom That Will Live in Infamy

NEWSWEEK's *Hilary Shenfeld went to the scene of Sen. Larry Craig's undoing with one mission: to get inside. How she did it—and what she saw:*

The hardest part was actually finding the bathroom. There are 86 public lavatories in the Lindbergh terminal of the Minneapolis-St. Paul airport, and every employee I asked sent me to a differ-

continued

National Affairs-100 | JANUARY

our reviews. I didn't agree with it. But there is a big fence around the White House. I didn't know how I could get in there if somebody didn't want me to.

How did it escalate?

When the OVP spokesperson made public this idea that because they have both legislative and executive functions, that requirement doesn't apply to them. I thought that was a rather remarkable position. So I wrote my letter to the attorney general [asking for a ruling that Cheney's office had to comply]. Shortly after, there were [e-mails from OVP aide David Addington to a National Security Council task force] to change the executive order that would effectively abolish [my] office.

What was your reaction?

I was disappointed that rather than engage on the substance of an issue, some people would resort to that.

Ultimately, the White House said the president never intended that the vice president would have to comply. This must have been frustrating—to be publicly thwarted doing what you saw as your job.

Well, you know, I've had 34 years of frustration. That's life in the big city.

Is too much government business conducted in secret?

I've never met anybody in this town who says we have too few secrets. I truly believe we need to introduce a new balancing test. Yes, disclosing information may cause damage, but withholding that information may even cause greater damage. The global struggle that we're engaged in today is

---

ent one. I finally found it: across from the food court, in the shadow of a giant statue of Snoopy and Woodstock. There was no sign on the door, nothing that read "Larry Craig was here." I waited until late to go inside, figuring that foot traffic would die down and I could minimize the awkward stares. Around 11 p.m. I stopped a friendly-looking guy and persuaded him to escort me (sorry—bad pun) inside. It's pretty big in there: a tiled cavern with nine stalls along the left wall. Craig's was the second from the back. I was only in the bathroom for a couple of minutes, but the entire time I was thinking, Eww. I scoped out the stalls, jotted down some notes, then got the heck out of there.

an ideological struggle. And in my mind, that calls for greater transparency, not less. We're in a situation where we're attempting to win over the hearts and minds of the world's population. And yet, when we restrict information, we're often ceding the playing field to the other side. We allow ourselves to be reduced to a caricature.

IMMIGRATION

The View From Both Sides

On the campaign trail this year, no issue burned hotter than immigration—particularly on the Republican side, where each candidate seemed determined to prove that he would build a taller fence than the next guy. For all the bluster, though, it's largely been a one-sided conversation. Americans rarely hear a perspective from across the border in Mexico. Jorge Bustamante is a U.N. immigration expert and president of El Colegio de la Frontera Norte, a Tijuana university that specializes in border studies. He spoke with NEWSWEEK's Monica Campbell about the issue—and how Americans get it wrong.

Do Mexicans interpret the immigration issue differently from Americans?

In Mexico, we see it as a labor phenomenon, not a crime. It's a binational problem involving supply and demand, not a domestic issue that can be solved with unilateral decisions enforced by the police. Everyone here knows that illegal immigration is a result of the demand for cheaper labor in the U.S. and supply from Mexico, which is produced by our own internal economic problems. It's worrying that many people in the U.S. believe undocumented immigrants have no rights and are committing a crime. At the same time, there's a lot of indifference in Mexico when it comes to this issue, particularly among the upper classes. But talk to poorer people and you will hear them full of indignation about how immigrants are treated in the U.S.

> It's worrying that many people in the U.S. believe undocumented immigrants have no rights and are committing a crime.

What's your take on proposals to make undocumented workers go home before they can apply to return to the United States?

Look at what President Bush said: the massive deportation of millions of undocumented immigrants is not realistic. It just can't work. There will always be a way to cross.

Do you say "illegal alien" or "undocumented immigrant"?

"Undocumented immigrant." I think that describes the situation most accurately. "Illegal alien" sounds fundamentalist.

Critics recently slammed a New York proposal to allow illegal immigrants to obtain driver's licenses. What was your take?

It reflected the hypocrisy of the debate. People see immigrants as workers, but not as human beings who deserve a driver's license. Dropping the proposal went against the interest of Americans. It could've improved highway safety.

What's missing from the debate?

More talk about human trafficking, particularly of women and children. It's an abhorrent, growing problem.

WEEK OF JANUARY 14

INVESTIGATIONS

A Scramble At the CIA to Lawyer Up

Attorney General Michael Mukasey's decision to launch a full-scale FBI probe into the destruction of CIA interrogation tapes has sent several alarmed agency employees scrambling to find lawyers. To lead the probe, the A.G. named John Durham, a hard-nosed veteran prosecutor who is assembling a team of deputies and FBI agents. Some CIA veterans fear the move is tantamount to unleashing an independent counsel on Langley. "A lot of people are worried," says one former CIA official, who asked not to be identified talking about sensitive matters. "Whenever you have the bureau running around the building, it's going to turn up some heads. This could turn into a witch hunt." Justice officials say Durham was assigned to investigate the 2005 decision to destroy the tapes—not the activities recorded on them, including the use of waterboarding on Al Qaeda suspects. But at this point, Durham has no formal mandate on the probe's scope, giving him the freedom to expand it if he chooses. "We're going to follow this wherever it leads," says one Justice official, who asked not to be identified discussing an ongoing probe.

One key figure, Jose Rodriguez, the former CIA chief of clandestine services who gave the order to destroy the videotapes, has retained Robert Bennett, a renowned defense lawyer who represented Bill Clinton in the Paula Jones lawsuit. Another potential witness, George Tenet, who was CIA director when the tapes were made, will be represented by former FBI general counsel Howard Shapiro. Roy Krieger, a Washington lawyer who has represented about 100 CIA employees, says that two agency officers have approached him about representation, though neither has retained him yet.

For the CIA spooks involved, cost is a serious issue. Krieger says legal expenses for each employee could reach "hundreds of thousands" of dollars; the CIA will not foot the bill. In anticipation of just such a scenario, however, the agency some years ago began encouraging its employees to purchase special liability-insurance policies from Wright & Co., a Virginia firm that specializes in coverage for government investigators. A Wright spokesman had no response to questions about whether claims have been filed for legal fees in connection with the tapes inquiry. CIA spokesman Paul Gimigliano confirmed the agency does not pay its officers' legal bills, but added "only a very, very small subset of agency activities ever become the subject of litigation or investigation."

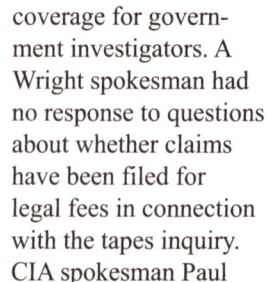

—Mark Hosenball and Michael Isikoff

WEEK OF JANUARY 21

CIA

Hunt on for More Tapes

The CIA has launched an internal search for more audio- or videotapes depicting interrogations of suspected terrorists, according to two U.S. officials familiar with the matter. The hunt is part of the agency's response to several investigations—by the Justice Department, Congress and the CIA's own inspector general—into the destruction in 2005 of videotapes documenting CIA interrogations of two senior Qaeda operatives. Current and former officials said they doubt the agency itself recorded any other interrogations, but added that the CIA might have received recordings made by friendly intelligence services that questioned Qaeda suspects. (The officials asked for anonymity when discussing sensitive matters.)

The agency has already acknowledged that it found some interrogation tapes beyond those destroyed in 2005. In a letter sent in October to the federal judge who jailed 9/11 collaborator Zacarias Moussaoui, prosecutors said the CIA had informed them about two videotapes and one audiotape apparently documenting the interrogation of suspects. Details are still classified, but the recordings appear to relate to the interrogation of suspects held by foreign intelligence agencies. The destroyed videos covered hundreds of hours of interrogation. They are understood to have included evidence of CIA officials using aggressive interrogation techniques such as "waterboarding" on Qaeda captives Abu Zubaydah and Abd al-Rahim al-Nashiri. The officials noted that if agency employees do find video- or audiotapes, they will probably turn them over directly to investigators without first viewing them—thus shielding themselves from accusations of interfering with the investigations. The CIA declined any comment on the ongoing investigations.

Congressional inquiries into the destruction of the agency's interrogation videos appear to be encountering snags.

Meanwhile, congressional inquiries into the destruction of the agency's interrogation videos appear to be encountering snags. People close to the investigation say Jose Rodriguez Jr., the former head of CIA undercover operations who ordered the tapes destroyed, is refusing to testify at Capitol Hill hearings without a grant of immunity from Congress. (Rodriguez's lawyer, Robert Bennett, declined to comment.) The Justice Department has also asked congressional committees not to allow witnesses to see documents that the department regards as critical to its own investigation, a move which may discourage other witnesses from giving congressional testimony. —MARK HOSENBALL

EDUCATION

No Child Outside the Classroom

When no child left Behind became law in 2002, teachers suspected there'd be some casualties—they just didn't think field trips would be one of them. Since the federal government's landmark overhaul of U.S. schools, class trips have plummeted at some of the country's traditional hot spots for brown-bag learning. The new emphasis on standardized testing has resulted in "a reluctance to take kids out of the classroom," says Natalie Bortoli, head of the visual-arts program at the Chicago Children's Museum, which has lost more than a tenth of its field-trip business since 2005. At Mystic Seaport, a maritime museum on the Connecticut coast, school traffic has slowed more than a quarter since 2005, while Boston's New England Aquarium has lost nearly the same amount since 2003. Even NASA's Johnson Space Center has started to see its figures stagnate, says marketing director Roger Bornstein, "and stability is not our goal."

Teachers blame the bear market in part on No Child Left Behind, which requires schools to get students up to state targets in reading and math by 2014 or face sanctions that could result in school takeovers or closings. "Curriculums are so much tighter than they used to be," says Susan Lewis, an elementary-school teacher in San Antonio, Texas. Add in rising transportation costs, and field trips are fast becoming history. Compton Avenue Elementary School in Los Angeles has halved its trips in the past three years. "They were all academically based," says principal Claudia Ross, but they no longer fit a budget focused on test scores, not general enrichment.

Museums are coming up with new strategies to lure schools back. The Chicago Children's Museum sends teachers a checklist that highlights how the museum can help them meet Illinois state

> **The new emphasis on standardized testing has resulted in "a reluctance to take kids out of the classroom."**

standards, while representatives from the New England Aquarium visit schools in Massachusetts to explain how its programs can give kids a boost. Many museums have also started giving their young visitors clipboards, worksheets, science journals and the chance to quiz a resident historian or scientist. "We know it's directly linking into the standards," Bortoli says. "But I don't think the kids notice." They're happy as long as they don't get left behind.

—ROXANA POPESCU

WEEK OF FEBRUARY 18

INTELLIGENCE

Back on the Tape Trail

Newly released documents suggest that the U.S. government videotaped more Qaeda suspects than it has publicly disclosed. Court filings unsealed last week show that federal prosecutors recently informed a judge about videos depicting the questioning of a key figure in the case of convicted Qaeda operative Zacarias Moussaoui. Although the witness's name was redacted, a U.S. official (who asked for anonymity discussing sensitive matters) acknowledged that it was Mohammad al-Qatani, the reputed "20th hijacker," who has been detained at Guantánamo Bay since 2002. A Qatani video could create problems: his treatment was the subject of an extensive investigation by the U.S. Southern Command. The probe, whose results were released in 2005, found that he'd been forced to wear a bra, stand naked in front of female guards, wear a leash and "perform a series of dog tricks." The Southern Command report concluded that while these practices were "abusive and degrading," they did not rise to the level of "inhumane treatment" barred by law. But the existence of video footage could become a factor if, as The New York Times reported last week, Qatani is among those likely to face charges by the Pentagon for his alleged role in the 9/11 plot. "This is critical to determining the lawfulness" of Qatani's interrogation, said ACLU lawyer

Jameel Jaffer. The ACLU plans to file a motion demanding that the Pentagon release the tapes.

Qatani may not be the last witness to turn up on interrogation tapes. Another newly released document shows that the State Department permitted foreign intelligence services to question Gitmo detainees in June 2002 under the condition that the United States would record audio and video. It's unclear how many of those tapes still exist. A spokesman for the U.S. military at Gitmo told NEWSWEEK that base officials are "not required to tape interrogations and did not routinely do so."

—MICHAEL ISIKOFF and MARK HOSENBALL

WEEK OF MARCH 3

INTELLIGENCE

Antiterror Help Wanted

In October 2007, National Counterterrorism Center director John Scott Redd, a retired Navy vice admiral, told a TV interviewer that the invasion of Iraq "probably" did not make the U.S. safer from terrorism. A few days later, Redd resigned, citing health concerns. Bush administration officials denied that Redd's departure had anything to do with his comments, and the post has remained vacant—which is odd, since the NCTC is one of the few undisputed bright spots of post-9/11 intelligence reform legislation. Since Redd left, the NCTC has been run on an interim basis by one of his deputies, Michael Leiter, a former Navy aviator and federal prosecutor whose leadership has won praise from intel officials and congressional monitors.

But until very recently, the White House has appeared reluctant to name Leiter as permanent NCTC chief. Instead, it spent months on a fruitless search for a higher-profile director, according to two government officials who asked for anonymity when discussing sensitive matters. Several possible candidates, including military officers and CIA executives, turned the job down. Administration officials and Republican congressmen concluded that candidates were scared off by the prospect of the Senate confirmation process—especially since the job could be short-lived, with only a year left in the Bush presidency.

So why hasn't the White House offered the post to Leiter? One factor could be his political credentials. According to his official biography, Leiter, a Harvard law graduate, once clerked for Supreme Court Justice Stephen Breyer, a liberal Bill Clinton appointee. A White House spokesman did not respond to a request for comment; a spokesman for the office of National Intelligence Director Mike McConnell declined to comment. Just hours after NEWSWEEK first inquired about the NCTC position, however, one government official indicated that the White House may well nominate Leiter in the near future.

—MARK HOSENBALL

FAST CHAT

A Reformer Who Keeps 'The Faith'

Recent popular books by atheist authors have spawned a new generation of Christian apologists. The latest rebuttal is "The Faith: What Christians Believe, Why They Believe It and Why It Matters," by Chuck Colson, the convicted Watergate felon turned prison reformer. Colson was Nixon's special counsel, a man so ruthless that, according to legend, he once said he'd kill his own grandmother for his boss; now he argues on behalf of Jesus. He spoke with NEWSWEEK's Lisa Miller.

Why did you write this book?
Christians are making a very poor case in public about what we believe. [Christopher] Hitchens's book is literally an embarrassment. We're being defined by people outside of the faith . . . Christianity in its radical form, its apostolic form, is a dynamic story, a powerful force that shaped Western civilization. In prisons, what resonates is the story of Jesus, a poor man riding on a borrowed donkey, born in a borrowed manger. That's the story that's resonating in the Third World. In South America, Africa, Asia, they're preaching the real thing.

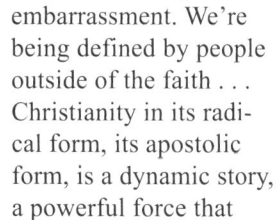

In your book, you use the word "orthodoxy" to describe the kind of Christianity you advocate. How does that jibe with the American ideal of pluralism?
Pluralism means a plurality of points of view. It doesn't mean you have to treat them all as equal. When people talk about pluralism, they say all religions are alike and that's absolutely not true.

What is "orthodox Christianity," then?
Right thinking and right beliefs. It doesn't change as times change. It's eternal truth if it's true at all.

Do you think the religious right is weakening or fracturing?
I think evangelicals have grown up, are more mature. Our influence as a power bloc has weakened, yes. But that's only because of the candidates. If you had a candidate who really expressed all the traditional moral values—

Well, doesn't Huckabee do that?
He was a minor candidate who has emerged as one of the last men standing. My hunch is that before the fall, most evangelicals will be organized behind McCain.

What does McCain have to do to win Christian conservatives?
He's got to emphasize his pro-life credentials, which are pretty good. He's got to pay a lot more attention to values.

What do you think about a McCain-Huckabee ticket?
I don't have any inside track ... but I have heard it discussed by people in the McCain campaign.

How much power do old-guard evangelicals, like Dr. James Dobson of Focus on the Family, still have in Washington?
[Dobson] said he wasn't going to vote [if McCain was the nominee]. I thought that was a mistake, I told him that before he said it ... It's a sin in my opinion not to be involved in your civic duty.

Should evangelicals stay out of politics?
No, of course not. You should stay in and fight, but not as a power group.

WEEK OF MARCH 10

RACE

When Hate Becomes Hurt

It began like any other policy fight, but the tension surrounding immigration reform has escalated into hate, according to the National Council of La Raza, the country's largest Hispanic civil-rights group. Last month, it accused cable news networks of letting hosts and guests inject a "hateful tone" into the debate, specifically citing CNN's Lou Dobbs and Glenn Beck. "It is palpable," says La Raza president Janet Murguía, who worries that descriptions of immigrants as "invaders" or "aliens" have contributed to a rise in anti-Hispanic violence. Since 2004, the number of anti-Hispanic hate crimes has jumped 25 percent, according to the FBI. In the past, experts have noted a link between hateful language and violence.

Now La Raza, which has launched a Web site to document instances of immigrant bashing, is demanding that the TV networks stop "handing hate a microphone." They've also asked presidential candidate Mike Huckabee to renounce the endorsement he received from Jim Gilchrist, cofounder of the Minuteman Project to patrol the U.S.–Mexico border and a frequent guest on cable news shows. In response, Fox News issued a letter defending the network's programming decisions, while CNN met with La Raza behind closed doors. (A CNN spokes-person acknowledged the use of strong language but declined to call it excessive.) MSNBC, meanwhile, has agreed to a meeting this month. But Huckabee is standing by his man. Huckabee said in an e-mail to NEWSWEEK that while he has sympathy for groups like La Raza, "I am glad [Gilchrist] supported my immigration plan."

> La Raza has asked the cable news networks to stop "handing hate a microphone."

The Anti-Defamation League, meanwhile, is standing behind La Raza. "When we saw the rhetoric shift from a legitimate debate to one where immigrants were dehumanized, we believe it inspired extremists and [some] mainstream Americans to act," says Deborah Lauter, the group's civil-rights director. But according to Dan Stein, president of the Federation for

---

THE DIGNITY INDEX

How About We Send Him to Afghanistan?

A weekly mathematical survey of dubious behavior that measures, on a scale of 1 to 100, just how low a person can go

Despite the fact that 99.62 percent of the country voted for someone other than him in 2004, **Ralph Nader** says he's running for president again. Score: **23**

Georgia GOP Rep. **Jack Kingston** blasts Obama on MSNBC for not wearing an American-flag lapel pin—while not wearing one himself. How patriotic. Score: **60**

Internet gossip jockey **Matt Drudge** gets our highest score yet for jeopardizing multiple lives when he posted the "Prince Harry at war" news. Score: **98**

Immigration Reform, La Raza is "trying to stop a legitimate public policy debate." If La Raza can't settle its dispute with the networks then it plans to take the fight to the sponsors. If that doesn't work, the next stop is November—and the voting booth.

—JESSICA RAMIREZ

WEEK OF MARCH 17

CRIME

An Arms Dealer's U.S. Ties

U.S. officials are thrilled about the arrest in Bangkok of accused Russian arms trafficker Viktor Bout following a lengthy undercover sting by the Drug Enforcement Administration. Dubbed the "Merchant of Death," Bout had been a top target for years. But if, as expected, he is extradited to New York, where he faces charges of conspiring to provide weapons to Colombian guerrillas, the case could also embarrass some U.S. government figures. As recently as four years ago, Bout's companies were employed by the Pentagon to fly troop supplies for the Iraq War into U.S. military bases—an issue he will likely exploit at his trial. "This shows the incompetence of the way the war was being run," said Lee Wolosky, a former White House national-security aide who led efforts to apprehend Bout during the Clinton administration. "While Bout was being pursued by one part of the

> "I feel like our kindergarteners are sitting there like sitting ducks."
> —*AZ state senator Karen Johnson, March 2008*
> Perspectives

U.S. government, another part was rewarding him with fuel agreements and subcontracts."

Bout's Iraq work continued even after President Bush signed a July 2004 order forbidding U.S. citizens from doing business with Bout after he allegedly supplied weapons to Liberian dictator Charles Taylor's regime. (Bout has not yet been assigned a U.S. lawyer. His brother told a Moscow radio station that he was a "simple businessman" who "only transported cargo.") But in a 2005 letter to Congress, the then Deputy Defense Secretary Paul Wolfowitz confirmed that "both the U.S. Army and Coalition Provisional Authority did conduct business with companies" that had subcontracted with Bout. Among those firms: Halliburton, the oil-services giant formerly headed by Vice President Dick Cheney. Pentagon records show Bout's aircraft landed 149 times at U.S. bases. A Pentagon official, who asked not to be identified discussing sensitive matters, said the firms flying into U.S. air bases had not been officially linked to Bout; the department revoked their landing rights later in the summer of 2004 after they refused to disclose who employed them. The arrangement, this official said, reflected the Pentagon's thinking at the time. "It was a case of, 'If the troops need it, get it to them and we'll clean up the paperwork later'." DEA operations chief Michael Braun said he's not worried about the prospect of Bout's raising at trial his past work for the U.S. government. "We're just happy we took his butt off the street," he said. —M.I.

WEEK OF MARCH 24

SCANDALS

Spitzer in Mind, the D.C. Madam Makes Her Case

If there's one woman who might take some small comfort in the Eliot Spitzer sex scandal, it's Deborah Jeane Palfrey, a.k.a. the "D.C. Madam." Her trial on federal charges of prostitution-related racketeering and money laundering is set to begin in April. Palfrey's "Pamela Martin & Associates" escort service boasted some 10,000 clients, including powerful D.C. figures. Sen. David Vitter, a family-values Republican from Louisiana, admitted he was on Palfrey's customer list and apologized. Deputy Secretary of State Randall Tobias, an anti-prostitution crusader, resigned last year after admitting he was also a Palfrey client. He insisted that he received only massages, not sex.

All along, Palfrey has claimed she was running a perfectly legal "adult fantasy" service that stopped short of sex; the Feds say it was an old-fashioned call-girl ring. If she's found guilty, she could face 55 years in prison. But now, she hopes, Spitzer's fall may give her claims an unexpected credibility boost. Part of Palfrey's defense has been that call girls charge much more than no-sex escorts. Exhibit A: Spitzer, who allegedly paid $4,300 for a session with "Kristen," the Emperor's Club prostitute who met him at Washington's Mayflower Hotel. "We charged between $200 and $300," Palfrey tells NEWSWEEK. Even if the Emperor's Club rates were inflated New York area prices, Palfrey says, her business "wasn't even in the prostitution price range. This whole scandal helps my case considerably."

She can hope so, anyway.

> "This whole scandal helps my case considerably," says Palfrey.

Prosecutors are trying to make their case on a provision called the Travel Act, which prohibits use of the mail and interstate travel to promote gambling, unlawful distribution of narcotics and prostitution. Like Kristen, who went by Amtrak from New York to Washington to meet Spitzer, Palfrey's D.C.-area employees allegedly crossed state lines to see clients in the District, Virginia and Maryland. Since Palfrey was based in California, prosecutors say, every phone call and payment from clients violated the law.

Meanwhile, Palfrey is already at work on, of course, a memoir. In the 100 pages she's written so far (and which she shared with NEWSWEEK), she portrays herself

---

THE DIGNITY INDEX

Eliot: The Wind Beneath Our Wings

Thumping the fallen Luv Gov is too easy, so this week's edition focuses on related figures and their dubious deeds

On 'The View,' **Dr. Laura Schlessinger** stands up for the sisterhood by implying that the Spitzer mess is ... his wife Silda's fault for not satisfying her man? Now that's progress. Score: **31**

Still kicking, part one: Detroit Mayor **Kwame Kilpatrick**, who says the media and his race, not the affair he tried to hide, are the reason his career's on life support. Score: **56**

Still kicking, part two: Remember this guy? Despite the guilty plea, despite the hypocrisy of being an anti-gay politician who solicited gay sex, **Larry Craig** remains a U.S. senator. Score: **62**

as a helpless victim of hypocritical "federales," "Bible thumpers" and heartless prosecutors out to conduct a "witch burning." She writes of growing up in a Pennsylvania steel town and dreaming of a better life. "Had I not left ... my life could have existed of stamping price stickers on cans of green beans at the local A&P supermarket." After failing to find "Mr. Right" or a solid career, she went to San Diego, where she was sentenced to 18 months in prison for running a prostitution ring. On her release, she moved north to Vallejo, Calif., and in 1993 opened her "little cottage industry," Pamela Martin & Associates. For 13 years, she ran her "snooze fest" of an escort service from a desk next to her washer and dryer, daily from 2 to 9, "except for holidays and snow days."

In Palfrey's telling, she was a model citizen. "I paid my taxes on time every April 15th," she writes, and says she filed tax forms for her employees with the IRS. "Empowerment was the goal," writes Palfrey. She says many of the 143 escorts who worked for her throughout the years were college graduates, and some held doctorate degrees. She urged them to save and invest. When the Feds came calling in 2006, she realized that "the government in the course of a 24 or so hour period could wipe out my entire life's work and savings. And I had to take it." The former governor of New York couldn't have put it better himself.

—Eve Conant

IMMIGRATION

Decades of Assimilation

Social scientists rarely get more than a passing glimpse as minority groups struggle to achieve the American Dream. But a pair of UCLA experts have just published a new book that offers a unique, 35-year, time-lapse view of economic and social changes among Mexican-American families. In 2000, Edward Telles and Vilma Ortiz led a team that interviewed more than 1,500 Mexican-Americans in Los Angeles and San Antonio whose families had taken part in a novel, mid-1960s survey designed to gauge how successive generations are assimilating into mainstream America. The short answer: full integration remains a long way off.

The original questionnaires that propel the book, titled "Generations of Exclusion," were lost for years before being unearthed during a library renovation project. In some ways, recent generations of Mexican-Americans follow typical patterns blazed by earlier, European immigrants. Countering critics who say Mexican-Americans don't want to learn English, the study found that nearly everyone spoke and read English by the second generation, though they remained bilingual. "Retaining Spanish wasn't done at the expense of English," Ortiz says. Later generations were more likely to become Protestants, vote Republican and marry non-Latinos. Even musical tastes shifted: three quarters of the immigrants liked Mexican styles best; half of later generations preferred black American music.

But other findings are less rosy. Mexican-American neighborhoods are more segregated today, thanks largely to a new influx of immigrants. The study also found that, unlike earlier Europeans, who caught up to American averages in income, wealth and education by the third generation, Mexican-Americans continue to lag. The authors blame the loss of middle-class manufacturing jobs, prejudice fueled by the immigration debate and subpar school systems. Overall, years of education rose substantially for the children of immigrants, but high-school graduation rates actually decreased slightly by the fourth generation. "I can't think of another [immigrant] group" for whom that's been true, says Telles. To reverse the slide, the authors call for an education-focused "Marshall Plan" to boost school spending. Without it, they say, too many Mexican-Americans may be running in place for generations to come. —ANDREW MURR

HISTORY

How to Sound Presidential

The orations of politicians, George Orwell once complained, "vary from party to party, but they are all alike in that one almost never finds in them a fresh, vivid, homemade turn of speech." It's an opiate-of-the-masses view of political jargon—one that's soundly rebuffed by William Safire, The New York Times's "On Language" guru, whose Political Dictionary will be rereleased next month in time for party conventions and the general election, both historical hotbeds of new "po-lingo."

Safire, a speechwriter for President Richard Nixon, hardly views the language of politics as Orwellian brainwashing. That said, he's the first to acknowledge that our vocabulary shapes, as much as it reflects, the way we think about the world. The names of laws ("death tax," "Clear Skies Initiative") and the characterizations of would-be leaders ("bull moose," "amiable dunce") have unconscious effects on even the savviest voters. It's why spinmeisters stay in business and why a politician's word choice can make a legend (FDR's "nothing to fear but fear itself") or break a career (George Allen's "macaca" blooper in 2007).

So what makes for effective political slang? Safire says that alliteration usually spawns memorable phrases ("Ban the bomb," "Tippecanoe and Tyler too"), as does borrowing from the Bible ("wilderness years"), zoology ("doves and hawks," "lame duck") and horse racing ("running mate," "shoo-in"). But Safire's not choosy: both the wildly successful and the widely derided of American political argot are included in his 829-page dictionary. What began in 1968 as a Beltway junkie's labor of love

> **Safire hardly views the language of politics as Orwellian brainwashing.**

'Po-Lingo': The Greatest Hits

Every campaign, every presidency offers up a few gems to our rich political history of sloganeering. A few of Safire's favorite phrases, dating back to World War II:

IN THEIR WORDS

G. W. BUSH
"Axis of evil,"
"shock and awe,"
"the Decider"

G.H.W. BUSH
"Read my lips,"
"voodoo economics,"
"vision thing"

CARTER
"Lust in my heart,"
"three-martini lunch,"
"ethnic purity"

JOHNSON
"Coonskin on the wall,"
"finger on the button"

EISENHOWER
"Bigger bang for a buck,"
"massive retaliation"

CLINTON
"Triangulation,"
"Whitewater,"
"I didn't inhale"

REAGAN
"There you go again,"
"morning in America,"
"evil empire"

NIXON
"Silent majority,"
"nattering nabobs of negativism"

KENNEDY
"Profiles in Courage,"
"life is unfair,"
"Peace Corps"

TRUMAN
"Do-nothing Congress,"
"whistle-stopping"

has turned into an authoritative collection of whistle-stopping campaign slogans and vicious slings and arrows of partisan attacks that stretches all the way back to the Founding Fathers (who came up with terms like "electioneer" and the party "ticket").

Last updated in 1993, before the U.S. political lexicon had acquired "soccer moms" (1996), "fuzzy math" (2000) and "Swift Boat spot" (2004), the book's newest version includes rich linguistic bequeathals from both the Clinton and second Bush White Houses. Inevitably, the language of the Bill-and-Hil years is riddled with scandal-related phrases: "Whitewater," "I didn't inhale" and "Monicagate," with its attendant "vast right-wing conspiracy."

But Clinton's coinages hardly match those of "Dubya," whose grammatical befuddlement has given us "the Decider" and "misunderestimate" (called "Bushisms," as were his father's lapses), and whose administration's post-9/11 "War on Terror" and Iraq invasion have spawned "axis of evil," "regime change," "shock and awe" and "mission accomplished." Language snobs may snicker at Bush's malapropisms, but his tenure could be remembered as the most linguistically fertile since the era of Safire's old boss. As Bush noted in 2001, "My critics don't realize I don't make verbal gaffes; I'm speaking in the perfect forms and rhythms of ancient haiku." Wonder what Orwell would say to that.

—KATIE BAKER

WEEK OF MARCH 31

THE DIGNITY INDEX

New York's Motto: Thank God for New Jersey

A weekly mathematical survey of dubious behavior that measures, on a scale of 1 to 100, just how low a person can go.

New Yorker journo **Malcolm Gladwell** plays fast and loose with the truth about office high jinks during his early days at The Washington Post. Pal, you are not helping. Score: **9**

Meet the Luv Guv, part two: New York's **David Paterson**, who fessed up— on his Inauguration Day! —to "several" extramarital affairs. Can it get any more nuts? Score: **60**

Yes! Anything N.Y. can do, Jersey can do sleazier. Outed ex-gov. **Jim McGreevey**, his wife and their chauffeur give new meaning to the term "triangulation." Score: **61**

WEEK OF APRIL 14

ABORTION

How Would Jesus Choose?

Adam Hamilton does not call himself "pro-choice." He prefers "pro-life with a heavy heart." What that means, as he explains in his new book "Seeing Gray in a World of Black and White," is that he believes abortion should be available and legal, that there are instances in which it might be necessary and that those instances should be very rare. Further, he says, the abortion debate has been too hot for too long, and that, as a Christian minister, his job is to try "to support people no matter what decision they make." As an evangelical megachurch pastor in Kansas, a man educated at Oral Roberts University, Hamilton speaks carefully, aware that he's staking out a controversial position.

Or maybe not. About a third of white evangelicals say that abortion should sometimes or always be legal, according to the Pew Research Center—a number that hasn't changed in a decade. In recent election seasons, however, these

> **These moderate voices have been drowned out by hard-line shouting on both sides.**

moderate voices have been drowned out by hard-line shouting on both sides. In the past, an evangelical who might condone abortion in the case of his ailing wife or 14-year-old daughter would never say so in public. Now, the abortion rhetoric has faded somewhat as evangelicals turn their attention to other things: AIDS, the environment, Darfur. In 2004, megapastor Rick Warren announced that abortion was a "nonnegotiable" for evangelical voters. This year, he's been silent. What's new, then, is not that a pastor like Hamilton would take a softer approach to abortion, but that he would feel comfortable enough to say so from the pulpit and in print.

Hamilton wants pro-choice and pro-life advocates to join forces to reduce the number of abortions and he enumerates seven areas where they could find common ground. Let both sides agree that adequate information about birth control can help prevent pregnancy, he says. And let both sides agree that the longer a pregnancy progresses, the more morally problematic an abortion becomes.

As for his heavy heart, Hamilton comes by it honestly. Seven years ago he received a letter from a parishioner describing her own teenage pregnancy in the years before *Roe*, the pressure from her parents to abort and her refusal to do so—in spite of the cost. That letter was from his mother.

—LISA MILLER

WEEK OF APRIL 21

POLITICS

State and Defense: For Once, Opposites Attract

Some of the most bitter battles in Washington have been fought between the secretaries of State and Defense. They are often competitors for resources and the president's ear, though not always along predictably dovish or hawkish lines. In the Clinton administration, the interventionist was the secretary of State, Madeleine Albright, while Defense Secretary William Cohen resisted sending forces into harm's way. In the Reagan administration, Secretary of State George Shultz was constantly sparring with Defense Secretary Caspar Weinberger over arms control. In the Truman administration, Defense Secretary Louis Johnson and Secretary of State Dean Acheson openly despised each other. Johnson fed so much damaging information to the press about Acheson that Truman forced his Defense secretary, weeping, to resign. In George W. Bush's first term, Secretary of State Colin Powell felt cut out by Defense Secretary Donald Rumsfeld. After a trip to Australia in the first year, Powell did not travel abroad with

> **The comity between the two is a "180-degree turn" from Rumsfeld and Powell.**

Rumsfeld; Powell's chief of staff Lawrence Wilkerson doesn't even recall the two men aboard Air Force One at the same time.

So Washington insiders have noted with interest that Rumsfeld's Pentagon successor, Robert Gates, has taken three trips in the last 10 months with Secretary of State Condoleezza Rice. For security reasons, the two secretaries tend to fly separately even when headed to the same place. But last summer Rice abandoned her C-32 official aircraft to fly with Gates from Egypt to Saudi Arabia aboard his more cushy E-4B (similar to the jets that serve as Air Force One). In the past year, Rice and Gates have traveled twice together to Russia.

The two are not just traveling companions but allies in every significant way. Both Russian experts, they served in national security during the Bush 41 years (Gates was Rice's boss). "They are friends, not just colleagues," said Gates's press secretary Geoff Morrell. The two secretaries' tandem travels are a "great indication of how well State and [the Pentagon] are working together," said Sean McCormack, Rice's chief spokesman. A senior official, who declined to be named discussing sensitive relationships, described the comity between the two secretaries as a "180-degree turn" from the fractious Powell/Rumsfeld dynamic.

Rice and Gates are both believers in "soft power," emphasizing economic and diplomatic ties. Some right-wingers complain that the Rice/Gates axis is producing a moderate foreign policy, isolating a small circle of hard-liners around Vice President Dick Cheney (who remains influential). But even some conservatives see a plus side to State-Pentagon cooperation. "A lot of people in the [Pentagon] believe that the State-Defense feud went too far" during the run-up to the Iraq War, says Michael Pillsbury, a conservative Pentagon consultant on China. "People are relieved at the détente."

At a speech at Kansas State University last November, Gates spoke out for giving the State Department more tools for soft power, including more diplomats and economic aid, as well as a "dramatic increase" in funding and personnel for the Pentagon's old bureaucratic rivals at the State Department. In Washington, where budgeting is often a zero-sum game, that's true love. —MARK HOSENBALL *and* EVAN THOMAS

POLYGAMY

New Homes in a New World

In the largest child-welfare intervention in Texas history, authorities last week raided the Eldorado ranch of the Fundamentalist Church of Latter-day Saints (FLDS), a breakaway polygamous sect not recognized by the Mormon Church. Officials were responding to repeated phone calls for help from a 16-year-old girl who said she was the fourth wife of a man who beat and raped her. Now the state has 416 kids in temporary custody amid fears they were ensnared in a system of forced marriage that often involved underage girls.

What will happen to them? For now, they're being housed in shelters in nearby San Angelo. In an unusual arrangement, more than 130 adult women from the compound are being allowed to stay with them. "You can imagine this is a whole new world for them," says Marleigh Meisner, a spokesperson for Child Protective Services. Each child is being assigned an attorney and a guardian and will receive counseling and medical services (some of the kids have chickenpox, which they apparently weren't vaccinated against). An April 17 court hearing will provide the children's parents their first opportunity to respond to the abuse allegations. If a judge rules against them, the kids will likely be placed in foster care and could eventually be adopted by new families. (FLDS lawyers did not respond to calls for comment.)

For now, officials say they're focused on easing the kids' transition. Most have had virtually no contact with the outside world and have never seen TV or the Internet. Among those helping authorities

> **The 416 kids, says Price, are "much like a refugee population."**

is Shannon Price, director of the Diversity Foundation, a group that assists boys pushed out of FLDS. Don't give them a Barbie doll or stare while they wash their undergarments, which are considered sacred, she advises. And keep them together as much as possible. They're "like a refugee population," says Price. "These children will need each other. They are very connected." Which makes their potential separation an unfortunate, if perhaps necessary, option.

—GRETEL C. KOVACH *and* ARIAN CAMPO-FLORES

WEEK OF APRIL 28

ENOUGH ALREADY

'__gate'

Everything wears out its welcome eventually. In this periodic feature, we say when.

After the news broke that Cindy McCain may have swiped a pasta recipe, pundits instantly dubbed it "Farfallegate," as if Bittergate and Spitzergate weren't enough. Please, can we stop hanging the suffix on every hint of impropriety, no matter how trivial? (The trivialization began early: after Watergate, the French labeled a scandal over Bordeaux "Winegate." Since then we've survived—just to name a few—Irangate, Travelgate, Skategate, Filegate, Monicagate and *two* Troopergates.) The device is beyond hackneyed. But worse, it's an exercise in hysterical hyperbole. Remember, the original case refers to a break-in that caused *the downfall of a U.S. president.* Farfallegate? It's barely a kerfuffle. —JENNIE YABROFF

THE DIGNITY INDEX

Hey Pope, You Rule. Am I Right or Am I Right?

A weekly mathematical survey of dubious behavior that measures, on a scale of 1 to 100, just how low a person can go.

After the pope's remarks at the White House, **President Bush** tells him he gave an "awesome speech." Awesome? You're talking to the pope, not Mylie Cyrus. Score: **12**

The presumptive GOP nominee's wife, **Cindy McCain,** gets caught passing off someone else's recipes as her own on her Web site—and she blames an intern for the deed. Score: **54**

Gratuitous commercial breaks, endless gutter-ball questions . . . **Charles Gibson** and **George Stephanopoulos** preside over the season's worst debate. ABC gets an F. Score: **80**

WEEK OF MAY 5

JUSTICE

In the Rezko Trial, a New Name Surfaces: Karl Rove

The trial of Chicago developer and political fixer Antoin "Tony" Rezko has been closely watched for any mention of the defendant's onetime friend, Barack Obama. But last week, prosecutors threw a curveball, telling the judge that one of their witnesses is prepared to raise the name of another prominent Washington hand: Karl Rove. Former Illinois state official Ali Ata is expected to testify about a conversation he had with Rezko in which the developer alleged Rove was "working with" a top Illinois Republican to remove the Chicago U.S. attorney, Patrick Fitzgerald.

The allegation, which Rove denies, quickly reverberated in Washington. Democrats in Congress now want to question Ata. They believe he can help buttress their theory that Rove played a key role in discussions that led to the firings of U.S. attorneys at the Justice Department in 2006. The House Judiciary Committee "intends to investigate the facts and circumstances alleged in this testimony," panel chairman Rep. John Conyers of Michigan said in a statement to NEWSWEEK.

THE DIGNITY INDEX

Remember That Thing I Just Said? I Never Said It.

A weekly mathematical survey of dubious behavior that measures, on a scale of 1 to 100, just how low a person can go.

To the tune of "White Christmas," conservative radio host **Rush Limbaugh** sings that he's "dreaming of riots in Denver," site of the Democratic convention. Score: **10**

During a live radio interview, **Bill Clinton** says the Obama campaign "played the race card on me," then claims the very next day that he said no such thing. Score: **58**

Over public objections from her own national party and likely nominee John McCain, North Carolina GOP boss **Linda Daves** airs a race-baiting, anti-Obama attack ad. Score: **63**

Investigators are intrigued by the timing of the alleged conversation about Fitzgerald. According to the Rezko prosecutors, it took place in November 2004—weeks after Fitzgerald had subpoenaed Rove to testify for the third time in another matter he was aggressively investigating, the Valerie Plame CIA leak case. A source familiar with Ata's testimony (who asked not to be identified talking about sensitive matters) said that Ata was meeting regularly with Rezko that fall. The two men shared a concern about Fitzgerald's ongoing probe of Illinois public officials. In one of those conversations, the developer allegedly told Ata that Bob Kjellander, a prominent GOP state lobbyist, was talking to Rove about getting rid of Fitzgerald. The reason: to "get a new U.S. attorney" who would not pursue the Illinois corruption probe, the source said. Ata, who has pleaded guilty to corruption-related charges and is now cooperating with the Feds, has no evidence that the conversation took place other than what Rezko allegedly told him, the source says.

Kjellander denies that he told Rezko anything of the kind. "I never had a discussion with Karl Rove or any other person on the White House staff" about firing Fitzgerald, said Kjellander, now a top GOP official in charge of this summer's convention. Rove's lawyer, Bob Luskin, told NEWSWEEK that Rove "does not recall" a conversation with Kjellander about Fitzgerald. He added that Rove "never talked to anybody in the White House about removing Fitzgerald."

Conyers's investigators apparently are not convinced. They've filed a civil-contempt lawsuit to force the White House to turn over documents about the U.S. attorney firings. In recent court papers, lawyers for the full House of Representatives charge that the White House has "stonewalled"

They've filed a civil-contempt lawsuit to force the White House to turn over documents about the U.S. attorney firings.

efforts to sort out the U.S. attorney firings; they cite an e-mail disclosed last year showing that Rove visited the White House counsel's office in 2005 and asked "how we planned to proceed regarding US attorneys . . . he said the matter was urgent." (In the e-mail, Rove wanted to know if all the attorneys would be asked to resign "or only some of them.") Conyers, whose staff has been probing other allegations of White House meddling in criminal prosecutions, recently renewed a demand for Rove to testify. If he refuses to appear, Conyers said, "the committee is prepared to resort to compulsory process"—i.e., a subpoena.

—MICHAEL ISIKOFF

WEEK OF MAY 12

FAST CHAT

A Family of Readers—And Writers

The old saw goes, "Write what you know." Long before she became First Lady, Laura Bush was a librarian; for two years during her tenure as First Daughter, Jenna Bush worked as a schoolteacher. So naturally their first collaboration as authors—"Read All About It!"—is a children's book set in a library. The two spoke about reading, teaching—and how time flies in the White House—with NEWSWEEK's Jon Meacham.

It's been a long seven years.
LAURA: It's gone by like a flash. I mean, my girls went from freshmen in college to 26-year-old grown women.

What about for you, Jenna?
JENNA: I'm ready for somebody else to be on CNN. I mean, I think [my father has] done a great job. And I admire anybody that would put themselves out there like that. [But] I'm ready for somebody else to try to do it. I'm ready to have my parents back.

Why this book now?
LAURA: Jenna and I have been talking about this book for about a year.
JENNA: She's been a teacher and a children's librarian. That was her career. Now she's a First Lady. So when she started talking about what she would write, this rang the most true, being in the classroom and inspiring kids. That's what she did for so many years.

Growing up, what's your first literary memory?
LAURA: I remember the Little Golden Books. Those were the ones that my mother could afford,

that you could buy at the grocery store. But I also remember when she read "Little Women" to me—that's a pretty adult book for a child. But it was a very powerful memory for me. When Beth died, for instance, Mother cried, we cried together. I loved the "Little House on the Prairie" books. I particularly identified with Laura because she had my same name and brown hair and—

JENNA: And she lived out on the prairie.

LAURA: She also had that pioneer spirit that I think even people in Midland, Texas, in the 1950s had. I think it's a very important book in American children's literature.

JENNA: I loved Toni Morrison's "The Bluest Eye." In middle school, something about that book really changed me.

You both talk to teachers around the country, and one of their frustrations is that so much falls to them. What advice do you have for how to bring order to a classroom and inspire learning?

JENNA: I taught in inner-city

ANALOGY CHECK

In Politics, It's All About Who You Know

History repeats itself, but not without a few wrinkles. We make the comparison—then pick it apart.

THE COMPARISON

The controversy over Barack Obama's former pastor, the Rev. Jeremiah Wright Jr., calls to mind another personal association that nearly clipped a rising-star politician. In 1987, John McCain intervened in the investigation of a savings and loan run by his friend and patron Charles Keating, whose company later headlined the S&L crisis.

WHY IT WORKS

Both inconvenient friends undercut the public image of their pals in office, and both candidates made politically tin-eared choices by consorting with them. The Reverend Wright is hot and divisive, while Obama's message is cool and inclusive. And Keating served four years for fraud, while McCain campaigns as an ethics crusader.

WHY IT DOESN'T

McCain's favor to a well-heeled friend and Obama's allegiance to a fiery black minister raise very different questions of character. Also, while McCain faced down expulsion from the Senate and jail for corruption—since Keating had given $114,000 to McCain's campaigns— Obama's worst case is a lost election. —TONY DOKOUPIL

D.C., and it is difficult to manage everything. One of the things that I've learned is that it's really important for parents, for principals, for people of the community to support your teachers. Even though they were working, my parents would still come in and help when [my students] were going on a field trip. And when I taught in inner-city D.C., we took the bus. So, of course—

LAURA: You needed help.

JENNA: The Metro bus with 24 kids and me. But I did it.

LAURA: What I see when I visit schools all over the country, all over the world, is that most really excellent teachers are called to teaching. It's a calling, and they love it and they love their children. As difficult as teaching is—and there are very few professions as challenging as trying to deal with 30 kids—I think it's also one of the most rewarding. You're never bored. There might be some terrible moments, but you're never bored with teaching.

WEEK OF MAY 26

THE DIGNITY INDEX

We Shall Fight Them on the Fairways

A weekly mathematical survey of dubious behavior that measures, on a scale of 1 to 100, just how low a person can go:

The NFL has moved on, but Eagles-obsessed Sen. **Arlen Specter** wants to keep investigating the Patriots spying scandal. Don't senators have anything better to do?
Score: **14**

Clinton booster **Terry McAuliffe** tells Tim Russert that Russert's father "up in heaven" would support Hill's staying in the race. The problem? "Big Russ" is alive and well.
Score: **38**

President **George Bush** claims that he quit golf in August '03 out of solidarity with the troops. Some sacrifice, right? But even worse: Dubya hit the links two months later.
Score: **84**

WEEK OF JUNE 2

INTELLIGENCE

Cyber Spying for Dummies

Congressional experts fear that Defense intelligence agencies are not making wide enough —and smart enough—use of the vast pool of "open source" information now available in cyberspace. The House Armed Services Committee, in a report approved last week on the House floor, worried that clumsy attempts by Pentagon agents to download useful intelligence from the Web could compromise U.S. spy operations by putting potential enemies on notice that U.S. intelligence is interested in them.

Last week the Federation of American Scientists made public a U.S. Army field manual, stamped FOR OFFICIAL USE ONLY, outlining procedures for open-source intelligence collection by Army units. The manual says Army agents "must use Government computers to access the Internet" unless they have special authorization to do otherwise. One U.S. official, who asked for anonymity when discussing sensitive information, said that, in an effort to track people behind Web sites giving detailed instructions on how to build sophisticated IEDs, counterterrorism experts two years

THE DIGNITY INDEX

Some Things Just Aren't Funny

A weekly mathematical survey of bad behavior that measures just how low a person can go

Fox News host **Bill O'Reilly** tries to pin the death of American troops in Iraq on GE chief Jeffrey Immelt. The evidence? Health-care-equipment sales to Iran. Score: **10**

CNN contributor and GOP consultant **Alex Castellanos** defends the word "bitch" as "accurate" when describing women like Hillary Clinton. What a jerk. Score: **42**

Right-wing radio host **Michael Savage** plays a song by the Dead Kennedys to make fun of Ted's brain tumor and makes cancer "jokes." Score: **94**

ago asked Pentagon brass for permission to log on to the Web sites using fake identities. The official said the plan was abandoned when lawyers and policymakers insisted that the counterterrorism officials log on using computers with telltale ".gov" or ".mil" domains—a ruling that would have tipped off potential bad guys.

A Capitol Hill official who also asked for anonymity said that congressional overseers were concerned that using U.S. IP addresses to search the Net could "complicate [the] ability to go deep into Web sites to extract information." One way for the Pentagon to get around such restrictions would be to hire private contractors, but this raises questions about protecting the rights of Americans. A Pentagon spokesman told NEWSWEEK: "We've seen an increased appreciation within the Department of Defense regarding the value of open-source intelligence."

—MARK HOSENBALL

CLOSURE

Behind The Lens

News stories captivate us for a moment and then vanish. We revisit those stories to bring you the next chapter.

STARTING POINT

November 2000: With the presidential race too close to call, Florida law mandates a recount. In contested Broward County, Judge Robert A. Rosenberg steps in as county elections supervisor to oversee the process.

FEVER PITCH

While "hanging," "pregnant" and "dimpled" chads become household terms, Rosenberg's image is plastered across the news, becoming a symbol of the drama. He appears with a magnifying glass, switching between glasses and no glasses, and using eyedrops.

PRESENT DAY

Rosenberg, still a circuit-court judge in Broward County, keeps a large framed picture of the iconic image in his office, but donated his magnifying glass to the Smithsonian. He wouldn't need it anyway. Unlike in 2000 when candidates could request a manual recount, if there is another close election Florida legislation now limits recounts to be done by machine only. As for the HBO movie "Recount," Rosenberg was not contacted during the production of the film, and his character does not appear in it. Rosenberg was offered two tickets for the premiere, but was not able to attend. —SCOTT SPJUT

TRANSITION

HAMILTON JORDAN, 63, POLITICAL STRATEGIST

Hamilton Jordan, who died last week of cancer, may be remembered, wrongly, as the good ole boy who got Jimmy Carter elected president in 1976 and was bizarrely investigated (though never charged) with snorting cocaine at New York City's Studio 54. A self-described "political animal," and the youngest ever White House chief of staff (at 34), Jordan—pronounced *jer-dun*—could be funny and profane, especially when chewing up a self-important Washington pooh-bah. House Speaker Tip O'Neill sometimes referred to him as "Hannibal Jerkin." He was, a friend of recalls, "a Southerner through and through, yet completely clear-eyed about the region's problems. He could smell hypocrisy a mile away, and found lots of it regarding race relations."

Volunteering as a civilian relief worker during the Vietnam War, he was exposed to Agent Orange, which may have caused his illness. A welldisguised intellectual deeply read in history, Jordan devoted much of his life to helping the sick, raising money for research and relief in the war on cancer. With his wife, Dorothy, a former oncology nurse, he founded Camp Sunshine near Atlanta for kids with cancer and wrote a moving memoir of his own 20-year battle with four different types of the disease, entitled "No Such Thing as a Bad Day."

—Evan Thomas

WEEK OF JULY 7/JULY 14

CIA

Headway on Tapes Probe

A criminal investigation into why the CIA destroyed hundreds of hours of videotapes recording harsh interrogations of two Al Qaeda leaders will stretch on at least another six months—and could ultimately result in indictments, according to a recent federal court filing obtained by NEWSWEEK. In his affidavit, John Durham, the veteran federal prosecutor on the case, said he is examining whether anyone "obstructed justice, made false statements, or acted in contempt of court or Congress in connection with the destruction of the videotapes." He said that he is specifically trying to determine whether the destruction of the tapes violated any judge's order. But progress may be slow. Two sources close to former intelligence officials who are potential key witnesses in the case, both of whom asked for anonymity when discussing the inquiry, said that these officials have not been summoned to give grand-jury testimony; one of them hasn't even been questioned by the FBI yet.

Intel officials acknowledged last year that the CIA taped interrogations— which included the use of "waterboarding"—of pre-9/11 fixer Abu Zubaydah and Persian Gulf boss Abd al-Rahim al-Nashiri. The tapes were stashed at the CIA station in Thailand, where, in late 2005, they were destroyed on the order of Jose Rodriguez, then head of CIA clandestine operations. Current and former counterterrorism officials, who also asked for anonymity, said many top spies believed the use of harsh techniques had been foisted on the agency by hard-line Bush politicos. One former counterterrorism official close to the investigation told NEWSWEEK that spies involved believed they had legally "dotted all the i's and crossed all the t's" and therefore will not be prosecuted. Robert Bennett, the prominent D.C. lawyer who represents Rodriguez, had no comment. "The CIA has cooperated vigorously with official inquiries into the destruction of the tapes," said CIA spokesman Paul Gimigliano, "and is fully prepared to let the facts take us where they may." —MARK HOSENBALL

THE DIGNITY INDEX

We're Messin' With Texas

A weekly mathematical survey of dubious behavior that measures, on a scale of 1 to 100, just how low a person can go.

Texas oil tycoon **T. Boone Pickens** reneges on his vow to pay $1 million to anyone who provides proof that the Swift Boat Vets for Truth were wrong about John Kerry. Score: **24**

Unhappy with a bullpen demotion, Houston pitcher **Shawn Chacon** grabs his own G.M. by the neck and tosses him to the ground. Result: a demotion off the team. Score: **67**

Karl Rove says Obama is "the guy at the country club" who "makes snide comments about everyone." The best part: Rove made his snide comment at ... the Capitol Hill Club! Score: **78**

WEEK OF JULY 21

SURVEILLANCE

Uncle Sam Is Still Watching You

The domestic spying measure approved by Congress last week will impose new rules on government wiretapping. But it will leave largely untouched what some experts say is the most sweeping part of the secret surveillance activities ordered by President Bush after 9/11: the National Security Agency's collection of phone records and other personal data on millions of U.S. citizens. The NSA's massive "data mining" program—in which the agency's computers look for call patterns that might point to suspicious behavior—has never been publicly confirmed by the Bush administration. But industry and government officials, who asked not to be identified talking about classified matters, say the practice is a big part of what the telecoms did for the spy agency, and a key reason the companies fought so hard for the immunity from lawsuits granted by the new bill.

After 9/11, the White House asked MCI (now Verizon), AT&T, Sprint and Qwest for help obtaining call records on U.S. numbers found in laptops and cell phones captured in Qaeda hideouts. Normally such data is easy to come by for law enforcement, but in the post-9/11 world, the premium was on speed. So the White House bypassed the established legal protocols. Qwest balked, but the other three carriers went along— because, as one industry official put it, "nobody wanted to be responsible for the next terrorist attack."

Over time, requests for call records grew into the thousands—often two or three calls removed from the original targets. And, without court oversight, the demands for these and other personal data ultimately sparked fierce protests from inside the Justice Department itself. Congressional and industry sources

Troubling questions remain about the collection of so much personal data.

say the effort was subsequently put on firmer legal footing, with requests approved through still-secret court procedures. But data mining has continued—and even expanded—with little oversight or debate. Thanks to other secret post-9/11 orders, the NSA's computers have access to—and crunch—wire transfers, bank transactions and reams of other personal financial data collected by the Treasury Department, says a former top official. (An NSA spokeswoman did not respond to requests for comment.) But regardless of the legal standards used to collect the information, privacy experts say there are still troubling questions about the government's accumulation of so much personal data. "This affects far more people—and has a lot more risk of sweeping in innocent contacts—than the actual interception of phone calls," says Jim Dempsey, vice president of the Center for Democracy and Technology, a privacy group. "It's bizarre that this has not been discussed more." Or addressed in the hotly debated new law.

—MICHAEL ISIKOFF

DISASTERS

Summer Fires, Take Two

As California Gov. Arnold Schwarzenegger discussed the "unprecedented wildfire siege" that since late June has burned more than 700,000 acres in his state, a handful of Buddhist monks in the Los Padres National Forest valiantly protected their monastery while fire crews from Mexico, Canada, Australia, New Zealand and elsewhere in the United States, including 2,000 California National Guardsmen, prepared to lend a hand to state efforts. Just another summer day in California.

The Buddhists won their bat-

THE DIGNITY INDEX

Land of the Free, Home of the Whiners

A weekly mathematical survey of dubious behavior that measures, on a scale of 1 to 100, just how low a person can go.

Harlem, N.Y., Rep. **Charles Rangel** defends his reported deal on four rent-stabilized apartments (half off!), while some constituents are getting evicted. Score: **62**

McCain adviser and former senator **Phil Gramm** says the U.S. is "a nation of whiners," and that we're in a "mental recession," not an actual one. See? It's all just in your head! Score: **74**

Are we thumping a man of the cloth for being so crass? Or a politician for being so dumb? For being testy, or for being nuts? No matter. The Rev. **Jesse Jackson** is our high scorer of the week. Score: **81**

tle—their retreat was spared—but the war rages on. A mere month into the burning season, the toll has

Just another summer day in California.

already eclipsed the more than $1 billion in damage sustained from fires in 2007, when the bulk of the flames stayed south, in San Diego and Orange counties. But this year, they're touring the north, and spreading to some of California's most treasured landscapes—Big Sur among them.

So far nearly 20,000 personnel, in an army of planes and 1,590 fire trucks, have been deployed to stop them, dousing the scenery with 4 million gallons of water and flame retardant. After three weeks, they're exhausted, having pulled 24-hour shifts in weather that's unseasonably hot. And there's no relief in sight. "The fire season is going to last for the next few months. This is only the beginning," Schwarzenegger told reporters. His message to D.C.: send more funds, stat. And, we'd add, if at all possible, more monks.

—Jennifer Ordoñez

WEEK OF JULY 28

POLITICS

An Empty Seat and An Exotic Getaway

House Democrats were fuming recently when Karl Rove defied a congressional subpoena and refused to show up at a House Judiciary Committee hearing into whether he meddled in Justice Department prosecutions. Instead of grilling the former White House political chief under oath, the members found themselves talking to an empty chair. What they didn't know is where Rove was that day: on a jet flying to a speaking engagement at Yalta, the historic Black Sea resort in Ukraine. Rove, who generally charges a reported $40,000 per talk, appeared on a premier panel (along with Democratic strategist Bob Shrum) on the upcoming U.S. election at the fifth annual conference of the YES Foundation, a confab of world luminaries bankrolled by billionaire Victor Pinchuk, the Ukrainian steel magnate and son-in-law of the country's former autocratic president, Leonid Kuchma.

Democrats on the judiciary panel were outraged when they heard about Rove's overseas jaunt on the day he'd been ordered to testify. "That's just extremely contemptuous—it shows the disdain that he has for Congress and which he has encouraged in the Bush White House," said Rep. Steve Cohen of Tennessee. But Robert Luskin, Rove's lawyer, said the criticism was "fatuous" because, before he took off, Rove had been directed by White House counsel Fred Fielding not to show up. The reason: as a former presidential adviser, the White House views anything he might say to the panel as covered by executive privilege. "What was he supposed to do, sit at home with his lights off?" said Luskin. "I understand that people are unhappy that he didn't show up." But the no-show "was not something we concocted so he could make money in Yalta." Rove himself did not respond to a request for comment. But last week in an appearance on Bill O'Reilly's Fox News show, Rove dismissed the Democrats' demand for his testimony: "They want a circus," he said.

The dispute is far from over. Democratic members and aides said they expect judiciary chair Rep. John Conyers to push for a vote holding Rove in contempt of Congress—an act that would likely end up as part of an ongoing court battle over another executive-privilege dispute involving White House chief of staff Josh Bolton and former chief counsel Harriet Miers, both of whom also ignored subpoenas involving the U.S. attorney firings. (The White House also last week invoked executive privilege in refusing to turn over to another House panel an FBI interview of Vice President Dick Cheney in the CIA leak case.) Democrats acknowledge they have few good options to enforce their subpoenas. But they hope to vent their frustrations at an upcoming hearing called by Conyers on "the imperial presidency," where they will give Rep. Dennis Kucinich an opportunity to argue his case for President Bush's impeachment. Republicans, for their part, derided the upcoming hearing as a waste of time. This is "merely political theater," said Rep. Lamar Smith, the judiciary panel's ranking Republican. —Michael Isikoff

> **Democrats acknowledge they have few good options to enforce their subpoenas.**

CRIME

An Equal-Opportunity Crackdown?

It's 90 degrees in downtown Flint, Mich., and Jayson Miguel is shirtless in a pair of gray sweatpants. He's hanging out, minding his own—and breaking the law. It's not that he's loitering, it's his pants: they're sagged to reveal a pair of boxer shorts. "I've been sagging since the fourth grade," the 28-year-old says. It's "cool."

Some might call that a style choice. But for David Dicks, Flint's new police chief, it's a national nuisance. Dicks has ordered his officers to start arresting saggers on sight, threatening them with jail time and hefty fines for a fad he calls "immoral self-expression." He's even said the style could give officers probable cause to search those saggers.

It's a move other towns have tried before on a style that's been around for decades. But Dicks is taking a particularly harsh approach—and one the ACLU believes is downright illegal. So far he has issued only warnings, but he's made it clear that anyone with pants that don't cover the butt—whether or not they've got on underwear—is violating the city's disorderly-conduct ordinance, punishable by 93 days to a year in jail, and fines of up to $500. The local ACLU, meanwhile, says that's an incorrect interpretation of the law, which states that a person must have "open exposure" of the "genitals, pubic area" or "buttocks" to be disorderly. So it's given

---

THE DIGNITY INDEX

It's Hard to Top Andy Dick

A weekly mathematical survey of dubious behavior that measures, on a scale of 1 to 100, just how low a person can go.

Off-duty N.Y.C. cop shoots madman in street brawl. Turns out cop is drunk; stripped of gun. Days later, comish **Ray Kelly** flip-flops, calls him "hero." Which is it? Score: **7**

With his eye on the VP prize, **Mitt Romney** tells newscaster that McCain authored the surge philosophy. It's not just historical revision, it's downright brownnosing. Score: **19**

The name already says it all. **Andy Dick** has made a career of undignified behavior. But groping random 17-year-olds? That's even sadder than his mug shot. Score: **65**

JULY | **National Affairs-137**

Dicks an ultimatum: stop, or we'll see you in court. "This man has basically taken his personal dislike of a style of dress and made it a violation of criminal law," says Flint ACLU president Gregory Gibbs.

Dicks declined to comment for this story—but has until this week, says Gibbs, to make his move. In the meantime, residents like Miguel—who, at 6 feet 3, wears a size 3X—are just plain confused. Flint is one of the most violent cities in America. Why allocate resources to regulating trousers? "Clearly there are more important things going on in Flint," says Todd Boyd, a cultural critic at the University of Southern California. But perhaps it's what's behind the fashion more than the fashion itself. Sagging is in part a relic of the prison system—inmates sagged because they weren't allowed belts—and some still associate it with a gangster lifestyle, says Boyd. Others see it as just plain crass. "Who in the world wants to see a butt in public?" asked 81-year-old Flint resident Minnie Boyd. Certainly not Dicks.

—JESSICA BENNETT *and* MARY CHAPMAN

> **Why allocate resources to regulating trousers?**

CRIMINAL INTENT

Flint Police Chief David Dicks has ordered his officers to arrest on sight people with their trousers sagged. A breakdown of the new policy, inch by inch.

A WARNING: Pants sagged but above butt
DISORDERLY CONDUCT: Pants below the butt
INDECENT EXPOSURE: Below butt with skin

HEALTH

A Bump on Tobacco Road

In North Carolina, the governor may be the top public official, but for the past 200 years, tobacco has been king. The state grows half of all the tobacco in the United States, and the original cash crop remains its economic backbone. But beginning next month, North Carolina will be home to one of the nation's toughest youth smoking laws, with a ban on tobacco use in public schools. Most students can't smoke at school anyway, but the law applies to everyone on campus, year-round: parents in the stands at football games, maintenance crews in the school garage, teachers in the parking lot.

Getting the law passed was no simple feat in a state that still depends on people lighting up. North Carolina spends just 4 percent of its annual $426 million of tobacco revenue on smoking prevention (less than half the minimum federal recommendation), and, at 35 cents, maintains one of the country's lowest cigarette taxes. In all, it took six years of local advocacy and the votes of all 115 of the state's school boards. "It wasn't easy," says Mark Ezell, the state's tobacco-free-campus director. "I got called a Nazi a few times." Health advocates who want the state to go further are likely to be called a few more things.

—MATTHEW PHILIPS

WEEK OF AUGUST 4

THE DIGNITY INDEX

Bob Novak Has Had Better Weeks

A weekly mathematical survey of dubious behavior that measures, on a scale of 1 to 100, just how low a person can go.

First, he whines that John McCain may have used him to peddle veep-selection rumors to distract from Obama's trip. Really? You think? Score: **12**

While driving in Washington, the conservative pundit hits a pedestrian and briefly fails to stop, claiming he didn't realize he'd hit anybody. Score: **54**

The best part of the traffic incident? Apparently the 77-year-old Novak drives a black Corvette convertible. Score: **60**

WEEK OF AUGUST 11

ANTHRAX

A Case's Last Bizarre Turn

When the FBI was scrambling to unravel the 2001 anthrax attacks, one of the first scientists they turned to for help was Bruce E. Ivins, a veteran researcher at the U.S. Army bioweapons lab in Fort Detrick, Md. But last week, the protracted anthrax probe took its most bizarre turn yet: Ivins was found unconscious in his bathroom and later died of an apparent self-inflicted drug overdose—just as agents were about to charge him with sending the tainted letters that killed five people. Ivins, a devout churchgoer who played the keyboard at Sunday services, recently had been committed to a psychiatric hospital, and had allegedly made death threats against a social worker. In her protective order, the social worker, Jean Duley, wrote that Ivins has a history of "homicidal threats, actions, plans." She added: "FBI involved, currently under investigation & will be charged w/ 5 capital murders."

For years, the Department of Justice pursued another researcher, Steven Hatfill, but he was finally exonerated in June when he received a legal settlement of $5.8 million after accusing the government of violating his privacy. Following Ivins's death, Justice issued only a terse statement noting recent "significant developments" in the case. According to a source who was briefed on the matter, but who requested anonymity while the evidence remains sealed, the

> **The FBI was about to charge Ivins with murder.**

CLOSURE

A Long Fall From Grace

News stories captivate us, then vanish. We revisit those stories to bring you the next chapter.

STARTING POINT

In 1985, **Ted Haggard** starts New Life Church. It grows to 14,000, and in 2003, he's made head of the National Association of Evangelicals. He is also an adviser to President Bush.

FEVER PITCH

In November 2006, prostitute **Mike Jones** alleges that Haggard has paid him for monthly meth-fueled sex. Haggard, who is married with five kids, admits to "sexually immoral conduct." He's fired from his own church, resigns from NAE and enters a "restoration" program.

THE END RESULT

Haggard is deemed "completely heterosexual" by a church official and moves to Phoenix in April 2007 to study for a master's and preach at a halfway house. He asks for donations to help support his family to be sent through a charity later found to be run by a convicted sex offender. A New Life Church official tells newsweek Haggard returned to Colorado in June, with plans to sell life insurance. Haggard didn't return calls, but his voice mail says he's working for a company called Mortgage Protection Group. —BRIAN NO

FBI began zeroing in on Ivins some time ago thanks to an "earth-shattering scientific breakthrough" which enabled agents to identify the precise origin of the anthrax spores used in the attacks. Another former U.S. official, who also requested anonymity, confirmed the chain of events. Ivins's own behavior fueled suspicions: according to the Los Angeles Times, he acknowledged misleading investigators by failing to report anthrax contaminations in his work area shortly after the letters were mailed.

If he was guilty, his motive remains a mystery. According to one of NEWSWEEK's sources, investigators theorize that Ivins may have mailed the letters as a "wake-up call" for the country about the dangers of a bio-attack. Paul Kemp, a lawyer who had been appointed to represent Ivins, said the "relentless pressure of accusation and innuendo . . . led to [Ivins's] untimely death" and that Ivins was prepared to defend his "innocence" at trial.

—MICHAEL ISIKOFF *and* SUZANNE SMALLEY

WEEK OF AUGUST 18/AUGUST 25

ANTHRAX

The Case Still Isn't Closed

When the FBI publicly branded the late Dr. Bruce Ivins as the anthrax killer, it unsealed court affidavits suggesting a possible motive for the mailing to one target: NBC anchor Tom Brokaw. According to the affidavits, Ivins was angry about repeated Freedom of Information Act requests from Gary Matsumoto, identified as "an investigative journalist who worked for NBC News" who was looking into Ivins's work on an anthrax vaccine. "Tell Matsumoto to kiss my ass," the affidavit says Ivins wrote in an Aug. 28, 2001, e-mail, noting that was "weeks" before the Sept. 18, 2001, anthrax mailing addressed to Brokaw. But Matsumoto told NEWSWEEK the FBI never interviewed him as part of its investigation. If it had, he says, he could have told them he'd actually left NBC News five years earlier. At the time he was bombarding Ivins's lab with FOIA requests, he was employed by ABC. "They're trying to connect dots that don't connect," he said.

Justice Department official Dean Boyd said

"there was no mistake in the affidavit" because Matsumoto had been employed by NBC in the past and Ivins told investigators he "believed" he still worked there. Still, the reference is one of a number of seemingly misleading passages, gaps and omissions that are raising questions about just how airtight the government's case against Ivins actually is. At a press conference last week, U.S. Attorney for the District of Columbia Jeffrey Taylor said Justice officials were "confident" that Ivins, who committed suicide last month, was "the only person responsible for these attacks." Among the FBI's evidence: new scientific tests that officials said traced the genetic material

> **The FBI could not find any trace of the deadly anthrax in Ivins's home, cars or clothing.**

from the anthrax used in the deadly mailings to a flask in Ivins's lab at the U.S. Army's research facility at Fort Detrick, Md. But many of Ivins's former colleagues are unconvinced, noting unanswered questions about the FBI's scientific tests, most of which have not been peer-reviewed, as well as the lack of direct evidence showing Ivins actually mailed the fatal letters.

Despite repeated searches, for instance, the FBI could not find any trace of the deadly anthrax in Ivins's home, cars or clothing. "I'd say the vast majority of people [at Fort Detrick] think he had nothing to do with it," said Jeffrey Adamovicz, who served as one of Ivins's supervisors in the facility's bacteriology division.

Paul Kemp, Ivins's lawyer, said some of what's presented in the unsealed affidavits are "speculative" theories that would never be admissible in court. An example: that Ivins might have sent anthrax letters to pro-choice Sens. Patrick Leahy and Tom Daschle, because Ivins and his wife were anti-abortion. "I don't know what that has to do with anything," Kemp said. What's more, Kemp said, the FBI omitted evidence that might have been exculpatory, including that Ivins kept his security clearance after passing a polygraph in which he was questioned about the anthrax investigation. "He was told he had passed [the polygraph] because we thought he did," said Justice official Boyd. But after the FBI learned of Ivins's history of psychological problems, it had experts re-examine the results, and they concluded he'd used "countermeasures" such as controlled breathing to fool the examiners. All that and more is now likely to be reviewed by Congress. "There are clearly a lot of unanswered questions," said Iowa GOP Sen. Charles Grassley, who asked for a full probe. —MICHAEL ISIKOFF

SECURITY

A Hassle at The Border

Next time you visit Canada, don't forget your doctor's note. Travelers who've had recent radiation treatment, like a bone scan or thyroid therapy, could face unexpected hassles when they enter U.S. border checkpoints from Canada and Mexico. They're being pulled over for "secondary inspections," detained while officers search their cars and themselves—adding time to an already lengthy process.

It's all because they've undergone medical procedures with nuclear isotopes, which set off alarms in "radiation portal monitors" installed to foil terrorists who might be smuggling nukes or "dirty bombs." The trouble is, these travelers aren't terrorists—yet they account for the "vast majority" of radiation alarms, along with people transporting tile, kitty litter, granite and bananas, says Erlinda Byrd, a spokeswoman for the Homeland Security Department's Bureau of Customs and Border Protection, which operates the sensors.

Worse, NEWSWEEK has learned, is that out of 270 million vehicles examined by the sensors—resulting in 1.5 million alarms—not a single one has turned out to be an actual terrorist threat. According to Homeland Security officials, given permission to speak on the condition of anonymity, the Bush administration began the $300 million radiation-monitoring project in October 2002. It now includes 270 sensors along the Canadian border that screen 83 percent of U.S.-bound passengers, and 350 on the Mexican side that screen 95 percent. (Cargo shipments are screened even more closely.) And though Homeland Security first said results of those screenings were "classified," the anonymous officials later conceded that the total number of terrorists spotted by the scanners is *zero*.

Which is why Dr. Manuel Brown, a radiologist at Henry Ford Hospital in Detroit, has begun issuing doctor's notes to some of his traveling patients, explaining why they might trigger an alarm. He says facilities in his region perform about 100 radiation procedures a day. While the amount of radiation used in less-serious procedures would trigger the alarms for only a day or two, more-serious therapy (like thyroid treatment) can set off alarms for weeks. Remember that on your road trip.

—MARK HOSENBALL

ALASKA

The Veep's Pipeline Push

A two-year-old letter by Vice President Dick Cheney that pushed a controversial Alaska natural-gas pipeline bill is getting renewed scrutiny because of recently disclosed evidence in the Justice Department's corruption case against Sen. Ted Stevens. In a conversation secretly tape-recorded by the FBI on June 25, 2006, Stevens discussed ways to get a pipeline bill through the Alaska Legislature with Bill Allen, an oil-services executive accused of providing the senator with about $250,000 in undisclosed financial benefits. According to a Justice motion, Stevens told Allen, "I'm gonna try to see if I can get some bigwigs from back here and say, 'Look . . . you gotta get this done'." Two days later, Cheney wrote a letter to the Alaska Legislature urging members to "promptly enact" a bill to build the pipeline. The letter was considered unusual because the White House rarely contacts state lawmakers about pending legislative matters. It also angered state Democrats, who accused Cheney of pushing oil company interests. The executive director of Cheney's energy task force later worked as a lobbyist for British Petroleum, one of three firms slated to build the pipeline.

Stevens confirmed to NEWSWEEK last week that he asked Cheney to write the letter. "We wanted the federal government to tell the state to act quickly on it," he said. (A spokesman for Alaska's other senator, Lisa Murkowski, said her office also had contacts with Cheney's office.) A Cheney spokeswoman said his office does not comment on pending legal matters.

In the motion, prosecutors said they want to show that Stevens, who has pleaded not guilty, used his political clout to benefit Allen's business interests while the oil exec was paying for renovations on the senator's home. As an example, the motion points out that Stevens discussed contacting the Federal Energy Regulatory Commission about the pipeline; soon after, FERC issued a report on the project "similar to the

> **Stevens told Allen, "I'm gonna try to see if I can get some bigwigs from back here and say, 'Look . . . you gotta get this done'."**

message delivered by Stevens." But the Justice motion made no mention of Cheney's letter. A department spokesman did not respond to requests for comment about why prosecutors did not also include the letter or whether they expect Cheney to come up at Stevens's trial, now slated to begin next month.

—MICHAEL ISIKOFF
and TONY HOPFINGER

WEEK OF SEPTEMBER 8

OIL

Drill Here? Why Now?

John McCain's proposal for a gas-tax holiday went over like a ton of bricks. But his proposals to open up the continental shelf for drilling have struck a chord. A recent CBS/New York Times poll showed that Americans back offshore drilling, 62-28; a bipartisan group of senators is at work on a compromise, and House Speaker Nancy Pelosi has signaled openness to the issue. Expect to hear a continuous chorus of "Drill here, drill now" in Minneapolis this week. But as a short-term fix, offshore drilling is just as lame as a gas-tax holiday. Exploring off the beaches of south Florida won't bring new supplies to the market for several years. And when offshore oil does arrive, the amounts will be so small compared with global demand that they won't have much impact on the price we pay. So why has drilling resonated? NEWSWEEK's economics expert Daniel Gross offers five theories:

■ **Vast right-wing conspiracy:** The gas-tax holiday was derided by the economic-policy wing of the Republican Party. By contrast, the Republican noise machine—the Wall Street Journal editorial page, Washington think tanks, talk-radio blowhards, the dwindling core of Capitol Hill Republicans—has marched in impressive message lock step for drilling.

■ **Vast Marxist conspiracy:** By sapping the highway trust fund of construction funds, the gas-tax holiday was a potential job killer. Domestic drilling, by con-

> **Wildcatting for oil taps into romantic notions about how the nation was built by pioneers.**

trast, is something akin to a jobs program for highly paid blue-collar workers.

■ **Screw the foreigners:**

Call it national security, or call it chauvinism, but drilling for domestic oil sets up a zero-sum game. Every barrel of oil produced here is one we don't have to buy from our long and growing list of enemies: Venezuela, Iran and Russia. By contrast, a gas-tax holiday just offers more opportunities to enrich Hugo Chávez and Mahmoud Ahmadinejad.

■ **Mytho-historical:**

Wildcatting for oil conjures up legendary fortunes (Rockefeller, Getty, Hughes) and feeds into romanticized notions of how the nation was built by pioneers who tapped into the natural bounty of this resource-rich land. Think John Wayne and "There Will Be Blood." Gas-tax holidays conjure up images of accountants. Think David Schwimmer.

■ **Freudian:**

The language and imagery surrounding the issue—drills penetrating the earth's crust in search of gushers—tap into deep-seated subconscious desires. A gas-tax holiday? Not so much.

CLOSURE

Mishap on a Texas Ranch

In the mass-media age, news stories captivate us, then vanish. We revisit those stories to bring you the next chapter.

STARTING POINT

In February 2006, while hunting quail, Vice President Dick Cheney accidentally shoots his friend, 78-year-old Texas lawyer **Harry Whittington,** in the face, spraying birdshot into his head, neck and torso. Whittington is helicoptered to a hospital.

FEVER PITCH

Whittington suffers a heart attack from a migrating pellet. A few days later, Cheney fesses up: "You can't blame anybody else ... I'm the guy who pulled the trigger." Then Whittington apologizes to him.

PRESENT DAY

Whittington still practices law in Austin. He says he's fully recovered, though pellets in his larynx changed his voice, and he still has birdshot in his chest, throat and eyes. Though Cheney's been "very kind" and calls him to check up, Whittington is no longer involved in Republican politics. "My biggest question," he tells NEWSWEEK, "is trying to figure out, 'Lord, why me?'"

—JESSE ELLISON

WEEK OF SEPTEMBER 15

THE DIGNITY INDEX

Nation of Whiners II: Still Whining

A survey of dubious behavior that measures, on a scale of 1 to 100, just how low a person can go:

After he was cut by the Detroit Lions, **Tatum Bell** allegedly took a locker-room souvenir: the Gucci luggage of the man who replaced him. Bell says it was a misunderstanding. Score: **41**

Georgia **Rep. Lynn Westmoreland** calls the Obamas "uppity," then claims he had no idea the word was a slur. Lynn, no one uses that term anymore *except* as a slur. Score: **55**

At a meeting with banking-industry lobbyists, former McCain economic adviser **Phil Gramm** doubles down on his "nation of whiners" line, dropping the W word yet again. Score: **58**

WEEK OF SEPTEMBER 29

THE DIGNITY INDEX

You're Doin' a Heckuva Job, Bushie!

A weekly survey of dubious behavior that measures, on a scale of one to 100, just how low a person can go.

Microsoft honcho **Bill Gates**'s dead-on-arrival ad campaign with Jerry Seinfeld gets yanked after just two weeks on the air. Congrats, Bill! You're the new New Coke! Score: **6**

Hillary fund-raiser **Lynn Forester de Rothschild** says she'll back McCain because Obama (as opposed to, say, a Rothschild) is an "elitist" who talks down to "rednecks." Score: **38**

After 72 hours of silence during a giant financial crisis, **George W. Bush** emerges to read a two-minute prepared statement. He got bold by week's end. Better late than never? Score: **51**

WEEK OF OCTOBER 6

RECOVERY

Overlooked: The Littlest Evacuees

Within hours of Hurricane Ike's landfall in Texas, San Antonio officials had compiled precise statistics about their evacuee situation. They knew the city would need to care for 5,303 people (561 of whom had special medical needs) and 642 pets, including a turtle named Nibbles. But there was one key group for which they had no figures: children. "No one knew" how many, says Kate Dischino, a staff member with nonprofit Save the Children, who's been working in the shelters.

The oversight is by no means unique to San Antonio; disaster-relief experts say kids are rarely counted in evacuations. It's symptomatic, they say, of a larger problem: three years since Hurricane Katrina there are still no national guidelines for how to protect children in disaster areas. "There are myriad issues with children, from preparedness and recovery to repatriation to communities" that remain unaddressed, says Gregg Lord, a senior policy analyst with the Homeland Security Policy Institute at George Washington University. Shelters have reported shortages of essentials such as baby wipes and diapers. Lacking a suitable place to bathe infants post-Ike, some evacuees have used sinks set up next to Porta Potties. Save the Children's Jeanne-Aimee De Marrais was working at a flood-victim shelter in Iowa this summer and witnessed a 3-year-old wandering outside by a busy road. How'd it happen? There were no cribs to keep mobile toddlers safe. "Everyone assumes these things are taken care of, but they're not," says De Marrais. Such oversights can heap more trauma on kids already shaken by disaster. In a study of 665 families displaced by Katrina, nearly half reported at least one child with emotional or behavioral difficulties.

Disaster-relief experts say kids are rarely counted in evacuations.

In December 2007, Congress created the National Commission on Children and Disasters to identify gaps in planning and recommend policy solutions. But because of squabbles over funding, the commission has yet to meet, blowing an opportunity to prepare for this summer's heavy hurricane season. Commission chair Mark Shriver says he's frustrated, especially given the smooth sailing for the 2006 legislation providing resources for pets in disaster situations. "If we can do this for dogs and cats," Shriver says, "we can do it for kids." Maybe next hurricane season.

—Sarah Kliff and Catharine Skipp

WEEK OF OCTOBER 20

VIEWPOINT

Bad? It's Just a Flesh Wound.

The new NEWSWEEK poll shows that 86 percent of adult Americans are "dissatisfied with the way things are going" in this country. That is a shocking number, but what's even more incredible is that 10 percent of American citizens continue to be "satisfied." Consider the implication: more than 22 million men and women think the country is on the right track.

Who are these people? One in 10 Americans can't be repo men or Bush relatives. Satisfied? *Now?* Nobody's that Republican. Do these 10 percenters live in caves without TV, magazines, newspapers and the Internet—yet somehow still have a phone? And if you lived in a cave without HBO, would you really be "satisfied"?

The obvious guess is that the responders misunderstood the question. So maybe a few old ladies thought the nice NEWSWEEK pollster said, *Are you sad it's tied?* And they said "yes" because they thought their guy had a big lead. If that's true, Gallup had the same problem: its poll found 9 percent were satisfied.

Meanwhile people are selling their gold teeth and losing their homes. Corporate behemoths like

> **Satisfied? *Now?* Who are these people? One in 10 Americans can't be Bush relatives.**

Lehman Brothers, Merrill Lynch, Bear Stearns—even Linens 'n Things—have been swallowed up or bitten the dust. EBay is laying off people, the Postal Service is talking about layoffs—and over

22 million people are satisfied with how things are going? I guess if you worked for Bed, Bath & Beyond, you'd be happy about the Linens 'n Things thing, but is that kind of schadenfreude good for America?

Maybe the people who are satisfied just can't admit to what's happening. Seriously, who could have predicted that giving out loans like Halloween candy to people with mini-salaries to buy mini-mansions—who then used their home equity to buy gas-guzzling Hummers—would ever backfire?

"Satisfied" is not a puny word. It's what you'd say after a great steak dinner or when your team wins the World Series. So perhaps these people are just eternal optimists, the type who make Norman Vincent Peale look like Sylvia Plath. We all have friends who say stuff like, "Turn that frown upside down," or mimic the woman from the movie "Office Space" who said, "Uh oh, sounds like somebody's got a case of the *Mondays*."

It's easy to keep bloviating about these mysterious 10 percenters from afar . . . which is why I've been doing it. But in these heady times, when print journalism strides like a colossus across the American landscape, NEWSWEEK spared no expense or effort to get the real story—so I took the elevator downstairs, walked a block to the White House and talked to some tourists.

One of the first people I met was "satisfied"—but she'd also been drinking that afternoon and wouldn't let me use her name. (I

THE DIGNITY INDEX

Psst! He Also Picks Wings Off Flies!

A weekly mathematical survey of dubious behavior that measures, on a scale of 1 to 100, just how low you can go.

Four months after advising viewers to "buy buy buy," hysterical CNBC stock picker **Jim Cramer** says oops, it's time to pull your money out of the market. And change the channel. Score: **45**

AIG execs go on a $440k spa junket days after scoring an $85 billion bailout. "Standard practice," says new CEO **Edward Libby**. Wrong answer. Score: **56**

Does **Sarah Palin** really believe that Obama "pals around with terrorists" or does she just enjoy stirring up angry mobs? Cool it, Guv. Score: **62**

directed her to the closest bar.) Later I found a really sweet couple satisfied with the way things are going in America, because they live in Canada. Then I talked to Warren DeSmidt, 65, of Cedarburg, Wis., who quite convincingly told me he thinks the economic mess is just "a bump in the road . . . and order will be restored." Lynda Race, of Arlington, Va., who is "almost 50," boiled it down: "I love America. Where else would you be *more* satisfied?" By the end of my interviews, I agreed with their criticisms of the mainstream media and with the fact that Chris Matthews has totally lost it.

I'm betting the NEWSWEEK Poll's 10 percenters are like the ones I met on Pennsylvania Avenue: *über* optimists who see this financial-core meltdown as "just a flesh wound," like the Black Knight in Monty Python's "Holy Grail" who keeps fighting after King Arthur lops off his arms and legs. "I've had worse," the knight says. So has the United States, and maybe that's what the "satisfieds" understand that the rest of us don't.

—STEVE TUTTLE

WEEK OF OCTOBER 27

THE DIGNITY INDEX

I Feel Vindicated. Even Though I Wasn't.

A weekly mathematical survey of dubious behavior that measures, on a scale of 1 to 100, just how low you can go.

In a YouTube video, **Ringo Starr** tells the world to quit sending him fan mail because he has "too much to do." How long does it take to answer three letters? Score: **29**

Florida Rep. **Tim Mahoney**, who replaced Mark Foley (the Capitol Hill male-page guy), gets his own sex scandal: cops to multiple affairs. Something in the water? Score: **52**

Responding to the Troopergate report, Gov. **Sarah Palin** says she's "pleased to be cleared" of "any kind of unethical activity." Nice try. The report said exactly the opposite. Score: **67**

WEEK OF NOVEMBER 3

PUBLISHING

The Rupe Faux Kerfuffle

Vanity Fair columnist Michael Wolff's new book, "The Man Who Owns the News: Inside the Secret World of Rupert Murdoch," won't hit bookstores for another month. But in a time-honored publishing-industry tactic, the book has already spawned a suspiciously opportune controversy. According to a New York Times article, Murdoch was upset about Wolff's characterization of Murdoch's relations with two top executives in his empire, News Corp. president Peter Chernin and Fox News boss Roger Ailes. In a copy of the manuscript read by this reporter, which may differ in minor ways from the final version, Murdoch complains that neither Chernin nor his college-age children read newspapers. Wolff also concludes that Murdoch, under his third wife Wendi's influence, is growing cool to hard-right politics, the viewpoint widely attributed to his Fox News, run by Roger Ailes.

News Corp. sources say Wolff has exaggerated the "controversy." Wolff declined to comment, but venting merrily last week to the Times, the author described how Murdoch obtained an embargoed

---

THE DIGNITY INDEX

I Condemned That Joke Before I Cracked It

A weekly mathematical survey of dubious behavior that measures, on a scale of 1 to 100, just how low you can go.

Under fire for a joke about John McCain and Depends, Sen. **John Kerry** blunders through a squirrelly defense, reminding us why he's not *President* Kerry. Score: **12**

Former New York mayor (and gifted attack dog) **Rudy Giuliani** stars in a McCain robo-call that pushes racial buttons by calling Obama soft on killers and sex offenders. Score: **34**

After insulting his constituency by calling western Pa. "racist," Rep. **Jack Murtha** backtracks, saying he meant the area was "redneck" until a few years ago. Nice save? Score: **49**

manuscript, copies of which are circulating (loosely, it seems) from Europe to North America, and then complained to publisher Doubleday about the Fox News and Chernin passages. But with a few exceptions, a Murdoch spokesman said, "Wolff's portrayal of Rupert, the company and the family is accurate and vivid."

Wolff notes repeatedly in 450-plus pages that the mogul mumbles in an impenetrable Australian accent. Likewise, Wolff writes that Murdoch's hearing has deteriorated— but that no one inside his bubble dares to tell him. Can it be that the author and subject simply couldn't understand each other?

Whatever the case, the book should do well regardless of the manufactured contretemps. If readers can survive the turgid prose, Wolff delivers an incisive portrait of Murdoch, who surely must be placing a huge preorder just in time for the holiday season.

Wolff's book is already drawing notice for a suspiciously opportune controversy.

—JOHNNIE L. ROBERTS

International Affairs

YEAR IN REVIEW

With the world's lone remaining superpower tied up in two lengthy wars and a crippling economic crisis, while being led by an increasingly unpopular and ineffectual president, the ripple effects across the globe were bound to be significant. In 2008, a thin veil of anxiety settled over the international community. Peace-loving nations watched nervously as the struggles of the U.S. coincided with provocative behavior by Russia, China, Iran, Zimbabwe and Venezuela, all of whom acted with confidence that no one was well-positioned, or sufficiently motivated, to stop them. Many Europeans have grumbled over the last decade about the outsized influence of the U.S. on the world stage; the events of the past year suggested that they should perhaps be careful what they wish for.

No international development was more alarming than the retrograde behavior of Russia and its steely leader, Vladimir Putin, who spent the year doing his best impression of a Soviet-style premier. Precluded by law from running for another term as president, Putin installed a hand-picked successor, Dmitri Medvedev, who then promptly appointed Putin as the country's new prime minister. This all but ensured that the new boss would be the same as the old boss. And after the international community defied Russia by backing Kosovo's Feb. 17 declaration of independence from Serbia, Putin cunningly flipped the situation to his advantage, using Kosovo as a pretext for unleashing his nation's military might in Georgia (a former Soviet republic). Two ethnically-mixed provinces there, South Ossetia and Abkhazia, sought to break away and rejoin Russia. The lopsided war between Russia and Georgia was brief, lasting just a few bloody days, but the message was sent: Russia, under Putin, was once again determined to do whatever it wanted. The will of the world be damned.

News out of the Middle East was no rosier, as Israel struggled through an especially grim year, marked by defeat in a lightning war with Lebanon in May and by scandal at the highest reaches of its government, which by year's end had resulted in the resignation of Prime Minister Ehud Olmert. With Iran inching ever closer to nuclear capability, and its president Mahmoud Ahmedinejad making increasingly aggressive statements about its intentions toward Israel, President George W. Bush scrambled in the waning months of his administration to salvage a foreign-policy achievement for his presidency. But he had little clout—and the concerned parties in the region had little motivation—leaving the next president to inherit a stalemate more precarious than ever.

WEEK OF JANUARY 7

BURMA

In This Life, Or the Next

Autocrats worry about Buddha power. In much of Southeast Asia, monks occupy the loftiest of moral high ground. According to the Buddhist concept of reincarnation, misdeeds in past lives affect problems in the current one. Do something bad in this life and you'll probably come back as a "sentient being" in your next one—but not necessarily a human. During Burma's bloody crackdown in September, some soldiers tried to "defrock" monks prior to detaining them, in a bid to soften their own karmic crimes. In 1988, I saw a Burmese soldier trying to give alms to Buddhist monks, who refused him by turning their begging bowls upside down. The guy seemed upset. He didn't want to be reincarnated as a toad, I suppose.

Authorities in Beijing, who've been criticized for supporting the Burmese junta, have reason to be queasy about monk-led protests both at home and abroad. Opposition to the Chinese occupation of Tibet in 1951 erupted first in Buddhist monasteries. Resentment still simmers. On Nov. 19, two teenage Tibetan monks quarreled with a Chinese shopkeeper and were detained. Some 200 sympathizers protested and five were arrested for "fanning the riot," according to the state-run Xinhua news agency. After the Dalai Lama was awarded the U.S. Congressional Gold Medal in October, clashes broke out between Chinese security forces and Buddhist monks. Celebrations were quashed and 3,000 police reportedly surrounded the Drepung Monastery near Lhasa, where monks learned of the award through Web sites and YouTube.

> **Celebrations were quashed and 3,000 police reportedly surrounded the Drepung Monastery near Lhasa.**

Tibet's "living buddhas" are a special case. Revered as reincarnated deities, they are said to exert an unusual amount of control over their future lives. Which led to the recent spat between Beijing and the exiled Tibetan leader the Dalai Lama over the politics of reincarnation. It began when Beijing authorities decreed that reincarnated deities must be Chinese citizens authorized by the religious-affairs bureau, meaning no reincarnations in exile.

International Affairs-158 | JANUARY

The exiled Dalai Lama responded by suggesting a variety of novel ways he might come back. At 72, Tenzin Gyatso is the 14th Dalai Lama; he once told me he could return as two Dalai Lamas. Later, he said he might help choose his own successor, or come back as a woman, or have his power pass to a legislative body. Buddha power at the ballot box? That sounds like double trouble for Beijing. —MELINDA LIU

FAST CHAT

The Man in The Middle

It's been a long year for Tony Blair. After stepping down as Britain's prime minister in June, under fire for his Iraq policy, he took on what many consider the hardest job in the Mideast: representative of the Quartet—the United States, Russia, the European Union and the United Nations—to the Palestinians. He spoke with NEWSWEEK's Kevin Peraino.

You've heard a lot of resentment among Palestinians for your support of the Iraq War. Can you get past that lack of trust?

For the Palestinians, it is essential for them to have someone who can deal with the Americans and with the Israelis. This is a tough thing to say, but it's true: if you are not a friend to Israel, you will play no very helpful part in bringing about a solution to this.

Do you favor direct negotiations with Hamas?

You can't have negotiations about a two-state solution with a party that's not prepared to accept that there should be two states.

Were you surprised by the U.S. National Intelligence Estimate that says Iran halted its nuclear-weapons program in 2003?

Not particularly, no. But I think people should read the whole report. It's not saying that we can forget about Iran.

Does this report make it likely that Israel may act unilaterally?

I think all of us will try to react rationally. If there's a serious threat posed, we've got to confront it. If we can avoid that confrontation, all the better.

Your successor, Gordon Brown, plans to cut British troop levels in Iraq by half. Is it difficult for you to watch?

One thing I absolutely don't do is comment on what's happened after me. I don't think that's fair to my successor, who I support 100 percent.

You sold a memoir recently for $9 million. How did you convince your publisher that you can write it and make peace in the Middle East at the same time?

Look, I'm a politician—I can convince a lot of people of a lot of things [*Laughs*].

FIRST PERSON

I Flew Halfway Around The World—For This?

White House correspondent Holly Bailey spent a week traveling overseas with the vice president. The trip didn't go quite as planned.

"Breakfast was excellent." Along with six other reporters, I spent more than a week in February traveling overseas with Vice President Dick Cheney, and through the first eight days those were just about the only words he spoke to us. (OK, he took one question during a quick press conference with Australia's prime minister. But that was it.) We'd been promised access to Cheney during a trip to shore up relations with top allies in the War on Terror. Mostly, though, the promise was empty. On day four, I used the stopwatch on my iPod to time how long I actually saw Cheney: 41 seconds here; 38 seconds there. I'd flown 27 hours, crammed into a middle seat on Air Force Two, for this?

The last few days, though, made it worthwhile. Cheney's aides told us we'd make surprise visits to

> **They ended up taking us to one of the few temporary barracks available, and it had only a few blankets, no sheets and hardly any pillows.**

Pakistan and Afghanistan. We flew to Baghram Air Force Base, where Cheney met briefly with troops, but a snowstorm prevented us from taking off for Kabul. He and his top aides quickly found beds for the night, but the rest of us weren't so lucky. The soldiers at the base were embarrassed and apologetic; they weren't prepared for overnight guests. They ended up taking us to one of the few temporary barracks available, and it had only a few blankets, no sheets and hardly any

JANUARY

pillows. A trip to the dining hall was canceled because there wasn't enough food, so we ate packages of Cheez-Its from the plane.

Just after dawn we were taken to the mess hall, where Cheney was dining with soldiers. "How was breakfast?" a reporter yelled. "Breakfast," he replied, "was excellent." That's all we got. Then our adventure resumed. As we waited to board the plane for Kabul, sirens went off and a plume of smoke rose in the distance. A suicide bomber with links to the Taliban had blown himself up at Baghram's main gate, killing 15 people. Aides worried that Cheney's security had been compromised, but we took off anyway. Once we landed, we buckled up for a white-knuckle motorcade ride to the presidential palace, speeding at more than 100mph past bombed-out buildings—a grim reminder that a meal of Cheez-Its wasn't so bad. An hour later, we were headed home. During the flight, Cheney finally spent a few minutes talking to us. Twelve minutes.

> "Dick Cheney is still a war criminal. Hillary Clinton is still Satan. And I'm back on the radio."
> —*Radio personality Don Imus, January 2008*
> *Perspectives*

WEEK OF JANUARY 21

MIDDLE EAST

Bothersome Intel on Iran

In public, President Bush has been careful to reassure Israel and other allies that he still sees Iran as a threat, while not disavowing his administration's recent National Intelligence Estimate. That NIE, made public Dec. 3, embarrassed the administration by concluding that Tehran had halted its weapons program in 2003, which seemed to undermine years of bellicose rhetoric from Bush and other senior officials about Iran's nuclear ambitions.

But in private conversations with Israeli Prime Minister Ehud Olmert last week, the president all but disowned the document, said a senior administration official who accompanied Bush on his six-nation trip to the Mideast. "He told the Israelis that he can't control what the intelligence community says, but that [the NIE's] conclusions don't reflect his own views" about Iran's nuclear-weapons program, said the official, who would discuss intelligence matters only on the condition of anonymity.

Bush's behind-the-scenes assurances may help to quiet a rising chorus of voices inside Israel's defense community that are calling for unilateral military action against Iran. Olmert, asked by NEWSWEEK after Bush's departure on Friday whether he felt reassured, replied: "I am very happy." A source close to the Israeli leader said Bush first briefed Olmert about the intelligence estimate a week before it was published, during talks in Washington that preceded the Annapolis peace conference in November. According to the source, who also refused to be named discussing the issue, Bush told Olmert he was uncomfortable with the findings and seemed almost apologetic.

Israeli and other foreign officials asked Bush to explain the NIE, which concluded with "high confidence" that Iran halted what the document describes as its "nuclear weapons program." The NIE arrived at this finding even though Tehran continues to operate uranium-enrichment centrifuges that many experts believe are intended to develop material for a bomb, and despite the CIA's assertion that it had, for the first time, concrete evidence of such a weaponization program. Most confusing of all, the document seemed to directly contradict a 2005 NIE that concluded—also with "high confidence"—that Iran *did* have such a weapons program. Bush's national-security adviser, Stephen Hadley, told reporters in Jerusalem that Bush had only said to Olmert privately what he's already said publicly, which is that he believes Iran remains "a threat" no matter what the NIE says. But the president may be trying to tell his allies something more: that he thinks the document is a dead letter.

—MICHAEL HIRSH

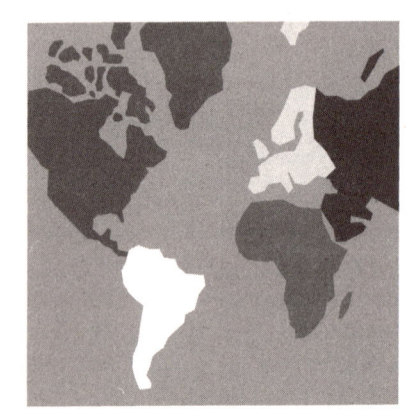

WEEK OF JANUARY 28

IRAN

High Stakes In the Gulf

Eager to avoid future confrontations between Iranian boats and U.S. warships in the Persian Gulf, the U.S. government has quietly sent word to Tehran asking for dialogue. The stern four-paragraph message, dated Jan. 10, was delivered to Tehran via a Swiss intermediary. The communiqué, a copy of which was obtained by NEWSWEEK, notes that Washington had sent an earlier request on Nov. 21, 2007, to limit "the possibility of miscommunication and misunderstanding" in the Gulf, but that "we have not received a response to that message. We believe it is in Iran's interest to consider [it] and avoid any further provocative actions."

U.S. officials say they are not hopeful that Iran will respond now, given its silence before. In December, after the first message was sent, there were two encounters in the Strait of Hormuz; one led the U.S. captain to fire warning shots. During the most recent provocation on Jan. 6, five Iranian launches careered around three U.S. warships for close to half an hour, at one point dropping objects in the path of one of the vessels, according to the Navy. A radio transmission from an unknown source declared a U.S. ship would "explode." "They came at us as a group of five, in a formation," said Cmdr. Jeffrey James, skipper of the destroyer USS Hopper. "They knew what they were doing."

Though Pentagon officials, speaking anonymously because of the topic's sensitivity, stress there is no proof, Navy analysts at Fifth Fleet headquarters in Bahrain have concluded that the Jan. 6 confrontation was most likely a deliberate effort by Iran's Islamic Revolutionary Guard Corps to persuade U.S. vessels to open fire on them. The purpose: to create an incident prior to President George W. Bush's visit to the region, which was intended in part to rally support from Arab countries against Iran. (An Iranian national-security official called the accusations "fabricated." Insisting on anonymity, he said they were a "show for the Arab countries.") The increased "buzzing" of U.S. warships by IRGC launches comes as the guard has taken more control of Gulf operations from Iran's regular Navy.

—JOHN BARRY *and* MICHAEL HIRSH

WEEK OF FEBRUARY 4

AFGHANISTAN

As Karzai Loses His Grip, A Familiar Face Looms

It wasn't long ago that Afghan President Hamid Karzai was seen as a dependable U.S. ally on par with Pakistani leader Pervez Musharraf. But as Afghanistan has fallen into violent chaos—along with Pakistan—tensions have erupted between Karzai and the United States and Britain. One of the most worried U.S. officials is Zalmay Khalilzad, the Afghan-born ambassador to the United Nations, who is seriously considering running for Karzai's seat himself when the next elections are held in 2009, according to several U.N. and U.S. government officials. Last Friday, Karzai blocked the appointment of British politician Paddy Ashdown, the former U.N. High Representative for Bosnia, as envoy to Afghanistan. During a meeting with U.N. Secretary-General Ban Ki-moon at the World Economic Forum in Davos, Switzerland, Karzai said that he and many Afghan parliamentarians did not want Ashdown in the post, according to a Western official briefed on the discussions who would only speak about them anonymously. Ashdown's formal role would have been to coordinate international relief programs. But American and British officials were hoping that Ashdown might also act as a kind of viceroy, bringing order to an Afghan government that finds itself besieged by a resurgent Taliban. Karzai's opposition grew as Ashdown sought to establish what his powers as "superenvoy" might be, one official says. The Afghan leader could still be persuaded to change his mind, but the same official says it is "unlikely." "Karzai has been under a lot of pressure and criticism, and he might feel that he was being marginalized," says Jim Dobbins, the former U.S. ambassador to Afghanistan.

U.S. and British officials have grown increasingly disenchanted with Karzai, who is now viewed as isolated in Kabul and surrounded by corrupt or incompetent ministers. Things are not much better next door in Pakistan, where militant Islamist groups have grown bolder and the embattled Mushar-

> **A senior Bush administration official says that Khalilzad is actively exploring a run in Afghanistan.**

raf is under pressure to step down. Like Karzai, Musharraf has begun lashing out publicly against what he sees as Western interference.

Khalilzad had a successful stint as U.S. ambassador to Kabul after the Taliban fell, helping to form the Karzai government. He also served as U.S. ambassador to Iraq and was one of the principal drafters of a 1992 "grand strategy" for U.S. global dominance that became known as the "Pentagon paper." Even so, in a 2005 interview with NEWSWEEK, Khalilzad said that one thing he had learned during his term in Afghanistan was that its people "don't want to be ruled by a foreigner."

Khalilzad has not directly denied that he is considering a run. His spokeswoman, Carolyn Vadino, told NEWSWEEK that "he intends to serve out his post as long as [President Bush] wants him in office. And then after that, he hopes to find a job here in the private sector in the U.S." But a senior Bush administration official who knows Khalilzad (and who asked for anonymity because he was not authorized to discuss Khalilzad's plans) said the U.N. ambassador was actively exploring a run. Kenneth Katzman, Afghanistan expert at Washington's Congressional Research Service, said that "most observers think he would stand only if Karzai decides not to run." During an interview this week with NEWSWEEK's Lally Weymouth (page 47), though, Karzai seems to leave the door open for a re-election bid.

—JOHN BARRY *and* MICHAEL HIRSH

ISRAEL

In Gaza, Borderline Insanity

A debate has opened among Israeli policymakers about how best to deal with the newly porous border between Egypt and the Gaza Strip. Last week, Hamas militants blew down part of the barrier, letting thousands of Palestinians pour into Egypt. The exodus was seen as a PR coup for Hamas and a setback for U.S. efforts to turn Gazans against the party. But now Israelis are quietly wondering whether the chaos might play into their hands. After the 2005 withdrawal from Gaza, hawks argued that they were no longer responsible for the welfare of the 1.5 million Palestinians there—a view that human-rights groups vigorously oppose. With Egyptian President Hosni Mubarak appearing to sanction the furlough, at least for now, the view has gained traction.

"This is a blessing in disguise," says one well-placed Israeli source, who asked for anonymity so he could speak more frankly. "We can forget about them and throw away the key."

Others, though, speculate that the border breach could create momentum for a larger incursion into Gaza, something Israel's Prime Minister Ehud Olmert, chastened by his disastrous 2006 invasion of Lebanon, has so far avoided. A large-scale ground attack is now "much more likely," says Yuval Steinitz, a member of the Likud party who sits on a key defense committee. An open border, he argues, will make it easier to carry in long-range rockets too big to smuggle through tunnels. "We have no other alternative," Steinitz says. For their part, the Egyptians appeared eager to slow the tide. Police formed a human chain along the fence permitting Gazans to flow in only one direction: home.

—KEVIN PERAINO

WEEK OF FEBRUARY 11

CHINA

This Little Piggy Shortage

A new breed of criminal has emerged in China: "pigjackers." Soaring pork prices in the People's Republic have sent thieves roaring off with truckloads of hogs—and sometimes with smaller hauls, as was the case with the gang that was busted last year in Shenzhen trying to make off with 275 pounds of pork on a motorbike. A local newspaper valued the meat at upwards of $420, or roughly three times what a stolen motorbike might fetch in the city. Police easily caught the getaway bike; it couldn't handle all that weight.

> **Soaring prices have resulted in thefts of hogs by the truckload.**

The porcine crime wave is no joke to China's leaders. They see it as a sign of a much larger problem: even more than they worry about a repetition of Tiananmen Square, they dread the kind of mass unrest that could erupt out of a spike in pork prices. A full 65 percent of the country's total protein consumption is pork. The threat of a spontaneous uprising has been made worse by a freak blizzard that paralyzed central China last week—the region's worst in 50 years—stranding mobs of migrant workers on their way home for the Lunar New Year and disrupting shipments of the pig meat that is essential to holiday feasts. Food prices in general, and pork in particular, have been skyrocketing for months. Economic boom times are boosting demand even as the supply has plunged because of shrinking farmlands, rising grain prices and a "blue ear disease" epidemic that forced pig raisers to cull many thousands of hogs.

In an effort to head off serious trouble, Beijing has tapped the country's official "pork reserve." That's no joke, either; it's the actual term for the special stash of meat the Chinese government keeps frozen in case of a sudden crunch—not unlike America's Strategic Petroleum Reserve. But snowbound shipments of pork probably won't reach many Chinese families' tables in time for the holiday. And the country's underlying agricultural shortages will only get worse. The prospect is something for the whole world to worry about. Experts predict that China, long a major exporter of corn products, will soon become a net importer—possibly this year. When that happens, global grain prices could jump like this year's oil market.

—MELINDA LIU *and* SAM SEIBERT

WEEK OF MARCH 3

PAKISTAN

Elections Usher in a New Face

Washington can expect to get along reasonably well with Pakistan's next prime minister. The Pakistan People's Party, the dominant partner in the newly elected ruling coalition, has chosen the eminently trusted politician Makhdoom Amin Fahim for the job, according to a PPP official who asked not to be named prior to the official announcement. Fahim, 68, is notoriously lacking in charisma, but he does have a demonstrated ability to get things done. Better yet, he possesses an attribute that makes him a rarity among the country's senior politicians: an immaculate reputation for honesty. And he's known to favor close military and economic ties with the United States.

Like most other Pakistanis, though, he's convinced his country needs to recalibrate its relationship with Washington—particularly regarding America's aggressive strategy against extremists on the Afghan border. Blaming the former Army chief, President Pervez Musharraf, for taking a disastrous course in the tribal areas, the new civilian leaders think they can do better by negotiating with tribal elders.

Fahim has shown before what he thinks of Musharraf. Back in 2002 the president, urgently seeking partners for his own jerry-built party, tried to recruit the PPP vice chairman as prime minister, asking only that Fahim not take direction from the PPP's exiled leader at the time, Benazir Bhutto. Fahim refused. Late last week he told party associates that the offer was made and rejected a total of four times.

Fahim says he has no regrets. Personal ambition doesn't seem to be what drives him—which is one reason the ambitious party heads are trusting him with the job. Bhutto's widower, PPP co-chairman Asif Ali Zardari, may be planning his own bid to step in as prime minister after stability returns. In any case, Zardari is counting on Fahim to hasten that return. Like the late Bhutto, Fahim is the scion of a landed feudal family in southern Sindh. His father was a locally venerated Sufi holy man, the Pir of Hala, and a founder of the populist PPP with Bhutto's father, Zulfikar Ali Bhutto. Fahim in fact retains the Sufi title of pir, which he inherited from his father. Nevertheless he's a thoroughly secular, moderate and pragmatic social democrat. He writes mystic poetry on the side.

> **Fahim has a rare quality among the country's leaders: a reputation for honesty.**

Will Fahim change course in the tribal areas? Washington's top ranks seem unworried about what the new civilian leaders might decide. "We're going to let them have their rounds of discussions," says a senior administration official who was not authorized to speak on the record. "We still expect the [Pakistani] Army is going to take the necessary military action." Count on an interesting transition.

—Zahid Hussain, Ron Moreau *and* Michael Hirsh

KOSOVO

To Block a Nation's Birth

The world's eyes were fixed on Belgrade last Thursday when some 2,000 rioters broke off from a protest march against Kosovo's Feb. 17 declaration of independence and torched the U.S. Embassy. But the more telling attack came two days earlier, when angry Serbs burned down U.N. border posts between Kosovo and Serbia. In an interview with B92 Television in Belgrade, the Serbian minister for Kosovo, Slobodan Samardzic, gloated, "We saved part of Kosovo!"

Not quite—NATO quickly retook the sites. But Serbia seems to feel that if it can't have the entire former province, no one can. While the United States and major European countries now recognize Kosovo, Russia and others are balking, worried about their own restive regions. Russia's Security Council veto can block any move to affirm Kosovo as an independent country, not a U.N. protectorate. Meanwhile, Serbia announced that its judges would start holding court in northern Kosovo, where ethnic Serbs are clustered. When NATO peacekeepers shut the border for a day, Serb officials and traders took mountain paths.

Officially, no one wants partition. But that seems to be what's happening by default. "They can't control it, so what are they going to do about it?" Aleksandar Vasovic, an analyst with Belgrade's Balkan Insight journal, says about the European Union mission that hopes to take over from the United Nations in Kosovo. "It is a de facto partition already." An EU official, unnamed because of the issue's sensitivity, confirmed there's no timetable for establishing Kosovo's international borders. "We'd have to see what precise arrangements were made," the official said. "It's unwise in the present circumstances to make precise predictions."

Serbia's leaders won't settle for

"Kostunica will never put his signature on anything recognizing the partition of Kosovo."

part of Kosovo, says Ljiljana Smajlovic, editor in chief of the newspaper Politika, who is close to Serbia's ardently nationalist president, Vojislav Kostunica. "They'll do everything they can simply to treat Kosovo as part of Serbia, provide Serbs there with all the government services they can," she says. "But Kostunica will never put his signature on anything recognizing the partition of Kosovo." Instead, she says, Belgrade will keep trying to bar Kosovo from international organizations and sporting events while calling on other countries to reject Kosovo's. The point? "To make [Kosovo's independence] less real."

—ROD NORDLAND *and* ZORAN CIRJAKOVIC

WEEK OF MARCH 17

ISRAEL

The Trouble With Silence

Despite flaring Israeli-Palestinian violence, a chorus of security officials, academics and ordinary Israelis is urging direct negotiations with the radical Islamist group Hamas. In a recent Haaretz-Dialog poll, 64 percent of respondents favored such talks. Even among those from the hawkish Likud bloc, the idea was backed by 48 percent.

Israelis are fed up with what they see as a failed Gaza policy. Hamas's attacks keep spoiling the peace efforts of moderate President Mahmoud Abbas, and Israel's retaliatory strikes in Gaza have backfired. Public opinion was hit hard earlier this month when Israeli raids killed more than 50 Palestinian civilians. "Hamas is not going to disappear," says Shlomo Brom, a former Israeli military chief of strategic planning who advocates indirect negotiations. Damascus-based Hamas leader Khaled Meshaal told NEWSWEEK last year that his organization was open to direct talks, as long as there were no preconditions.

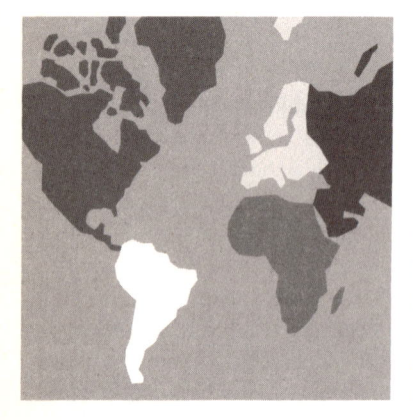

High-profile meetings are all but unthinkable. Israeli Prime Minister Ehud Olmert, his popularity hovering in the single digits, doesn't dare alienate the right-wing parties that are keeping him in power. And which Hamas should Israel deal with? Since seizing control in Gaza last June, the organization has split into a pack of independent power bases. "When you talk to Hamas, you don't have one address," says a former Israeli intelligence operative who has held direct talks with the Islamists in the past and who asked for anonymity on such a delicate topic. "You have to deal with several figures in order to achieve approval for anything."

That hasn't kept Israel from quietly holding behind-the scenes talks—especially with jailed Hamas representatives. Last summer Ofer Dekel, a former Shin Bet intelligence officer assigned to negotiate the release of captured Israeli soldier Gilad Shalit, met with senior Hamas officials at Israel's Hadarim prison. Lawyers for Shalit's father, Noam, are also seeking a sit-down with Hamas in Gaza. So far the Israeli government has withheld travel permission. But one thing is sure: ignoring Hamas hasn't made it go away.

—KEVIN PERAINO *and* JOANNA CHEN

WEEK OF MAY 5

ESPIONAGE

North Korea On the Spot

Newly declassified spy photos suggesting North Korean involvement in the construction of a Syrian nuclear reactor, which was heavily damaged in an Israeli bombing raid last year, have raised fresh questions about the facility's murky history—and about whether the disclosure of the images could derail a pending nuclear disarmament deal between Washington and Pyongyang. Prior to last week's unveiling of the photos, U.S. and Israeli officials had refused to discuss publicly the September 2007 raid. Even now, U.S. officials acknowledge that they're still withholding key information about the provenance of the photos in order to protect sources and methods. But according to one senior intelligence official, who spoke only on the condition of anonymity, the "handheld" photos taken from inside the reactor were gathered "over a period of time," indicating that whoever took them was somehow able to breach the building's inner sanctum on a consistent basis. Among the few photos released to the media: a shot of a fuel-rod system whose design closely resembled the one at

North Korea's Yongbyon plutonium plant.

Intelligence officials briefed select congressional leaders on the Syrian plant after the Israeli bombing raid. At a media briefing last week, a senior official said that the administration decided to keep the public—and the full membership of congressional intel committees—in the dark at Israel's request, and to avoid provoking Syrian retaliation. Pundits speculated that the timing of the North Korea-Syria disclosures hint at a plot by marginalized administration hard-liners, such as Vice President Dick Cheney, to sabotage the nuclear-disarmament deal. But two current U.S. officials said that, in fact, the disclosures are part of a well-crafted diplomatic strategy to nudge Syria toward peace with Israel and to pressure North Korea to disclose its nuclear-proliferation activities. One of the officials told NEWSWEEK that Secretary of State Condoleezza Rice briefed Chinese officials about the Syrian reactor project late last year. After examining the evidence, the official said, Beijing agreed to toughen its stance toward Kim Jong Il's regime. —MARK HOSENBALL

TERRORISM

A Tense Impasse in Yemen

During a Mideast trip earlier this month, FBI Director Robert Mueller made an unpublicized detour to Yemen in order to press an issue of serious concern to Washington: why has the Yemeni government refused to turn over an accused Qaeda terrorist charged in the October 2000 bombing of the USS Cole, which killed 17 U.S. sailors? The meeting between Mueller and Yemeni President Ali Abdullah Saleh did not go well, according to two sources who were briefed on the session but asked not to be identified discussing it. Saleh gave no clear answers about the suspect, Jamal al-Badawi, leaving Mueller "angry and very frustrated," said one source, who added that he's rarely seen the normally taciturn FBI director so upset.

The fate of Badawi is one of a number of terror-related cases that has generated tension with Yemen. U.S. officials only recently learned that another indicted Cole bomber, Fahed al-Quso, broke out of a Yemeni jail along with Badawi two years ago and remains a free man. Yet another accused Qaeda operative, Jaber Elbaneh, a 41-year-old American citizen with a $5 million bounty on his head (stemming from charges that he was part of a suspected Buffalo-area terror cell), was recently seen walking into a Yemeni court—and then nonchalantly walking back out again. The cases last Friday prompted President George W. Bush to have his own phone call with Saleh—a leader he once warmly praised for his cooperation in the War on Terror. "We are not fully satisfied yet,"

> **The fate of Badawi is one of a number of terror-related cases that has generated tension with Yemen.**

said one national-security official familiar with the conversation.

The impasse with the Yemeni government coincides with an escalation in attacks from a resurgent Qaeda organization. In recent weeks, Westerners based in the country have been besieged by bombings and mortar fire aimed at the U.S. Embassy, a housing complex for foreigners and a Canadian oil-company facility. The State Department has evacuated all non-emergency personnel. Counterterrorism analysts say Saleh, preoccupied with tribal unrest, may be too weak to crack down on anti-U.S. terrorists. But if the Bush administration presses too hard for the Cole bombers, said analyst Brian O'Neill, an expert in the region, it could undermine Saleh even further and accelerate Yemen's devolution into a "failed state." Mohammed al-Basha, a spokesman for the Yemeni Embassy, said his country remains committed to fighting terrorists. "It is common that any allies will have bumpy roads from time to time," he said. —M.I.

WEEK OF MAY 12

PAKISTAN

The Price of Peace Deals

As Pakistan's new government pursues peace deals with Islamic militant leaders in tribal regions along the Afghanistan border, some U.S. counterterrorism officials fear their "worst nightmare" is unfolding: a scenario in which Al Qaeda leaders in the area will have more freedom than ever to recruit and train new members. But the Bush administration is internally divided about how best to approach the situation. U.S. officials say they are particularly alarmed by the new coalition government's negotiations with Baitullah Mehsud, a fierce tribal boss and Qaeda sympathizer based in South Waziristan province whom Pakistan's own government has accused of orchestrating the December 2007 assassination of former prime minister Benazir Bhutto. (Bhutto's widower, Asif Ali Zardari, now heads her political party and is one of Pakistan's senior leaders.)

According to several U.S. officials, who asked for anonymity when discussing internal debates, many intelligence officials believe the United States must press Pakistan to resist going too far with its accommodations. "We continuously say that this is where bad things happen," said one of the officials. But other administration officials, including State Department diplomats, believe Pakistan's new leadership needs to be given some room to sort out its own problems. "The new government wants to distance itself from the policies of [Pakistani President Pervez] Musharraf," one senior U.S. official said. "They want to fight terrorism in their own way." The official said that the Bush administration is willing, for a time, to go along with Islamabad's efforts—provided that the government and tribal leaders "enforce" whatever peace deals they strike.

"Silence is probably the best American posture in public," said Bruce Riedel, formerly one of the CIA's top experts on the region, because "it's very clear the new Pakistani government is not going to listen to [Washington] on this issue." On the other hand, he noted, the recent resurgence of terror in the border regions began when Musharraf announced his own peace overtures in 2005. "This is a formula," Riedel said, "whose track record has been discredited."

—MARK HOSENBALL

WEEK OF MAY 26

LEBANON

Hizbullah Awaits the Next Round

Even as Hizbullah leaders cut a deal to remove their troops from Beirut's streets last week, the Islamist group's on-the-ground commanders were quietly making plans to consolidate their military gains. "Our units are still patrolling the area," said one Hizbullah military commander, who asked not to be identified because he didn't have authorization from his superior. "We still have guns, but we're hiding them now." The Islamists are particularly focused on expanding their network of intelligence collection. Starting about a year ago, Hizbullah operatives began meticulously surveilling Sunni security guards with close ties to Saad Hariri's Future Movement, according to the Hizbullah commander. By the time fighting erupted in Beirut two weeks ago, the operatives had compiled a comprehensive list of names and phone numbers that were used to intimidate Sunni enemies during the fighting. As Hizbullah's guerrilla army swept through Beirut's streets, operatives phoned the Sunni gunmen they had been shadowing. "How are you?" the unidentified caller would begin. "How's your wife?" And then: "We can see you now. You have three minutes to evacuate."

At a safe house in Beirut's predominantly Shiite southern suburb of Dahiya last week, the Hizbullah commander triumphantly showed a NEWSWEEK reporter photographs from the clashes that he had taken on his cell phone. Yet the militant—sporting a green Dolce & Gabbana baseball cap, wraparound sunglasses and a Browning pistol tucked into his jeans—believes "we're still in a state of war." The

> **"The prospect of Sunni-Shiite strife has always been Hizbullah's Achilles' heel," says Amal Saad-Ghorayeb.**

commander says Hizbullah is also prepared for renewed fighting with Israel. In recent months the Islamists have imported batches of new Russian-made Kalashnikovs and other arms.

Still, Hizbullah's political leadership knows that long-term fightingis likely toharm the guerrillas' image in the eyes of ordinary Lebanese. "The prospect of Sunni-Shiite strife has always been Hizbullah's Achilles' heel," says Amal Saad-Ghorayeb, a Hizbullah scholar in Beirut. That's one more reason why Hizbullah believes low-profile intel operations could workbetter than open war. Before leaving, the Hizbullah commander offered one last piece of advice. "I'm being followed," he said quietly. "You're being followed." The message: even if Hizbullah's forces have largely left Beirut's streets, its invisible eyes remain.

—Kevin Peraino

WEEK OF JUNE 30

IRAN

Back on the Black Market

Tehran is pushing back against Bush administration efforts to crack down on Iranian agents who buy U.S. military equipment on the black market. In a development

> **U.S. officials are furious that Beijing may have ordered Hong Kong to cave to Tehran's wishes.**

that angered and baffled American investigators, Hong Kong authorities recently freed, without explanation, an alleged Iranian operative named Yousef Boushvash, who is wanted by the United States for conspiring to obtain embargoed U.S. military-airplane parts. In a similar incident, Iran accused Britain of surrendering its sovereignty to U.S. intelligence agencies by preparing to extradite a former Iranian diplomat, Nosratollah Tajik, accused of trying to buy night-vision gear for Tehran.

Ever since military sales to Iran were frozen after the 1979 Iranian revolution, U.S. agencies have regularly cracked down on Iranian efforts to circumvent the embargo. British authorities arrested Tajik in November 2006; earlier this year U.K. courts ruled in favor of his extradition, which was authorized for early June but has been delayed due to Tajik's ill health.

More disturbing to U.S. officials, though, is the case of Boushvash. In an e-mail to a U.S. supplier, Boushvash claimed his customers operated a fleet of "about 200 light aircraft"; in reality, he allegedly was buying fighter-jet parts for shipment to Tehran. Last August, agents filed a complaint in Manhattan federal court seeking Boushvash's arrest, and he was picked up in Hong Kong during an undercover sting in October. An extradition hearing was scheduled for April 14, but according to a Justice Department letter obtained by NEWSWEEK, U.S. prosecutors were notified on April 10 that Hong Kong had canceled the extradition. Boushvash was released the next day. He disappeared and is now the subject of an Interpol arrest notice. U.S. officials, who asked for anonymity when discussing a continuing investigation, said they believe Tehran confirmed to Beijing that Boushvash was Iran's man, but complained he had been set up. Whatever the reason, Washington is furious at the Chinese government, blaming Beijing for ordering Hong Kong to cave to Tehran's wishes and free someone they very much wanted to meet face to face.

—Mark Hosenball

WEEK OF JULY 7/JULY 14

ELECTION IN ZIMBABWE

An Underground Diary

Some details, such as timing and description of movements, in the following are altered for the safety of NEWSWEEK's *reporter. For longer versions of each entry, visit Newsweek.com.*

Wednesday, June 25: Arriving after dark in Harare, Zimbabwe's capital, we see gangs of young men jogging down a wide avenue, half hidden by trees. They have signs and clubs; these are the ZANU-PF youths, Robert Mugabe's young party activists, who have been prowling the best neighborhoods, gathering at the gates of the well-off and demanding that they send out their servants for "re-education."

My first contact, ominously, is a no-show. I reach him on the phone and his voice is tense. "I'm very sorry. I can't meet you because we got called away when one of our friends was abducted and we found him shot in the head; he's in the hospital now, but we don't think he's going to make it. Another one we think is dead, but we can't find his body." The victims were party activists; some details I have to disguise, for safety reasons. Even three days after Morgan Tsvangirai announced he wouldn't run in Friday's election, the violence continues.

Thursday, June 26: Nearly every minibus in Harare has a poster of Mugabe. I asked around and there's a very simple reason. These privately owned vehicles, which carry most people to work, can rarely find fuel at official prices and so must revert to the black market, at some US$8 to US$10 a gallon. But if they have a Mugabe poster, they're allowed to refuel at government depots at subsidized prices of only 60,000 Zimbabwean dollars per gallon. That's essentially free, since the Zim dollar is trading at 18 billion for each U.S. dollar; it has doubled in a week and is going up nearly 20 percent a day, for an inflation rate in excess of 30 million percent a year.

Friday, June 27: What if they held an election and no one came? Today's vote was pretty much like that. Downtown was a virtual ghost town. Most stores and businesses had closed up shop for the day, out of fear of violence. Many people were warned that they'd be attacked if ZANU-PF found fingers that hadn't been dipped in ink. Normally this is done to prevent people from voting more than once; in this case, it was to scare people into voting. It clearly didn't work in most cases. The scenes today were in marked contrast to the March 29 presidential poll, which Tsvangirai won. That election took place in a carnival atmosphere. Queues were measured in hundreds rather than twos and threes, and people waited happily.

Fast-forward to today: whenever there was a short queue, it was sad and sorry-looking. People waited their turn of shame with downcast eyes and grim expressions. Voter Charles Mutema, an employee at the Ministry of Justice, didn't look happy as he dipped his finger in the telltale ink. "We need a president," he said, "so we have no choice."

—Rod Nordland

> **What if they held an election and no one came?**

WEEK OF AUGUST 4

INTERNATIONAL

Where Karadzic Drank 'Blood'

Tomas (Misko) Kovijanic has been drinking all day, which may help explain why he sounds a touch maudlin as he recalls the fugitive who had become a regular at the Mad House, the tiny café Misko runs in New Belgrade. Nearby, in one of the neighborhood's identical socialist-era apartment towers—in Block 45, Building 267—Radovan Karadzic had lived for at least the past year. Not only had he been hiding in plain sight, the ex-president of the Bosnian Serbs had adopted a disguise so outrageous it turned heads wherever he went. With a huge gray beard, spectacles the size of saucers, and long locks tied up in a topknot, he looked more like an aging hippie who'd dropped too much acid than one of the International War Crimes Tribunal's two most-wanted. "It was impossible not to notice him," Misko says, speaking slowly, either so every word could be written down, or to keep from slurring them, or both. "I said, 'Who could this strange person be? Maybe a saint who came down from the mountains, or a white magician, or even a prophet'."

For a man who was always a moth to the limelight, it's not surprising that Karadzic would be drawn to the Mad House, a nationalist hangout where pride of place is given to Karadzic's own picture, along with pictures of fellow war-crime indictees Gen. Ratko Mladic and ex-dictator Slobodan Milosevic, who cheated justice by dying at The Hague. Although Karadzic had disguised himself with a new persona as an alternative-health guru named Dragan Dabic, slimming down on nonfat yogurt and macrobiotics, he remained the serious drinker he had always been, quaffing glass after glass of Bear's Blood wine, which Misko is drinking now in his honor. The café is an uncomfortably intimate place, a service bar and four little tables, crammed with as many as 20 drinkers, all men of Balkan-war age. "One educated Serb is more precious than a million educated Americans," Misko says passionately, adding, "No offense."

In their cups, habitués of the Mad House often turn to the *gusle*, a single-stringed fiddle used to accompany Serbian epic poetry. Some of these poems celebrate Karadzic's own exploits. Despite that—or perhaps because of it—one memorable recent night Karadzic himself picked up Misko's gusle, carved from a single piece of maple, its headstock in the form of an eagle. "In his hands the gusle was playing the most beautiful sounds we ever heard," Misko recalls, splashing another dollop of Bear's Blood into a glass. "He said, 'My children, listen to me, you are the future of Serbia. Our epic poems will preserve our past and proclaim our future'." Misko caught sight of a tear in the war criminal's eye (there's one in his, too, at this recollection). "I could see happiness on the face of Radovan Karadzic, a.k.a. Dragan Dabic, that night."

That happiness would prove

> **"He is convinced that with the help of God, he will win."**
> **—Serbian lawyer Svetozar Vujacic, on client Radovan Karadzic, August 2008**
>
> *Perspectives*

short-lived. Last week three Serbian secret policemen were already aboard the Route 73 bus when Karadzic climbed on, presenting a bus pass he got using the ID card of a dead Serb from Bosnia. "Old man, come with us," they said, and ignored his feeble protests of innocence as they manhandled him into a waiting car, en route to The Hague after 13 years on the run. Misko says he and his friends will be waiting for him to come back, this time to play the gusle under his own name. "History is not written in one single day, and eventually it will show us who really was Radovan Karadzic." After a few more glasses, at the Mad House, that may even seem plausible.

—ROD NORDLAND

CHINA

Thanks for the Offer, But . . .

Officials in China's devastated Sichuan province are getting a crash course in a novel concept: accepting philanthropy. Since the May 12 earthquake that killed nearly 70,000 people and destroyed homes across the region, millions may have been lost because officials were leery of taking money from nongovernmental organizations and private donors.

In just one county, Mianzhu, a team from McKinsey Greater China recovered $2.2 million in a single week, says Qiu Tian, project manager for the pro bono effort. Her team scoured the local government's departmental logbooks for unreturned phone calls, rang back 50 neglected donors and persuaded 15 of them to renew their offers.

The problem isn't corruption or even plain incompetence. All public life in China was state-controlled until recently (anything sensitive still is), and many not-for-profit groups are barely legal even now. Local officials can't help being nervous about working with them; in other parts of the world NGOs have been criticized as Trojan horses for the West because of their efforts to open up societies and demand individual rights. Qiu says the head of one town where seven schools collapsed turned away an NGO offering psychological counseling to pupils; he worried about "involving strangers working in his area" and lacked the expertise to conduct background checks, she says. Such caution tends to be strongest among lower-level officials in outlying townships. The hope is that better coordination will build trust between the two groups in China. Qiu and her team of consultants, for instance, are training members of a new Mianzhu government team, the Social Resources Coordinating Council. They'll be tasked with recovering more donations, and then with channeling contributions to where they're most needed. The team's newly launched Web site is seeking some $1 million to build an orphanage for 78 children, and roughly $870,000 to rebuild roads to three shattered villages.

Redirecting donations is a vital task. Mianzhu's Education Bureau is flush with cash, thanks to the public's widespread horror at the deaths of some 13,000 Sichuan schoolchildren—while other necessities like road repair have less appeal. Qiu tells of one man who wanted to rebuild an entire primary school and hoped to spend some $250,000. Tough post-quake building codes meant the sum was too small to do the whole job, and overstretched local officials reflexively said no to his offer without thinking to coordinate with other departments. The SRCC quickly called him back to discuss other important projects that could fit his budget. At this point just about everything in Sichuan is proceeding by trial and error—but they're learning. —MARY HENNOCK

WEEK OF AUGUST 11

PAKISTAN

A Bid for Control Backfires

Washington is losing faith that Pakistan's new civilian government can stop the expansion of Al Qaeda-linked terrorism in that country's tribal regions. One big problem: tensions between the ruling party of slain leader Benazir Bhutto and the Pakistani military. The latest evidence emerged just as the new prime minister, Syed Yousuf Raza Gilani, left for Washington last week to meet President Bush, NEWSWEEK has learned. In a maneuver attributed to Asif Ali Zardari, Bhutto's widower and head of the Pakistan People's Party, the government tried to wrest control of Pakistan's powerful intelligence service—the Directorate of Inter-Services Intelligence, or ISI—by placing it under the control of Rehman Malik, a Zardari associate who is de facto Interior Minister. That was a "rookie move," says a U.S. official, who declined to be named discussing a sensitive matter, and it backfired.

Before making its move against the ISI, U.S. and Pakistani officials say, the civilian government failed to consult with some top military brass, including President Pervez Musharraf, who until recently was the Army chief of staff. According to a senior Pakistani official who would speak only on condition of anonymity, Musharraf heard about the decision as he was leaving to attend a wedding. In disbelief, he called the ISI's director general to verify the news. "Were you consulted?" he asked. The answer was no. Another senior Pakistani government official, who also requested anonymity, blamed the fumble on Malik, saying he misworded the announcement to make it seem as if the Interior Ministry was taking over the entire ISI, when in fact it is only seeking control of "domestic operations." (Malik did not return calls. Zardari, reached on his cell phone, declined to comment.)

Malik's gambit followed a series of visits to Pakistan by CIA and other senior U.S. officials, who complain the ISI is still riddled with Islamist sympathizers. In fact, U.S. officials believe the ISI provided support to the perpetrators of the fatal July 7 bombing of the Indian Embassy in Kabul, Afghanistan. According to a Taliban commander who serves under Jalaluddin Haqqani, the militant leader implicated in the blast, Haqqani's forces moved their base after the ISI alerted them about the U.S. (Pakistan's ambassador to the U.S., Husain Haqqani—no relation—told NEWSWEEK that his government "has not been presented with evidence of any ISI connection.") Islamabad could be in for more bad news. The government is bracing for the fall publication of a memoir by Pakistan's rogue nuclear scientist, Abdul Qadeer Khan. Officials fear that Khan may disclose secrets about the country's nuclear capability.

> **Officials are bracing for the autumn publication of a memoir by jailed A.Q. Khan.**

ZAHID HUSSAIN,
MICHAEL HIRSH *and*
MARK HOSENBALL

WEEK OF AUGUST 18/AUGUST 25

MIDDLE EAST

A Murder Mystery in Syria

What happens when a cloak-and-dagger general is shot dead in an Arab country where the regime is secretive and the press regularly gagged? It ignites a blogosphere bonanza. The assassination early this month of Syria's Mohammed Suleiman got limited coverage in the printed press, but it spawned streams of commentary on Web sites devoted to the Middle East and to military matters. Suleiman, who was killed while vacationing at a resort on the Mediterranean coast, was a close confidant of Syrian President Bashar al-Assad. Nicknamed "the imported general" for his pale complexion and foreign looks, Suleiman had been linked to some of Syria's most criticized policies and programs, including its dealings with North Korea and Iran, an alleged nuclear facility that Israel bombed last year, and its support for Lebanon's militant Hizbullah group. He'd been a key aide to Assad since the mid-1990s. Among the more intriguing whodunit theories circulating: Iran whacked him to avenge the death earlier this year of master bomber Imad Mughnieh, or Assad ordered him killed because Suleiman knew too much about the 2005 assassination of former Lebanese prime minister Rafik Hariri.

In Washington, three current and former officials familiar with the Middle East told NEWSWEEK that Israel's Mossad has to be near the top of any shortlist of suspects. All refused to be identified discussing sensitive matters.

Israel has long complained that Syria funnels Iranian arms to Hizbullah and gives the group rockets from its own arsenal. (Both Syria and Iran say their ties to Hizbullah are their own business.) An Israeli diplomatic source told NEWSWEEK last week that Suleiman was Syria's main liaison to the group and had helped Hizbullah triple its arsenal of rockets and missiles in the past two years. But a spokesman for Israeli Prime Minister Ehud Olmert, asked about Suleiman's assassination, said Israel had "no direct knowledge and no comment on this matter." —DAN EPHRON, MARK HOSENBALL *and* KEVIN PERAINO

> Among the theories of who ordered the assassination: Iran, Israel or Syria's president.

WEEK OF SEPTEMBER 8

PAKISTAN

Fears About a Would-Be Leader's Mental Health

If Pakistan's upcoming election goes as expected, Asif Ali Zardari, widower of assassinated leader Benazir Bhutto, will succeed Pervez Musharraf as the country's next president, giving Zardari at least partial sway over the Muslim country's nuclear arsenal. Concerns spiked last week with the disclosure of medical records indicating that as recently as last year, doctors hired by Zardari had diagnosed him with mental problems including dementia, depression and post-traumaticstress disorder. While Zardari's spokespeople say he has been cured, multiple U.S. officials, among them Rep. Pete Hoekstra, the ranking Republican on the House Intelligence Committee, told NEWSWEEK that word of Zardari's mental-health history took them by surprise. "Typically," said Hoekstra, "[The U.S.] wouldn't want that kind of person" involved in a nuclear chain of command.

Lawyers for Zardari argued in London's high court that he was too ill to testify in corruption-related cases, and they submitted recent mental-health evaluations as evidence. In March 2007, the Financial Times reported, New York psychologist Stephen Reich concluded that Zardari was "chronically anxious and apprehensive" and had thoughts of suicide, though he had not acted on them. The newspaper wrote that a New York psychiatrist, Philip Saltiel, found that Zardari's long imprisonment in Pakistan while facing corruption probes had left him with "emotional instability" as well as memory and concentration problems. Dr. Reich declined to comment; Dr. Saltiel could not be reached.

Two American officials, who asked for anonymity when discussing a sensitive issue, said that Washington regarded Zardari's medical diagnoses as a legal ploy designed to stall corruption cases against him. Pakistani officials and Zardari supporters said all the allegations against him were trumped up by his enemies. (Last week, days after Newsweek.com reported that Zardari might use his new political clout to try to shut down a Swiss corruption probe, Geneva's prosecutor announced that he had ended his inquiry—a development that Jacques Python, a Geneva lawyer who formerly represented Pakistan, called "extremely shocking.") Zardari's supporters added, however, that the prison stresses were real. In an e-mail to NEWSWEEK, Husain Haqqani, Pakistan's U.S. ambassador, wrote that Zardari "obviously was affected by the torture of imprisonment without conviction . . . A similar diagnosis is usually made for former POWs immediately after their release but that does not preclude their full recovery and subsequent running for high political office. Mr. Zardari has no current condition requiring psychiatric help or medication."

Hoekstra said he did not recall being briefed about Zardari's claims of mental incapacity; two other U.S. foreign-policy officials said they found the revelations surprising and disquieting. But a U.S. official familiar with intelligence, who also asked for anonymity, said any elision was unintentional. "No one here should think information was deliberately withheld or suppressed," the official said. "Nor should they simply accept at face value assertions made with the apparent goal of warding off legal proceedings." According to one of the officials, the U.S. government believes Pakistan's nukes are tightly controlled by elite elements of its military—and that the nuclear authority of elected officials, including the president, would be "extremely limited."

—MARK HOSENBALL

> **Doctors hired by Zardari had diagnosed him in 2007 with dementia, depression and PTSD.**

WEEK OF SEPTEMBER 15

GEORGIA

Russia's Nervous Neighbors

Since Russia's rout of the Georgian armed forces in August, Prime Minister Vladimir Putin has suggested that Washington secretly provoked the conflict. But the Americans wanted no such thing, according to Lt. Col. Robert Hamilton, who ran the U.S. military training program in Georgia until six weeks ago. (He's now on a year's fellowship at the Center for

Strategic and International Studies in Washington.) "At no time did the U.S. attempt to train or equip the Georgian armed forces for a conflict with Russia," he says. "In fact, the U.S. deliberately avoided training capabilities [that] were seen as too provocative" to Russia. That's one reason Georgia's troops crumpled so fast—precisely because their training didn't cover conventional-warfare topics like tanks, artillery and helicopters.

America's military involvement in Georgia began with a mission that was supposed to reduce Moscow's jitters. The Russians were complaining that Chechen rebels with suspected ties to Al Qaeda were holed up in Georgia's Pankesi Gorge. In 2002 the Pentagon stepped in, training and equipping Georgia's ragtag Army to clear out the unwelcome guests. After that mission ended in 2004, Georgia joined the Coalition in Iraq, and the training's focus shifted to counterinsurgency and peacekeeping duties.

Now U.S. military planners are facing two questions. Should America help rebuild Georgia's armed forces? And if so, should the focus be on combating a Russian threat? Moscow's potential reaction is only the first obstacle to new U.S. military aid to Georgia. More than that, however, the debacle in Georgia has exposed an issue that NATO has carefully swept aside for the past decade: how the alliance expects to defend its new members. Georgia is not a NATO member. But if America sets out to solidify Georgia's defenses, can it fail to do likewise for the 10 nations that have joined NATO since 1999?

Under Article 5 of the group's charter, the 1949 North Atlantic Treaty, an attack on one member will be regarded as an attack on all. Even so, NEWSWEEK has learned, NATO didn't bother to formally assess any of the new members' defense needs before they joined. "The attitude was, the more the merrier," says retired U.S. Air Force Gen. Charles Wald, deputy commander of U.S. forces in Europe through the early years of this decade. "NATO didn't really look at the Article 5 part of it."

In fact, Wald adds, NATO actively dissuaded its new mem-

> "Russia's actions have cast grave doubts on Russia's intentions, and on its reliability as an international partner."
> —*Vice President Dick Cheney, September 2008*
> Perspectives

bers from beefing up their defense capabilities. Romania and Bulgaria wanted to build modern air forces by buying several hundred top-of-the-line aircraft. "They were told, don't do that," he says. "They were advised they should concentrate on making a 'niche contribution.' Which meant counterterrorism and counterinsurgency forces to operate outside Europe." The Global War on Terror took priority over conventional defenses. But that was before Russia and Georgia raised the stakes.

—JOHN BARRY

WEEK OF SEPTEMBER 22

NORTH KOREA

The Plan Post-Kim: No Plan

Some thoughts are even more disturbing than the idea of Kim Jong Il's controlling an arsenal of poison gas, germ-war cultures and nuclear devices. Like what if the North Korean leader suddenly *didn't* control those weapons of mass destruction? The question grew urgent last week after Kim failed to show up at a parade marking the Stalinist regime's 60th anniversary. The Dear Leader hadn't appeared in public for weeks, and senior North Korean officials soothed no one's doubts when they broke their usual silence to deny that Kim had suffered a stroke. With no solid information on Kim's health, Washington could only hope North Korea wasn't on the verge of a succession crisis.

That's the last thing the region needs. Kim, 66, a former smoker who's more than fond of good food and drink, has no designated successor. Rivalries at the top might get ugly, South Koreans worry. What really scares them is the North's desperately poor civilian population. If the demilitarized zone were to disappear the way the Berlin wall did, the South's economy would be crushed by the overwhelming poverty of the North.

Despite those fears, Washington and Seoul have no real contingency plans if Pyongyang implodes.

> "The major players are completely unprepared. The South Koreans don't want to touch it, and the U.S. takes its lead from the South."

"The question has been completely taboo," says Andrei Lankov, a North Korea expert at Seoul's Kookmin University. "The major players are completely unprepared. The South Koreans don't want to touch it, and the U.S. takes its lead from the South." The closest thing to an emergency protocol was CONPLAN (Concept Plan) 5029, which outlined nonmilitary steps to cope with refugees, WMD risks and other problems if the North fell into chaos. But three years ago the Americans sought to add military measures to the deal, and Seoul said no, citing concerns for national sovereignty. The two sides agreed to "upgrade" the original deal instead.

Still, U.S. officials seemed surprisingly calm. The odds are that Kim is recovering, they said. And if he doesn't, North Korea's ruling circle will likely form a governing committee to take over as smoothly as possible. None of Kim's three sons seems ready to fill his shoes, but the new regime would likely include a token family member if only for the appearance of continuity.

In case of problems, the Bush administration is betting that Beijing and Seoul will go all-out to stabilize things. Neither neighbor wants a flood of refugees, and the Chinese already exert a powerful hold on Kim's country. The North imports more than 80 percent of its daily necessities from China, and Chinese firms control much of its natural-resource output. "While Seoul and Washington sat idly, Beijing vigorously prepared for any emergencies in the North," says Park Young Ho, a fellow at the Korea Institute for National Unification.

No matter how bad the chaos might get, no one is likely to drop the bomb—or auction one off. Military analysts say there's no evidence Pyongyang has anything close to a deliverable nuclear weapon (as opposed to the test devices that have been detonated deep in the northern mountains). Kim's stockpiles of plutonium probably aren't going anywhere either, thanks to U.S. monitoring technology. The end of the Kim era may not be catastrophic. But that doesn't mean it won't get rough.

—B. J. LEE *and* MARK HOSENBALL

ISRAEL

Iran Nukes: Out of Reach

It wasn't an official military assessment, but retired Gen. John Abizaid's remarks at a Marine Corps University conference last week appeared to echo the thinking of at least some in the upper echelons of the U.S. military: Israel is incapable of seriously damaging Iran's nuclear program. Abizaid, who oversaw military operations in the Middle East as head of U.S. Central Command until 18 months ago, caused a stir last year by publicly asserting the United States could live with a nuclear-armed Iran through a strategy of cold-war-style deterrence. Last week, when asked to reflect on the possible consequences of an Israeli strike on Iran's nuclear facilities, Abizaid said he doubted whether "the Israelis have the capability to make a lasting impression on the Iranian nuclear program with their military capabilities." An Israel–Iran confrontation, he said, would be "bad for the region, bad for the United States [and would] ultimately move the region into an even more unstable situation."

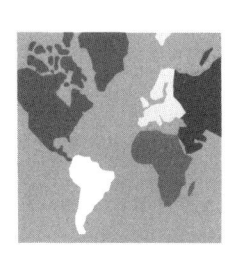

Israel believes Tehran might be within a year of crossing the uranium-enrichment threshold and has made clear it would not tolerate a nuclear-armed Iran. (Iran says its program is peaceful.) A year ago, Israel sent warplanes to Syria to destroy what it believed to be a budding nuclear facility. But according to several officers

> **Israel believes Tehran might be within a year of crossing the uranium-enrichment threshold.**

and Pentagon analysts who spoke to NEWSWEEK, the U.S. military thinks Israel would face huge challenges in reaching Iran, refueling its warplanes along the way and penetrating hardened nuclear targets. Earlier this month, the United States agreed to sell Israel 1,000 small-diameter bombs known as GBU-39s, capable of piercing several feet of concrete—an arms deal that analysts believe is linked to the Iran issue. But a spokesman for Boeing, which makes the bombs, estimated that they would not be delivered before 2010. And thus far, according to a source familiar with talks between the two countries, the United States has not granted Israel's request for additional equipment. That order from the Israelis, said one Pentagon analyst who monitors the Middle East and did not want to be named discussing sensitive issues, reinforces the notion that its military does not have the means to conduct a large-scale attack.

—DAN EPHRON

WEEK OF OCTOBER 13

PAKISTAN

The Mystery Spymaster

As Pakistan copes with a spate of terrorist violence and political unrest, Bush administration officials worry that they know too little about the man who was just appointed to lead the Muslim nation's sprawling spy agency, the Inter-Services Intelligence directorate. Last week, Islamabad disclosed that ISI's new chief will be Lt. Gen. Ahmed Shuja Pasha, Pakistan's former director of military operations and a protégé of Gen. Ashfaq Kiyani, the country's top commander. Kiyani, who once headed ISI and took training courses in the U.S., is admired and trusted by American defense and intelligence officials. But they don't know much about Pasha beyond his close ties to Kiyani and that he ran operations against militants who turned tribal regions along Pakistan's border with Afghanistan into a terrorist safe haven.

Two U.S. counterterrorism officials, who asked for anonymity when discussing sensitive information, said they believe that U.S. complaints about alleged collaboration between ISI and Taliban fighters played a role in the departure of ISI's former commander, Gen. Nadeem Taj. This past summer, according to one of the officials, the U.S. presented Pakistan with a dossier outlining alleged treachery inside ISI, including purported contacts between ISI representatives and Taliban militants who attacked India's embassy in Kabul on July 7.

Washington's chief concern is whether the new ISI boss, who is not a career spy, will have the skill and clout to purge the agency of

elements sympathetic to Al Qaeda and the Taliban. Some U.S. experts say the service is so inscrutable that it may harbor secret factions that are working at cross-purposes to the interests of the U.S. and Pakistan. "Nothing tells me they are ready to break the link between ISI and Afghan Taliban," said Bruce Riedel, a retired CIA expert on the region. Washington relies heavily on ISI for intel on militants. Historically, says a former senior U.S. intelligence official, who also asked for anonymity, 80 percent of credible U.S. intel about terrorists in Pakistan originated with ISI.
—Mark Hosenball

ADOPTION

Wanted: A Bundle of Joy

If Brangelina is any indication, American interest in adopting foreign children is stronger than ever. So why is the United States adopting fewer of them? According to early projections by the State Department, foreign adoptions have dropped an estimated 10 percent from last year—the fourth straight year of decline since the high-water mark of 22,884 in 2004. Experts say the downward trend is likely to continue as countries such as Russia, Guatemala and China, which in recent years had been among the largest providers of orphans for adoption, have either dialed back their programs or ended them entirely. "It's not that American interest has diminished at all, or that there are fewer kids who need homes," says Chuck Johnson of the National Council for Adoption. "The declines are directly the result of bureaucratic or political issues."

In China, a process that used to take a year—and was lauded for being efficient, transparent and affordable—now takes 31 months

A process in China that used to take a year now takes 31 months—and could get longer.

and is expected to get longer. China says increased prosperity in the country means fewer abandoned children. Russia, Ukraine and South Korea, all facing declining birthrates, are encouraging domestic adoption. The U.S. government stopped new adoptions from Guatemala early this year because the country failed to comply with the Hague Adoption Convention's standards. And Vietnam shuttered its program last year following allegations of fraud and corruption.

Advocates hope the tide will turn back soon. Guatemala has signaled that it plans to overhaul its program when the adoptions currently in the pipeline are com-

pleted. In Vietnam, negotiations are underway to restart adoptions following the arrest of 24 police as part of a crackdown on abuse. And there are encouraging signs that adoptions from Mexico, Colombia and Ethiopia will soon increase, proving that as some doors close, others are bound to open wider.
—PAT WINGERT

WEEK OF NOVEMBER 3

IRAN

Nukes: Too Deep to Hit

Western intelligence experts believe that Iran's nuclear facilities are so deep underground that it would be difficult for Israel to wipe them out, or even significantly damage them, with a quick airstrike. In order to deal a serious setback to Iran's nuclear program, at least four key sites inside Iran would have to be hit, said one Western official, who asked for anonymity when discussing sensitive information. The facilities, however, are located in tunnels fortified by barriers more than 60 feet thick. According to this official and other U.S. experts, Israel does not possess conventional weapons capable of knocking out the facilities. Breaking through the thick shell would require, at minimum, several bunker-buster bombs striking precisely the same spot. "These targets would be very hard to destroy," said former U.N. nuclear expert David Albright. Theoretically, Israel could do a lot more damage with a nuclear strike. But U.S. and other Western experts say there is no reason to believe the Israelis will abandon their policy against

> **Israel could do a lot more damage with a nuclear strike.**

shooting first with nukes.

U.S. and allied efforts to keep tabs on Iranian nukes suffered a blow recently because of a "spy vs. spy" mixup in Germany. For more than 10 years, according to two Western counterproliferation officials, the BND (Germany's equivalent of the CIA) employed an Iranian-Canadian informant known by the code name "Sinbad." Sinbad peddled technology to the Iranians, and, in turn, brought the BND high-quality Iranian government documents, including what Germany's Der Spiegel magazine described as pictures of tunnel-digging machinery and briefing papers on nuclear delivery systems. But the espionage operation recently ran aground when German Customs officers, unaware of Sinbad's role as a spy, busted him for illegal missile-technology shipments to Iran. Sinbad had concealed extracurricular schemes from the BND, and the spy agency had no power to stop the investigation. One of the counterproliferation officials said that Sinbad's arrest was a significant setback to espionage efforts against Iran's nuclear program.

—MARK HOSENBALL

The Economy

YEAR IN REVIEW

Like a tidal wave gathering force a mile offshore, our troubled economy was on everyone's mind at the start of the year, with home prices already in free fall, jobs disappearing from the market and vague murmurs about a bursting bubble already seeping onto editorial pages. But it took until late summer before a downturn that had already chewed up the middle class turned into a cataclysmic collapse that rocked the entire world, and led some to proclaim it an "economic 9/11." Viewed in hindsight, the late-September implosion of one bank after another—Lehman Brothers, Merrill Lynch, Wachovia—was the inevitable outcome of a get-rich-quick system built out of little more than empty paper, irresponsible mortgages, overextended credit, and a laissez-faire government asleep at the switch.

Once America got wise to the gravity of the situation—in early autumn, at the zenith of the presidential campaign—a furious debate broke out over a "bailout" of Wall Street, and whether using taxpayer money to rescue the very same people who endangered the economy amounted to the ultimate example of "moral hazard." Should we give a golden parachute to those who piloted us straight into the eye of a hurricane? During a tenuous 10 days of Congressional negotiations, Americans kept one eye on the stock market and the other on their 401(k)s, praying both would stabilize once a deal was struck.

The most potent way to distill 2008's economic story down to a single issue would be to look at the price of a gallon of gas. Prices soared well over $4 by the second half of the year, crippling the average American family while oil companies celebrated record profits. After Hurricane Ike ravaged the Gulf of Mexico, wreaking havoc with the nation's energy center, drivers in several American cities spent hours in lines at gas stations, evoking the frustration of the Carter-era 1970s. It became a flashpoint in the election, with candidates scrambling to come up with ways to promise immediate relief for a problem that only has patient, long-term solutions. Both John McCain and Barack Obama drove home the desperate need to wean America off of its dependency on foreign oil—whether by domestic drilling or by investing in the development of alternative fuel sources, such as solar and wind power. Ironically, it is the same mantra that could not get Al Gore elected just eight years ago. In 2008, you could not get elected without it.

WEEK OF JANUARY 7

FIRST PERSON

A (Dollar) Sign of the Times: It's Not Easy Being Green

NEWSWEEK's *financial columnist Daniel Gross covered a number of economic calamities in 2007. He writes here about the U.S. currency plunge.*

In late June, with no local currency in my pocket and a case of jet lag that only a doppio espresso could cure, I stumbled into a familiar London storefront. I whipped out my Starbucks card, which still had about $8 left on it. But when the barista rang up my coffee and newspaper, his smile crinkled into a frown. "I'm afraid you're all out," he said. "That'll be another 40 pence. Cheers!" I had just been punked by the weak dollar.

In 1971, Treasury Secretary John Connally told foreign counterparts that the dollar is "our currency, but your problem." Well, 2007 may have been the year the slumping dollar became our problem, too. Thanks to several macroeconomic factors—a slowing economy, the Federal Reserve's accommodative interest-rate policy and a lack of confidence in the U.S. financial system due to the subprime debacle—2007 was a bad year for the greenback. The dollar last summer hit a 27-year low against the British pound and a 31-year nadir against the Canadian dollar. The trade-weighted dollar index—a measure of strength against six major currencies—was off 38 percent from its 2002 peak.

> **The long-term decline threatens the dollar's status as the world's reserve currency.**

The long-term decline threatens the dollar's status as the world's reserve currency, which it has enjoyed since World War II. The dollar is the currency in which German department stores pay Vietnamese garment factories, Indian distributors purchase Saudi Arabian oil and black marketers around the world conduct business. All those dollars floating around the world not spent here are essentially free loans to the United States from foreigners—and they help keep U.S. interest rates low.

But nobody likes to hold on to declining assets. So it's no surprise that passengers in 2007 began to bail from the listing USS Greenback. The rumor that Brazilian supermodel Gisele Bündchen no longer wanted to be paid in dollars turned out to be false. But in May, Kuwait untethered its currency from the dollar and moored it to a basket of more buoyant currencies. In November, India said tourists could no longer pay admission fees at 120 tourist sites (including the Taj Mahal) in dollars. Russia, China and Japan have been quietly rebalancing their foreign-currency holdings.

> "The U.S. economy in 2008 will be like a cat on a hot tin roof that has already used up eight of its nine lives."
>
> —*Stuart Hoffman, chief economist for PNC Financial Services Group, January 2008*
>
> Perspectives

"We have a strong dollar policy," President Bush said in November. But the strong dollar policy consists of little more than saying just that. Currency strategists say that because the items that weighed on the dollar in 2007—fiscal imbalances, a slowing economy, credit issues—aren't likely to turn around any time soon, they don't expect a sharp reversal in the dollar's fortunes. So if you can't get through the day—at home or abroad—without a pit stop at Starbucks, load those cards with everything you've got. Cheers!

WEEK OF JUNE 2

ECONOMY

States of Emergency

Gov. Arnold Schwarzenegger is in a jam. Even after $10 billion of proposed cuts, California still faces a $17 billion budget gap. Most voters and lawmakers don't like his plan to fix it by borrowing billions against the state's lottery, meaning the Governator will likely have to resort to raising taxes, something he vowed never to do, and bump the state's sales-tax rate by one cent.

Arnold isn't the only governor facing a killer budget crunch. After two years of surpluses, the housing market and national economy have plunged more than half the states—29, and the District of

Columbia—into red ink this spring. Altogether, the total budget shortfall is $42 billion for the rest of this fiscal year and for fiscal year 2009; the biggest gaps are in states where the housing boom-and-bust was most pronounced, such as Arizona, Nevada and Florida, which are now coping with too many unsold houses and tanking property values. And the bottom is at least a year away, says Mark Zandi, a chief economist with Moody's. "You have to go back to the Depression to see a decline this big," he says.

Unlike the federal government, states aren't allowed to run deficits, so most are choosing to cut spending rather than raise taxes. That means deep cuts to education and public-health programs, as well as hiring freezes, which has stalled one of the few economic sectors that had been holding strong. Tennessee Gov. Phil Bredesen wants to cut 5 percent of his state's workforce to cover a half-billion-dollar gap; Florida lawmakers, grappling with what they call the state's worst-ever budget year, cut spending by more than $4 billion. All those cuts take a toll. "They tend to hurt the most vulnerable, those who depend on public health care and can't afford private schools," says Iris Lav of the Center on Budget and Policy Priorities.

Economists are predicting a prolonged crisis that could rival the one that began in 2001 and peaked in 2004, when 42 states faced a combined $84 billion deficit. "Everyone's holding their breath," says Scott Pattison of the National Association of State Budget Officers. "We haven't seen the worst yet."

—MATTHEW PHILIPS

> **Economists are predicting a prolonged crisis that could rival the one that began in 2001 and peaked in 2004.**

WEEK OF JULY 21

ENERGY

T. Boone Pickens's Mighty Wind

It's beginning to feel like 1992, and not just because economic woes are dominating the presidential campaign. Last week a billionaire Texan with a disarming drawl started a media blitz to focus attention on a dire financial and public-policy problem. In 1992, it

The Economy-200 | JULY

was H. Ross Perot and his charts on the deficit. Today, it's T. Boone Pickens, the 80-year-old oilman. In ads on CNBC and CNN and in newspapers—and before NEWSWEEK's editors—Pickens laid out his plan to stop the madness of spending $700 billion each year on foreign oil. "We have to take control of our own destiny as far as foreign oil is concerned." But unlike Perot, Pickens isn't interested in public office. Now running a hedge fund, and a big investor in wind energy, he's going green to make green.

Drawing pie charts and crude maps on a whiteboard, Pickens shows how the United States' need to import 70 percent (and rising) of the oil it requires has been a national disaster. Short term, Pickens believes we should drill everywhere we can. "But don't stop there, because we must do everything." That includes conservation, ethanol, nuclear and renewables.

His big idea? Harness the mighty wind that sweeps through his beloved Texas and Oklahoma—and the rest of the Great Plains—and use it to displace natural gas as a fuel for generating electricity. That would free up the plentiful domestic source—"the only fuel that would help with our transportation system right now"—to power cars instead of turbines.

That would reduce imported oil by 38 [percent], about $300 billion p[er year].

Of course, it's no[t sim]ple. Building the infra[structure to] allow for (a) the transmission of electricity from the Great Plains to population centers, and (b) the use of natural gas as a mainstream transportation fuel would require massive investments. The car-crazy United States has only 142,000 vehicles that run on natural gas. But given the potential benefits, government should step in. "This

> **The car-crazy United States has only 142,000 vehicles that run on natural gas.**

has to be done with the urgency that was used when Eisenhower built the interstate highways," says Pickens.

Pickens isn't waiting for the government. He's buying a Honda Civic GX, which runs on natural gas. And he's building a $10 billion wind farm in the Texas panhandle, where he's persuading neighboring ranchers to plant turbines in their fields. But even Pickens isn't averse to the sort of NIMBY-ism that has impeded new energy infrastructure. "There are no turbines on my ranch, because I think they are ugly."

—DANIEL GROSS

AUGUST 4

REAL ESTATE

Moscow on the Hudson

In this summer of high-end real-estate purgatory, New York real-estate circles are abuzz over some good news. In early July, a town house on a gilded block of East 64th Street changed hands for $42.5 million. The buyer hasn't been publicly identified. But speculation is centering on Leonard Blavatnik, a Russian oil magnate who last fall paid $50 million to buy the neighboring house from Seagram's heir Edgar Bronfman Jr.

A quarter century after the debut of "Red Dawn," in which Patrick Swayze and Charlie Sheen fought back against a Soviet invasion of a bucolic Colorado town, Russians are again occupying promontories in the Rockies. This time they come bearing hard currency rather than Kalashnikovs. Roman Abramovich, the Russian billionaire whose holdings include London's Chelsea soccer team, in May paid $36 million for a 200-acre ranch in Aspen. Recently, Dmitry Rybolovlev, a 41-year-old fertilizer multibillionaire (net worth: about $13 billion), agreed to pay Donald Trump $95 million for his 62,000(!)-square-foot beachfront mansion in Palm Beach, Fla. According to the hyperboleprone Trump, it was the most expensive purchase of a single home in the nation's history.

And you didn't see many Americans at Trump's open house. The credit crunch has removed an important source of support for the penthouse floor of the housing market. When they made their millions, subprime barons and hedge-fund parvenus cemented their status by purchasing (frequently gauche) trophy properties. Just in time, a new class of nouveau riche buyers with dubious taste and a penchant for conspicuous consumption has arrived on the scene: Russian oligarchs.

Booming commodity markets have turned entrepreneurs from the steppes of Central Asia into gazillionaires. Several factors—the weak dollar, concern about stability at home and the age-old international playboy's desire to establish footholds in global capitals of fabulousness—are bringing them here. No truth to the rumor that

> **The credit crunch killed a needed source of support for the elite housing market.**

The Economy-202 | AUGUST

HGTV is developing a new show about the makeovers: "Flip This Dacha."   —DANIEL GROSS

POVERTY

Hope Amid A Downturn

The real-estate bust is creating an unexpected benefit: housing for the homeless. Even as the foreclosure crisis pushes some low-income families into shelters, chronic homeless rates are shrinking thanks in part to the foreclosed and vacant buildings social-service agencies can now afford to buy. In Denver, persistent homelessness is down 36 percent since 2005, as nonprofits have turned seized apartment buildings and run-down motels into 1,242 rooms, complete with access to addiction treatment and health care. A Wooster, Mass., nonprofit will soon close on five multifamily duplexes that will provide 20 to 30 units for the homeless, and Ventura County, Calif., is in talks with local banks to take over 100 homes for permanent use. "These are opportunities we haven't seen in decades," says Philip Mangano, the Bush administration's homelessness czar.

> **Historically, economic downturns are good for the homeless.**

Historically, economic downturns are good for the homeless, just as booms tend to be bad. During the 1990s, despite record spending and increases in shelter beds under the Clinton administration, homeless rates jumped 50 percent. "The prosperity always trickles up, not down," says Mangano. For now, advocates are grabbing what they can.
—MATTHEW PHILIPS

WEEK OF AUGUST 18/AUGUST 25

REAL ESTATE

On Realty Road, It's a Rough Ride

Real-estate agents are an optimistic bunch, but it's hard to put a positive spin on the nation's deepening housing bust. In the past year, the average U.S. home has lost 16 percent of its value, and the number of homes changing hands has dropped by one third since the market peak in 2005. Since most agents make money only when houses actually sell (most earn no salary), that's leading to a sense of desperation in some hard-hit regions. In one Los Angeles-area brokerage office, an agent told NEWSWEEK, the outlook is so bad they've even set up a food pantry with pasta and canned goods so struggling agents won't go hungry.

Consider the scene at Prudential California Realty in Cypress, a community in well-heeled Orange County. Manager Christine McGowan says she's watched a number of her employees lose their own homes to foreclosure. Among them is Michael Vasquez, a veteran broker, who lost his—and his marriage—when financial stress contributed to his divorce; he was forced to move in with a friend. He hasn't taken to moonlighting, yet. But colleague Chrysteen Bandy has: she works three hours each evening selling Marriott time-share vacations. "It's been a major struggle for everyone," says McGowan. "I just don't think people fully realize what [agents] are going through."

In Florida, at the center of the housing bust, conditions aren't much better. Jack Meeks, owner of Real Estate Professionals of America, has downsized from 123 agents to 55—and the entire office is selling just 10 homes a month. In some parts of the state, analyst Jack McCabe says, homes are selling at a rate of less than one per year per agent—and nearly a third of sales are foreclosures, which are often done without an agent. "The truth is, [agents] are getting destitute," he says.

Meanwhile, membership in the National Association of Realtors has dipped by just 7 percent since 2006, to 1.3 million. And it's not clear those ranks will fall much further, since many agents sell homes only part time, or rely on a spouse's income to support them through down markets. If nothing else, the current market may help counter the boom-time image that selling houses was an easy ticket to quick riches. The reality is a whole lot tougher. –JAMIE RENO *and* CATHARINE SKIPP

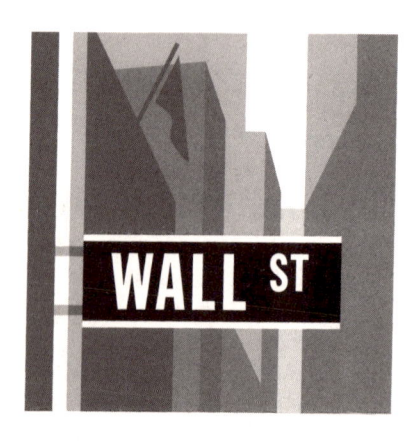

> "The truth is, [agents] are getting destitute."

WEEK OF SEPTEMBER 8

ENVIRONMENT

Paper or Plastic? It'll Cost You.

Economist Peter Nickerson, 56, is a proud resident of Seattle, arguably the capital of green America, so it almost goes without saying that he supports aggressive environmental policies. He'd like to see his city make public transit free to reduce vehicle emissions. He wants to ban pesticides in rivers where salmon swim. He's a devoted recycler who even composts his own trash. Surely, then, he must love Seattle's new bag tax? (Starting in 2009, it would require drug, grocery and convenience stores to charge 20 cents per disposable bag.) Actually, Nickerson thinks it's a terrible idea.

A tiny tax with big environmental potential would seem like a natural fit for Seattle. Other U.S. cities, such as San Francisco, have banned certain disposable bags; Seattle would be the first to tax them. "We know it won't solve global warming," says Mayor Greg Nickels, "but a small change in behavior can make a big difference." According to a city survey from late 2007, though, 63 percent of Seattleites oppose the tax. And last week, an advocacy group called the Coalition to Stop the Seattle Bag Tax submitted a petition with more than 20,000 signatures, enough for a popular vote on it next year. In Seattle, it turns out, there are many shades of green—and for some, the "green fee" isn't green enough. Either the city government is "ill informed," says Nickerson, who's been studying the plan for the Northwest Economic Policy Seminar, or it's just looking at a town full of eco-warriors and picking off some low-hanging political fruit.

> **Experts say "harm charges" are the future of policy.**

In defense of the fee, Nickels points to Dublin, Ireland, where a similar tax reduced bag use by 90 percent. But a recent study found the majority of Seattleites already recycle bags or reuse them for sack lunches and cleaning up after pets. And what if, Nickerson asks, residents begin replacing disposable (or "type 2") plastic bags with more durable, fabric-like polypropylene (or "type 5") bags—which are not recyclable? Even if residents opt for canvas, Nickerson estimates, people must reuse each bag some 300 times to offset the resources that go into making it. (The city disputes his figures.)

Others, even those who consider themselves plenty green, grumble about a levy that—in a progressive town—seems to hit regular folks the hardest. For Tim Rafferty, 49, who's currently on disability and already reuses his plastic bags as trash-can liners, the tax is just more money he doesn't have coming out of his pocket. "I'd hate to have the [store] bagger ask, 'Do you want to double-bag that?' and then be thinking about whether I want to spend the extra 20 cents," he says.

Whether Seattle's green fee survives or not, experts say "harm charges"—requiring consumers and companies to pay for environmentally unfriendly behavior—are the future of policy. The Seattle tax is "the leading edge of a broader trend," says Daniel Esty, director of the Yale Center for Environmental Law and Policy. Soon green living might be the law of the land, not just a lifestyle choice.

—Sarah Kliff

WEEK OF SEPTEMBER 22

PAGE TURNER

Let's Rally Around the Green Flag

In "Hot, Flat, and Crowded," New York Times columnist and globalization exponent Thomas Friedman pleads for Americans to wake up to the perils and opportunities of an emerging resource-strapped world. The author comes across as a blend of Will Rogers, Jack Welch and Norman Vincent Peale—a plain-spoken citizen outraged at the bullheadedness of U.S. politicians, yet optimistic about the power of ingenuity and finely crafted policy to avert disaster.

The Problem: The world is getting crowded and hot. More people tapping computers and on the road means more competition for resources, more emissions. It's all "intensifying the extinction of plants and animals, [and] strengthening petro-dictatorship." If we don't act, life in 2040 could look like a cross between "Waterworld" and "Mad Max."

The Answer: Ignore the calls to drill here and now. We need a Code Green: a national project that includes subsidies for alternative energy, as well as mechanisms to make emissions more expensive, promote public and private research projects and change individual behavior. We should conserve here, be more efficient now.

The Result: Friedman believes that rallying around the green flag will create jobs, save the polar bear, allow China to develop without destroying the environment and restore our national greatness. All we need is leadership and focus. Of course, judging by the media-political complex's recent obsession with swine cosmetics, it sure looks like we're failing.

—MARY CARMICHAEL

> "I'd rather play America's hand than any other country."
> —New York City Mayor Mike Bloomberg, September 2008
>
> *Perspectives*

WEEK OF OCTOBER 6

FINANCE

Paulson's Goldmen

Critics of Henry Paulson's effort to put together a financial bailout worry that the Treasury secretary is getting too much of his advice from aides who were his colleagues at Goldman Sachs, where he was the CEO before joining the Bush administration in 2006. Paulson has recruited three former Goldman execs—Ken Wilson, Ed Forst and Dan Jester—in recent weeks to help him create and execute a bailout plan. A fourth, retiree Steven Shafran, is one of Paulson's "senior advisers." Treasury spokeswoman Michele Davis said Wilson and Jester joined Treasury as advisers in August; Forst, who left Goldman this summer to become a senior administrator at Harvard, joined Paulson's crisis squad in September. "This is a time when the American people need all the experts at Treasury that they can get," Davis said, adding that the ex-Goldmen are getting paid "de minimis" as "contractors."

Administration critics expressed concern that Paulson's

team is heavy with Wall Street expertise but short on Main Street perspective. A senior commercial banker, who asked for anonymity discussing bailout politics, said that the relationship between the investment business, which will be a major beneficiary of any bailout, and the Treasury team is "very incestuous." A GOP congressional adviser, who also asked for anonymity, said Paulson's Goldman-heavy kitchen cabinet "narrow[s] their window of input." Democrats also have close ties to Goldman. Ex-Treasury secretary Robert Rubin, a top adviser to Barack Obama, was the investment firm's co-chairman until 1993. According to OpenSecrets.org, the Obama campaign has received about $690,000 from Goldman-affiliated donors. The Obama campaign says it "receives advice from a wide range of economic experts."

—MARK HOSENBALL

> "If money isn't loosened up, this sucker could go down."
> —President George W. Bush, during negotiations on the federal bailout plan, September 2008
>
> *Perspectives*

WEEK OF OCTOBER 13

ECONOMY

A Salve for Slumping CEOs

Feeling blue because you're an embattled CEO getting blamed for bringing down the U.S. economy? Jerry Levin feels your pain. The deposed Time Warner chairman, who oversaw the disastrous 2000 merger with AOL, is now the presiding director of the high-end Santa Monica, Calif., treatment center, Moonview Sanctuary. Last week, the center issued a press release offering "executive resilience summits" for down-on-their-luck masters of the universe facing "the toughest times in their careers" and looking to "bounce back." The price tag for a three-day session restoring your equilibrium: $15,000 for a one-on-one, or $30,000 for a group of 10.

Levin insists that the workshops—a mixture of role-playing games, personality tests and lectures on the toll of relentless overachievement—are aimed at all overworked executives, not

ENOUGH ALREADY

Where the Streets Have Two Names

In politics, every crisis gets its own cliché, and the near collapse of the U.S. financial system has already spawned a groaner: the false dichotomy pitting "Wall Street" versus "Main Street." Whenever Barack Obama and John McCain babble about our

"Wall Street" versus "Main Street."

dueling American boulevards—and they both do it, a lot—you can practically hear the implied sound effects. Wall Street: *hiss!* Main Street: *yay!* In this climate, boosting soda fountains and sliming investment bankers carries about as much political risk as declaring that America is awesome.

Never mind that the majority of us don't live on either street,

Wall Street: *hiss!* Main Street: *yay!*

or that, if pressed to admit it, we envy the perks of both—the warm simplicity of Main Street and the lucrative grandeur of Wall Street. The problem lies in suggesting an

just Wall Streeters. They're also part of Moonview's expansion beyond chemical-dependency, chronic-pain and personal-crisis treatment to optimal performance seminars for athletes, performers and business people. "I'm putting my life experience out there to help others," says Levin, 69. "We didn't anticipate Hank Paulson's drive to save the world."

But the timing sure is convenient. And Levin isn't the only businessman selling luxury during these decidedly unluxurious times. In layoff-ridden New York, some posh restaurants are slashing prices, offering coupons and discounts once seen mainly at chain eateries. New York's Jack Bistro tried cutting its entrees a penny for every point the Dow would drop on any given day. On Craigslist last week, one poster got attention for touting "Recession specials for your Hamptons getaway!" The catch: the five-bedroom house is nowhere near the beach. Levin, for his part, says he doesn't know if anyone has signed up for his summits, but he believes executives are "more open now than before" to nontraditional ideas. Good, because their schedules are wide open, too.

—ANDREW MURR

antagonistic relationship where a symbiotic one exists. Economic health depends on the recovery of both places, not one or the other. And like all political shorthand, the more frequently it's used, the less sincere it sounds. For both candidates, "Main Street" has become a two-word crutch to flash concern for a place that neither guy seems to know very much about.

—DEVIN GORDON

WEEK OF OCTOBER 20

TREASURY

The Boss of The Bailout

As recently as June, the man anointed by the Treasury Department to steward Wall Street's bailout package was playing down the subprime-mortgage crisis in presentations to private industry groups. In a PowerPoint presentation to Nevada bankers, Neel Kashkari, a former Goldman Sachs banker who is now interim assistant Treasury secretary for financial stability, suggested that only 9 percent of U.S. mortgage holders were behind in their payments compared with "50 percent seriously delinquent in the 1930s." Other slides touted the success of Hope Now, a program to help struggling homeowners renegotiate mortgage terms. But two industry officials who attended the presentations, and who asked for anonymity when discussing private meetings, said Kashkari's overall theme was that massive federal intervention was unnecessary. The message, according to one of the bankers: "There is no problem here." Steven Adamske, a spokesman for Rep. Barney Frank, the Democratic chair of the House Financial Services Committee, said the panel got similar briefings and concluded that the numbers were "dubious."

At the time, chief Treasury spokeswoman Michele Davis acknowledged in e-mails to

> **"This plan is immoral."**
> **—Rep. Dennis Kucinich, explaining why he voted against the bailout bill, September 2008**
>
> *Perspectives*

NEWSWEEK, "Neel was reflecting the Department's view that drastic legislation wasn't needed to deal with the housing correction . . . but that housing posed the biggest downside risk to the economy." Even though the Bush administration wasn't expecting a meltdown, Davis added, Treasury Secretary Henry Paulson had earlier "directed Neel and others . . . to do contingency planning . . . to examine the various policy options out there so if we needed to take stronger action, we'd be prepared to do so." That contingency planning, however, yielded Treasury's initial three-page bailout proposal—which Congress swiftly discarded. A Treasury official, who also asked for anonymity, insisted that the proposal was purposefully thin "so that Congress could add to the proposal to make it their own."

—MARK HOSENBALL

WEEK OF OCTOBER 27

SENIORS

Ready to Move, Stuck In One Place

The market crush is hurting most Americans, but it's especially painful for senior citizens who are ready to move into retirement communities but can't sell their homes to get there. Seniors pay out of pocket for most of their long-term housing needs, and because entrance fees for retirement communities can cost as much as a house, making a move is often contingent upon a sale. "The idea is that a senior has built up equity in [a] house, and this assures that they can have care for the rest of their lives," says Larry Minix, of the American Association of Homes and Services for the Aging. But not if they can't find a buyer. And with a glut of houses on the market, even reduced asking prices don't always lure prospective buyers. Ruth Scher, 85, put her condominium in Delray Beach, Fla., on the market last year and "nobody came," she says. The clogged market helps explain why vacancies in senior living facilities are on the rise—most dramatically in areas where the market is most distressed. In Tampa, for instance, 12 percent of senior housing units are unoccupied, up from 4 percent last year.

Already pinched by high food and utility costs, some retirement-home operators are hiring real-estate agents to help their new residents hasten the sale of their old homes. But agents say that selling an elderly person's home can be a challenge: "It takes so much more than just the for sale sign," says Debbie Miller, an agent in Arlington, Va. Outdated wallpaper, old appliances and poor maintenance often deter buyers. According to a 2008 survey from the American Seniors Housing Association, nearly a quarter of seniors haven't made a home improvement in 10 years, and 41 percent say they won't spend money to attract a buyer. Few have the money anyway, says Robert Kramer, the president of the National Investment Center, an industry research group. Just as the real-estate bust has cheapened the value of their primary asset, seniors have watched their retirement accounts shrink, too, as the market plummets.

> **Selling a senior's home, real-estate agents say, takes "more than just the FOR SALE sign."**

Some seniors have made their peace with staying put. Preston Dixon, of Dallas, wants to move into an independent-living facility, but he won't budge from his home until the market improves. "If I get my target price, fine," says Dixon, 85. "If not, I don't move." That might be the smart play financially, but holding out can be perilous. According to Jeffrey Love of the AARP, money trouble can cause some seniors to pinch pennies on things they really need, such as heat, medication or nutrition. With winter coming, those are choices many of them can't afford to make.

—CAITLIN MCDEVITT

WEEK OF NOVEMBER 3

BUSINESS

Vice: The Recession-Proof Bet

It's 8:30 p.m., the stock market is down 700 points, and Rick's Cabaret in Manhattan is packed. Drinks are flowing, women in electric-blue gowns are peeling off layers onstage, and if the Wall Street clientele is stressed, the guys aren't pinching pennies. Sabrina, who offers $20 neck rubs at the bar, is making a killing. "I'm happy," she says, "but I'm sorry it's for this reason." Margo, a stripper, tells NEWSWEEK she just wired $1,000 to her dad, a plumber who recently got sacked. Claudia, another dancer, says her tips are "consistent," but she's losing clients in her day job as a fitness trainer. This stability isn't news to Rick's CEO, Eric Langen, who has seen stock in his chain of gentlemen's clubs nose dive even as his revenues nearly double. "I wouldn't say we're recession-proof," he says, "but we're recession-resistant."

Even in tough times, people don't give up their guilty pleasures. Analysts tout industries such as alcohol, tobacco and gambling—known as "vice" or "sin" stocks—as "defensive": they're beacons of hope in grim financial times. "Not only do people drink and smoke regardless of the economy, but they do it around the world," says

> **Even in tough times, people don't give up their guilty pleasures.**

Charles Norton, manager of the Dallas-based Vice Fund (VICEX). The fund is down 27 percent this year—"We're in a hundred-year storm," Norton admits—but he's one in a choir of analysts who maintain that while all industries are suffering, the business fundamentals of vice remain strong and will rebound faster.

With the word "depression" on some people's lips, says Caroline Waxler, author of "Stocking Up on Sin," "the more lowbrow the vice, the better it will do." Condom sales will rise, she predicts. (Indeed, Durex sales have soared in Europe.) Local casinos will do better than travel destinations such as Las Vegas. And we'll all become Joe Six-Pack. "People have their routines—a beer at the end of the day, a pitcher after the softball league," says California beer distributor Terence Fox. "Remember, a bad year for the beer industry means we're down 4 percent; a bad year for high-tech means losses of 30 percent." As other industries flail, the company that makes Camel and Salem cigarettes just posted better-than-expected quarterly profits. At Rick's, where happy hours have been extended, the current mantra is affordability *and* escape. "Just look!" says one customer, a tax accountant, surveying a packed room. "I don't see any recession here."
—Eve Conant

War

YEAR IN REVIEW

Five years is a long time for a war—a symbolic number, and not a proud one. So it probably should not have come as a surprise that the fifth year of the war in Iraq was a transformative one, both on the ground in the Middle East and in the mind's eye of a war-weary nation back home. In 2008, the urgency to end America's involvement in Iraq reached a fever pitch, in part because a cynical, economically strapped country was ready to see Iraq's own government take over, but also because Afghanistan—the forgotten front in the war of terror—was gradually re-emerging as both the more pressing threat to U.S. national security and the war's true central front. (Though many in the foreign policy community would argue that such was always the case.)

The first major news story of the new year set the tone for 2008, because of its setting: Pakistan, where a dazed and divided nation was mourning the brutal Dec. 27, 2007, assassination of Prime Minister Benazir Bhutto. The subsequent unraveling of the Muslim nation's government culminated with the Aug. 18 resignation of U.S.-backed Pakistani President Pervez Musharraf, the army general who had seized power in a coup d'etat nearly a decade ago, and ruled over a military state until the threat of impeachment over the summer capsized his administration. The power vacuum destabilized a country already in a pitched battle with forces of radical Islam, Al Qaeda, and the fundamentalist former government of Pakistan's neighbor, Afghanistan. With no powerful central government to check the influence of Islamic militants, the remote regions of Pakistan thrived as a launching ground for attacks inside Afghanistan that threatened to wreck the democratic government there led by President Hamid Karzai.

The increased volatility in Afghanistan and Pakistan, combined with the success of the U.S. military's "surge" strategy led by General David Petraeus, helped the Iraq war fade into the background for Americans. It slipped off the front pages of newspapers and out of the nightly news broadcasts and, for long stretches, it receded as a presidential campaign issue. But it was a collective delusion, at best, that Iraq was no longer a dangerous place, or that its days of sectarian chaos were safely behind it. Still, by the late months of 2008, something of a consensus about Iraq had emerged: it was time for the U.S. to get ready to leave and place the fate of the country back in its own hands—a view shared by Iraqi president Nuri al-Maliki, Democratic presidential nominee Barack Obama, and even President George W. Bush, the man who staked his administration on the war and resisted a timetable for its end.

WEEK OF JANUARY 7

BLACKWATER

A Price Tag for Mistakes

The state department is still mulling how to rein in private security firms like Blackwater USA, whose employees dominated headlines in September when they shot dead 17 Iraqi civilians. But in 2008 a series of lawsuits currently working through the U.S. court system could have more impact. In all the cases, Iraqi victims represented by American lawyers are seeking restitution for abuses allegedly committed by contractors. While U.S. law shields military members from such suits, a judge in one case last month against CACI International Inc. left open the possibility that private contractors would not enjoy the same immunity. Peter Singer, an expert on private contractors at the Brookings Institution, says the possibility of a huge payout is already making companies review

FIRST PERSON

In Iraq, a Season of Disquieting Silence

As NEWSWEEK*'s Baghdad bureau chief, Babak Dehghanpisheh often faces the war right on his doorstep. His thoughts on the year of the surge:*

The first rocket streaked low over our house with a crackle at about 8 p.m. I was riding an exercise bike in the front yard, and before I could take cover, the rocket slammed into the pavement behind our house, shattering windows up and down the block. The dust had hardly settled before another rocket flew in. Whump. And another. Whump. A few weeks later, a rocket landed in front of our house and shrapnel hit a neighbor's guard. My NEWSWEEK colleague Larry Kaplow watched the man die in the street as medics tried to treat him.

For six months, starting in the spring, insurgents pounded our area with disturbingly close mortar and rocket fire that the military

continued

their practices. "Liability is the one thing they fear more than accountability," he says.

The suit against CACI, brought by 256 former inmates at Abu Ghraib, is a test case. Susan Burke, the lead attorney for the Iraqis, says CACI interrogators took part in torture at the prison in 2003 and 2004. She has argued that CACI employees were not just following military personnel's instructions but even directed some of the abuse. ("There's nothing in any of the Abu Ghraib investigations that accuses CACI personnel of having anything to do with rape or murder or torture," CACI attorney Bill Koegel said in response.)

Singer says Blackwater has already grasped the liability risk of its security unit and is quietly shifting its focus to safer ventures, such as private intelligence gathering. (The company did not respond to a request for comment.) If so, the Iraqi petitioners can claim one victory before their trial even begins.

—DAN EPHRON

---

calls IDF—or indirect fire—because there isn't a direct line of sight between shooter and target. But there's nothing indirect about a mortar that comes crashing down close by, with a schedule you could set your watch to: a volley around 10 a.m., another around 2 p.m. and a nightcap around 6. The average was about 10 explosions a day. I imagined the mortar teams meeting up for breakfast or lunch, shooting off a few shells and then heading back for a nap before starting the next round.

The attacks continued like that for months. Then one day . . . they stopped. It was late August, and the silence was so sudden we didn't know what to make of it. The U.S. military had been beefing up their troops in Baghdad as part of the surge, and cleric Moqtada al-Sadr had told his armed supporters to stand down. But would the attacks really stop for good? It seemed hard to believe. A week passed. A month. Then two. Shops were staying open later and life returned to some no-go zones. It's been three months now since we had a significant IDF attack near our house. Like many Baghdad residents, we're waiting to see if the lull in violence is only temporary. I persuaded myself to get back on the exercise bike after the close call. But I've been practicing my duck-and-cover drills ever since.

FIRST PERSON

Meet the New Generation Of War Veterans

In 2007, Newsweek.com launched a blog called Soldier's Home, by Iraq War veteran David Botti. With combat heading into its sixth year, Botti shared his thoughts on battles here at home.

I grew up in an era when war veterans were the aging men at Memorial Day parades wearing triangular hats. It never crossed my mind that a vet might someday be a kid like me. If it had never crossed yours, either, this year probably changed all that. At my graduate school in New York, I can count at least five classmates who know an Iraq War veteran firsthand—and that's just one class, in one school. More than 1 million veterans have returned from Iraq and Afghanistan, lifting our collective profile by the sheer weight of our numbers.

During the past year, veterans' issues were all over the media—and often the news was grim. In February the Walter Reed hospital scandal broke, with revelations about decrepit housing and substandard care. Next came a series of reports on Iraq War data: we learned that the Army suicide rate had reached a 26-year high in 2006; that there'd been 4,698 desertions during the 2007 fiscal year, an 80 percent increase since 2003; that the number of Iraq vets diagnosed with mental-health issues triples during their first six months at home. I followed these stories with a strange sense of relief. For too long, people seemed to think veterans came home and simply melted back into society. Now vet issues were finally getting attention—even if it took bad news to make it happen.

When I started my blog this year, I wondered if there would be enough news about veterans to get me through one day. I couldn't have been more wrong. There we were in the rhetoric of politicians, in countless newspaper features, even on reality TV. For the blog, I've made an effort to examine not only the challenges that my fellow veterans face but also their accomplishments. As one Wall Street Journal columnist wrote, "The media struggles in good faith to respect our troops, but too often it merely pities them."

> "The media struggles in good faith to respect our troops, but too often it merely pities them."

Stories like the Walter Reed scandal can invite this kind of pity and overshadow the fact that most of us are immensely proud of our service. A single tour in Iraq or Afghanistan can define a person's entire life; collectively, our experiences will echo for decades. If 2007 was the year when veterans' issues entered the public's consciousness, we need to make sure they don't go away in 2008.

WEEK OF JANUARY 21

FIRST PERSON

In Diyala, a New Offensive

The GI's marched in silence, placing their feet carefully to avoid tripwires that could detonate an IED. In the no man's land between Shakarat and Sinsil, small villages about 60 miles north of Baghdad, the only sounds that pierced the midnight darkness were the murmurs of platoon leader Capt. Travis Batty into his radio, and the crunch of boots hitting sand. The military's Operation Iron Harvest—a major offensive to drive Al Qaeda in Iraq from Diyala province—was underway, and the troops from Blackfoot Company were in the vanguard, tasked with securing the area for their comrades in the rear. I was along to watch.

Diyala province is the latest battleground in the fight against Al Qaeda, and since the operation began last week, at least nine U.S. soldiers have been killed. The insurgents holed up here remain tenacious, unleashing suicide bombers and planting lethal explosives that can blow anything off the road. And they've upped the ante. A severed head turned up last week in a deserted market in Shakarat, a mere 500 yards from the U.S. military's combat outpost. It was the 10th head discovered in two weeks—gruesome warnings of what will happen to anyone who helps the Americans. "They stuck the head of one of my brothers on the bridge close to the camp," a local farmer, Nazem Aziz Habib, told me as he walked by with his two children.

The idea behind Operation Iron Harvest was to kill or capture the approximately 200 Qaeda members who've been hiding out in the Diyala River Valley, an area known as the Bread Basket because much of the nation's produce is grown here. But Al Qaeda apparently got wind of the offensive beforehand; some locals say they were tipped off by Iraqi Army sources. The insurgents set booby traps, then disappeared.

As morning arrived, we set up camp at a large house in Sinsil. Inside, soldiers questioned a young man, Maad Khalaf Darweesh, about Al Qaeda's presence in the town. He seemed suspicious, coughing and sweating as First Sgt. Ken Brantley grilled him about a strange drawing. But it turned out to be the building's electrical grid, and the soldiers realized Darweesh was actually ill with a nasty cold. A medic gave him antibiotics, and gradually, the platoon relaxed. "Sit down over there so you don't get shot by snipers," a 22-year-old sergeant told me.

The calm didn't last long. A 50-pound IED rocked the house and sent a 25-ton Army vehicle bouncing into the air. Smoke billowed, and we took cover while the company rushed out to investigate. Inside the vehicle, four soldiers and a freelance reporter were injured. "It blew up right under my feet," the writer, Rick Tomkins, told me. "I was just holding my breath wondering if there would be another blast." The soldiers found no Qaeda operatives. Like phantoms, the culprits had slipped away yet again, with the soldiers of Operation Iron Harvest right behind them. —LENNOX SAMUELS

WEEK OF MARCH 31

PAKISTAN

With a Quiet Blessing, U.S. Attacks on Al Qaeda Spike

The United States has stepped up its use of pilotless planes to strike at Qaeda targets along Pakistan's rugged border area, a measure that in the past drew protests from President Pervez Musharraf but now has his government's tacit approval. Since January, missiles reportedly fired from CIA-operated Predator drones have hit at least three suspected hideouts of Islamic militants, including a strike last Sunday on a house in a South Waziristan village called Toog.

The surge began after visits to Pakistan at the beginning of the year by senior U.S. officials, including intelligence czar Mike McConnell, CIA director Gen. Michael Hayden and Adm. William Fallon, who recently resigned as commander of the U.S. forces in the region. Some news reports said at the time that Musharraf had "rebuffed" U.S. proposals to step up combat operations inside Pakistan. But U.S. officials and

Pakistani sources, who asked for anonymity discussing sensitive information, said the recent wave of Predator attacks are at least partly the result of understandings the high-level visitors reached with Musharraf and other top Pakistanis, giving the United States virtually unrestricted authority to hit targets in the border areas.

One former official said that the United States has been relying on its own intel to uncover terror targets because Pakistani intelligence agencies are weak on espionage in the tribal areas. By contrast, U.S. forces have a heavy presence on the Afghan side of the border. Bruce Riedel, a retired CIA expert on the region, said that a new wave of terrorism inside Pakistan—there were 62 suicide attacks last year, after just six in 2006—has forced Musharraf and the new military chief, Gen. Ashfaq Kayani, to acknowledge that the same extremists threatening Americans now also pose a growing threat to Pakistan's internal security. Another reason for the rise in Predator strikes, according to a current U.S. official: Washington fears that any newly formed civilian government in Pakistan will be more hostile to U.S. operations there than Musharraf's current regime. Time to act, in other words, may be running out.

At least one top Qaeda operative has been killed in the Predator strikes. After a missile hit a home in North Waziristan in late January, reportedly killing 10 militants, U.S. officials confirmed that among the dead was Abu Laith al-Libi, a top field commander who was believed to be a liaison between Qaeda's fugitive leaders and Taliban fighters in Afghanistan. The CIA declined to confirm or comment on any of the reported attacks, but three current and former U.S. officials, who also asked for anonymity, said that the one-per-month strike rate is definitely higher than in previous years.

—MARK HOSENBALL, ZAHID HUSSAIN *and* RON MOREAU

The same extremists threatening Americans now also pose a growing threat to Pakistan's internal security.

WEEK OF APRIL 14

JUSTICE

A Top Pentagon Lawyer Faces A Senate Grilling on Torture

With little advance notice, Pentagon general counsel William Haynes quietly resigned at the end of February to take a top legal job at Chevron. But Haynes, a close ally of Vice President Dick Cheney, remains a key figure in a sweeping Senate probe into allegations of abuses to detainees in Defense Department custody.

Haynes was thrust back into the spotlight last week after the disclosure of a March 2003 Justice Department memo concluding that federal laws against torture, assault and maiming would not apply to the overseas interrogation of terror suspects. Haynes requested the memo (which was written by the then Justice Department lawyer John Yoo) and he and his boss, the then Secretary of Defense Donald Rumsfeld, later used it to justify harsh interrogation practices on terror suspects at Guantánamo Bay. The memo's disclosure raises new questions about the role that Haynes and other Bush-administration lawyers played in crafting legal policies that critics say led to abuses at Abu Ghraib and elsewhere.

It's a role that the Senate Armed Services Committee, overseen by Sen. Carl Levin and its ranking Republican member, Sen. John McCain, has been quietly but aggressively scrutinizing during a two-year investigation. Two sources familiar with the probe, who asked not to be identified discussing sensitive matters, say the panel's investigators have grilled a number of key players—including Special Forces operatives and FBI agents—who were never previously questioned. The panel notified the Pentagon in early February that it wanted to question Haynes. Before receiving any response, investigators learned on Feb. 25 that Haynes was leaving for Chevron in San Francisco. "How often

> "How often does somebody like that give two weeks' notice and leave town?"

does somebody like that give two weeks' notice and leave town?" said one government source familiar with the sequence of events.

Haynes's departure initially raised concerns about obtaining his testimony without a subpoena, especially after the panel learned that he had retained top criminal defense attorney Terrence O'Donnell, who represented Cheney during the Valerie Plame leak investigation. But O'Donnell told NEWSWEEK that Haynes has agreed to be interviewed, adding that the committee's probe "had nothing to do" with his resignation. A Pentagon spokeswoman said that Haynes had discussed his departure "some months ago" with Secretary of Defense Robert Gates and that he "looks forward to . . . enjoying a promising private-sector opportunity." —MICHAEL ISIKOFF

WEEK OF APRIL 28

IRAN

An Upside to a 'Bad Actor'

Against a backdrop of congressional testimony by Gen. David Petraeus and Ambassador Ryan Crocker, the two top U.S. officials in Baghdad, the Bush administration has stepped up its claims of Iranian interference in Iraq, suggesting that with Qaeda forces in Iraq now cornered, Iran has become the predominant troublemaker for U.S. troops. "If Iran makes the wrong choice," President George W. Bush said in an April 10 speech, "America will act to protect our interests and our troops and our Iraqi partners."

In fact, though, Iran's activity in Iraq—and in Afghanistan—is quite nuanced, according to several U.S. officials familiar with the relevant intelligence assessments. These officials, who asked for anonymity when discussing sensitive information, said that while Iran certainly has been a "bad actor" in Iraq, not all of Tehran's actions are negative. For instance, according to the officials, Iran used its ties with the rival Shia factions jockeying for power in Iraq to help broker the recent Basra ceasefire between the (Iranian-backed) Iraqi government's forces and (Iranian-supplied) "special groups" of Moqtada al-Sadr's Mahdi Army. One said

APRIL | **War-225**

the Iranians are playing a kind of poker, "placing their bets on all Shia positions at the table." Former CIA analyst Ken Pollack, now with Washington's Saban Center, said Iran was "incredibly helpful to us" in resolving the Basra flare-up. In parts of Afghanistan, one of the

> **Iranians are playing a kind of poker, "placing their bets on all Shia positions at the table."**

U.S. officials said, Tehran has occasionally played a benign—even constructive—role, competing with NATO forces to provide local warlords with money for economic and humanitarian projects while seeking little in return.

The degree of Iran's negative meddling in Iraq remains unclear. Last month, NEWSWEEK has learned, the U.S. military in Baghdad canceled a media briefing to provide evidence of Iranian interference. Prepared under Pentagon and White House supervision, the presentation by military spokesman Maj. Gen. Kevin Bergner was going to allege that Iran has smuggled improvised roadside bombs into Iraq; that Shia insurgents who plant the devices have been trained by the Quds Force, a branch of Iran's Revolutionary Guard, and that most of the munitions recently unleashed on Baghdad's Green Zone are believed to have come from Iran. Washington called off the presentation because of fighting in southern Iraq; it has been rescheduled for this week.

—MARK HOSENBALL

WEEK OF MAY 19

TERRORISM

A Plea Deal Vanishes

More than six years after it began imprisoning terrorist suspects at Guantánamo Bay, the Bush administration finally hopes to present evidence against one of them at trial next month and prove that its much-criticized military-commissions system can be fair. Yemeni national Salim Ahmed Hamdan, one of Gitmo's highest-profile detainees, faces charges of conspiracy and giving material support to terrorists while serving as Osama bin Laden's driver. But the commission's former lead prosecutor, Air Force Col. Morris Davis, now says the government weighed a plea agreement with Hamdan last year that would have halted a trial and presumably set a date for his release.

Davis told NEWSWEEK that Gen. Thomas Hartmann, the Pentagon's top legal adviser in the commission's office, made plans to fly to Gitmo last August with Neal Katyal, one of Hamdan's civilian defense attorneys, to hammer out a plea deal. Davis said the trip was postponed when he filed a complaint against Hartmann for interfering in prosecutorial decision making. Davis's complaint touched off a Pentagon investigation, and he resigned his post in October. "I think the turmoil just collapsed the whole plea bargain," Davis said. Hartmann refused to discuss the episode and Katyal said he "never comments publicly on the existence of plea negotiations."

Davis does not know what Hartmann was ready to offer Hamdan, who has repeatedly, and successfully, challenged aspects of the military-commissions process in court. The prosecution depicts Hamdan as a Qaeda terrorist—not just a $200-a-month chauffeur—whose alleged crimes merit life in prison. But a plea bargain the government agreed to months earlier with Australian detainee David Hicks would certainly have been viewed by Hamdan as a precedent. Hicks got nine months in exchange for a guilty plea to the charge of giving material support to terrorists. Prosecutors believe they have a stronger case against Hamdan. But a trial could prove embarrassing for the Bush administration if Hamdan describes being beaten during his interrogation. That is, if he even shows up in court: he promised earlier this month to boycott his own trial.

—DAN EPHRON

Prosecutors believe they have a stronger case against Hamdan.

INTELLIGENCE

Fighting Words, Revisited

Back in 2004, when the Senate intelligence committee began investigating whether public statements by U.S. officials about Saddam Hussein's pre-invasion Iraq were "substantiated" by existing intel, Republicans controlled Congress and the committee's inquiry was aimed at figures on both sides of the aisle. The idea was to examine the fighting words of President George W. Bush and Vice President Dick Cheney as well as prominent Democrats including Al Gore, Sen. John Kerry and Sen. Hillary Clinton. But Democrats, who took over the panel after winning Senate control in 2006, decided that the final report would examine only statements by "policymakers"—in other words, the Bush administration. So in the report, due out this week, no Democratic comments will be parsed. That includes an Oct. 10, 2002, speech by Clinton in which she criticized Saddam's WMD ambitions and accused him of giving "aid, comfort and sanctuary to terrorists, including Al Qaeda members."

According to three intelligence officials familiar with the inquiry, who asked for anonymity when discussing an unpublished report, even committee Democrats are expected to acknowledge that most of the prewar WMD statements were proved inaccurate only after the invasion. The forthcoming report, though, is expected to be more critical about prewar discussion of Saddam's terrorist links. During a Sept. 8, 2002, appearance on "Meet the Press," for instance, Cheney discussed a Czech intelligence report claiming that Muhammad Atta had met an Iraqi spy in Prague a few months before he led the 9/11 attacks. But a declassified July 2002 report by the Defense

The final report will examine only statements by "policymakers."

Intelligence Agency had already debunked that claim, pointing out that there was no "photographic, immigration or other documentary evidence" to support it. NEWSWEEK discovered another recently declassified Pentagon document that reported that Czech officials retracted some of their original claims about Atta's Prague visit when they realized they had "confused him with a Pakistani national with a similar name." A Cheney spokeswoman said that she could not comment on a Senate report that she had not yet seen.

—MARK HOSENBALL

WEEK OF MAY 26

AFGHANISTAN

Speaking With the Enemy

The Bush Administration may not be practicing what the president preaches when it comes to "appeasement." In a speech to Israel's Knesset, which was regarded as an attack on Barack Obama and other Democrats, Bush condemned as a "foolish delusion" the belief "that we should negotiate with terrorists and radicals." But the administration itself has sanctioned such discussions in Sunni areas of Iraq, Pakistani tribal areas and Afghanistan. Last week, Defense Secretary Robert Gates suggested that the United States "need[s] to figure out a way to develop some leverage with respect to the Iranians and then sit down and talk with them."

That notion evidently extends to elements of the Taliban. Mark Sedra, a Canadian expert on Afghanistan, says high-level U.S. officials, who he declined to name, admitted during a private Washington think-tank conference earlier this year that there was no purely military solution to Afghanistan's problems and expressed a "willingness" to negotiate with "moderate" Taliban figures. Four administration officials, who asked for anonymity when discussing policy deliberations, told NEWSWEEK that Washington has already assented to efforts by Afghan President Hamid Karzai to talk with Taliban factions that do not share the nihilist religious extremism of Supreme Leader Mullah Omar. "If the Afghans want to peel away so-called [Taliban] 'reasonables,' we're fine with that,"

"We say it's not negotiation. It's dialogue."

one of the officials said. Those inside the administration who object, said another of the officials, have been somewhat mollified by the use of semantic legerdemain: "We say it's not negotiation. It's dialogue."

—MARK HOSENBALL

WEEK OF JUNE 9

CLOSURE

The War's First Hero

News stories captivate us for a moment and then vanish. We revisit those stories, then bring you the next chapter.

STARTING POINT

March 2003: Three days after the U.S. invasion of Iraq, enemy forces capture 19-year-old Army Pvt. **Jessica Lynch** in an attack on her convoy.

FEVER PITCH

Eight days later, the Pentagon releases a five-minute video of Lynch's dramatic "rescue" from an Iraqi hospital and discloses that she had been abused by her captors. Lynch later accuses the military of exaggerating her story and turning it into propaganda.

PRESENT DAY

Now a sophomore studying education at West Virginia University, Lynch has a 16-month-old daughter with her fiancé. She also runs a charitable organization that collects stuffed animals for hospitalized children. In 2007, she testified to Congress about the military's misleading portrayal of her story. She still gets hate mail accusing her of lying about the rescue effort. "If they want to take out their hatred on me, that's OK," she tells NEWSWEEK. "At this point, I don't really stress about it."
—J.E.

WEEK OF JUNE 16

IRAQ

'Anything Not to Go Back'

As an internist at new York's Mount Sinai Hospital, Dr. Stephanie Santos is used to finding odd things in people's stomachs. So last spring when a young man, identifying himself as an Iraq-bound soldier, said he had accidentally swallowed a pen at the bus station, she believed him. That is, until she found a second pen. It read 1-800-greyhound. Last summer, according to published reports, a 20-year-old Bronx soldier paid a hit man $500 to shoot him in the knee on the day he was scheduled to return to Iraq. The year before that, a 24-year-old specialist from Washington state escaped a second tour of duty, according to his sister, by strapping on a backpack full of tools and leaping off the roof of his house, injuring his spine.

Such cases of self-harm are a "rising trend" that military doctors are watching closely, says Col. Kathy Platoni, an Army Reserve psychologist who has worked with veterans of Iraq and Afghanistan.

> **"Only a fool or a fraud talks tough or romantically about war."**
> **—Sen. John McCain, June 2008**
> *Perspectives*

"There are some soldiers who will do almost anything not to go back," she says. Col. Elspeth Ritchie, the Army's top psychologist, agrees that we could see an uptick in intentional injuries as more U.S. soldiers serve long, repeated combat tours, "but we just don't have good, hard data on it." Intentional injury cases are hard to identify, and even harder to prosecute. Fewer than 21 soldiers have been punitively discharged for self-harm since 2003, according to the military. What's worrying, however, is that American troops committed suicide at the highest rate on record in 2007—and the factors behind self-injury are similar: combat stress and strained relationships. "It's often the families that don't want soldiers to return to war," says Ritchie.

Soldiers have long used self-harm as a rip cord to avoid war. During World War I, The American Journal of Psychiatry reported "epidemics of self-inflicted injuries," hospital wards filled with men shot in a single finger or toe, as well as cases of pulled-out teeth, punctured eardrums and slashed Achilles' heels. Few doubt that the Korean and Vietnam wars were any different. But the current war—fought with an overtaxed volunteer Army—may be the worst. "We're definitely concerned," says Ritchie. "We hope they'll talk to us rather than self-harm."

—Tony Dokoupil

WEEK OF JUNE 23

TRIBUNALS

No Country For 270 Men

White House and Justice Department lawyers are bracing for a flood of new court battles as a result of last week's historic Supreme Court ruling, which granted Guantánamo Bay detainees the right to seek their freedom in federal court. But a more daunting problem lurks down the road: what happens if the courts actually do set them free? The largest block of Gitmo prisoners—nearly 100 of the remaining 270—hail from Yemen, a country that so far has resisted taking back detainees because of U.S. demands that they be put on trial back home (or, at least, that the Yemenis pledge to keep a close eye on them). "Of course, we want our citizens back," says Abdulwahab al-Hajjri, Yemen's ambassador to the United States. "But [the United States] has these conditions, so this is taking time." Other prisoners come from countries that allegedly engage in torture, such as Syria, Libya and China. Attempts to find countries in Europe willing to take them have hit a brick wall. "The most vexing problem," says one senior administration official, who asked not to be identified discussing diplomatic matters, "is nobody wants them."

One example is Suleman Al Nahdi, a Yemeni who's been in Gitmo for more than six years. In 2004, a special military tribunal declared him an "enemy combatant" and "a member of or affiliated with Al Qaeda"—a conclusion based on classified evidence that Al Nahdi never saw. (Last week's court ruling found such hearings unconstitutional.) Earlier this year,

> **"People escape from prison all over the world," says al-Hajjri, Yemen's ambassador. "It happens."**

though, the U.S. military changed its mind, telling Al Nahdi he was "cleared for release." His current lawyer, Rick Murphy, says Al Nahdi was thrilled when he got the news in February. But he still hasn't been let go and is now so disenchanted he refuses to meet with his attorneys.

The Bush administration is especially apprehensive about returning detainees to Yemen because of a massive jailbreak two years ago in which 13 Qaeda operatives escaped, including Jamal al-Badawi, who was indicted for the USS Cole bombing. FBI officials suspect that the jailbreak was an inside job and have demanded with no success that al-Badawi be returned to the United States. "People escape from prison all over the world," says al-Hajjri, Yemen's ambassador. "It happens." —MICHAEL ISIKOFF

WEEK OF JULY 21

IRAQ

Who Says Fewer Troops?

Barack Obama is taking heat for hinting that he might refine his 16-month timetable for withdrawing U.S. troops from Iraq. But a forthcoming Pentagon-sponsored report will recommend an even steeper drawdown in less time, NEWSWEEK has learned. If adopted, the 300-page report by a defense analysis group at the Naval Postgraduate School in Monterey, Calif., could transform the debate about Iraq in the presidential election. Expected to be completed in about a month, it will recommend that U.S. forces be reduced to as few as 50,000 by the spring of 2009, down from about 150,000 now. The strategy is based on a major handoff to the increasingly successful Iraqi Army, with platoon-size U.S. detachments backing the Iraqis from small outposts, with air support. The large U.S. forward operating bases that house the bulk of U.S. troops would be mostly abandoned, and the role of Special Forces would increase.

The report's conclusions have been discussed inside Secretary Robert Gates's Defense Policy Board, a body of outside experts. And they've found favor with some former members of the Iraq Study Group, such as former White House chief of staff Leon Panetta. "That's basically the approach we thought made sense—embedding some of our forces at smaller outposts, transferring major combat to the Iraqis," says Panetta. Like the Study Group, this report also calls for a regional diplomatic effort complementing negotiations with the Iraqi tribes, which echoes the previous recommendations of such analysts as John Arquilla, a professor at the Naval Postgraduate School. "Even with a small leavening of American troops the Iraqis perform quite well," he says. The biggest problem: Iraq commander Gen. David Petraeus, who oversaw the surge, is said to oppose the recommendations, according to a Defense contractor who is privy to the discussions. Asked about the report, Pentagon spokesman Bryan Whitman told NEWSWEEK that Gates "feels the most important military advice he gets is from his commanders on the ground." As the next head of Central Command, Petraeus will soon have responsibility for Afghanistan and Pakistan too, which could change his views on troop deployments and the new report. Spokesman Col. Steve Boylan says Petraeus "is focused on Iraq at this point and will continue to be."

—MICHAEL HIRSH

WEEK OF JULY 28

TERROR

The Politics Of Gitmo

A Federal judge's ruling last week threw a potential new curveball into the campaign debate over the War on Terror. Democratic-appointed Judge James Robertson gave the Pentagon a green light to start the first-ever military-commission trial of a Gitmo detainee this week—that of Salim Hamdan, an alleged Qaeda member who served as Osama bin Laden's driver. (Robertson said that if defense lawyers see the trial as unfair, they can challenge the results later in federal court.) But the ramifications of the ruling go beyond that one case. Pentagon officials say it allows them to proceed with a series of military-commission trials, hearings and new charges that (coincidentally or not) will play out in the middle of the election campaign. Among them are hearings, if not the actual trial, in the conspiracy case involving 9/11 mastermind Khalid Sheikh Mohammed. "We are moving forward," said J. D. Gordon, a spokesman for the Pentagon, noting that the next round of KSM hearings are slated for August and another commission trial, involving Canadian detainee Omar Khadr, is due to begin Oct. 8.

Aside from producing new testimony on Al Qaeda and terror plots, the proceedings could sharpen the debate between John McCain and Barack Obama. While both have said they want to shut down Gitmo, McCain backs the military commissions; Obama voted against the bill that created the panels in 2006. When the Pentagon announced its charges against KSM and five co-conspirators, Obama argued that the men should be tried either in a civilian court or by a military court-martial. But would he call a halt to trials already underway? Spokesman Bill Burton told NEWSWEEK Obama will "review any pending cases and make a judgment about how to go forward based on the best interest of the country." But the established "court systems . . . are capable of convicting terrorists." —M.I.

WEEK OF SEPTEMBER 1

IRAQ

Petraeus: The Exit Interview

Gen. David Petraeus has no intention of doing a victory lap on his way out of Iraq. So when his aides proposed a valedictory interview with NEWSWEEK, they made it clear the theme would not pick up from this magazine's 2004 cover CAN THIS MAN SAVE IRAQ? As the boss (that's what his subordinates call him) heads off next month to take over the U.S. military's Central Command, in charge of Afghanistan as well as Iraq, there would be no talk of, "So *did* this man save Iraq?" Little surprise there, from a military leader wise enough to quote Seneca around his troops and media-savvy enough to warn them, "Don't put lipstick on a pig."

OK, instead we'll talk about Al Qaeda in Iraq. They've lost Anbar province and Baghdad. They've vacated the Sunni Triangle. Virtually the entire Sunni Arab population has turned against them, and now not a single Sunni imam, politician or tribal leader of note inside

> "Every time you start to feel really good, there will be some kind of incident."

the country supports them. So why then don't we just say it: Al Qaeda in Iraq has been defeated.

"You won't find a single military leader in this theater who will say that," says Petraeus.

"You could be the first, General."

"Yeah, I could, but I won't be."

"At least can't we say strategically defeated?"

"We'll leave that to the academics. [U.S. Ambassador Ryan] Crocker and I explicitly, from day one, said that we have got to be coldly realistic and not let our enthusiasms creep into our assessments . . . [Success] is still not self-sustaining; there is still a degree of fragility to it, and it could be reversed."

Actually, it's right there in the general's counterinsurgency guidance to his troops: "Avoid premature declarations of success." He is far too politic to refer to President George W. Bush's "mission accomplished," but he won't make the same mistake. "The champagne bottle remains in the back of the refrigerator," he says.

Other players rush in where Petraeus declines to tread. "Al Qaeda is definitely defeated tactically," says Iraq's national-security adviser, Mowaffaq al-Rubaie. Recently, Rubaie says, intelligence agencies intercepted communications between Al Qaeda in Iraq and senior Qaeda officials in Pakistan. "They asked them not to send any more foreign mujahedin," only suicide wanna-bes. "This is very significant. It means they no longer have any territory to defend."

Wouldn't the general agree, then, that a tipping point has been reached in which al Qaeda is so weak that it no longer has the capability to affect how Iraqis live, much less spark a renewal of sectarian warfare? "Yes, Al Qaeda in Iraq has been significantly diminished, its capability substantially degraded," he says, "but we assess they remain lethal—what we call the wolf closest to the sled." And, he adds, "every time you start to feel really good, there will be some kind of incident."

Will he take along the lessons learned in Iraq to Afghanistan? "It's premature to say." On many days now, the violence there is actually higher than in Iraq. Secretary of Defense Robert Gates says he's waiting for Petraeus's assessment before deciding what to do there, but the boss is already managing expectations. Afghanistan, Petraeus says, "will be the longest campaign" in this long war.

—Rod Nordland

WEEK OF SEPTEMBER 8

IRAQ

Stay in the Closet, or Else

When Militiamen from the Mahdi Army came by the compact, two-story stone home in the Doura neighborhood of Baghdad, they weren't looking for Sunnis to harass. They were hunting gays. "Bring us your son's cell phone," one ordered the man who came to the gate. They wanted to check if his son, Nadir, had been calling

> **It's open season on homosexuals in Iraq. Since 2003, some 430 gay men have been murdered.**

foreigners. In fact, only hours earlier he'd called this reporter and had often called a London-based gay nonprofit, Iraq LGBT. Fortunately, Nadir was ready: he produced a "clean" phone and the soldiers left, vowing to return if they found evidence he was gay—or talking to undesirable foreigners.

Sometimes the act of reporting is as revealing as the story itself. This was the case when NEWSWEEK began looking into the problems of Iraq's homosexuals, many of whom are taking refuge from the militias' self-appointed morality police in safe houses around Baghdad. Iraqi authorities scoffed at the subject—when not scolding a reporter for even asking about it. A written request for an interview at the Legal Section of the Ministry of Human Rights was greeted with a suggestion to delete the word "gays." After weeks of inquiries, newsweek found Nadir and persuaded him to permit a visit to one of the safe houses he helps run. But the Mahdi militia—radical Shiite cleric Moqtada al-Sadr's armed wing—rousted him the night before. Terrified, he broke off the visit.

Now that Iraq's sectarian war has cooled off, it's open season on homosexuals and others who infuriate religious hard-liners. According to Iraq LGBT, more than 430 gay men have been murdered in Iraq since 2003. But many officials feel that in a country at war, there are more pressing concerns than gay rights. An adviser to Prime Minister Nuri al-Maliki's government said that of all the meetings he has attended, none ever touched on the rights—or even the existence—of homosexual Iraqis. "Most acts of homosexual people are being done in dark corners and, with corruption and paying bribes, they will be kept there for a long time," said a Ministry of Justice judge, who would not allow his name to be used discussing gays.

In such a climate, the only recourse for Iraqi gays seems to come from activists abroad. Iraq LGBT looks after about 40 young men between the ages of 14 and 28 in several Baghdad safe houses, where they sleep in cramped quarters. They stay away from neighbors and rarely leave their immediate area. "I hope you can see how sensitive and very important the security issue is for the safe houses," said Ali Hili, who fled Iraq and received asylum in Britain.

Hili continues to use a pseudonym to protect himself. He has not returned home in eight years but does visit Syria and Jordan to raise money and check on an underground railroad that helps spirit some gay men out of Iraq. Since the late-evening visit by the militiamen, Nadir has moved to another part of Baghdad and stayed away from home. "They said, 'We will get you even if you fly to God'," he says. Saif, one of the older residents at an Iraq LGBT house, recalls Saddam's repressive but secular regime wistfully. "Those were the most beautiful days of our lives," he says. "The fall [of Saddam] was the worst thing to happen."

—Lennox Samuels

WEEK OF OCTOBER 27

BATTLEFRONT

Why Iran Is Cooling Off

For reasons that remain unclear to the Bush administration and its allies, the level of violence attributable to Iranian-backed insurgents in both Iraq and Afghanistan is falling. Pentagon press secretary Geoff Morrell says the trend dates back to an Iraqi-government assault last spring on militants in the Basra region of southern Iraq. After the crackdown, Iranian-supported insurgents (known to U.S. officials as "special groups") fled into Iran, where they have since been cooling their heels. Still, according to one

U.S. counterterrorism official, who asked for anonymity when discussing sensitive information, some reports suggest that Iraqi militants are still actively being trained inside Iran for attacks on U.S. forces.

Iran is exercising restraint In its dealings with Afghan insurgents.

Meanwhile, in Afghanistan, intelligence reports last year indicated that Iran was also supplying terrorist-style arms to anti-American militants there. But the latest intelligence indicates that the level of bombing technology used by the Taliban in recent IED attacks is far less sophisticated than the devices used by Shia militants in Iraq—evidence that Iran is exercising restraint in its dealings with Afghan insurgents.

The question is, why? Another U.S. official, who also requested anonymity, said that Iran may be turning down the heat on American forces in the region in anticipation of a Barack Obama victory in the presidential election. According to this theory, Iran's theocrats fear an Obama presidency would greatly improve American esteem among European governments; the Iranians believe these leaders indulge Tehran now chiefly because of their disdain for President Bush.

A drop in Iranian-instigated paramilitary attacks does not mean that Tehran has ceased making mischief in the region. Recently, Morrell says, Iranian operatives have been actively pressing Iraqi politicians to oppose U.S. efforts to reach a new "Status of Forces Agreement" with the Iraqi government regarding the continued presence there of American troops. He said Iranian efforts have included trying to orchestrate anti-U.S. demonstrations in Shia neighborhoods and funding attempts to bribe Iraqi politicians. —MARK HOSENBALL

Culture and the Arts

YEAR IN REVIEW

It was bound to happen eventually, but 2008 was the year when *American Idol* finally lost its stranglehold over the country's collective consciousness. Sure, the Fox reality show was still plenty popular—TV's highest rated program for several seasons in a row—but it didn't consume the culture the way it had in the past, when even those who never watched a second of *Idol* could easily come up with the name of the winner. Not so in 2008. (The latest winner was David Cook, by the way.) Instead, sobering times sent Americans in search of more serious entertainment. The summer was dominated by a pair of dystopic tales about the importance of decency in cruel times: Pixar's *Wall-E*, a vision of a scorched-earth future in which robots have more humanity than the humans; and the Batman sequel, *The Dark Knight*, a box-office smash that made more money than any other film in history besides *Titanic*, and was seized upon by liberals and conservatives alike as an allegory for a nation divided by a war on terror. The accidental death of Heath Ledger, the talented young actor who delivered a bold, intoxicating performance as the Joker, could not alone explain the movie's astounding success. Director Christopher Nolan's film resonated with a moment of anxiety and moral weariness, and a wish for new heroes, even as it expressed skepticism that any hero could remain one in such a cynical age.

The breakthrough gadget of the year, Apple's iPhone, quickly became the sleek black symbol of an instant karma world, where nothing really happened unless it was captured on YouTube or Facebook. (Forunately, or unfortunately, it almost always was.) The gradual sea change in communication, from a television culture to an Internet culture, was all but complete by 2008, which helps explain how a TV series like *Gossip Girl* could have such an impact even though hardly anyone watches it. The entertainment industry, which began the year struggling through one workers strike and ended it with the threat of another, underscored the tension and opportunity of the moment, with no one quite sure how to reach people—and, more crucially, how to make money off them—in this new, unpredictable environment. Everything seemed to blur together. Just look at how the McCain campaign, frustrated this summer by its inability to get attention in the comet trail of Barack Obama, blasted the Democratic nominee as the product of a celebrity culture, comparing him to Britney Spears and Paris Hilton. Politics and popular culture, hand in hand, two sides of the same coin. At several moments during the presidential campaign, the only thing people anticipated more eagerly than what Sarah Palin would say or do next was how Tina Fey would spoof it on *Saturday Night Live*. Not that anyone watched SNL anymore, of course. They saw it on YouTube.

WEEK OF JANUARY 7

FIRST PERSON

A Hungry Crowd Smells iPhone, and Pounces

NEWSWEEK's *Senior Technology Writer Steven Levy is an authority on much-coveted gizmos. This year, one nearly got him trampled.*

Technology writers are seldom subject to frenzied, Beatlemania-esque paroxysms of public attention. June 29, 2007, was the exception. I was in the wrong place—Apple's Fifth Avenue store in Manhattan—with the right device. The iPhone.

Because I was one of four journalists who'd been given a pre-release iPhone for review, Fox News asked me to do an on-location interview. But as soon as I saw the swarming crowds of rabid fan boys and girls, it was clear that even a glimpse of the thing would set off a near riot. When the interview began, the crowd smelled iPhone, and ominously closed in. Suddenly a young man swooped behind us and made a grab—not for the iPhone, it turned out, but for the interviewer's microphone. He bolted with it, but was tackled by one of the Fox technicians, and the mike was recovered. (The interloper's point, it turned out, was to protest Fox News, not to swipe my prize; the whole sorry event wound up on YouTube.) Shaken but undaunted, we restarted. It got even scarier. People pressed in close, fingers stretching toward the device, Michelangelo style. Afterward, a production assistant warned me that I should have a bodyguard with me until the sale began at 6 p.m.

I made it through the day without extra muscle, but I still marvel at the phenomenon. For two weeks a gizmo took its place among Iraq and Paris Hilton as a dominant news event. Only part of this could be attributed to the marketing acumen of Apple, which has a sense of drama that no company can match. People are passionate about their mobile phones—and passionately unhappy about the general experience of using them to access the Internet. Apple's iPod success led them to believe an even bigger breakthrough was possible

> **I was in the wrong place— Apple's Fifth Avenue store in Manhattan— with the right device. The iPhone.**

Culture and the Arts-244 | JANUARY

with the iPhone. In some respects the iPhone hype overwhelmed even Apple. Criticism of its sudden price cut (from $600 to $400, after only 10 weeks) and its rejection of third-party software (Apple says it will address this early in 2008) was amplified by the expectations. But statistics show that the million-plus iPhone users are taking advantage of the device's breakthrough Web-browsing features. And even though I knew that a faster, flashier model would come out in 2008, I went to the Apple store when it was time to give back my loaner and I bought a replacement. This time the crowd wasn't nearly as bad.

FAST CHAT

He's Still a Bit Crushed

Everyone knows the most memorable scene in the June finale of "The Sopranos." But a close second had to be the outrageous death of Tony Soprano's nemesis Phil Leotardo (Frank Vincent), who was shot twice, then got his head smushed by an SUV. Vincent spoke with NEWSWEEK's Joshua Alston.

Were you disappointed Phil didn't get to take out Tony?
No. I didn't want Phil to die, but I figured he was going to. Tony is a very important character, so I assumed he wouldn't die.

Yours is the kind of death scene for which you have to prepare your friends and family.
I didn't tell anyone except my wife. I had to spend a whole day in makeup to make the prosthetic head. They made almost a dozen heads.

What a bizarre way to die.
Yeah, it was interesting because a lot of references were made during the season to Phil's gray hair. Lots of subtle references to his head. David [Chase] is a genius.

Did seeing it gross you out?
Yeah. I didn't know there would be all those reaction shots. The kids throwing up—that was pretty gross. But it's just a film trick. There's only so much they can show of my head being squashed because my head is not actually being squashed.

Right, because I'm talking to you now.
Absolutely. But it wasn't easy. I had to lie down in front of the car and we had to chain the car so it could only go a certain distance. It

had to come very close to my head, but then the dummy went in.

That must have been nerve-racking.

It was tense. It's not something you do every day.

Everybody has a theory about the final scene. What's yours?

I [don't] think Tony died. I think they rode into the sunset. That way there can be a sequel.

FIRST PERSON

'I'm Shy. I'm Sweet. I'm Normal. I'm Nice.'

It was a tough year for Paris Hilton, but at least she got to spend a couple of hours with NEWSWEEK*'s Ramin Setoodeh. His repast with the heiress:*

If you're having lunch with Paris Hilton, be prepared for a long wait. Remember, she didn't even arrive at court on time. More than an hour passed before she made her entrance at Fred Segal in Los Angeles, and it reminded me of the scene in "The Great Gatsby" when Daisy Buchanan is introduced, shrouded in white, like a vision from a dream. Only Paris was dressed all in black: a cutout dress and sunglasses, which she took off only for a few seconds, at my request. When she excused herself to go to the bathroom, I realized that the entire restaurant was looking at

---

FIRST PERSON

The Best of Times, the Worst of Times

National sports correspondent and Boston bureau chief Mark Starr had a sickening grin on his face all year; Senior Editor Devin Gordon, a lifelong New Yorker, spent the year just feeling sick. Here's why.

BOSTON

I'm a longtime season-ticket holder, so I've seen the worst, now maybe the best ever. The Patriots have answered a cheating bust with a scorched-earth run. Target: 19-0 perfection, and a fourth Super Bowl trophy in seven seasons.

We'd just put down our champagne glasses from 2004; now we're hoisting them again. No miracles, bloody socks or Yankees this time, but another playoff comeback and Series sweep. It was just so painful to have to wait three years.

The most-storied team in NBA history, dormant since Larry Bird's heyday, is reborn as a title threat with a new Big Three: Kevin Garnett, Ray Allen and Paul Pierce. Chemistry frets are soothed by the league's hottest start.

me, wondering how the hell I got a lunch date with Paris.

Just as Gatsby was infatuated with Daisy, we haven't been able to look away from Paris Hilton this year. Her fans probably aren't familiar with Fitzgerald, but she's come to embody qualities similar to fiction's best golden girl. Paris is a blonde with a voice full of money and happily plays the role of "a beautiful little fool" (to quote Daisy's description of what a woman must be). She hijacked our cable-news coverage during her 23-day jail stint this summer, and yet so many of us watched, transfixed.

Paris speaks in a low whisper, a kind of insincere sincerity mixed in the California sun. On the morning of our lunch in October, she was planning a good-will trip to Africa, which she then canceled a few weeks later. She said she wants to settle down and have kids, though she's been saying that for years. "Having a baby, it looks really painful," Paris said. "But everyone says once you see the baby, you don't remember the pain." The way Paris describes herself, you also don't remember all the trouble she's been in. "I'm very sensitive. I'm shy. I'm sweet. I'm normal. I'm nice," she said. At the end of our lunch, I walked her to the door, where the paparazzi had gathered. She kissed me on the cheek, landing us both on TMZ.com. It was a masterful performance. Paris, like Daisy, drives fast and never looks back.

> **She's come to embody qualities similar to fiction's best golden girl.**

NEW YORK

J-E-T-S once again stood for "Just End the Season," and it didn't help that our hated division rival (guess who?) was clubbing teams like they were baby seals. As for the Giants: yet another winter collapse, right on schedule.

The old, fat, steroidal Yankees choked on the Sox's dust. Speaking of choke, that's your cue, A-Rod! And still speaking of choke, my Mets pulled one for the ages, gagging away the biggest September lead in baseball history.

Just when I thought it couldn't get any worse: ladies and gentlemen, my 2007-08 New York Knicks! The sex-harassment rap, the incompetent GM-coach, the worst team that money could buy ... Anyone up for a game of Scrabble?

STEROIDS

Hit-and-Run Accusations

Eighteen months ago, federal authorities released a court document justifying a raid at the home of Jason Grimsley, an Arizona Diamondbacks relief pitcher suspected of using performance-enhancing drugs. The affidavit named a number of Grimsley's alleged cohorts in baseball's extensive steroid subculture. But in the public version, the names were blacked out. Months later the Los Angeles Times claimed to reveal six of the deleted names, including Roger Clemens and Andy Pettitte. The two star pitchers (and workout buddies) vehemently denied steroid use, and—in an unusual move—the U.S. Attorney's Office in San Francisco declared publicly that the Times got some of the names wrong.

Having watched with wariness how the Feds' laudable investigation of a cabal of fitness quacks had morphed into a seemingly obsessive crusade to take down superstar athletes—including Barry Bonds—I wondered whether the San Francisco investigation had degenerated into a drive-by character assassination of innocent players. I knew that Pettitte, in particular, had a straight-arrow reputation, so I set out to determine whether he (or others) had been unfairly smeared in a media frenzy. Law-enforcement officials confirmed to me that some of the names published by the Times were indeed inaccurate, but they refused to say which ones.

When an uncensored version of the Grimsley affidavit finally became public before Christmas, the names of Pettitte, Clemens and some others identified by the Times were not mentioned. But all the players they identified *did* turn up in December's Mitchell Report on "juicing" in baseball. My instincts were right, but I'm certainly relieved that I never wrote a story debunking the Times report, since Pettitte was the first noteworthy player named by Mitchell to confirm his use of human growth hormone. (He said he used it only briefly to speed his recovery from an injury. Clemens, on the other hand, claims to be innocent.) I'm still feeling uncomfortable, though, about the Feds' use of powerful criminal-investigation tools (search warrants, grand-jury testimony) to out athletes who may have cheated their competitors but were not even low-level drug distributors or money launderers.

A law-enforcement source told me that the San Francisco Feds got the final pieces of evidence they needed to complete their criminal case against Barry Bonds while the World Series was still going on, but decided to hold off on indicting him until after the Series because they didn't want to spoil the fun. (That chore was left to Alex Rodriguez and his agent.) This restraint suggests prosecutors had some sense of proportion about how to use their considerable powers. But Mitchell is right when he says that it's really the duty of baseball to police its own frontline cheaters. Don't the Feds have more important wrongs to right?

—MARK HOSENBALL

WEEK OF JANUARY 14

EXCLUSIVE

More Heat for the Rocket

Roger Clemens may have talked himself into a tight legal squeeze. Congressional officials say the chief reason that the House Oversight Committee has asked Clemens—and four others implicated in baseball's steroid scandal—to appear at a Jan. 16 hearing is that the seven-time Cy Young Award winner publicly challenged the credibility of December's Mitchell Report. "The committee thinks that's worth investigating," says a congressional aide who asked for anonymity when discussing an ongoing official inquiry. Philip Schiliro, the committee's chief of staff, told NEWSWEEK that the members expect the five men to testify voluntarily. But if they refuse, two congressional sources say, the panel may well issue subpoenas. The officials say that witnesses will be asked to testify under oath, emphasizing that they could be prosecuted for lying to Congress if their testimony is later proved to be false.

The committee, chaired by Democratic investigative ace Rep.

Henry Waxman, has also asked Clemens's longtime workout buddy Andy Pettitte to testify, as well as another prominent former New York Yankee, Chuck Knoblauch, and two admitted suppliers, Kirk Radomski and Brian McNamee, whose testimony was central to former senator George Mitchell's findings on alleged steroid use by major-league players. Mitchell said McNamee told him that he had personally injected Clemens with steroids. Clemens has vehemently denied ever using performance-enhancing drugs; in an interview with "60 Minutes" on Sunday, he said that McNamee had injected him with vitamin B12 and lidocaine, a legal painkiller.

> **"Roger is willing to answer questions, including those posed to him under oath."**

"Roger is willing to answer questions, including those posed to him under oath," said Clemens's lawyer, Rusty Hardin, in a statement. "We hope to determine shortly if schedules and other commitments can accommodate the committee on that date." A lawyer for McNamee could not immediately be reached for comment.

—MARK HOSENBALL

TELEVISION

Who Writes This Stuff?

Late-night talk shows are slaves to structure. The host takes shots at the president and the disreputable starlet du jour, spars with the band leader and chats up guests. Lather, rinse, repeat.

But when Jay Leno and Conan O'Brien returned to the air last week without their striking writers, the routine—and their routines—were shattered. The novelty of the situation mitigated the impact; darn-this-strike jokes carried both hosts the first night. But no one knows how long the impasse will last, and strike humor will soon get as old as . . . well, the strike. The test isn't the first night's show, it's the show a week—or, God forbid, a month—from now.

But the writers could end up suffering as much as their bosses. The truth is, most people don't really understand what they do, and the perception of their importance depends on the host's performance. Leno is an old-fashioned jokester whose material has to be prewritten (and doing so himself got him in trouble with the union), while O'Brien lives to riff (hence

battle, they had better hope their bosses don't upstage them.
—Joshua Alston

WORTH YOUR TIME

How to Act As If You're In 'Control'

In "control," a british biopic about the 1980s post-punk band Joy Division, Sam Riley, as lead singer Ian Curtis, approaches the microphone with an air of reluctance. With his tidy haircut and shirt buttoned to the top, he looks more like an introvert than a rock star. When he begins to sing, his voice is monotone. Gradually, though, he surrenders to the song, letting his body be overtaken by a frenzied, arm-pumping dance,

his sketch of spinning his wedding ring on his desk). Still, both shows felt a lot like their prestrike versions, which means that writers are there to be the brawn, not the brains.

In other words, the hosts could probably write it all themselves, but there are snarky Harvard grads happy to do it for them. If the writers are to continue winning the PR

THE DIGNITY INDEX

Let's Just Pretend My Guest Tonight Is Will Smith

A weekly mathematical survey of dubious behavior that measures, on a scale of 1 to 100, just how low a person can go.

In a rambling Web posting, **Michael Moore** says no to endorsing any of the "less-than-stellar" Democrats for president. Want to bet they're more than relieved? Score: **17**

A-list celebs won't cross a picket line, so über-lame (and union member!) **Bob Saget** is Conan O'Brien's first back-to-work guest. Scarier: it's downhill from here. Score: **28**

He won big in Iowa, but **Mike Huckabee** isn't getting off the hook for telling reporters he pulled an attack ad on Mitt Romney— right as he played the very same ad for TV cameras. Score: **66**

like a crazed cadet marching himself into the ground. His shirt grows dark with sweat; his eyes turn glassy and wide. Most films about musicians portray music as the one pure joy in their lives. But Riley's performance suggests that the truth is more complex. He has a heavy-browed, gangly-armed grace that reads as both boyish and weary, and his subtle expression of Curtis's rage makes other films' guitar-smashing, bottle-throwing displays seem sloppy and false. Watching Riley, I found myself wishing I'd seen the real Joy Division play live, and his performance left me in awe of the courage it takes to reveal oneself so completely before a crowd.

Curtis occasionally suffered epileptic seizures during shows, and in Riley's portrayal, the line between musical transcendence

---

A LIFE IN BOOKS

Khaled Hosseini

The Afghan-American author is known for a pair of wrenching novels about his childhood home: "The Kite Runner," a massive best seller and now a feature film, and more recently "A Thousand Splendid Suns." His picks, in no specific order:

MY FIVE MOST IMPORTANT BOOKS

1. **"Shahnameh: The Persian Book of Kings"** by Abolqasem Ferdowsi. This 11th-century epic is the jewel of Persian literature.
2. **The Qur'an.** Hypnotically poetic, the Qur'an is the central text of divine guidance for a billion people.
3. **The Bible.** The Christian holy text through which God reveals himself to man. Even "Harry Potter" can't compete with its sales.
4. **"The Origin of Species"** by Charles Darwin. The basis of modern biology, the primary model for the diversity of life on earth.
5. **"Crime and Punishment"** by Fyodor Dostoevsky. No novel captures isolation, guilt, spiritual unraveling and salvation like it.

A CLASSIC YOU REVISITED WITH DISAPPOINTMENT:

"The Catcher in the Rye" by J. D. Salinger. When I was a teen, I thought Holden Caulfield was brilliant. Now I find his self-absorption hard to forgive.

A BOOK YOU HOPE PARENTS WOULD READ TO THEIR KIDS:

"The Giving Tree" by Shel Silverstein. The ultimate tale of selfless, undying love.

and neurological breakdown is desperately fine. Maybe that's the point: you can see the struggle on his face as he becomes possessed by the music and fights to maintain control. As the band becomes famous, the singer's hesitation to turn himself inside-out onstage curdles into genuine dread. At one point he refuses to perform. "They don't understand how much I give, how much it affects me," Curtis tells the band's manager as the audience screams for him. Riley's restraint punctures the dangerously romantic notion that Curtis, who killed himself in 1980 on the eve of the band's first U.S. tour, died for his art. He uses the singer's illness, and the toll that each show exacted from him, to explore the ambivalence that an artist can feel for his audience. Riley, who sings all of Curtis's songs in the film, won a British Independent Film Award for his work. But so far he's been overlooked by U.S. awards committees. Don't make the same mistake. —Jennie Yabroff

> **You can see the struggle on his face as he becomes possessed by the music and fights to maintain control.**

WEEK OF JANUARY 21

WORTH YOUR TIME

Finally, Spike's First Joint

Filmmaker Tyler Perry has built a mini-empire in Hollywood by portraying a certain type of African-American character: articulate, urbane and upwardly mobile. But Perry ("Why Did I Get Married?") hasn't broken any creative ground. In 1986, a scrappy NYU film graduate named Spike Lee laid the foundation for Perry's empire, introducing like-minded characters in his debut feature, "She's Gotta Have It"—and when Lee did it, Perry would've been barely old enough to see the salacious dramedy without his parents. This week, more than two decades later, Spike's first joint is being released on DVD.

I saw the film when I was 13, a case of my parents' being absent-minded or progressive, but either way, a fluke. I had never seen a character break through the fourth wall, so it felt as if I were hallucinating when the movie opened with Nola Darling (Tracy Camilla

Johns) wriggling out of a neatly made bed and talking straight to the camera. "I want you to know," she says, "the only reason I'm consenting to this is because I wish to clear my name."

Nola seeks to defend her reputation from an evergreen double standard. She's making time with three suitors: Jamie, who's clearly her soulmate; prissy male model Greer, and hip-hop geek Mars Blackmon (played by Lee). Naturally, she's labeled a tramp for playing the field like a man. The film's gender politics are as polarizing now as then: does Nola own her sexuality? Or is that simply what she tells herself to justify bedding losers?

The fact that gender and sexuality, as opposed to race, are the film's conversation points is proof of its singularity. Unlike the blaxploitation-era directors who paved his way, Lee chose to make a film about people who happened to be black, rather than one about black people.

"She's Gotta Have It" is clearly not the work of a veteran director. The performances are middling, and the movie often looks so ramshackle you wonder what Lee did with the rest of his meager $175,000 budget. But he still managed to create a confident debut with hints of the voice and flair he later perfected. The denizens of Spike's world are smart, subtle and talky, kind of like the sophisticated black Brooklynite that I like to think I've become. The verdict on Nola? Still pending. But the referendum on Spike Lee's talent has long since come back in his favor. —JOSHUA ALSTON

FAST CHAT

Fallen 'Idol'? Not So Fast.

Finally, the race is on. Not for the White House —we mean for "American Idol," which returns on Jan. 15. How will the country's biggest show fare during the writers' strike? And did "Idol" fix last season's low notes? (So long, Sanjaya.) Executive producer Nigel Lythgoe spoke to Ramin Setoodeh.

How will the Writers Guild of America strike affect the new season of "Idol"?

Everyone says it's going to be much bigger because of the strike. But my gut feeling is that people are going to say, "I'm not going to watch TV." A lot of TV executives are so small-minded, and they think people will watch any old crap they put on. Well, they won't.

Culture and the Arts-254 | JANUARY

Are you auditioning the contestants any differently?
For the first time, we allowed them to play instruments. We had one drummer sing "Hooked on a Feeling." I think our big mistake last year was that we didn't let the public get to know the contestants as we should have.

Is there a new Sanjaya?
Somebody who will steal the limelight because of their hair? I don't think so.

Last season drew a lot of complaints for its meanness. Have you scaled back on that?
There's a little cruel streak in all of us. If Simon Cowell is bored, he'll yawn. But he's not doing it for the camera. It's because he's such an a– –hole.

WEEK OF JANUARY 28

THEATER

How to Act Presidential

If you're suffering from P.P.E.—Premature Political Exhaustion—and wondering how you'll make it to this fall's election, here's an antidote. "November," a new Broadway comedy by David Mamet, introduces you to a candidate you'd never vote for, no matter what your partisan leanings. Charles H.P. Smith (Nathan Lane) is a president who's about to fail, disastrously, in his bid for a second term. He's raised only $4,000 for his campaign, and his poll numbers "are lower than Gandhi's cholesterol." Why? he wonders, as he paces the Oval Office, which he's equipped with an exercise machine, golf clubs and a globe that doubles as a beer cooler. "Because you f——ed everything," says his chief of staff, Archie (Dylan Baker). "They hate you." Big laugh.

Despite the play's contemporary hooks—the country is at war in Iraq but not Iran, though it's unclear whether this prez can tell the difference—Mamet has denied that the character is based on Bush. And "November" isn't razor-sharp satire (like his "Wag the Dog"); it's comedy so broad, it borders on shtik. "Chuckie," as his aide calls him, tries to shake down the head of the National Association of Turkey Manufacturers and battles his gay Jewish speechwriter (Laurie Metcalf). The cast is hilarious, the play frothy. You want serious theater? Tune into C-Span.

—CATHLEEN McGUIGAN

WORTH YOUR TIME

The Secret Lives of Teens

We meet Austin on page 77 of "Class Pictures," a new book of large-scale color portraits by Chicago-based photographer Dawoud Bey, culled from 15 years that Bey spent visiting high schools across the country. Austin has a blond buzz cut, beefy arms and a flat, tight-lipped expression as he leans forward on his desk. "What up?" Austin writes in his accompanying essay. "My favorite class in school is Science. I like to go out Friday nights and chill." On the next page we meet Carolyn, who rests her head on one hand, letting her dark hair drape onto her desk. Like Austin, she accepts the camera's gaze head on, but there is a wistful look in her eyes. Her father died of Lou Gehrig's disease during her sophomore year, Carolyn explains in her essay. "Your memories are engulfed with all that sadness," she writes. "And you try to get beyond that, but it's so hard."

Chilling out on a Friday night, dealing with a parent's death: looking at Bey's photographs reminded me of the vast spectrum of experiences in a typical high-school class. What secrets, I wondered, had my former classmates harbored? Maybe, without knowing it, I spent my junior year next to a Kevin (page 108) whose father had been in jail, or a Julia (69) who hid her sister's eating disorder from her family. There are many Austins in the book, too—kids who seem as yet untouched by adult concerns. The inequity of sadness among Bey's subjects is stark, but his tender portraits afford them all the same dignity. It's striking to see teens portrayed with so little sensation: there isn't a Gossip Girl in the bunch.

—JENNIE YABROFF

WEEK OF FEBRUARY 4

MOVIES

Nothing But The Truth At Sundance

Every bone-chilled veteran of the Sundance Film Festival will tell you the same thing: *stick with the documentaries.* You can always count the decent movies in the dramatic competition on one hand; the nonfiction films are more likely

Culture and the Arts-256 | FEBRUARY

"Roman Polanski: Wanted and Desired" was the first movie sold here in Utah, and with good reason. Focusing on the trial that convicted the brilliant filmmaker of unlawful sexual intercourse with a minor, director Marina Zenovich talks to people who've never spoken before (including Douglas Dalton, Polanski's lawyer), casting the case in a new light. Polanski isn't let off the hook, but the true villain of the piece is Judge Laurence J. Rittenband, a vain, publicity-obsessed martinet who died in 1993 and whose manipulations of both the prosecution and the defense make Polanski's decision to flee the country seem justified.

Artfully blending the personal and the political, "Nerakhoon (The Betrayal)" is a wrenching and lyrical epic about a Laotian family forced to flee their country at the end of the war in Vietnam and resettle in the United States. Ellen Kuras's codirector, Thavisouk Phrasavath, is the main subject of the film, which documents the United States' brutal clandestine operations in Laos and the devastating repercussions for the Laotians who worked on our side. Arriving in New York, the family members are dumped in a crack house and left to fend for themselves in a completely alien culture. It's a chronicle of deraci-

---

THE DIGNITY INDEX

We Wish We Knew How to Quit *You*, Mr. Gibson

A weekly mathematical survey of dubious behavior that measures, on a scale of 1 to 100, just how low a person can go

After Obama airs a national TV ad, **Hillary Clinton's** campaign shrieks that he broke a pledge to skip Florida as punishment for the state's decision to move up its primary. But it's impossible to run a national ad *without* including Florida because, duh, Florida is part of the nation. Let's grow up, people. Score: **12**

Facing trial for perjury, **Barry Bonds** tries to get the charges dismissed by claiming that the questions from prosecutors were too confusing. Score: **39**

Fox News got a thin apology from him, but radio host **John Gibson** still tops the Index for two days of cracking crude Heath Ledger jokes. Score: **72**

nation and survival that packs an emotional wallop.

For sheer entertainment, few movies, fact or fiction, could match "Man on Wire." In 1974 the elfin French daredevil Philippe Petit stunned the world by wire-walking (illegally, with no net) between the Twin Towers of the World Trade Center. Mixing re-creations, old footage and interviews, British filmmaker James Marsh shows us how Petit pulled off his astonishing feat. Marsh wisely never mentions 9/11, but the fate of the towers gives this thrilling tale a ghostly undertone. —DAVID ANSEN

WEEK OF FEBRUARY 11

STEROIDS

Raise Your Right Hand

Embattled sports trainer Brian McNamee is intensifying his efforts to prove that famed right-handed pitcher Roger Clemens used steroids. McNamee has told federal investigators and former senator George Mitchell's Major League Baseball inquiry that he injected Clemens with steroids and human-growth hormone. Clemens insists that he has never taken steroids and that McNamee gave him

> **Congress is pursuing evidence that McNamee hopes will corroborate his account.**

painkiller and vitamin shots. Now Congress is pursuing evidence that McNamee hopes will corroborate his account, according to his lawyer and Capitol Hill officials.

This week McNamee, Clemens and Andy Pettitte—another former McNamee client who is also Clemens's friend and ex-teammate—will all give closed-door testimony to congressional investigators in preparation for a House committee hearing later this month on Clemens's public challenge to the Mitchell Report's findings. McNamee's lawyer, Earl Ward, told NEWSWEEK that in his testimony, his client will recount a conversation he had several years ago with Jim Murray, a representative of Clemens's agents, in which the two of them discussed

Culture and the Arts-258 | FEBRUARY

how Clemens might be in trouble if baseball tightened up its drug-testing policies. But according to a source close to the investigation, who declined to be identified discussing sensitive material, Murray did not substantiate McNamee's version of events during an interview with Congress late last week. Murray's lawyer, Lawrence Finder, said his client "answered all of the [committee's] questions" but declined to discuss the details.

Ward says that Pettitte's testimony should also corroborate McNamee's claims. In 2002, McNamee says, Pettitte expressed to him an interest in HGH. "Why didn't you tell me about any of this stuff?" Pettitte allegedly asked. McNamee believes Pettitte was prompted by an earlier discussion he had with Clemens, though Ward concedes that Pettitte did *not* explicitly say so to McNamee. Pettitte's lawyer, Jay Reisinger, declined to comment.

—MARK HOSENBALL

WORTH YOUR TIME

Up 'Close' and Personal

We see a lot of portraits in the new documentary "Chuck Close." Most are the celebrated artist's meticulous, highly detailed paintings of himself and his friends. But the film's most revealing portrait involves neither paint nor canvas. It comes when director Marion Cajori interviews the artist Brice Marden, Close's friend since the 1960s. In a movie filled with art-world talking heads (Kiki Smith, Robert Rauschenberg), Marden's segment stands out for its psychological intensity. He begins fondly, reminiscing about losing many of his early works to Close in pool games. Then the monologue grows darker. Close's portraits are "eerie" and "irritating," Marden says, shifting in his chair, leaving viewers to wonder if it's the paintings or the painter that irritates him. "Chuck's a very strange guy," he allows, then trails off. Marden

"Chuck's a very strange guy."

talks about the "immense struggle" evident in Close's process—and the more he develops this notion, the more he struggles with his own words, contradicting and correcting himself. I saw "Chuck Close" twice, and both times people in the audience began laughing halfway through the scene, a collective nervous reaction to the sight of a man dismantling both himself and someone he considers a friend.

But Marden's ramble also has

moments of insight. Other artists in the film argue that Close's paintings are ultimately about marks on canvas, that the biography of the subject is unimportant. Marden points out that Close made "Frannie," a picture of his grandmother-in-law, by repeatedly pressing his inked thumb against the canvas, creating a portrait made of thumbprints. "The harder he pressed the image away, the more the image comes up," Marden says, creating an elegant metaphor for the push-pull of intimate relationships. "It's as though you add up all the details and you get the soul." That's an apt description of the scene, too.

—Jennie Yabroff

FAST CHAT

Notes From the Crack Trade

In the 2005 best seller "Freakonomics," sociologist Sudhir Venkatesh inspired a chapter about why crack dealers live at home with their moms. The chapter was based on seven years Venkatesh spent trailing actual dealers. As a first-year graduate student, he walked into a notorious Chicago drug den, clipboard in hand, and asked: "How does it feel to be black and poor?" That intro earned him access to the gang and its leader, a man he identifies only as "JT." Now a Columbia professor, Venkatesh documents those years in a new book, "Gang Leader for a Day." He spoke with Jessica Bennett:

You say the drug trade is about power and money. But JT calls it a social organ-ization. Which is it?

I was surprised that a street gang thought of itself as a legitimate member of the community. But in these poor circumstances, people sometimes turn to a gang for basic services. There was no government, so the gang would help maintain the apartments. There was no security, so the gang provided escorts for the elderly. And residents hated that, but they had no choice.

Some say you've used people to make a name and left them behind.

[Not] a day goes by where I'm not conscious of the ways I've made my career selling poverty. But ultimately I think the best thing I can do is keep poverty on the map.

You describe taking part in a beating. Where's the line?

I didn't want to take part; I came to the aid of somebody, and in doing so, kicked his attacker. But the fact is, I was sent out to study a very violent world, and there was no way I was not going to find myself in unpleasant situations.

WEEK OF FEBRUARY 18

FASTCHAT

More Than Just a Month

February of every year is Black History Month, and it's easy to tell when it's here because we're inundated with images of Martin Luther King Jr. and other celebrated African-Americans. All of it can seem mostly pro forma political correctness with little context and even less thought. But a new eight-volume set of books released this month, the African American National Biography (AANB), blows the dust off Black History Month by telling the stories of 4,080 black lives in America—past and present, famous and obscure. The series is edited by Henry Louis Gates Jr., director of the Institute for African and African American Research at Harvard University. He's also the creator of "African American Lives 2," on PBS throughout this month, and editor in chief of TheRoot.com, a new Web magazine about black issues published by NEWSWEEK's owner, The Washington Post Company. Gates spoke with NEWSWEEK's Raina Kelley.

What is the African American National Biography?

It is the largest history-recovery project in African-American studies. We included people who were

---

THE DIGNITY INDEX

A Sore Loser's Last-Second Patriot Act

A weekly mathematical survey of dubious behavior that measures, on a scale of 1 to 100, just how low a person can go

We don't pick on washed-up celebs as long as they stick to reality TV shows, but **Corey Haim**'s taking out a full-page ad in Variety to beg for work is totally fair game. Score: **28**

Internet viral-video star Amber Lee Ettinger sat out her home state's primary. In other words, **Obama Girl** did not vote for Barack Obama. Score: **59**

Super Bowl loser **Bill Belichick** stomps off the field before the clock expires, completing his evolution from sports hero to cartoon villain. Score: **91**

important in their time but have been stuck in suspended animation. Now they will never be lost again.

What are your favorite entries?

Richard Potter, a ventriloquist and magician, who became a millionaire in the 19th century. George Washington Bush, a frontiersman who settled in Washington Territory and was so respected by his white neighbors that they petitioned Congress to allow him to own land, which they did. The slave Onesimus, who told his master, Cotton Mather, that in Africa they take a little bit of smallpox and scratch it into the skin. That saved Mather's colony. Henry (Box) Brown was a slave who mailed himself in a crate to freedom. Then there was Cathay Williams, who cross-dressed and enlisted in the Buffalo Soldiers as William Cathay. Or Alice of Dunks Ferry [Pa.], born in 1686. She took tolls in Bucks County, Pa., and actually lived in three different centuries. These people are characters, and they deserve to be remembered.

What did the AANB teach you about the history of African-Americans in this country?

The interaction between black and white people was always much more complicated than we imagined. It wasn't ideal, but I'm astonished that in a racist society, black people found ways to express themselves. Yes, there were great tragedies, but there were lots of black people who managed to succeed in the face of oppression. They made a way out of no way.

Who is the AANB aimed at?

Everyone. The story of these people's lives will become assimilated into African-American

> **The interaction between black and white people was always much more complicated than we imagined.**

history and then into all the history books that usually write about great men or women or anonymous social movements. We have this picture in our minds of black lives' being one of unmediated misery. But when you read these stories, you see that black and white people were dealing with each other from the very beginning in ways outside of the slave-master paradigm.

What is the lesson of the AANB for African-Americans today?

It lets the sensitive, ambitious African-American know that they are not alone. That black people just like them existed from 1619. That the sky is the limit for African-Americans.

TRANSITION

His Magical Mystery Tour

MAHARISHI MAHESH YOGI, 91, HINDU TEACHER
Born in central India, the one-time spiritual guru to the Beatles is credited with introducing the West to Transcendental Meditation. He died last Tuesday at his home in the Netherlands. NEWSWEEK's *Sharon Begley offers her thoughts on the Maharishi's contribution to science.*

What Maharishi Mahesh Yogi gave the Beatles is the stuff of pop-music legend. During their otherwise disastrous stay in his ashram overlooking the Ganges River in northern India in the spring of 1968, the Beatles minus Ringo (he bailed after a week, saying he couldn't stomach the food) experienced a creative surge unlike any they'd ever had before—much of which ended up on the "White Album." The other legacy the Maharishi gave the West is more controversial. In 1971, he founded Maharishi International University (now the Maharishi University of Management) in Iowa, which has become the center for studies of Transcendental Meditation.

Almost immediately, scientists there began researching the effects of TM on subjects, ranging from job satisfaction to blood pressure: one study found TM reduced hypertension in older African-American men; another, that it could moderate the harm of strenuous physical exercise on the immune system and that it reduced anxiety.

But many scientists were not fully convinced of those findings, particularly because the studies often compared people who meditated with people who didn't. If meditators have lower levels of

> **What Maharishi Mahesh Yogi gave the Beatles is the stuff of pop-music legend.**

stress than nonmeditators, they wondered, maybe it was because only already-mellow people choose to meditate and stick with it? Or the placebo effect might explain the claimed benefits of TM: if you expect an intervention to help you, it often does. So perhaps it's the belief that TM will do wonderful things that produces benefits, not the actual meditation.

Whichever way you sway, the Maharishi deserves credit for introducing the study of meditation to biology. Hospitals from

Stanford to Duke have instituted meditation programs to help patients cope with chronic pain and other ailments. Scientists unaffiliated with the movement have been emboldened to study the effects of other forms of meditation on diseases from depression to psoriasis, with impressive results. Whatever you think of the "White Album," give the Maharishi credit for helping launch what's become a legitimate new field of neuroscience.

TELEVISION

Latter-day Domination

Maybe Mitt Romney should have taken up tango. While some voters are still uneasy about a Mormon presidential candidate, Americans seem plenty comfortable voting for Mormons in another type of election: prime-

---

A LIFE IN BOOKS

Ann Patchett

Patchett landed on the best-seller list with her 2001 novel "Bel Canto," a PEN/Faulkner Award winner about a hostage crisis in South America that has sold more than 1 million copies. Her most recent work is "Run," the story of a fictional mixed-race Boston family. Her list:

MY FIVE MOST IMPORTANT BOOKS

1 **"So Long, See You Tomorrow"** by William Maxwell. A perfect Swiss watch of a book: it weighs in at a scant 135 pages.

2 **"Independent People"** by Halldor Laxness. Iceland's Nobel Prize-winning masterpiece: dismal, hysterical and stunning.

3 **"The Awkward Age"** by Henry James. I'm tempted to recommend a dozen others, because you can't go wrong with James.

4 **"Miss Lonelyhearts"** by Nathanael West. Sentence by sentence, one of the most beautifully constructed novels I know.

5 **"Loving"** by Henry Green. He's a master of form, dialogue, character and political tensions brought on by class and war.

A CLASSIC BOOK THAT, UPON REREADING, DISAPPOINTED: George Orwell's **"Animal Farm."** The last time I had read it I was 12. Now I don't think it holds up past the age of 13.

A BOOK YOU HOPE PARENTS READ TO THEIR CHILDREN: All of Laura Ingalls Wilder's **"Little House on the Prairie"** books. The girls grow up to be smart and resourceful. What could be better than that?

time dance shows. Mormons have already won "So You Think You Can Dance" and "Dancing With the Stars," and two of the front runners on ABC's current hit "Dance War" are, yes, Mormon. "Some of the greatest dancing on TV is coming out of this community," says Kenny Ortega, director of the "High School Musical" movies, both of which were filmed in Utah to capitalize on a hotbed of dance talent that Ortega noticed while choreographing the opening ceremony for the 2002 Olympics in Salt Lake City. "Dance is part of our culture," says Lee Wakefield, chair of Brigham Young University's dance department. "Mormons danced when they crossed the plains to Utah, and one of the first buildings they built was a dance hall." "Dance War" favorite Zach Wilson says he's happy to help shatter the notion that Mormons "can't dance and don't know how to have fun." Maybe Romney should have moved more on his feet, less on the issues.

> "Mormons danced when they crossed the plains to Utah, and one of the first buildings they built was a dance hall."

—SALLY ATKINSON

WEEK OF FEBRUARY 25

STERIODS

Beanball on Capitol Hill

It began as a juiced-up soap opera about steriods in baseball, but the congressional inquiry into whether legendary pitcher Roger Clemens used performance-enhancing drugs has morphed into a bizarre partisan slugfest between politicians. Prior to last week's hearing with Clemens and Brian McNamee, his chief accuser and former trainer, both Democrats and Republicans said they simply wanted to examine Clemens's claim that he had been smeared by Major League Baseball's steroid investigation. But the televised inquisition split along party lines. Democrats, led by House Oversight Committee chair Rep. Henry Waxman, hammered Clemens over his shaky denials; most Republicans fumed about McNamee's history of lying.

Partisan tensions only escalated after

the hearing. According to McNamee's camp, GOP committee members went easy on Clemens because he's a well-connected Republican. The pitcher "travels in the same circles as the Bushes," McNamee lawyer Richard Emery told NEWSWEEK. "It's more than logical. It's demonstrated." (Emery also told the Associated Press that the White House would pardon Clemens if necessary.) In response, Clemens's lawyer Rusty Hardin said he had "no idea" whether his client is a Republican. Hardin confirmed that Clemens is a longtime pal of former president George H. W. Bush and that the two men spoke the day after MLB's steroid report was released. Clemens and his lawyers also made a round of very public visits to members of Waxman's committee prior to the hearing. But apart from that, Hardin said, Clemens had no contact with other Republicans or Bush family members, including the current president. Jean Becker, the elder Bush's chief of staff, said that the former president "has done no lobbying of any kind to anyone on the Hill or the White House, nor will he." Scott Stanzel, a spokesman for the current president, said that Emery's claims are "ludicrous." A check of federal campaign-finance records showed that Clemens has made no contributions to any political candidate or party.

Hardin conceded that Clemens's credibility took a hit during the hearing. His client, he said, participated despite the knowledge that his testimony could result in a perjury investigation by the Justice Department. (A Justice Department spokesman had no comment.) A committee official, who asked for

> **Partisan tensions only escalated after the hearing.**

anonymity when discussing internal deliberations, said the committee won't decide for at least a week whether to call for a criminal investigation. If it does, Republicans might balk—but two committee sources said that Waxman could go ahead with a criminal referral anyway. —MARK HOSENBALL

SPORTS

Super Bowl, Super Bust

Every Super Bowl loser leaves piles of suddenly worthless merchandise in its wake, but the tease of the New England Patriots' perfect season produced unusual extremes. Nike and Reebok each sunk several hundred thousand dollars into stillborn commercials pegged to a Pats win, while team owner Robert Kraft planned for a bonanza of post-perfect merch. Before the game, he applied for trademarks to use phrases such as "19-0" and "Perfect Season" on a litany of gear including greeting cards, jigsaw puzzles, kites and temporary tattoos, according to a copy of the application obtained by NEWSWEEK. Fans are crying jinx, but "if that were true we would've lost the AFC title game," says Patriots spokesman Stacey James. One thing is for sure: "18-1" garb is selling big—to Giants fans.

—TONY DOKOUPIL

FAST CHAT

'Everything I Cook Is Good'

Best-known for his 1995 hit "Gangsta's Paradise," Compton, Calif.-born rapper Coolio, now 44, is trying to move beyond the microphone. He's the star of a new weekly Webisode series on mydamnchannel.com called "Cookin' With Coolio," in which he pimps out his culinary skills and shares recipes for dishes such as "Tricked-Out Tilapia" and "Finger-Lickin', Rib-Stickin', Fall-Off-the-Bone-and-Into-Your-Mouth Chicken." Coolio, born Artis Leon Ivey Jr., spoke with NEWSWEEK's Jessica Bennett.

Coolio, where have you been?
I'm about to release [a new] album, "Steal Hear." My six children have grown up. I've been divorced. Me and my new woman are working on a clothing line. And I've developed my culinary skills to a fine point. I've also changed my style of dress—I wear a lot of suits now.

Ah, so you're a businessman?
Well, you either *be* the business or you get *played* by the business.

Do you still have your braids?
I sure do. I have them in a *brohawk*—that's a mohawk for a brotha. My hairline has started to recede, so I had to change it up a little bit.

How'd the cooking show evolve?
I've been cooking for a while; I even got a little formal training. Me and my cousin were playing around in the kitchen one day and I said, "Damn, what if we had a cooking show?" It became something we realized could be a reality.

And you're having fun?
I'm *ecstatic*. I don't think I've ever used that word before. This show is our baby—she's really beautiful and she's an Amazon woman.

What do you cook?
I've taken a lot of traditional black recipes and made them healthy—taking the cholesterol out, taking the butter out. I also do fusion: Mex-Italian, Blasian [black Asian], Ghitalian [ghetto Italian].

What's your best dish?
Everything I cook is good.

What makes your show different from all the others?
We use foods that poor people can afford. I'll take a chicken outta Compton and make it taste better than Foster Farms. I'll take a cow from Brooklyn and you can go get some Kobe beef and mine will taste better.

What's with all the show references to Shaka Zulu?

A LIFE IN MOVIES

Michel Gondry

An Oscar-winning writer-director, Gondry is known for trippy music videos and mind-bending films including "Eternal Sunshine of the Spotless Mind." His latest is "Be Kind Rewind," a comedy about video-store employees who reshoot classic films. His list:

MY FIVE MOST IMPORTANT MOVIES

1 **"L'Atalante."** Full of surrealism without being part of the surrealist group, it's the most poetic love story told on film.

2 **"The Great Dictator."** Shot before America was clearly against the Nazi regime, it shows Chaplin once again on the side of good.

3 **"Le Voyage en Ballon."** The first film I ever saw was this simple tale of an inventor traveling across France in a balloon.

4 **"Groundhog Day."** The perfect example of an accessible comedy with an incredibly smart concept. Bill Murray is a genius.

5 **"Stuck on You."** I saw it after my girlfriend abandoned me, and I totally felt like Matt Damon and Greg Kinnear: separated twins.

A FILM THAT YOU RETURN TO AGAIN AND AGAIN: It's not a film, but **"Mr. Show,"** an HBO comedy series from the 1990s. I'm addicted to it and I know it by heart. It's still so complicated and unique.

A FILM YOU HOPE PARENTS WILL SHOW THEIR CHILDREN: Well, my son watches a lot of Stanley Kubrick, but I wouldn't really advocate that. **"Le Voyage en Ballon"**? Like pure poetry, it gives you the feeling of flight.

I say "Shaka Zulu" because I've got a bad habit of saying "motherf——er." So instead of saying "s—t" or "f——," now I say *Shaka!*

Who's your main competitor?

I like Rachael Ray, I like Bobby Flay, I like all them cats. But they are not the Gourmet Ghetto, baby. My motto is, I cook better than your *Shaka Zulu* mama. And I wash my hands a lot.

So, Coolio: rapper turned culinary connoisseur?

Yeah. We're gonna transfer this to frozen foods, to restaurants. I'm going all the way.

Are you making a profit?

Coolio do not work for free, let me just say that. Coolio got six children, and Coolio likes nice things. And Coolio likes voluptuous women.

OSCARS

She's Also Edith Piaf

Marion Cotillard could win an Oscar on Sunday night for her remarkable portrayal of French chanteuse Edith Piaf in "La Vie en Rose." But there's another amazing Piaf performance in the movie, and it's delivered by someone you never see: French vocalist Jil Aigrot, who re-recorded many of Piaf's songs—including the crowd-pleaser "Padam Padam"—for the big screen. (Yes, Cotillard was lip-syncing.) Aigrot was discovered by Piaf's own secretary, Ginou Richer, who had written a book about the icon. In 2005 Aigrot went to a book signing by Richer and performed a Piaf song right there on the spot. Richer was startled by the similarity, so

> "I'm very blessed that people think it was Edith Piaf singing," she says. "But it's also difficult because I'm an artist."

a few months later, she suggested that Aigrot audition for the film's director, who decided against using nothing but original Piaf recordings because some songs didn't exist or the quality wasn't good enough.

Aigrot says she's proud of her work, except for one thing: she thinks she sounds a bit *too* much like Piaf. "I'm very blessed that people think it was Edith Piaf singing," she says. "But it's also difficult because I'm an artist. I have a career. My name is often in the dark." Aigrot's debut album, "Words of Love," could change all that when it's released next month. Or maybe not. It's an album of *more* Piaf songs.

—RAMIN SETOODEH

WEEK OF MARCH 3

TRANSITION

HBO's Killer With a Code

OMAR LITTLE, 34, ARMED ROBBER

A charming, cunning shotgun surgeon who made his living robbing drug dealers, Omar Little had an aura of permanence—amazing considering he wasn't a real person, he was a TV character (played by actor Michael K. Williams). On "The Wire," HBO's Baltimore

> More than any other death on "The Wire," Omar's made us know the agony of caring for a murder victim—even one who, by all rights, had it coming.

THE DIGNITY INDEX

The Question Is Elementary, My Dear Watson

A weekly mathematical survey of dubious behaviors that measures, on a scale of 1 to 100, just how low a person can go.

It's come to this for **Lindsay Lohan**: she takes off all her clothes for a magazine spread and everyone agrees it's a smart career move. Wasn't she an actress once? Score: **20**

Mohamed Al Fayed, father of Princess Di's lover, Dodi, accuses the CIA, MI6, French police, the Easter Bunny and Posh Spice of conspiring to kill the couple. Let it go. Score: **51**

Chris Matthews pummels woefully unprepared Obama backer **Kirk Watson** when the Texas pol can't name one Barack accomplishment. Great TV, though. Score: **78**

Culture and the Arts-270 | MARCH

crime drama, we're used to lives ending abruptly. But the death of Omar—a cult figure among "Wire" fans, felled by a bullet to the head from a tween triggerman—was especially jolting. And the subsequent scenes, in which news of his death spread, were even more sobering: neither the cops nor the corner boys showed any affect, a response that was faithful to the world of the show, but created dissonance between the observers and the observed.

We spent years with Omar. In his way, he was principled, committed to hustling those who hustled others. ("A man got to

---

TELEVISION

The Joke's on Them

This primary season, the presidential candidates got off easy: the 14-week writers' strike meant fewer political jokes from late-night-TV hosts. But no one escaped entirely—and no candidate got it worse than the guy who's already got the job.

Target of joke	Sept. 3, 2007—Jan. 31, 2008	Total # of jokes
George W. Bush		175
Hillary Clinton		68
Rudy Giuliani		29
Mitt Romney		28
John McCain		26
Mike Huckabee		24
Dennis Kucinich		21
Tommy Thompson		19
Barack Obama		18
Fred Thompson		11
Sam Brownback		8
John Edwards		6
Chris Dodd		6
Tom Tancredo		4
Bill Richardson		4
Joe Biden		3
Duncan Hunter		2
Mike Gravel		1

■ Democratic presidential candidate

■ Republican presidential candidate

BASED ON AN ANALYSIS OF THE POLITICAL AND PUBLIC-AFFAIRS JOKES IN THE MONOLOGUES OR OPENING SEGMENTS OF "THE TONIGHT SHOW," "LATE SHOW WITH DAVID LETTERMAN," "LATE NIGHT WITH CONAN O'BRIEN," "THE DAILY SHOW" AND (SINCE JULY 1, 2007) "THE COLBERT REPORT." EXCLUDES REPEAT OR ENCORE PERFORMANCES. FIGURES REFLECT AN INTERRUPTION DUE TO WRITERS' STRIKE, BEGINNING NOV. 5. SOURCE: CENTER FOR MEDIA AND PUBLIC AFFAIRS. GRAPHIC BY STANFORD KAY—NEWSWEEK

have a code," he said once.) His moral compass so endeared him to viewers that he long outlived the seven-episode arc his creators had originally planned for him. More than any other death on "The Wire," Omar's made us know the agony of caring for a murder victim—even one who, by all rights, had it coming. For a moment, we knew how it felt to have someone close to us die, and to wait in vain for someone to give a damn.

—JOSHUA ALSTON

WEEK OF MARCH 10

STEROIDS

Roger Dodger vs. the Feds

Democrats and Republicans on the House Oversight Committee jointly agreed to ask the FBI to investigate whether baseball legend Roger Clemens lied during a Feb. 13 hearing about whether he used performance-enhancing drugs—but that doesn't mean the partisan divisions on display at the hearing have been resolved. In an 18-page memo summarizing their investigation, Democratic staffers on the committee raised fresh doubts about Clemens's credibility. Among other issues, the document noted that investigators could find little evidence and even fewer witnesses to substantiate Clemens's claim that Brian McNamee, his former trainer, and others had injected him repeatedly with vitamin B-12 and the painkiller lidocaine.

Although House Republicans signed on to the demand for an FBI probe, they did not endorse the Democratic staff dossier. One GOP official, who asked for anonymity when discussing committee deliberations, said that contradictory testimony by Clemens's former teammate and close friend Andy Pettitte justified an FBI probe—but that some other accusations in the Democrats' dossier were "extraneous" and "unsupported." Some Capitol Hill Republicans remain skeptical about whether the hearing turned up enough evidence to successfully prosecute Clemens

> **Some Capitol Hill Republicans remain skeptical about whether the hearing turned up enough evidence to successfully prosecute Clemens for perjury.**

for perjury, though they acknowledge that federal investigators may already have (or could gather) additional evidence to solidify the case.

The Feds are trying to clear up questions about who will do the investigating. Despite speculation that the case ultimately will be turned over to the San Francisco G-men who have pursued steroids-related probes of Barry Bonds and other prominent athletes, FBI spokesman Richard Kolko told NEWSWEEK that control of the case was likely to remain with the FBI's Washington office. In a written statement, Clemens's lawyer, Rusty Hardin, said he welcomed the probe because it would be conducted according to rules that "very specifically level the playing field." —MARK HOSENBALL

ART

Still Life With Beach Towel

The gift shop at the New Museum of Contemporary Art in New York doesn't sell standard museum fare—no Monet neckties or Jackson Pollock jigsaw puzzles. Instead, the NCMA, which just opened its new building in November, carries much edgier stuff. There are $540 smocks from a pattern by Andrea Zittel, an artist known for living out in the desert in mobile survivalist cabins. You'll also find $30 canvas totes by pop-noir draftsman Richard Pettibon and $68 beach towels by fey portraitist Elizabeth Peyton. "I've always thought that every artist ought to have a cheap line," says conceptual artist John Baldessari, who has a coffee mug inscribed with his cheeky aphorism TIPS FOR ARTISTS WHO WANT TO SELL available at the new Broad Museum of Contemporary Art in Los Angeles.

Artist-made museum merchandise is on the rise. The San Francisco Museum of Modern Art, the Museum of Contemporary Art in Chicago and Boston's Institute of Contemporary Art are all getting into the act, striking deals with artists involving flat fees and cuts of the take. Next month SFMoMA will unveil a line of T shirts, silicon place mats and word puzzles by artist-designer Rex Ray. It's a way of allowing visitors to feel like they're taking home a genuine work of art. But is it really art, or just a gussied-up tchotchke?

"Since I don't see our curatorial department trolling the gift store for additions to the permanent collection," says Boston ICA retail manager Victor Oliviera, "it's probably a good guess that the shop doesn't carry 'real works of art'." For some, though, what they do carry is close enough.

—Peter Plagens

DVD'S

Sure, We've Got That!

In an age of cable-on-demand, Netflix and BitTorrent, it can be tough running a mom-and-pop video store. But give a few of these independent retailers credit for ingenuity: they've come across a novel trick for turning the competition into part of their supply chain. Instead of paying $20 or more for every obscure foreign or documentary title a customer requests, a few stores have begun using Netflix accounts to procure the title, slip it in a blank case and re-rent it to customers. "It's nice to be able to offer the latest foreign title that no one has heard of," says one Massachusetts store owner, who typically rents out 10 to 15 Netflix discs a month, saving more than $2,000 in annual inventory costs. (The $4.50-per-disc rental revenue more than covers his three Netflix accounts.) Ted Engen, president of the Video Buyers Group, which represents 2,000 independent video stores, says a small number of retailers have been exploiting Netflix in this manner for years. He thinks the problem has waned as DVD prices have come down, but suspects it could grow as pricey Blu-ray discs

The Netflix customer agreement clearly states that DVDs are to be used only for personal enjoyment, not for renting or loaning to others.

(which cost up to twice as much as existing DVDs) become more prevalent. "We could see this fire back up," Engen says.

It's not just video retailers. Last month the Sanbornton Public Library in Sanbornton, N.H., put an article in its local paper inviting the public to sign out DVDs via the library's Netflix account, effectively piggybacking the town's 2,900 residents on a single account. Right now the library is using Netflix's $16.99 three-discs-at-a-time membership, but "if we get a lot of requests, we might go up to the next level," says librarian Martha Bodwell.

Netflix, aware of the practice, is not a fan. Spokesman Steve Swasey says the Netflix customer agreement clearly states that DVDs are to be used only for personal enjoyment, not for renting or loaning to others. However, with 1.8 million DVDs shipping from Netflix warehouses every day and no obvious way to catch rental bandits, Netflix has limited ability to police it. Swasey says anyone caught doing it will receive a reminder that they're breaking the terms of their contract. How about sending a copy of "There Will Be Blood"? —DANIEL MCGINN

WEEK OF MARCH 17

TRANSITION

He Chose His Own Adventure

GARY GYGAX, 69, CO-CREATOR OF DUNGEONS & DRAGONS
A hero to self-proclaimed geeks everywhere, Gygax watched his pioneering role-playing game explode into a $1 billion phenomenon. Warren Spector, creative director at Disney Interactive Studios, shared these thoughts about his late colleague with NEWSWEEK's *N'Gai Croal:*

Everybody in the electronic-gaming industry should get down on their knees once a day, face north and give thanks to Gary. As sophisticated and mainstream as videogames have become, we have them largely because of the work that he and Dave Arnesen, his partner, did back in 1974, when they were just playing games in the basement of the library in Lake Geneva, Wis. And to this day, if you look at most role-playing games now on consoles or on computers, you still find all the things that Gary and Dave created in their original Dungeons & Dragons rule set. Concepts like strength, intelligence, dexterity, wisdom—it's all still there. People are in some very real sense still playing D&D, even if they're not sitting around a table for eight hours on a Saturday, eating chips and drinking too much Dr Pepper.

> **There was this mad creative energy that emanated from him.**

I played D&D for the first time in 1978, when I was 22 or 23. It was a bunch of writers—these crazy, creative people playing this strange new game that, frankly, scared my mother to death. I had heard that there was this wild game that allowed you tell your own stories as you played. You mean I don't just roll dice and move around a board and win? I can really become the hero of my own adventure? That, I think, was the magic of it. Gary made so many of us who were outsiders, who were nerdy guys, feel special and creative. It quickly became an important part of my life. And it almost killed my graduate-school career.

I lived in Lake Geneva for a few years, so I met him a couple of times. There was this mad creative energy that emanated from him. You could totally see where D&D came from just by interacting with him. He was gracious and articulate. And theatrical. He was a larger-than-life sort of guy in a lot of ways—but maybe that was just me being a little bit of a hero worshiper. I'm really surprised how hard this news has hit me. I got the call about his death while I was driving, and I had to pull over. It's like a little part of my life that's just gone. I mean, I owe that man my career.

THE SECOND TERM

So You Think You Can Dance: A Presidency

It's not easy being a lame duck with low approval ratings. You've got to go the extra mile just to get attention. President Bush has found a new way, and the good news is, it's working. The bad news? It's working.

Feb. 21, 2008: Liberia. Just a few weeks ago, during his tour of Africa, Bush very nearly got jiggy with it. An inescapably white performance, and yet charming in its arrhythmic way.

April 24, 2007: The White House. This time, during Malaria Day festivities, he got a little too hot, throwing his arms up in the air like he just didn't care. He later commandeered a guest performer's drum.

March 5, 2008: The White House. An ambivalent, unfocused, time-killing performance as he awaited John McCain's arrival for a celebratory grip-and-grin. You're the *president*. Don't you have stuff to do?

DOCUMENTARIES

A Ticket Out of Hell

"See this right here?" says the young black man, dribbling a basketball in New York's rugged Coney Island. "This here can get you a long way." Some people are unsettled by the idea that a game can be such a potent symbol of escape for so many inner-city teens, but it's an ivory-tower argument at odds with street-level reality. Two new documentaries, one a conventional history lesson, the other a triumph of new-media storytelling, examine the past and present of hoop dreams as a ticket out of hell.

On March 16 and 17, ESPN will air director Dan Klores's four-hour "Black Magic," which examines the rise of basketball at black colleges during the civil-rights era, a time when hardwood floors were the only level playing field around. Klores's film has great stories to tell, such as the secret 1944 scrimmage between white Duke University students and a team from the North Carolina College for Negroes, a game that could've been deadly if word got out. (NCCN won, 88-44.) "Born Ready," meanwhile, is "Hoop Dreams" told in real time— and on the Web. Each week at bornready.tv, Fader Films will post a new four-minute episode tracing the ups and downs of Coney Island star Lance Stephenson's junior year: the windmill dunks, the pregame trips through metal detectors, the stupid fight that earns him a brief suspension. It's the story of a talented, temperamental kid whose future is bright, but not assured. Basketball, these two films argue, really can "get you a long way." The question, then and now, is how far?

—Devin Gordon

TEENS

Branding for Beginners

Chanel vamp lip gloss, Jimmy Choo heels, Gauloises cigarettes, Absolut vodka: they're the kind of brand-name products you'd expect to find in a glossy magazine. But they're popping up with astounding frequency in novels aimed at teen girls, according to a new study by Naomi Johnson, a communications-studies professor at Virginia's Longwood University. Johnson looked at six best-selling novels from the

"Gossip Girl," "A-List" and "Clique" series, and found that brand names appeared an average of more than once per page: 1,553 references in all. Among them were 65 allusions to brand-name alcohols, cigarettes or prescription drugs. The brand names helped drive plotlines and define characters, says Johnson, who also noticed a degree of snobbery at work: almost all 22 references to Keds served to label the girl wearing them a loser. Other lessons: don't wear Target bikinis; do wear Chanel. (A spokesperson for Alloy Entertainment, a marketing-firm subsidiary that holds the copyright for each line of books, told NEWSWEEK that it does not accept payment for product placement in any of its titles.) "The Judy Blume books I read as a kid were about life lessons and defining yourself," says Johnson. "The life lesson here is that you can buy your identity."

—Eve Conant

WEEK OF MARCH 24

WORTH YOUR TIME

Songs in the Key of Life

"Young @ heart" was a movie that I approached with dread. For starters, there was that title—so uncool. And a documentary about a chorus of senior citizens singing covers of the Clash, James Brown and Prince sounded like a recipe for cloying, life-affirming clichés.

How wrong I was. "Young @ Heart" is a gem I can happily recommend to anyone. It follows 24 men and women in Northampton, Mass., for seven weeks as they prepare for a nearby concert (they call themselves Young @ Heart). Their dedicated musical director, Rob Cilman, is a hard and gifted taskmaster—and at least 45 years younger than the oldest member, Eileen Hall, 92, who sings lead on "Should I Stay or Should I Go." The rehearsal sessions can be hilarious, as the group repeatedly stumbles through Allen Toussaint's "Yes We Can Can," but the specter of death is never far away: not all of them will make it to the final concert.

There are scenes in this exhilarating movie that startled

> **If I didn't hate the phrase, I'd even call it life-affirming.**

me with their power. The group performs at a low-security prison, and the reactions of the young, tough cons—caught by surprise by the deep feelings the concert evokes—are unforgettable. At the climactic concert, Fred Knittle, a heavyset man with a playful wit, sings a spare, heart-piercing rendition of Coldplay's "Fix You." His singing, informed by the recent death of one of the group's cherished members, contains the wisdom and emotional directness you hear in Johnny Cash's late acoustic recordings. "Young @ Heart," which opens April 9, sends you out of the theater transformed. If I didn't hate the phrase, I'd even call it life-affirming.

—DAVID ANSEN

MUSIC

Love Me, Love My Mix Tape

It took hours to make: every free moment curled by the boombox, the local radio station's song-request line set to speed dial, the volume knob turned loud enough to hear, but quiet enough not to wake Mom and Dad. Then, finally, the master product: a flawless combination of Alanis Morissette, Nirvana and Boyz II Men—decorated, doodled on and packaged in that familiar square case—that would become the soundtrack to a fleeting eighth-grade romance.

Ah, the mix tape. Philips first unveiled its cassette in 1963, but the durable plastic has long since been replaced by the MP3. Still,

> **"Cassettes are the last refuge of the music nerd," says Jay Cook.**

what's old is always new again eventually, and the cassette tape has a burgeoning cult following that, like the vinyl obsession of generations before, has made it hip again among the audio underground. "Cassettes are the last refuge of the music nerd," says Jay Cook, a New York DJ and cultural marketing specialist.

Today, DJs covet old-school mix-tape sets by artists like Dr. Dre, and dozens of companies have sprung up to convert your yesteryear mixes to CD. There's a podcast, Mixtape Songs, devoted exclusively to other people's dusty old mix tapes, an "International Mixtape Project" where fans exchange tapes by mail—even cassette-themed art, clothing and computer accessories. Remember the Casio ghetto blaster you tossed out on the curb, or the clunky

Sony Walkman you gave to your little brother? They're reselling for upwards of $100 on eBay. Brooklyn rockers MGMT recently sent out demos in cassette form (and a player with each package). And leave it to the usually gadget-snobby hipsters to carry their iPods inside the hollowed-out cases of vintage Walkmen—the retro *look* without the retro sound.

Cassettes may never rival the warm vibrations of vinyl or the crispness of an MP3. But to anyone reared in the 1980s or '90s, tapes remain a testament to youth, a reminder of the "love and ego involved in sharing music," as Sonic Youth frontman Thurston Moore put it in a 2005 tribute. And—assuming you've still got a tape deck—they'll probably last longer than any teenage romance.

—JESSICA BENNETT

WEEK OF MARCH 31

FAST CHAT

Glimpses of A Golden Age

While Major League Baseball opens its season Tuesday showcasing its future—the Oakland A's face the champion Boston Red Sox in Tokyo—former MLB commissioner Fay Vincent has kept a keen eye on the game's past. His second volume of oral histories, "We Would Have Played for Nothing," featuring stars of the '50s and '60s, hits stores next week. He talked with NEWSWEEK's Mark Starr.

That's a sentimental title.
It came from Brooks Robinson, who said, "The owners weren't very smart. We would have played for nothing." I wondered about the title because, of course, in some sense it's not true. But it does get at the generational difference. We're all looking back at what was considered to be a rosy time in baseball. It was never what we think it was.

Why are these oral histories so important?
I knew that my great friend, Larry Doby, the first black player in the American League, had cancer. I started this endeavor [be-

cause] I was concerned that people were going to die away and we wouldn't have their stories.

How distressed are you by recent issues about steroid use?

This off-season was awful. But people are voting with their feet. They go to the ballpark. Baseball is booming again.

Is MLB immune to the damage?

The cheating is a very big threat. There is the potential of losing the belief that it's a fair competition. I don't think fans will stay if the cheating is pervasive. Take the 100-meter dash. Will we ever again look at women running the dash and not think of Marion Jones cheating at the Olympics?

Does baseball have any credibility left in tackling this problem?

I think the Mitchell Report was a noble one. It was flawed only because the union wouldn't participate. The union's record is both consistent and abysmal. It never wants to deal with these issues.

Isn't baseball a special case because of the reverence for numbers? Has that been lost?

The last 10 or 15 years, everything is tainted. I don't know if we could have stopped it. Look, I was there, I was part of the problem. I never thought steroids was going to be as big an issue as it became because I thought it was a muscle-building drug. I looked at [Hank] Aaron and [Willie] Mays and they weren't muscle guys. It was all about quickness. I thought it was a football problem. I thought Jose Canseco was an anomaly.

TRANSITION

Through His Viewfinder

PHILIP JONES GRIFFITHS, 72, PHOTOGRAPHER

Photojournalism has lost one of its giants. A member of the esteemed Magnum photo agency since 1966, the Welsh-born Griffiths was a canny observer of daily life, as is evident in the pictures he made on walks through countless cities. But he'll be remembered best for his work during the Vietnam War, culminating with his 1971 book, "Vietnam Inc.," which helped accelerate the West's disillusionment with the conflict. "Not since Goya," said Henri Cartier-Bresson, "has anyone portrayed war like Philip Jones Griffiths."

—SIMON BARNETT

TRANSITION

A Futurist in A Hula Skirt

ARTHUR C. CLARKE, 90, AUTHOR

Clarke, who died of a heart attack last week in Sri Lanka, where he had lived since 1956, thrilled fans with his uncanny predictions and darkly prophetic stories, including "2001: A Space Odyssey." He co-wrote his final novel, "The Last Theorem," with Frederik Pohl, a longtime friend who shared these memories:

Arthur was a celebrity, but he was also a regular cut-up on the futurist circuit. We traveled the world together in the 1960s and 1970s, attending conferences and joking about the shape of things to come. Of course, Arthur's jokes had a way of coming true. He had so much confidence in his own ability—some people even called him "Ego Clarke"—that distant predictions didn't scare him. He talked in detail about moon landings and satellite communication before anyone else. In fact, he often joked that his visions were too distant to profit from—"the patent would be expired if I got it now." He was loquacious and intelligent, competitive and solitary, with very few close friends. But he loved to entertain a crowd. One min-ute he'd play the self-serious sage, the next he'd thrown on a hula skirt. During a break from a NASA conference in Georgia, when we were still young and spry, we bicycle-jousted with other colleagues. I pedaled, with Arthur on the handlebars. I don't recall if we won. With friends, he never kept score.

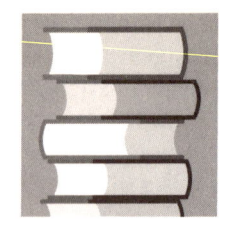

TRANSITION

The Talented Mr. Minghella

ANTHONY MINGHELLA, 54, FILM DIRECTOR

Anthony Minghella knew a lot about grief and loss. His first movie, "Truly, Madly, Deeply," a movie cherished by the few who saw it, is about a widowed musician (Juliet Stevenson) who's visited by her late cellist husband (Alan Rickman). Funny and incredibly moving, it showed off Minghella's rare sensitivity and intelligence as a writer and his gift for coaxing remarkable performances from his casts, a talent he would demonstrate again in his Oscar-winning "The English Patient," in the daring "The Talented Mr. Ripley" and in his Civil War epic "Cold Mountain."

But with the news of his untimely death, it's that haunting first film that springs to mind, for it understands so well the acute pain of mourning. I first met the man at a dinner in Los Angeles with director Randa Haines, whose movie "The Doctor" he had rewritten. His gentle, soft-spoken presence created an aura of intimacy that you wanted to share; it was easy to see why actors were drawn into his collaborative embrace. Yet under the warmth was the steel will necessary to marshal his epic, darkly romantic visions to the screen. A gifted playwright and an acclaimed opera director, Minghella considered himself a writer first, one lucky enough, he once said, to "be able to direct the films that I wrote." But not, it turned out, lucky enough to have the long and splendid career he deserved. —DAVID ANSEN

WEEK OF APRIL 7

VIRAL VIDEO

Bathing John Malkovich

John Malkovich's latest role is a bit of a shocker: the A-list thespian can be seen now in a fleshy video at Superdeluxe.com, sitting in a bathtub. With another man. Getting the business end of a loofah.

No, this is not another embarrassing celebrity sex video. Malkovich, who is apparently down for anything, is the first guest in a new Web-only talk show called "Bathing With Bierko," the sudsy brainchild of producer Robert Cohen and actor Craig Bierko ("Scary Movie 4," "Cinderella Man"). In the debut episode, we are confronted with the startling image of Bierko sitting behind Malkovich in a tiny tub. Both men appear to be naked (though, sadly, Bierko tells NEWSWEEK they both wore trunks) as the host squishes soapy water all over Malkovich's pate and leans in for a vigorous scalp massage, all while conducting perhaps the most peculiar interview ever pulled off with a straight face. (Bierko: " 'Portugal' is one of those words where if I repeat it over and over again it loses its meaning. Have you ever done that?" Malkovich: "No.")

It's funny, it's disturbing— and it's viral-video catnip: 30,000 people had watched the three-minute clip by the weekend. If you find yourself cringing through it, Bierko says that's the point—to spoof the awkward false intimacy of talk shows. He pitched it to Malkovich, he says, as "Charlie Rose, but it'll just be silly chatter. And [Malkovich] said, 'Yeah, I'll do it.' I had to refrain from asking him 'Why?'" Bierko's lining up more guests, including an Oscar winner, but won't spill any names.

He *is* happy to divulge, however, that the show's bathtub has an unlikely Hollywood provenance: it

30,000 people had watched the three-minute clip by the weekend.

used to be Bette Davis's. The tub is now in a house owned by Bierko's friend, the actress Carrie Fisher. Any chance she'll soap up next?
—BRIAN BRAIKER

WEEK OF APRIL 14

BLOGS

Stuff Other People Like

What do recycling, farmers markets and "The Wire" have in common? If you've ever read Stuff White People Like, the satirical blog that has clocked 20 million hits since its January debut, you'd have your answer. Random House handed the site's author a reported $350,000 book deal—and that might explain the proliferation of knockoff sites by minorities poking fun at their own. Now there's Stuff Educated Black People Like (No. 8: business cards), Stuff Asian People Like (No. 46: cutting in line), Stuff Jewish Young Adults Like (No. 4: Ultimate Frisbee) and more. The sites, of course, are a joke. "I'm not speaking the gospel here," says Charlee Renaud, the educated black creator of Stuff Educated Black People Like. It's true: her list shows that other EBPs prefer neo-soul.

—JESSICA BENNETT

GAMBLING

Go Ahead, Make Their Day

There's obvious allure in a film like the current box-office hit "21," a reality-based account of MIT students who took Vegas for millions at blackjack tables in the 1990s. Like its source, Ben Mezrich's bestselling book "Bringing Down the House," the film glamorizes card counting, the practice of tracking dealt cards to gain an edge over the house. But it provokes a question: why would casinos embrace a film that shows them getting scammed? "Casinos were lining up to host the premiere," says Jeff Ma, who led the real MIT team and appeared in "21," which was shot at the Planet Hollywood casino. That's because card counting isn't nearly as easy or profitable as it looks in the film— and Vegas is happy to let you learn that lesson the hard way.

> **Card counting isn't illegal, but casinos will boot you out if they catch you trying it.**

"This movie is great for Vegas. It perpetuates the myth that blackjack is beatable," says Ma, explaining amateurs will try it "and fall apart at the table."

Card counting is not a total sham. Blackjack is a game of probability, and each dealt card reveals valuable information about

---

THE DIGNITY INDEX

My Guest Tonight Is That Blind, Idiot Umpire

A weekly mathematical survey of dubious behavior that measures, on a scale of 1 to 100, just how low a person can go.

Five years too late, **Moises Alou** bails out hated Cubs fan Steve Bartman, saying he wouldn't have caught That Foul Ball even if Bartman had stayed out of his way. Score: **19**

Known for his softball questions, CNN host **Larry King** plays hardball at his 9-year-old son's Little League game, arguing a call so loudly that the umpire tells him to zip it or else. Score: **28**

Air America host **Randi Rhodes** gets caught on video calling Hillary Clinton a word that rhymes with (and is much nastier than) "bore." Score: **65**

the remaining cards. When the count is favorable—meaning the deck is laden with 10s and face cards—the advantage shifts to the player. But mastering the count takes impeccable concentration and years of practice, says Anthony Curtis, publisher of the Las Vegas Advisor, a monthly newsletter on how to keep your shirt in Sin City. Most people can't do it, and those who can earn only about 1 percent back on their bets over the long term. And that's if they get away with it: card counting isn't illegal, but casinos will boot you out if they catch you trying it. "People think it's an automatic winner and it's not," says one Planet Hollywood host, who asked for anonymity discussing casino strategy. "It's nothing that any of us lose sleep over." Try it, and you probably will. —TONY DOKOUPIL

FAST CHAT

You Say You Want an Evolution?

His resume is loaded: lawyer, economist, presidential speechwriter—and beloved monotone teacher. Now Ben Stein ("Bueller? Bueller?") is taking on the role of moral crusader. In "Expelled: No Intelligence Allowed," a documentary that opens April 18, Stein dissects Darwinism and what he calls its monopoly on American classrooms. He spoke with NEWSWEEK's Jessica Bennett:

Why did you make this film?
Darwinism is a brilliant theory, but to say it has all the answers would not be truthful or sensible. And today's students aren't learning that.

And academia has a role in that?
There are a number of scientists and academics who've been fired, denied tenure, lost tenure or lost grants because they even suggested the possibility of intelligent design. The most egregious is Richard Sternberg at the Smithsonian, the editor of a magazine that published a peer-reviewed paper about ID. He lost his job. Some of the people we interviewed wouldn't even talk on camera for fear of the repercussions. Our goal is to encourage free speech.

In the film you compare Darwinism to Nazism. Is that fair?
Darwinism was very popular with Hitler's Nazi party, who explicitly said life is about survival of the fittest. [That] led to horrible consequences.

Are you worried you'll be called the right-wing Michael Moore?
I don't purposely try to make myself look goofy or offensive. But if our movie ... provokes as much thought and consideration as his do, we'd be happy.

WEEK OF APRIL 21

TELEVISION

Anchored to The Ground

CBS News had a problem. It was 1952, and the network had dispatched its stars to the first nationally televised Republican National Convention. But CBS wanted to showcase an impressive rookie, Walter Cronkite. A young producer named Don Hewitt, later of "60 Minutes" fame, conjured up the image of a relay race: each journalist would do a segment, then hand off to the next. Cronkite would be the "anchor leg." Three weeks later Cronkite was on his way to becoming the "most trusted man in America."

CBS News now faces a far more difficult challenge, according to Hewitt, 85. The network says Katie Couric will lead its convention coverage this summer, but her ratings have dropped from 10 million households in September 2006 to about 6 million now, and gossips are predicting a post-election departure for her. She's not the only one struggling. Last year, according to the Project for Excellence in Journalism, ABC, CBS and NBC averaged a total of 23.1 million viewers a night for their network news programs, down 5 percent, or 1.2 million, from 2006, compared with an average annual slide of 1 million viewers over the previous 25 years. Hewitt thinks anchors no longer possess the magnetism to draw new viewers. "They're good but not great," he says. "There are no more Cronkites and Huntleys and Brinkleys." Also, with longer work hours and longer commutes, fewer people are home for 6:30 newscasts, and many turn to the Internet instead.

CBS wouldn't comment; NBC News president Steve Capus wasn't available. "Network news [is] still drawing by far the largest audiences in any media today," says a spokesman for ABC News. Even Hewitt isn't for tossing out the anchor format altogether. He thinks the shows should insert local news anchors into the national broadcasts in one- or two-minute spots to boost their regional appeal. Maybe today's anchors don't need to be the most-trusted people in America—just the most trusted on the block. —JOHNNIE L. ROBERTS

WEEK OF APRIL 28

WORTH YOUR TIME

Three Decades in Madrid

If Antonio Lopez-Garcia's "Lucio's Balcony" were not a great painting on its own, then the circumstances of its creation would clinch the matter. It took the 72-year-old Spanish realist 28 years to complete, from 1962 to 1990. That's partly due to his painting method: on site, same time of day, same season for each session. But it's also because he began the picture—which is now on view in a retrospective of his work at Boston's Museum of Fine Arts—as the setting for a portrait of friends, who soon moved away. Then the apartment changed hands three times. The most recent owners allowed López-García to set up his easel in the same spot and, decades later, finish.

The result is a brilliant combination of the artist's early "magic realism" and his mature style of planar symphonies dedicated to the architecture of his beloved Madrid. The work looks restrained, but López-García gets more chromatic melody out of his muted, chalky palette than most artists do from primary colors. When he decided "Lucio's Balcony" needed more space, he simply added more wood panels and let the seams show—realism within realism. As he explained some of the painting's nuances to me in Boston last week, López-García couldn't resist running his hands over the textures. "I suppose they have to allow *him* to touch if he wants to," said a viewer nearby.

López-García admires Edward Hopper and Andrew Wyeth, but his work is quintessentially Spanish—just go upstairs and look at the concurrent exhibition of Spanish painting from El Greco to Velázquez. Believe me, he doesn't suffer at all by comparison.

—PETER PLAGENS

BOOKS

In the Valley of the Dolls

There was a three-year period during my adolescence when Jessica and Elizabeth Wakefield, the heart-stealing twins of Francine Pascal's "Sweet Valley High" series, were, like, my best friends and biggest idols. I'd curl up in the library and speed through their adventures with boys and boobs. They were everything I wanted to be: pretty, popular and fun, with beach-bum boyfriends who all had names like Todd. To this day, those books are still a nostalgia bomb for most girls (sorry, *women*) my age. So when I heard they were being rereleased this month— updated to reflect modern teen tastes—I was giddy. As series editor Beverly Horowitz puts it, "School dramas, sister issues and California beaches never go out of style."

Actually, they do—at least for this former fan. The series updates are pretty minor (Liz writes a gossip blog on top of her duties at the school paper; the girls ditch their Fiat for a Jeep), but the characters I once loved now remind me more of the ice queens from "Gossip Girl" than figures from my own childhood. "Double Love," the first of the updated series, begins with Jessica whining about how fat and disgusting her "perfect size 4" body is. (Note: in the old books, Jessica was a "perfect size 6.") Later, she invents a sexual assault to drive a wedge between her sister and her crush. She's pathological and knifing—a "mean girl" to the core. Yet to everyone around her, she's still *so utterly cool*. I hope young fans see through her—but I sure didn't. Now? With my grade-school infatuation long gone, the girls read to me the way they really are: just a couple of bimbos from the Valley. —JESSICA BENNETT

WEEK OF MAY 5

FAST CHAT

New Hero of The High C's

Peruvian-born tenor Juan Diego Flórez, 35, sang "La Fille du Régiment" at the Metropolitan Opera last week, and was cheered wildly after the showpiece aria "Ah! Mes Amis," with its nine high C's. He then sang an encore, hitherto banned at the Met, with a single exception: Luciano Pavarotti during a performance of "Tosca" in 1994. Flórez spoke with NEWSWEEK's David Gates.

Why have you been the one to break the ban on encores?

I don't know. But since I began singing this opera the public has asked me for an encore, first at La Scala last year, then abroad, even in Tokyo. The word spreads, and it becomes like a tradition. At La Scala I didn't know I was breaking a ban of 75 years. It's better not to know.

Are you hurt now if they *don't* want an encore?

No, no, no. Because sometimes you're glad you're not doing all those C's again.

Is "Ah! Mes Amis" really as difficult as everyone says?

My repertoire is the bel canto and the high tenor, and in that repertoire everything's difficult. But for me, this piece is not *extremely* difficult, and often I quite enjoy singing it.

As a teenager, you had a different repertoire.

Yes, in Peru I had my rock band. I played guitar, keyboards, sang—I played the drums sometimes.

What kind of guitar?

I don't remember, because it was a cheap one. I didn't have money to buy a Fender. Something without a brand, maybe.

Do you perform tonight?

No. I'm doing an interview with [costar] Natalie Dessay at the Metropolitan Opera Guild. *That's* my performance for tonight.

WORTH YOUR TIME

A Writer's Brush With Fate

"Havanas in Camelot," a posthumous collection of William Styron's essays, transports us back to an era when being a novelist meant a kind of lustrous celebrity, as Styron and his contemporaries ("our vintage"—Norman Mailer, Truman Capote, James Baldwin) jockeyed to inherit the outsize mantles of Hemingway and Faulkner. Each of Styron's 14 pieces—mostly about life and writing in the '50s and '60s—is a gem. Here he is, a debut author, lounging around Paris cafés and smirking at the hordes of "leonine" Hemingway poseurs. Here he is, a short time later, a luminary on the rise, sailing off Cape Cod and smoking contraband Cubans with JFK (hence the title).

The collection's best piece is set at a moment when this heady future seemed impossible, during Styron's Marine training in 1944. It opens on the medical ward, where Styron's been diagnosed with syphilis—the "great pox" whose contraction would prevent a guy from ever making officer. Even on the venereal wing, syphilis had a dubious distinction. It was rare, which meant the getter must have gotten it in the most squalid of ways. "In square, church-going America at the time of my diagnosis," Styron writes, "a syphilitic was regarded . . . as a degenerate, and a dangerously infectious one at that."

It's a view held by Styron's own doctor, who misdiagnoses his patient. When the mistake is exposed, Styron is giddy to recover a life he'd counted as lost. Fighting in "the bloody Pacific" was a horror he could deal with, he writes; "in that gray ward, I'd nearly been broken by fears that were beyond imagining." Also beyond imagining, just then: Paris, the president, literary fame—the world his essays capture with a fleeting grace.

—Katie Baker

WEEK OF MAY 12

WORTH YOUR TIME

Rage Against the Machine

Filming a documentary in a war zone is no easy task. To make "Heavy Metal in Baghdad," a new film about Iraq's only known metal band, Eddy Moretti and Suroosh Alvi of Vice Films smuggled themselves into the country, shelling out thousands of dollars for security and dodging constant disorder. But for the members of Acrassicauda, the band those filmmakers set out to find, chaos is a way of life. To get to practice, they cope with roadblocks, curfews and death threats. To fuel their amps, they use gas generators. They play shows amid power outages and mortar rounds, and risk being thrown in jail for headbanging. At one point, their practice space—a rare solace amid the insanity of Baghdad—is blown up, sparing their lives but destroying all their equipment.

In many ways "Heavy Metal in Baghdad," which hits theaters in New York and Los Angeles this

---

THE DIGNITY INDEX

[Insert Your Own Pocket-Rocket Joke Here]

A weekly mathematical survey of dubious behavior that measures, on a scale of 1 to 100, just how low a person can go

Thirty years after the fact, **Barbara Walters** needlessly reveals that she had an affair with a married U.S. senator. Why now? Because she's got a new memoir to push. Score: **37**

At a panel on sports blogging, author **Buzz Bissinger** goes berserk on Deadspin blogger Will Leitch, bullying and cursing away what could've been some valid points about journalism. Score: **43**

Here's how bad it's gotten for **Roger Clemens**: all those alleged affairs come to light, including one with a country-music star that began when she was 15—and no one is shocked. Score: **55**

month, is a tale of Iraqi youth. Acrassicauda's young members—Tony, Marwan, Faisal and Firas—are educated and Westernized, and though they're intensely loyal to Iraq, they yearn for a place where a Slip Knot T shirt won't get you killed. Playing heavy metal in a Muslim country has never been encouraged, but there was a brief time— between Saddam's fall and the chaos that ensued—when, like many Iraqis, they hoped real change would come. Their music, though, only underscores how the song remains the same: the grinding percussion and wrenching lyrics of tunes like "Massacre" conjure the whizzing missiles, mortar blasts and shotgun fire of daily life.

"Sometimes, if I don't play drums as hard as I can, as fast as I can, [I feel like] I'm going to kill someone," says Marwan.

"Sometimes, if I don't play drums

A LIFE IN BOOKS

Randall Kennedy

In "Sellout," Kennedy—a Harvard law professor best-known for his 2002 history of the N word—investigates another fraught subject: betraying your race.

MY FIVE MOST IMPORTANT BOOKS

1. **"The American Political Tradition"** by Richard Hofstadter. It ignited my interest in history.
2. **"Black Boy"** by Richard Wright. It indelibly imprinted on me the horrors my grandparents and parents faced as blacks in the pre-civil-rights Deep South.
3. **"Reconstruction: America's Unfinished Revolution, 1863–1877"** by Eric Foner. A magnificent scholarly edifice.
4. **"Our Undemocratic Constitution"** by Sanford Levinson. A fearless examination of the Constitution by one of the most adventurous (and overlooked) U.S. intellectuals.
5. **"Four Quartets"** by T. S. Eliot. Because it contains the poem "East Coker," in which one finds the lines: "For us, there is only the trying. The rest is not our business."

A CLASSIC BOOK THAT DISAPPOINTED

W.E.B. DuBois's **"The Souls of Black Folk"** is one of the most lauded books in the African-American canon, but I found it disappointingly thin.

A CLASSIC YOU'VE NEVER READ

Leo Tolstoy's **"War and Peace."** Why? Laziness.

as hard as I can, as fast as I can, [I feel like] I'm going to kill someone," says Marwan. Whether you love or hate metal, Acrassicauda's struggle to stay together—and alive—will rock you.

—JESSICA BENNETT

TELEVISION

The ABCs of Wartime TV

After three decades of trying to make basic math and reading fun, "Sesame Street" is tackling a more serious subject: war. Its new series, "Talk, Listen, Connect: Deployments, Homecomings, Changes," uses Elmo, the lovable red puppet, and his pal Rosita to teach children of military families how to cope when a parent is deployed—or returns home wounded. "Military children serve alongside their parents and they suffer just as much as their parents do," says Gary Knell, president of Sesame Workshop, the nonprofit behind the PBS show.

The four videos, developed with input from military and

> **"Sesame Street" is tackling a more serious subject: war.**

childhood psychologists, are the second phase of Sesame's military initiative—available free by request. The first installment, released in 2006, addressed parents going away for long periods of time. The new chapters go deeper, tackling the baggage of a spiraling war by teaching children how to adjust to redeployments and the scars that soldiers bring home. In one clip, Rosita asks how she can still dance with her dad even though his legs "don't work like they used to." The answer? Rolling to the beat—in Daddy's wheelchair.

Maj. Jennifer Lange, who recently returned from a tour in Iraq, says the videos have comforted her two young daughters and given her and her military husband "a lot of ideas for how to approach these sensitive topics." The DVDs leave out some of the complexities of war, such as where Daddy is going or who hurt him. Instead, Daddy Elmo simply tells his son that he must leave to do "grown-up work."

—DANIEL STONE

WEEK OF MAY 19

MOVIES

Attack of The Clones

The archetypal hero, said mythologist Joseph Campbell, embarks on an odyssey through a realm of strange forces and finally triumphs, gaining the prize of self-knowledge. Campbell, the philosopher-king of "Star Wars" fanatics, also could've been describing the archetypal heroine. Or *heroines*: four of them, who set off to conquer a larger-than-life version of New York, battling against bad sex, couture crises and men who wouldn't commit. By the end, they'd won it all: true love, self-worth and fabulous shoes.

Now the prospect of seeing the "Sex and the City" girls go through one more mytho-poetic cycle is

---

A LIFE IN BOOKS

Claire Tomalin

Britain's literary grande dame is known for sweeping, scrutinizing biographies like "Jane Austen" and "Samuel Pepys." Her latest, "Thomas Hardy," reveals the class anxiety behind Hardy's ambitions.

MY FIVE MOST IMPORTANT BOOKS

1 **"La Chartreuse de Parme"** by Stendhal. Conjures the post-Napoleonic period, from the battlefield of Waterloo to the intrigues at an Italian court where politics conflict with love.
2 **"The Oxford Book of Sixteenth Century Verse"** edited by E. K. Chambers. Here are the glories of English poetry: Wyatt, Campion, Shakespeare, giving sparks of genius as they play with words and verse forms.
3 The Complete Works of Shakespeare. One of the twin jewels of the English language. The other? Below.
4 The Bible. No one can live without the Bible in the Authorized Version.
5 **"The Diary of Samuel Pepys"** edited by Latham and Matthews. Pepys was a young man on the make; I love his openness and lyrical appreciation of London.

A BOOK YOU HOPE PARENTS READ TO THEIR KIDS

Charles Dickens's **"David Copperfield."** Humorous, delicate and intense, it's a story every child responds to, and never forgets.

causing epic preparations. To celebrate the movie's May 30 opening weekend, devotees can enter a "SATC" look-alike contest at Boston's Underbar, brunch with Baltimore's "Girls in the City" social club or indulge in a package at New York's Mandarin Oriental hotel featuring "Mr. Big Apple-tini" cocktails and trips to Jimmy Choo. Patricia Field, the show's costume designer, is peddling bejeweled apple pendants and cosmo flasks on her Web site.

Most fans, though, will just round up their posse and head to the theater in style; a few plan to dress as their favorite characters. "I've always identified with Carrie," says Rozy Lewis, a Manhattan party planner who's leaning toward a ball gown-and-cardigan ensemble. By dressing up, viewers may be trying to capture the myth's magic—like men wearing Yoda costumes to see "Star Wars." But before you smirk at the attack of the Carrie clones, consider this: at least the ladies look good in *their* outfits.

—KATIE BAKER

WEEK OF MAY 26

TRANSITION

A Marvelous Object Maker

ROBERT RAUSCHENBERG, 81, Artist
In a legendary 1953 stunt, Robert Rauschenberg painstakingly erased a Willem de Kooning drawing. But the modern master, who died last week at his home in Captiva, Fla., will be remembered for what he gave the art world, not what he took away. His "combines" incorporated paint, found objects, text and sometimes even sound. Long before the computer age, he was a true multimedia artist, culling beauty from the detritus of modern life. Choreographer Merce Cunningham shared these memories of his longtime friend and frequent collaborator.

I first met Bob at Black Mountain College in North Carolina, where I'd come to give dance classes for the summer session. I remember his feet. They were not very flexible, but they were interesting—the size and the shape. At Black Mountain, [composer John] Cage devised this evening, the first Happening. It was Cage, [musician] David Tudor, Rauschenberg, [poet] M.C. Richards, myself. We could do whatever we wanted. I remember Bob at the top of a ladder, with an old-fashioned Victrola that you wound up, playing records. The record player was probably something he had in his room. He had this gift of being able to use anything he saw. Later on, in New York, we became friends. I asked him to make something for me, and two or three weeks later I went to his loft to see it. There was this star-shaped object made of materials from the street—sticks of wood, sheets of plastic, bits of newspaper, comic strips. All different colors. It was this marvelous object. You didn't know what it was, but there it was.

Bob was all humor. He was marvelously open to the world that way. When he traveled with us in the Volkswagen bus, he'd sing popular songs. He didn't really have a singing voice—it was like he talked them through. I see him in India, in Delhi, trying to hang something from the top of the stage. It turned out to be a bicycle, and that turned out to be the whole set for the dance. His theory of art was to do what nobody else does. He made so much work; his facility was extraordinary. He had such energy about art.

Bob rarely talked about his childhood. I didn't even know he'd changed his name until someone told me his real name had been Milton. I do know he didn't have any connection with art until he was in the Navy. He was in San Diego and he went to a museum, and

> **It was this marvelous object. You didn't know what it was, but there it was.**

he saw paintings and he thought, "I could do that." I'm sure it was that kind of directness. I think with Bob, dying was not an end, it's a transition. He's probably out there someplace trying to hook up the stars with the planets, trying to find some way to use the material at hand.   *as told to* JENNIE YABROFF

WORTH YOUR TIME

His Better 'Last Lecture'

When it comes to goofing off, there are few Web sites that offer the rich resources of YouTube. Since last fall millions of people have visited the site to watch "The Last Lecture," terminally ill Carnegie Mellon professor Randy Pausch's hourlong address on reaching your dreams. The lecture, which formed the basis for the best-selling book published by

Hyperion last month, is funny, instructive and uplifting—but it's not Pausch's best. "The talk that I'm actually most proud of is the talk I've given over the years on 'Time Management'," Pausch wrote on his blog this spring.

He gave a version of that oration to 850 people at the University of Virginia last fall, and it's also now available on YouTube. "At this point I'm an authority on what to do with limited time," Pausch, 46, told the audience while displaying CT scans of his pancreatic cancer. (Last August doctors projected three to six months of "good health"; since then he's suffered heart and kidney failure, but last week his strength was returning.) While less inspirational than his celebrated lecture, this one is filled with practical tips on Pausch's passion: becoming more productive by setting priorities, multitasking, efficiently dealing

A LIFE IN BOOKS

Louise Erdrich

A Native American novelist and poet, Erdrich is known for haunting stories of racism and reservation life, such as "Love Medicine." Her 13th novel, "The Plague of Doves," recounts the slaughter of a farm family in a North Dakota town. Her list:

MY FIVE MOST IMPORTANT BOOKS

1 **"The Portable Chekhov"** edited by Avrahm Yarmolinsky. I can easily carry it anywhere for literary solace.
2 **"Austerlitz"** by W. G. Sebald. The final novel of a fractured and supernal mind in search of its own history.
3 **"Everything That Rises Must Converge"** by Flannery O'Connor. This line electrified me: "Go back to hell where you came from, you old wart hog." It made me want to write.
4 **"The World Without Us"** by Alan Weisman. The most shattering and consoling book I read this year.
5 **"Winter in the Blood"** by James Welch. A book of terse and desperate grace, perhaps the best novel about reservation life.

A BOOK TO WHICH YOU ALWAYS RETURN

"Wide Sargasso Sea" by Jean Rhys. Savage, strange and perfect.

A BOOK YOU HOPE PARENTS WILL READ TO THEIR CHILDREN

William Steig's books, including the original **"Shrek!"** Simple, beautiful, funny, and an adult can read them without suffering brain damage.

with e-mail, managing meetings and minimizing distractions from chatty colleagues. While many of the tips will be familiar to fans of efficiency books like "Getting Things Done" or productivity Web sites like LifeHacker.com, some of Pausch's tactics are extreme. He's hooked three monitors to his PC (to maximize his electronic workspace), put uncomfortable chairs in his office (to keep visitors from lingering) and he stands up while talking on the phone (as an incentive to finish quickly).

> **The goal is not to become some superhuman office drone, he says, but to make it easier to get back home.**

The goal is not to become some superhuman office drone, he says, but to make it easier to get back home, where one's real living is done. "Time is all we have, and you may find one day you have less than you think," says Pausch, whose three children are all under age 6. One thing's for sure: if his Web video results in less time sucked away by YouTube, somewhere Pausch will be smiling.

—Daniel McGinn

MUSIC

Songs in the Key of Cheese

Pop-trivia question: what do James van der Beek (of "Dawson's Creek") and Osama bin Laden have in common? In their youth, both dabbled in a cappella. According to "Pitch Perfect: The Quest for Collegiate A Cappella Glory," by author Mickey Rapkin, the teenage bin Laden—who opposed the use of instruments —organized a group with his pals. That discovery "was pretty weird," says Rapkin. "It just shows that a cappella is everywhere." Love it or hate it, he's right: there are 1,200 college groups in the United States, uniting some 18,000 kids under ivy-covered archways to belt out Coldplay tunes. But Rapkin's book reveals a world with as much discord as harmony. One group (the Beelzebubs of Tufts University) dropped more than $30,000 to record a CD; another (the University of Virginia's Hullabahoos) traveled to the Philippines to sing. The two narrowly avoided a drunken postperformance brawl with each other.

Most a cappella singers don't pursue careers in music; still, their passion is all-consuming.

"They stay up all night debating one song," says Rapkin, himself a former performer. It's about the lure of fame, he says. The Hullabahoos can draw 4,000 fans to a show. Harvard's Krokodiloes annually rake in $300,000 from gigs and CD sales. For just as many people, listening to 15-man harmony is the ninth ring of hell. "Khaki pants, vests and snapping are never going to be cool," Rapkin says. "You have to embrace the humor of it." Or run away screaming.

—SARAH KLIFF

WEEK OF JUNE 2

TELEVISION

Absolution For Couch Potatoes

The knock on television news has long been that it emphasizes style over substance. But style, it turns out, may have some serious substance of its own. In their forthcoming book, "Image Bite Politics," Indiana researchers Erik Bucy and Maria Grabe offer absolution for couch potatoes, defending the flickering tube as a source of valuable political information. Their study begins like a typical broadside, reporting that between 1992 and 2004, network TV coverage of the presidential race got even flimsier: the average length of each candidates' TV sound bites continued to fall, from a high of 40 seconds in 1968 to less than eight seconds in 2004, while image bites—the generic footage that rolls while reporters narrate—swelled to more than a quarter of all coverage. Image bites are primarily nibbles of B-roll: soundless shots of John McCain grilling burgers, Barack Obama bowling or George Bush on wheels.

But Bucy and Grabe see an upside to this dumbing-down trend. Image bites may look like empty filler, they note, but those fleeting pictures are actually rich windows into each candidate's emotional and physical readiness to lead. "We are hard-wired to pick up on hints of fear, evasion and secondary status based on a quick read of someone's face," says Bucy, explaining how a superficial reading can be as informative as hard analysis. "Show a completely uninitiated person a 10-second video clip of candidates running for office," he adds, "and even with the sound off they will accurately predict nearly 70 percent of the time who won the race." The authors also unpack sound bites, concluding that nearly 70 percent of them are "essentially issue-focused," dealing with policies and qualifications.

> **"The candidate that looks stronger on TV isn't always the better president. Bush vs. Gore proved that."**

In his 2005 book "Blink," Malcolm Gladwell collected similar cases, including students who can tell from just a few minutes of video whether a teacher receives positive reviews, and a psychologist who can read a couple's three-minute conversation for whether they are destined to split. By the same token, researchers say, television provides voters with the raw material to sniff out lies. What's still unclear is how people factor in other sources of information, like newspaper articles, when they interpret TV images. As Bucy points out, perception does not always equal truth: "The candidate that looks stronger on TV isn't always the better president. Bush vs. Gore proved that."

—TONY DOKOUPIL

FAST CHAT

Pitchforks For Change

In his new book, "The Uprising," author and populist gadfly David Sirota argues that a "fist-pounding, primal screaming" revolt is brewing in America—and it's about to boil over. He spoke with NEWSWEEK's Tony Dokoupil:

What kind of uprising are you talking about?

It's actually more than a dozen separate uprisings, connected by a common backlash against the elite domination of government. On the left, it manifests itself as a backlash against the war, economic inequality and conservatism; on the right, it's a backlash against illegal immigration and liberal elites.

They sound more different than the same.

They are different in the specific issues they focus on, but the same in what they are reacting against: the establishment and the status quo.

If the people are always right, what keeps them down?

Social and cultural divides, territorialism and a kind of vanity. There is a huge amount of power to be wielded on the local level, but all the focus is on national targets, like Congress and the White House. Becoming a movement would require less of the glamorous stuff, like the presidential race, and more community organizing, far from the media spotlight. It also requires more democracy. I reserve some tough criticism for organizations whose leaders are not elected and thus face no accountability. Moveon.org, for instance—its leaders are great individuals, but the organization has an undemocratic structure that expresses a lack of trust in the people they serve.

What would a cohesive movement look like?

Something akin to history's past movements—multicultural, locally based and broadly themed so that different individual issues fit under the movement's umbrella.

Why is the time right for a populist revolt?

There is an extremely intense wave of dissatisfaction building right now that mirrors the wave in 1980 that helped the conservative uprising explode into a full-fledged conservative movement.

Do you worry that you'll turn off elite readers with a pitchfork mob on your book cover?

Not at all, because this book wasn't written for the establishment crowd. It's not a book by Tom Friedman. It's not a book for wealthy people.

And yet you're rather establishment, as the son of a Philadelphia doctor.

"Establishment" is a point of view—do you worship power or challenge it? No one who knows my work would say it is establishment.

WORTH YOUR TIME

The NASCAR Of the Age Of Ragtime

It's hard to fathom the America that Charles Leerhsen recaptures in "Crazy Good," his wire-to-wire biography of Dan Patch, one of the early 20th century's most celebrated athletes— who also happened to be a horse. Today's racehorses don't command the same spotlight unless they have tragic injuries, like Eight Belles at the Kentucky Derby in May, or Triple Crown chances, like Big Brown at next week's Belmont Stakes. But before World War I, horse racing was the nation's leading sport, and harness racing, in which the horse pulls a rider on a light cart, was more popular than the Thoroughbred game. Because most people still traveled by horse-drawn carriage, it was like the NASCAR of the ragtime era: a chance to cheer on a faster version of something you have at home. Dan Patch in his prime—he raced from 1900 to 1909—was the fastest, most electrifying form of transportation available. More than 100,000 people would flock to watch his exhibitions of blinding speed, where he frequently pierced the two-minute-mile mark, and eventually shaved the record to 1:55. He earned close to $1 million a year at a time when baseball's great Ty Cobb was making just $12,000, and his fame floated a bonanza of Dan Patch merchandise, including pancake syrup,

> **More than 100,000 people would flock to watch his exhibitions of blinding speed.**

washing machines and cigars. "In this one animal, humbly bred and congenitally malformed, had come together all the virtues the horse-drawn world had ever imagined," writes Leerhsen.

One of the many satisfactions of "Crazy Good" is that it goes farther than "Seabiscuit"—Laura Hillenbrand's popular resurrection of another unlikely superstar—in explaining how a horse could be so feted, then forgotten. By the time of his death in 1916, the horse-and-buggy world had been upended, and Dan Patch's departure didn't resonate with a society where the automobile reigned. With wit and a winking charm, Leerhsen, an executive editor at Sports Illustrated, makes sure this handsome brown stallion resonates in ours. He overcomes the obstacle of a main character who never spoke a word by stuffing his story with the outsize personalities of trainers, owners and local legend-keepers, and the details of an era when "fast food meant oysters." From start to finish, this book has legs.

—Tony Dokoupil

PUBLISHING

Blog Books Go for Broke

It's the latest ploy to get rich quick: create a quirky blog, solicit a following and—*voilà!*—six-figure book deal. Last year Collins signed the creators of the photo blog Passive Aggressive Notes for a reported six figures; Christian Lander, whose blog Stuff White People Like has clocked 20 million hits this year, signed for $350,000 with Random House in March. Now loyal contributors to Postcards From Yo Momma can revel in anthologized maternal mail as well as the knowledge that the site's creators sewed up a "comfortable" deal with Hyperion.

But are publishers being smart? Many bloggers just repackage what they've already done. That can work, à la Robert Lanham's 2003 "The Hipster Handbook," which has sold 40,000 copies. But usually "the reading experience for a book needs to go deeper," says Brettne Bloom of the Kneerim & Williams agency. The media bloggers at Gawker, whose readership has topped a million a month, certainly learned that lesson after signing a rumored $250,000 deal with Atria last year. Sales to date? Fewer than 1,000, according to Nielsen. The fashion and lifestyle newsletter Daily-

> **Many bloggers just repackage what they've already done.**

A LIFE IN BOOKS

Jane Yolen

The author of more than 280 books, Yolen, a writer of folklore fantasy and children's literature, is best known for her Holocaust novella "The Devil's Arithmetic." Her latest work, "Naming Liberty," tells the story of a Russian girl and the designer of the Statue of Liberty.

MY FIVE MOST IMPORTANT BOOKS

1. **"Moby-Dick"** by Herman Melville. It's a book I reread every 10 years, which is coming up again. I even love the whale parts.
2. **"Winter's Tales"** by Isak Dinesen. It has two of my favorite Dinesen stories, "Sorrow Acre" and "The Sailor-Boy's Tale."
3. **"The Complete Poems of Emily Dickinson."** Her poems taught me to "tell all the truth/but tell it slant."
4. **"Where the Wild Things Are"** by Maurice Sendak. This stood the world of children's picture books on its head in 1963.
5. **"The Great Stink"** by Clare Clark. I read this mystery novel set in the London sewers in one long, stinking sitting.

A BOOK YOU HOPE PARENTS WILL READ TO THEIR KIDS

James Thurber's **"The Thirteen Clocks."** This perfect fairy tale will get inside you from your guggle to your zatch.

A CLASSIC YOU REVISITED WITH DISAPPOINTMENT

L. Frank Baum's **"The Wonderful Wizard of Oz."** All I could see were the repetitions, the unvarying sentences and the paper-thin characters.

Candy was another flop: its highly anticipated 2006 release has sold 11,000 copies. For Random House to earn back its advance on "Stuff White People Like," it'll have to sell 100,000 copies—a figure that would likely land the book on the best-seller lists. Next up on the reading list: how to get a book deal by blogging—and get people to buy it. —Jessica Bennett

WEEK OF JUNE 9

TRANSITION

In a Formula Town, a Genuine Artist

SYDNEY POLLACK, 73, FILMMAKER, ACTOR
A master of the star-studded, mainstream Hollywood movie, Pollack, who died of cancer last week, was the rare director who managed to please the critics, the suits and a wide public—though not always with the same film. His best, 1986's "Out of Africa," with Meryl Streep and Robert Redford, won Oscars for best director and best picture. But he took a turn with his last film: 2005's "Sketches of Frank Gehry," about the architect, was his only documentary. Gehry, a longtime friend, remembers Pollack:

I met Sydney's wife, Claire Griswold, through my shrink in the 1970s. She was an actress, but she was interested in architecture and came to work in my office one summer before going to architecture school. No more gorgeous creature on earth existed! So, I'd see Sydney at dinner from time to time. I was a little intimidated in the early days—it was the Hollywood thing—and I remember being very judgmental about the commercialism of moviemaking. Where was the art? I was talking to him one night, and there was probably a little edge to my voice, asking him what he was doing. I was being holier than thou, self-righteous—and I was poor and suffering and making architecture that nobody wanted. He didn't take umbrage, he just started talking about it. If you do a Western, he said, it's pretty set, there's a formula the studios want. But there's a space in there to make art—10 to 20 percent—and it's enough to swing it. I'll never forget it because I went back and looked at my own work, and I was in the same box he was in. An office building is an office building—it's pro forma. But I also had 10 to 20 percent wiggle room. He made me understand that like no one had. He

Culture and the Arts-304 | JUNE

could've gotten pissed at my question but he didn't.

He was also a pilot. He had a Citation X. At the opening of the Guggenheim Bilbao [in 1997], I was standing in the atrium when I saw him outside peering in. I started screaming, "Sydney!" He said, "I was flying my plane from London and to tell you the truth, I was curious to see this." He had this little yellow drugstore camera with him, and a few weeks later he sent me about 10 pictures. They were the best pictures of the building—they had people in them. Later, a friend was helping me sort offers from people who wanted to make a documentary about me. She innocently asked who'd taken the best shots of the museum, and I said, "Sydney Pollack." But then I told her, don't badger him. Of course she did, and Sydney said, "You've got to be kidding! I've never done a documentary, I don't think I can do this, I'm busy." Three weeks later, he was doing the movie.

> **"He was quoted once saying he that wasn't 'a visual stylist.' But he had an incredible eye!"**

His work? "Three Days of the Condor"—I thought that was incredible. I thought "Tootsie" was amazing. In his obituary, he's quoted as saying he never had a good eye, he wasn't "a visual stylist." But he had an incredible eye! Whether you liked "The Interpreter" or not, the last scene was a Renoir picture—that watery image. He was tough, he was a control freak, like a director has to be. He would follow through on every detail, every meeting, even going to dinner. But he was extraordinarily modest—he didn't have that pushy, self-important thing going. He was this big handsome guy with a beautiful smile. When I saw him a few weeks ago, he knew he was dying. His voice was lower than usual. He knew there was no way out. But he was still smiling.

—*As told to* CATHLEEN MCGUIGAN

WEEK OF JUNE 16

TRANSITION

Rock and Roll's Founding Father

BO DIDDLEY, 72, Musician

With those big black glasses and that guitar shaped like a cigar box, Bo Diddley just radiated strange. But a good kind of strange—the kind that made you want to work your way through the crowd and hang onto the edge of the stage all night long while he played.

Diddley (he got the name from high-school classmates; he was born Ellas Bates) was not a happy camper while he lived, so there is not a chance in a hundred that he went gently last week when he died of heart failure. He was always ornery, especially when it came to getting his due. (If you'd invented as much as he did and didn't get the credit, you'd be ornery, too.) In Diddley's case, he thought he'd invented nothing less than rock and roll. He was out there before Elvis or Chuck Berry or Little Richard, tearing it up with an electric guitar and a trademark beat that landed somewhere between a shuffle and the clave rhythm of Latin music. The very phrase "rock and roll" was coined by disc jockey Alan Freed in the early 1950s to describe what his listeners were about to hear: Diddley, "a man with an original sound, who is going to rock and roll you right out of your seat."

Even when he got his due, the prickly side was there. When it was pointed out how much he'd influenced music, he said it "didn't put no figures in my checkbook." And the way he saw it, he didn't influence people; they *stole* from him. "Everybody tries to do what I do," he said. "I don't have any idols I copied after." He never needed them.

—MALCOLM JONES

WORTH YOUR TIME

All-American Arms Race

I went into the new documentary "Bigger, Stronger, Faster*" expecting an exposé of steroid use in sports. What I got was something far more provocative and ambivalent: a meditation both personal and political on our culture's obsession with winning at any cost. The subtitle of Christopher Bell's movie—"The Side Effects of Being American"—perfectly reflects the range of this funny, disturbing and complex tale.

Bell grew up in Poughkeepsie, N.Y., idolizing Arnold Schwarzenegger, Sylvester Stallone and Hulk Hogan, whose admission of steroid use shattered the filmmaker's illusions. Both his brothers, "Mad Dog" and "Smelly," suffered from crippling feelings of inadequacy and ended up on steroids; their struggles to succeed at sports are poignant tales of dashed dreams.

Bell disapproves of steroid use, but the deeper he researched the subject the more he began to suspect that its public demonization rested on wobbly science, skewed moralism and political posturing. We see Joe Biden denounce the use of steroids as "un-American"—but what does that mean when everybody's using them? And what does it say about the U.S. military, which supplies amphetamines to its fighter pilots? Bell's net keeps getting wider: he compares the deregulated $24 billion dietary-supplement industry to "snake oil" and asks us to ponder why some performance enhancers—Tiger Woods's Lasik surgery, for instance, which gave him perfect vision—are legal while others are not. When I emerged from this rousing doc, I didn't know what to think—but I had plenty to think about. It'll shake up your beliefs not just about steroids but about competition, hypocrisy, body obsession and American notions of masculinity.   —DAVID ANSEN

> **When I emerged from this rousing doc, I didn't know what to think—but I had plenty to think about.**

WEEK OF JUNE 23

CHILDHOOD

Wet Hot American Summers

It was a place of many firsts: the first time away from home, the first campfire and—for a few zillion kids—the first kiss. It began with the long trip on a schoolbus with puke-colored seats, and it ended with friendships that faded by fall but roared back the next summer. Ah, camp: the hot-weather ritual where cheesy singalongs, Popsicle-stick sculptures and swimsuit wedgies were totally awesome, at least until August.

If you're already feeling nostalgic, a quirky new book called "Camp Camp" is a "love letter" to the whole experience, say authors Roger Bennett and Jules Shell. The glossy book is stuffed with 301 pages—whittled down from thousands of submissions—of Polaroid snapshots, mess-hall memories, packing lists and diary entries from former campers whose recollections are so vivid you can practically smell the pine cones. Best are the tales of first-day jitters, the inevitable first-night homesick sniffles and, of course, the clumsy preteen sexuality: the purity tests, the bra-size competitions and the endless debates about what really constitutes going to second base. In one entry, a once chubby camper waxes about the girls he got to "actually French me at the Saturday night social."

> **"Camp Camp" is tapping into a larger yearning to revisit those days of cabin fever.**

"Camp Camp" is tapping into a larger yearning to revisit those days of cabin fever. There are hundreds of camp alumni groups

---

THE DIGNITY INDEX

Oh, the Humanity

A weekly mathematical survey of dubious behavior that measures, on a scale of 1 to 100, just how low a person can go.

Baseball's richest franchise, led by boss **Hank Steinbrenner**, wants New York City to fork over an additional $350 million of public money to finish the new Yankee Stadium. Score: **15**

Feigning nobility, **Katherine Heigl** says she doesn't deserve an Emmy and pulls out of the race—but then blames it on "Grey's" writers for lame scripts. Score: **34**

Fox News mouthpiece **Bill O'Reilly** has a new memoir in the works, and the title is "A Bold Fresh Piece of Humanity." Yes, the title refers to him. And yes, he appears to be serious. Score: **51**

Culture and the Arts-308 | JUNE

on Facebook, and a Web site, CampAlumni, has built a business on re-uniting old buddies. The Web page for "Camp Camp," meanwhile, has become a mini-encyclopedia of bunk brothers and counselor crushes. "There's a vast army of former campers out there who are still braced for a color war at any moment," says Bennett. How about right now?

—JESSICA BENNETT

TELEVISION

Burning Down the House

Where there's smoke, there's fire. So it should have come as no surprise to fans of "Weeds"—Showtime's hit series about a single mom who sells mari-

---

A LIFE IN BOOKS

Michael Lewis

A master of nonfiction narratives, Lewis skewered 1980s Wall Street in "Liar's Poker" and tackled sports in his last two books, "Moneyball" and "The Blind Side." His picks:

MY FIVE MOST IMPORTANT BOOKS

1 **"A Confederacy of Dunces"** by John Kennedy Toole. It's among the funniest books ever written.
2 **"Huckleberry Finn"** by Mark Twain. It gave me a new sense of the pleasure to be had from books.
3 **"The Education of Henry Adams."** The book I kept nearest at hand when I wrote my own first book.
4 **"Writing Home"** by Alan Bennett. Reminds me of how much interest can be got from paying attention to the most picayune details of life.
5 **"The Right Stuff"** by Tom Wolfe. It put to rest any fears about the limits of the nonfiction narrative.

A BOOK TO WHICH YOU ALWAYS RETURN

George Orwell's **"Collected Essays, Journalism and Letters"** reminds me of the force of a writer working to strip his prose of pretension and nonsense.

A BOOK YOU HOPE PARENTS GIVE TO THEIR CHILDREN

"His Dark Materials" by Philip Pullman. Even my 8-year-old could sense she was in the grips of a master storyteller.

juana in her California suburb—when Nancy Botwin torched her house just in case the encroaching wildfires didn't do the job. What may surprise viewers is how much changes on the show as a result. In the season premiere, Nancy (Mary-Louise Parker) has relocated her family to a Mexican border town, leaving behind her old life and a few key characters. "Things run their course," says "Weeds" creator Jenji Kohan. "When it's time to move on, you move on."

It's a gutsy move, but narrative reboots have become commonplace for shows in need of a jolt. Thrillers such as "24" and "Lost" have tinkered with skewed timelines and new settings. Now

> **Narrative reboots have become commonplace for shows in need of a jolt.**

melodramas and comedies are taking the same liberties. The surgical drama "nip/tuck" relocated from Miami to Los Angeles for its fifth season. This season of "Desperate Housewives" featured a devastating tornado and, in its finale, jumped five years into the future.

There's freedom in freshening staid storylines—but also a risk that fans won't stick around. Critics lauded the new directions of "Lost" and "nip/tuck," and both rebooted shows handily won their time slots. But they later hemorrhaged so many viewers that their respective season finales were the least-watched yet. Kohan is confident her fans will remain loyal. "What surprised us is that despite how much we changed, it still really feels like 'Weeds'," she says. And if the experiment fails, well, who says you can't go home again?

—JOSHUA ALSTON

WORTH YOUR TIME

A New King Of the Idiots

The Foot Fist Way," a new comedy made for pennies by a bunch of pals from the North Carolina School of the Arts, is not a particularly good movie. Many of the actors can't act. Whole scenes fall flat. And you'll find more sophisticated camerawork on YouTube. But you should see the movie anyway, because what it does have is Danny McBride, the most hilarious man you've never heard of, heir to Will Ferrell's throne as king of the idiots. Last year McBride was the funniest thing in two deeply unfunny star vehicles for Andy Samberg ("Hot Rod") and Ben Stiller

Culture and the Arts-310 | JUNE

("The Heartbreak Kid"). "The Foot Fist Way" is something of a first: a star vehicle for a guy who's not even close to a star.

McBride plays Fred Simmons, a strip-mall tae kwon do instructor who bullies his 6-year-old students ("Your weakness disgusts me") out of the delusion that he's preparing them for a world in which a man is defined by how many planks of wood he can break with his palm. To Simmons, life is just one long version of the tournament scene in "The Karate Kid," only in *his* version, the jackhole *sensei* from the Cobra Kai dojo is the hero, not Daniel-*san*. McBride is blessed with a face that oozes dumb. His eyes are always at half-mast, and that black scrapple of fuzz on his lip is not, to put it mildly, a thinking man's mustache. But that's why his whipsaw comic timing always catches you flat-footed. When it comes to stupidity, McBride is a borderline genius.

—DEVIN GORDON

WEEK OF JUNE 30

(NOT) WORTH YOUR TIME

America's Least 'Wanted'

The trailers for the action movie "Wanted" promise some hot romantic sparks between stars Angelina Jolie and James McAvoy. "Is this when we start to bond?" asks McAvoy. "Would you like to?" Jolie purrs. Then there's a shot of the two smooching. The thing is, that first rooftop scene isn't even in the movie and the kiss (which is) has nothing to do with romance. There is no love story. At all.

So much for truth in advertising. The rest of the trailer, however, gives you a fair taste of Russian director Timur Bekmambetov's hyperbolically violent movie. The filmmaker, whose Russian sci-fi fantasies "Day Watch" and "Night Watch" broke box-office records in his homeland, whips this preposter-

> **Here's a movie that offers mass murder as a cure for the 9-to-5 blues.**

ous tale of an ancient secret society of assassins into an expressionistic frenzy, relishing every slo-mo bullet through the skull. McAvoy is an anxious, cuckolded office drone who's recruited by the Fraternity and transformed into the superhuman super assassin he was born to be: it turns out his murdered father was this nutty organization's greatest killer. Its sagacious leader (Morgan Freeman, natch) explains that they are just restoring order to a chaotic world. "Trust your instincts," he advises, which should give you an inkling of the script's originality.

Jolie, radiating slinky, lethal glamour, is one of the more accomplished death-dispensers, though when she punches out McAvoy

---

BOOKS

Sex, Lies and Pillow Talk

William Butler Yeats once said that sex and death are the only things that can interest a serious mind. If that's the case, Pulitzer Prize–winning author Robert Olen Butler is one serious guy—and seriously clever. His last book, "Severance," was told through the voices of recently severed heads. His latest, "Intercourse," is about, well, sex—but it's not erotica. It's the inner monologues of coupling couples throughout history, all (OK, most) based on actual period research.

THE COUPLE	THE PLAY-BY-PLAY
Adolf Hitler **Inga Arvard**	**The place:** Berlin, 1935. Hitler's office, during an interview with the reporter. "It was a long session, and people speculated on the teeny bit that came out of it," says Butler. Hitler's thoughts: Jews, and the perfect Aryan mouse beneath him. Hers: his violet eyes.
Robert F. Kennedy **Marilyn Monroe**	**Ten minutes and counting, 1962:** RFK compares himself to John. "I can hear her saying inside her head, Oh, General, yes, you are ever so much better in bed than the President." And Marilyn? Says Butler, she's "trying to find her identity with all these men."
Bill Clinton **Hillary Clinton**	**Late spring, 1971:** Even in bed, Hillary has her eye on the prize, says Butler. Bill thinks of Coltrane, meanwhile—and of his bride-to-be: "She's smart and she's tough and I don't want to lose her but before she's done here I've got to figure out how to get on top."
Santa Claus **An Elf**	**The North Pole, 2008:** Butler even researched elf tradition for this one. Poor Mrs. Claus has turned a blind eye, and Santa's XXXmas wish is to ravish one of his elves without thinking of his wife. Too bad his elf is thinking of the Easter bunny.

—JESSICA BENNETT

(during his training) you fear her needle-thin arms will crack on the spot. Somebody needs to give this beautiful assassin a Fatburger.

"Wanted" has one good plot twist in store (though it makes little sense), and its sense of humor about its own silliness keeps the fantasy afloat for a while. But as the body count rises, so does the portentous tone, and the relentlessness of Bekmambetov's overamped style becomes oppressive. The astonishingly versatile McAvoy does more than keep a straight face; he works his butt off to anchor the tale in real emotions, and almost pulls it off. Here's a movie that offers mass murder as a cure for the 9-to-5 blues. Is that Russian, or what? Personally, I'd have preferred the love story.

—DAVID ANSEN

A LIFE IN MOVIES

Andrew Stanton

The animation guru's Pixar résumé dates back to his script for 1995's "Toy Story." He won an Oscar for "Finding Nemo," and his latest is the robot tale "WALL-E."

MY FIVE MOST IMPORTANT MOVIES

1 **"Lawrence of Arabia"** David Lean, the master of filmmaking. I've watched this movie on a big screen over 20 times. His sense of staging and editing is awe-inspiring.
2 **"The Lion in Winter"** Not the most cinematic film, but you'll never encounter better dialogue.
3 **"Gallipoli"** Peter Weir's WWI story of friendship and purpose is deeply engaging. A seminal movie for me.
4 **"Close Encounters of the Third Kind"** Sheer wonder has never been captured better, before or since.
5 **"Cool Hand Luke"** What a character. What an allegory. A man's movie, introduced to me by my father, and I've introduced it to my son.

A CLASSIC FILM YOU HAVEN'T SEEN

"La Dolce Vita" I know, I know … I'll watch it tomorrow.

A CLASSIC FILM THAT, UPON REVISITING, DISAPPOINTED

The home footage of my sixth-grade performance as a fence painter in "Tom Sawyer." It's a classic in our house. I thought I was amazing, but, man, I was bad.

WEEK OF JULY 7/JULY 14

FASHION

A New Color Clash on The Catwalk

Chanel Iman Robinson, a 17-year-old model from Los Angeles, is celebrated enough in the industry to drop her last name, in the style of Naomi, Cindy and Tyra. But she still gets passed over for jobs. "I will fly to London for what is supposed to be 20 casting calls and won't get but 15 because the other five designers don't want black models," she says. "That's not going to happen to white models. It's upsetting and insulting and totally backwards."

In a year when Donatella Versace dedicated her men's spring-summer collection to Barack Obama, others in the fashion world are lamenting the absence of black faces on runways. "This is not the conversation I thought I would have to have at this point," says model Naomi Campbell. "You think you've broken the barriers and then the game changes. So you have to fight all over again." Campbell, along with black supermodels Beverly Johnson, Iman and Tyra Banks, gained worldwide fame in the 1980s and 1990s. But after Banks left for TV and Campbell worked on her left jab, designers such as Miuccia Prada turned chiefly to Eastern European girls. Prada's spring show featured just one black model, Jourdan Dunn—and she was the first in 11 years for the label. (Prada New York declined to comment.) Pale skin, blue eyes and curve-free figures became the desired esthetic and, according to many in the fashion world, caused an industry that once led on racial diversity to slip backward. "Two years ago, I attended Fashion Week and saw girl after girl who looked exactly the same," says Bethann Hardison, an ex-model who discovered Campbell and Tyson Beckford. "I immediately phoned Iman and any other black model I knew and said, 'We have to do something'."

The talk became so loud that

> **"Two years ago, I attended Fashion Week and saw girl after girl who looked exactly the same," says Bethann Hardison.**

Culture and the Arts-314 | JULY

Diane von Furstenburg, head of the Council of Fashion Designers of America, sent out an e-mail prior to casting for this year's Fashion Week asking designers to be "mindful of diversity." July's Italian Vogue features only black models; the magazine's editor, Franca Sozzani, said she wanted to address the industry's lack of diversity. Models in the issue, including Alek Wek, say they're delighted with the message it will send to publications such as American Vogue, whose only recent black cover models have been NBA star LeBron James and actress Jennifer Hudson. But Hardison says more needs to be done. "We don't want to be separated in our own issue—we want to be included," she says. "A few articles and an all-black issue isn't enough to make this go away."

—ALLISON SAMUELS

LINGO

'Jump the Shark,' Meet 'Nuke the Fridge'

Early in the new "Indiana Jones" sequel, our creaky, 65-year-old hero stumbles onto a nuclear test site, and the warning siren is blaring. Panicked, surrounded by Potemkin houses, he folds himself inside the lead-lined cavity of a refrigerator. Kaboom: the blast sends Indy hurtling across the New Mexico desert, a mushroom cloud rising behind him. He lands and, logic be damned, tumbles out unscathed. The franchise, though, will never recover.

In TV land, this phenomenon is known as "jumping the shark": the moment when a once proud series swan-dives into putridity. It's a reference to a dreadful, late-era episode of "Happy Days" in which a water-skiing Fonz lofts himself over the fin of a great white. But Indy fans were so demoralized, they coined a new phrase just for movie-franchise meltdowns. Ergo: "nuking the fridge."

The phrase was born on May 24—two days after the film opened—and it went viral on movie message boards. In barely a month, it has blown through several Web. 2.0 benchmarks: YouTube tributes, "fridge" haikus, merch-hawking Web sites, "Word of the Day" status on UrbanDictionary.com. "You're expecting [the movie] to be as great as you remembered it," says Beth Russell, creator of nukingthefridge.com, "and after the fridge scene, it was like, 'Oooo-K'." A new legend is born, for all the wrong reasons.

—SARAH BALL

WEEK OF JULY 21

ARTS

Help Wanted: Museum Boss

The White House isn't the only American institution about to change hands. In an unprecedented wave of turnovers at the top, several of the country's most prominent museums, including the Metropolitan Museum of Art, the Guggenheim Foundation and the Philadelphia Museum of Art, are looking for new directors. "We are facing a generational shift right now," says Millicent Gaudieri, executive director of the Association of Art Museum Directors. "It's been 15 years since we've had this many openings."

Twenty U.S. art museums are without directors. That's a lot of shoes to fill, considering the demands of running a modern museum. Art institutions today function much like corporations, with huge staffs and budgets, satellite museums scattered around

> **Twenty U.S. art museums are without directors.**

the world, retail divisions and, of course, the constant pressure to generate revenue by securing private donations and attracting foot traffic to their "blockbuster" exhibits. The Guggenheim is scheduled to open a branch in Abu Dhabi in 2012, and the Philadelphia Museum of Art is undergoing a $590 million expansion. Trustees want a museum director who can collect like a connoisseur but compete like a CEO. "Ideally a candidate has a Ph.D. in art history but also an M.B.A.," says Ford Bell, president of the American Association of Museums.

But traditionalists question the importance of a business background. "Art is very much still at the core of the job description," says Maxwell Anderson, director of the Indianapolis Museum of Art. "A business degree is not necessary, just some good business sense." In 2006, Elizabeth Easton, former president of the Association of Art Museum Curators, started the Center for Curatorial Leadership, a fellowship program where Columbia Business School professors train qualified curators in the administrative skills they need. One of the program's fellows is currently in the running for the top job at the Met. "We don't want museums to become entertainment centers with art as the byproduct," says Easton.

Finding a director who can

—Oscar Raymundo

WORTH YOUR TIME

One Funny Appetizer

Sure, "Wall-E's" a hit, but Pixar's exuberant (and unbilled) short "Presto" steals the show—before the show even begins. A quickwitted throwback to old Warner Bros. critter capers, "Presto" stars pompous stage magician Presto DiGiotagione, a headliner whose one gag is pulling a rabbit out of his hat. Only today, that rabbit, Alec Azam, is in a diva's snit. Alec is overdue for a carrot and won't budge 'til he's dined—not even when an indignant

CLOSURE

Bartman!

News stories captivate us for a moment and then vanish. We revisit those stories to bring you the next chapter.

STARTING POINT

Oct. 14, 2003: The Chicago Cubs are just five outs away from their first trip to the World Series since 1945 when 26-year-old superfan **Steve Bartman** interferes with a foul ball that Cubs left fielder Moises Alou appears primed to catch. The Florida Marlins score eight runs, force a Game 7 and win the pennant.

FEVER PITCH

For weeks, Bartman is besieged by death threats, and TV trucks surround his house. The governor of Illinois suggests he join the Witness Protection Program, while Florida Gov. Jeb Bush offers him asylum. The ball fetches $100,000 at auction and is publicly exploded.

PRESENT DAY

The Cubs are in first place in their division and Bartman-mania has resurfaced, though Bartman remains reclusive as ever. Family friend Frank Murtha, who handles interview requests and has granted none in the past five years, says only that Bartman "has not put his life on hold." He still lives with his parents in Northbrook, Ill., and continues to work at a consulting firm and, presumably, root for the Cubbies. —Matthew Philips

Presto insists the show must go on. But hell hath no fury like a hungry bunny, and Alec smacks down—hard. The ensuing finger-crimping, egg-hurling and electrocuting dazzles the magic-show audience, who misinterpret it all as part of the act. Like a lot of Pixar's shorts, the Doug Sweetland-directed "Presto" (now on iTunes) is dialogue-free, focusing instead on superb visuals. Each frame is a richly toned pastiche of Victoriana, the camera lingering on vibrant circus posters and saffron-fringed curtains, and the score is classic, cymbal-happy Hollywood. In the end, of course, the two resolve their differences and Alec gets his carrot—exeunt all. It has not a whiff of "Wall-E's" moralistic tone. But with its goofy charm, "Presto" is the perfect foil.

—SARAH BALL

A LIFE IN BOOKS

Matt Taibbi

Rolling Stone political columnist Matt Taibbi has written three books since 2006: two collections of essays and his latest, "The Great Derangement," a mass skewering of modern Americans, from 9/11 conspiracy theorists to mega-church goers. His picks:

MY FIVE MOST IMPORTANT BOOKS

1. **"Dead Souls"** by Nikolai Gogol. I've probably read this book 50 times. A great novel about how human society is basically an unbroken string of tragic misunderstandings.
2. **"Gulliver's Travels"** by Jonathan Swift. See above. A lot of the books I like are sort of about the same thing.
3. **"Anna Karenina"** by Leo Tolstoy. The thing I love about Tolstoy is his way of making you realize that the seemingly dull details of ordinary day-to-day existence can be dramatic and terrible.
4. **"The Gulag Archipelago"** by Aleksandr Solzhenitsyn. Of all the books ever written, this one is probably the least like "Chicken Soup for the Soul," which has to count for something.
5. **"Papillon"** by Henri Charrière. I think this is the greatest true-adventure tale ever, a great story of perseverance and the will to live. Always amazed by how beautiful the writing is.

A BOOK TO WHICH YOU ALWAYS RETURN

I read **"Candide"** about once every two years. It's great if you have a talent for forgetting jokes.

Culture and the Arts-318 | JULY

WEEK OF JULY 28

FAST CHAT

Living a Second Life Online

We've all heard the warnings: addiction, isolation, a waste of time. But some 50 million people log on to online role-playing games like The Sims and Second Life—and many of them never log off. The makers of a new documentary called "Second Skin," which hits theaters in September, followed seven hard-core gamers to find out why. Victor Piñeiro, the film's producer, spoke with NEWSWEEK's Jessica Bennett:

Why make a film about gamers?
It all started with a teacher friend who got so into Star Wars Galaxy that he was leading a double life. He'd run home from work during lunch, 10 blocks, to check what was going on inside the game. He was staying up all night and would show up to class with bags under his eyes. From the outside it looked crazy. But from the inside it was kind of amazing. He'd become the mayor of his

---

ENOUGH ALREADY

I'm Sick of Your Dirty Job

From "Dirty Jobs" to "Deadliest Catch," "Ax Men" to "Ice Road Truckers," the airwaves are overrun by TV shows about people—er, men—with dangerous, physical, soot-collar jobs. If people want to come home from a hard day's work and watch other people put in a hard day's work, more power to them—these shows attract tons of viewers. What's annoying is how they suggest there's a fascinating character study happening beneath the surface. What makes someone do this for a living? they seem to ask. We've got a theory: money, and lots of it. Want to see a really dangerous job? How about a woman working for minimum wage at a big-box retail store who can't afford health insurance? Marvel as she scans groceries, aggravating the carpal tunnel for which she can't go to a doctor. It might not be as visually compelling a show, but it would certainly be more relevant. —JOSHUA ALSTON

town and was leading hundreds of people.

What's the lure of such games?

What it comes down to is trying to find fulfillment and like-minded individuals. In a virtual world, you can choose your destiny. There's satisfying work, the chance to be good at something. From outside you might say, "Oh, that person's a nerd." But inside these people are well known and respected.

One of your subjects games 16 hours a day, sleeps by the computer and does it all over again.

Yes, and there's of course a point where people go too far—many lives are wrecked by gaming. But these games are very fulfilling to people, and to some that's not addiction, it's an extension of living.

Some of your sources say they found true love in virtual reality. Do you think that's possible?

In many cases I think real love blossoms best in a virtual world. We hung out with countless couples who met inside these games, and many were among the most madly-in-love people I've met. Each will say they had no expectations of falling in love, but that they really got to know each other from the "inside out."

What was the most unexpected thing you discovered?

There was a guy we met in Second Life who was really great: affable, funny, smart and fun—we really connected. Months later, we were shocked to find out he was completely disabled by cerebral palsy, to the point where he could only work one finger on one hand and couldn't talk. In that moment, the power of virtual worlds to enhance people's lives really crashed down on us.

WORTH YOUR TIME

A Man Walks Into a Bar . . .

"Stop me if you've Heard This," Jim Holt's new history and philosophy of jokes, isn't a topnotch book. It jumps around, from Palamedes to Sarah Silverman (chart), and the closest it comes to a big idea is that jokes "come and go." But there are at least 10 pages (28–38) that everyone should read. They're about Gershon Legman, a "self-taught scholar of the dirty joke," who claimed to coin the phrase "Make Love, Not War," invent the vibrating dildo and introduce origami to the West. (He wasn't kidding.) Born in Pennsylvania in 1917, Legman's life has a gripping, Forrest Gump-like quality to it. He moved to New York after high school, and found work as an erotic-book hunter for Alfred Kinsey, before breaking away to pursue his true calling. By his death in 1999, he'd amassed one of the world's largest dirty-joke collections, more than 60,000 variants filed away on index cards under amusing headers like THE BIG INCH and ZOO-PHILY. Holt's book isn't quite that funny, but the pages on Legman are seriously worth the read. —TONY DOKOUPIL

Palamedes (Greek legend): Mythical inventor of the joke.

Poggio Bracciolini (1380-1459): Ran a "fib factory" for storytellers at the Vatican and compiled Europe's first joke book.

Sarah Silverman (1970-): Master of the dirty joke.

1000 | B.C. A.D. | 1000 | 2000

Sigmund Freud (1856-1939): The author of "Jokes and Their Relation to the Unconscious."

Gershon Legman (1917-99): A "self-taught scholar of the dirty joke," credited with amassing the largest collection of blue humor in the world.

WEEK OF AUGUST 4

BOOKS

Why Are You a Democrat?

To compile "why I'm a Democrat," editor Susan Mulcahy recruited more than 50 fellow party faithful, including celebs like Tony Bennett, Isaac Mizrahi and Nora Ephron, along with farmers, waitresses and one billionaire (insurance mogul Bernard Rapoport). Some of their reasons are predictable (civil rights, JFK), while others are amusing ("because I'm already enough of an a—hole," says Presidents of the U.S.A. guitarist Dave Dederer). But while the values praised in the book may have been exclusively Democratic

> **"I'd rather be Barney Frank than Larry Craig."**
> —*Paul Weitz*

back in the Depression or even in the '70s—compassion for the less fortunate, opportunity for new

> "Democrats at least work toward making things fair."
> —Tony Bennett

Barack Obama, who ran circles around the populist John Edwards. In this light, the book comes off as simplistic partisan cheerleading, particularly the foreword by former Anita Hill-bashing GOPer David Brock, which reads like a parody of Gingrich-era bickering: "Re-Americans—times have changed. As this year's primaries showed, voters now identify with pro-immigrant, socially progressive Republicans like John McCain and tough-on-defense, down-on-handouts Dems like Hillary Clinton and

> "Because I'm not mean and selfish enough to be a Republican."
> —Isaac Mizrahi

A LIFE IN BOOKS

Cristina García

The Cuban-born novelist has written four books, including "Dreaming in Cuban," a National Book Award finalist, and her latest, "A Handbook to Luck." Her picks:

MY FIVE MOST IMPORTANT BOOKS

1. **"Labyrinths"** by Jorge Luis Borges. Intelligence and imagination have never been so ecstatically merged.
2. **"Collected Stories"** by Anton Chekhov. No one writes with as much generosity or understanding of human nature.
3. **"Mrs. Dalloway"** by Virginia Woolf. Her language and powers of observation are second to none.
4. **"Autobiography of Red"** by Anne Carson. This epic poem will carve room in your soul for unlikely creatures.
5. **"The Emigrants"** by W. G. Sebald. It questions what we think we know and how history gets made.

A BOOK YOU ALWAYS RETURN TO

Juan Rulfo's **"Pedro Paramo"** grows more mysterious and miraculous with each reading, and reminds me the dead continue to live among us.

A BOOK YOU HOPE PARENTS WILL READ TO THEIR KIDS

Norton Juster and Jules Feiffer's **"The Phantom Tollbooth."** I missed this as a kid but read it to my daughter some years ago. We were both hooked.

publicans believe that deep down, we're all fundamentally bad." It's an attitude more suited to the politics of 1998, or even the Swift Boating of 2004. But in an election cycle when the Dem has invited a GOP senator along for his world tour—and when McCain's biggest supporter is Joe Lieberman—"Why I'm a Democrat" comes four years too late. —KATIE BAKER

> "I read the labor history—what the Irish did in America—and it was all Democratic."
> —*Frank McCourt*

SPORTS

Needed: A Real Bat Man

Major League Baseball fans, take note: you might consider swapping your glove for a helmet next time you head to a game. A recent surge in exploding bats has sent bystanders ducking for cover. In April, a woman was rushed to the hospital after being hit in the face by a bat barrel at a Dodgers game, leaving her jaw broken in two spots. In June, umpire Brian O'Nora was bloodied after he was hit in the face while behind the plate. There are no of-

---

TWO WOODS DIVERGING

Maple bat
ADVANTAGES
The wood is stronger and harder, for better contact. It's also less likely to break into shards.

DISADVANTAGES
A more brittle wood. Its grain is also hard to see, which makes proper grading difficult.

Ash bat
ADVANTAGES
A lighter wood, ash has a long grain, making fractures less violent. Cracks are easier to see, so bad bats can be replaced.

DISADVANTAGES
Ash is not as strong or as dense as maple. It tends to flake apart more, and is prone to rupturing into shards.

IT'S WHAT'S INSIDE THAT COUNTS

To ensure maximum strength, wood grain should ideally run parallel to the length of the bat. If not, cracks will form an oval-shaped split.

ficial statistics kept on broken bats, but there has been about one per game in July, prompting MLB's Safety and Health Subcommittee to study what's causing it. One theory is that maple—a denser wood that peaked in popularity when Barry Bonds used it to hit 73 home runs in 2001—shatters more easily than traditional ash. Another is design: many players now request fatter barrels and slimmer handles to increase the torque on the ball. Roland Hernandez, a wood expert who presented his findings to MLB two weeks ago, says it's a combination of the grade of the wood and certain designs that breaks bats.

—ADAM DE JONG

WEEK OF AUGUST 11

COMIC BOOKS

Sketching The Deluge

To this day, the images are haunting: entire neighborhoods submerged by toxic water, bodies packed into the Superdome like sardines. Seeing them rendered in a comic book—dialogue balloons filled with cries of anguish, inked and colored corpses—is, as it turns out, no less horrifying. But that's what makes "A.D.: New Orleans After the Deluge," a 14-part Web comic series about Hurricane Katrina, so good. The brainchild of New York cartoonist Josh Neufeld and produced by Smith Magazine, "A.D." tells the story of six real-life New Orleanians who survived: a couple in their 20s; a sixth-generation native; an Iranian-born supermarket owner; a high-school student, and a local doctor. The series culminates this month with the hurricane's third anniversary, and hits bookstores next year with a contract from Pantheon.

"A.D." is raw and painful—

> **For many New Orleanians, the story hits all too close to home.**

down to the detailed depictions of ruined homes and the frenzied dialogue among friends. It reaches a climax in chapter 13 (above), with army vehicles whizzing past the frail and thirsty, crying children and a dying old woman. The language, too, is authentic—and foulmouthed—which is in part what makes it all so powerful. "It's one thing to imagine what happened, and to hear these stories from people you've never met," says Neufeld. "But I really tried to make these characters real people you feel like you knew." For many New Orleanians, the story hits all too close to home.

—JESSICA BENNETT

MOVIES

A 'Pineapple' Pot Plot Ploy

How do you hawk a film to a mainstream audience when even the meaning of the title is too illicit to explain? Simple—you make it look like something else. Ads for the new Judd Apatow-produced stoner comedy, the Aug. 6 release "Pineapple Express," shill the movie as an action flick about two dimwitted pals inadvertently swept into a crime thriller. The cleverly edited promos have all the retro stylings of a screwball "Dirty Harry"—Seth Rogen sports polyester lapels while James Franco thwarts grisly bad guys with a Glock and a ninja headband. Only the occasional background wisp of smoke suggests there might be reefer behind that madness.

But drugs are the theme, not a sideshow. These guys aren't low on IQ points—they're just perpetually stoned. They're not even bud-

---

THE DIGNITY INDEX

That Song Is Beyond Ridiculous

A weekly mathematical survey of dubious behavior that measures, on a scale of 1 to 100, just how low a person can go.

In a divorce filing, **Alex Rodriguez** says his wife's claims that he's a cheater are "immaterial." Legally? Maybe. In the court of public opinion? Nope. Score: **12**

"Nightline" co-anchor **Martin Bashir** lets out his inner caveman, joking—at a diversity conference, with ABC's Juju Chang right at his side—that Asian women sexually arouse him. Score: **48**

On the one hand, **Ludacris**'s new pro-Obama, anti-Hillary and McCain rap song is garbage. On the other hand, his name is *Ludacris*. Still, way to put your own guy in a bind. Score: **51**

dies; as stoner and dealer, they're more like business associates. And they're not on the lam from mobsters—they're entangled in a police chase over the eponymous "pineapple express," a powerful strain of psychoactive marijuana. So why the vanilla marketing in an age of moms dealing pot on cable? Sony Pictures didn't return NEWSWEEK's requests for comment. But as Robert Thompson, a pop-culture and television professor at Syracuse University, puts it: "It's the old bait-and-switch, but in reverse"—rather than lure with controversy, Sony has made the film seem tame. The worry, he says, is that you'll get "a whole bunch of people who really want to see a standard action adventure, and all of a sudden it's Cheech and Chong for the new century." With movies, as with drugs, what you see isn't always what you get.

—SARAH BALL

A LIFE IN BOOKS

Darin Strauss

The former Guggenheim fellow (and husband of a newsweek senior writer) is adapting his 2006 book, "Chang and Eng," into a screenplay with actor Gary Oldman. His picks:

MY FIVE MOST IMPORTANT BOOKS

1 **"Portnoy's Complaint"** by Philip Roth. This is what made me think I'd try this crazy career. Crude as hell, yet a literary triumph.
2 **"Anna Karenina"** by Leo Tolstoy. It doesn't seem like you're reading a novel, but watching big, messy life play out in front of you.
3 **"Pnin"** by Vladimir Nabokov. "Lolita" is more famous, "Pale Fire" more ambitious. But this is his most accessible, warmest book.
4 **"Time's Arrow"** by Martin Amis. The book shows that, with the right idea, every single sentence can be made interesting.
5 **"Collected Stories"** by V. S. Pritchett. A latter-day Chekhov. But his sentences, forgive the blasphemy, are better than Chekhov's.

A BOOK TO WHICH YOU ALWAYS RETURN

"Herzog" by Saul Bellow. I almost put this in my top five. His prose is so energizing. Read a paragraph and you'll want to start writing.

A CLASSIC BOOK THAT, UPON REVISITING, DISAPPOINTED

"Portnoy's Complaint." While it was important to me, I think that its humor has dated badly.

WEEK OF AUGUST 18/AUGUST 25

MOVIES

Back on the 1960 Campaign Trail

With the conventions almost here, the timing seems just right for "Primary," one of three JFK documentaries by filmmaker Robert Drew, re-released on DVD. In 1960, Drew gained access to John F. Kennedy and Hubert Humphrey as they canvassed in battleground Wisconsin. The film opens with Humphrey on smalltown Main Streets, shaking hands and cracking hokey jokes. Rural Midwesterners considered Humphrey an insider; the film even catches a radio host predicting his easy win.

But when the camera cuts to people screaming and straining just to touch the junior senator from Massachusetts, it's clear who will emerge victorious. While Humphrey harangues half-empty union halls, Jack displays his oratorical flair in front of packed auditoriums. At his side, doe-eyed Jackie is alluring in white gloves and pearls. The couple sparkles with an energy that makes poor Humphrey look as exciting as a tree stump.

It's hard not to draw comparisons to the present race, where

THE DIGNITY INDEX

Some Sauce With Your Indignity?

A weekly mathematical survey of dubious behavior that measures, on a scale of 1 to 100, just how low a person can go.

On one of Beijing's smoggiest days yet, Olympic committee prez **Jacques Rogge**, a doctor, praises China for doing all "humanly possible" to clean up the air. Inhaler, anyone?
Score: **6**

It's not often regular citizens make it to the Index, but **Reginald Peterson** of Florida is that good. He called 911—twice!—because his spicy Italian Subway was missing its sauce.
Score: **38**

Hats off to our first **100**-point scorer. **John Edwards** outclassed the competition by cheating on his wife, who has cancer, and then lying about it during the campaign. Ouch!

another older "straight-talking" senator with a penchant for snooze-inducing town-hall speeches faces a charismatic politician whose rock-star presence has energized the youth vote (though in 1960, it's religion, not race, that's the elephant in the room). In JFK's case, as Drew's later films show, his idealism helped him navigate the challenges he later faced, like ending segregation. If only we had the benefit of fast-forward this time around. —KATIE BAKER

WORTH YOUR TIME

What's Your City Saying?

It makes city governments cringe. But graffiti can be provocative, inspiring and poetic—sometimes even a tool for public discourse. That's what San Francisco designers Axel Albin and Josh Kamler say in their new book, "Written on the City."

A LIFE IN BOOKS

Jonathan Kozol

The activist and National Book Award winner is best known for his works on public education. His latest is "Letters to a Young Teacher." His picks:

MY FIVE MOST IMPORTANT BOOKS

1. **"The Sound and the Fury"** by William Faulkner. A work of relentless, triumphant prose. I couldn't write for a year afterward.
2. **"The Power and the Glory"** by Graham Greene. A soaringly spiritual book, by a man every bit as cynical as an Englishman can pretend to be.
3. **"The Souls of Black Folk"** by W.E.B. Du Bois. Unlike most political books, it is also a work of artistry and beauty. It captured my soul.
4. **"The Brothers Karamazov"** by Fyodor Dostoevsky. Still the most overwhelming and engrossing work of fiction I've ever read.
5. **"Collected Poems"** by William Butler Yeats. Reminds me of the worth of pushing back against the worst that life can do to you.

A BOOK TO WHICH YOU WILL ALWAYS RETURN

"The House at Pooh Corner" by A. A. Milne. No other book reflects so tenderly the magic of childhood.

A CLASSIC BOOK THAT, UPON REVISITING, DISAPPOINTED

"The Four Quartets" by T. S. Eliot. I don't think he had enough red wine or erotic juices in his veins. Dry as British skeleton bones.

They've compiled their favorite "message graffiti" from cities around the globe—the musings, rants, political statements and cultural observations of artists who risk jail to have their voices heard. The best examples are poignant ("One week that we've been separated," reads an image of two lovers), funny ("You looked better on MySpace," jokes another) and thought-provoking ("Create beautiful children. Marry an Arab," says a wall in Tel Aviv). The original spray paintings are likely covered up by now: cities spend millions each year to do so. But the authors believe their photographs can tell us something about the dialogue happening around us. "People want to talk about graffiti as this kind of raw, urban, danger-of-the-city kind of thing," says Albin. "But this project is really more human than anything else."

—JESSICA BENNETT

WEEK OF SEPTEMBER 1

WORTH YOUR TIME

A Place on 'The Black List'

After the Washington Post ran a series of surveys and stories called "Being a Black Man" in 2006, comedian Bill Cosby lambasted the project for being too rosy. "I'm not interested in hearing that things aren't as bad as they seem,"

> **A new documentary on HBO, is bound to irk Cosby-esque pessimists.**

Cosby told an audience. Now, with Obamamania at a fever pitch, the black community is under a microscope (see: CNN's hotly debated "Black in America" documentary) and every examination of it invites the criticism that the view is either too dismal, or not dismal enough.

"The Black List: Volume 1," a new documentary on HBO, is bound to irk Cosby-esque pessimists. It features interviews with 22 prominent African-Americans from all walks of life: former secretary of State Colin Powell shares the frame with guitarist Slash. Interviewer Elvis Mitchell and director Timothy

Greenfield-Sanders don't strive to paint a full portrait of black America (as if that would be possible). Instead, they engage with some of its most esteemed members and, in doing so, pose intriguing questions. What is the secret of black achievement? Why does being black seem to motivate some, but enervate others?

When Nobel Prize-winning author Toni Morrison speaks about how her father pushed his daughters to succeed and how being outside the white establishment freed her to create, it's evident that her success came because she's a black woman, not in spite of it. Too rosy? Perhaps, but just as real and valid as any other black experience.

—JOSHUA ALSTON

FAST CHAT

Sex and the Single Girl

In her new memoir, "Epilogue," author Anne Roiphe chronicles her sudden widowhood and attempts, at age 72, to date again in the Internet era. She spoke with NEWSWEEK's Katie Baker.

Have e-mail and the Web made things easier than when you dated as a young woman?
This is a great addition to my life. Most of the people I know *don't* know anybody who is single and available. If I go to a party, there *aren't* single men there. Let's start with that. So I would never meet anybody.

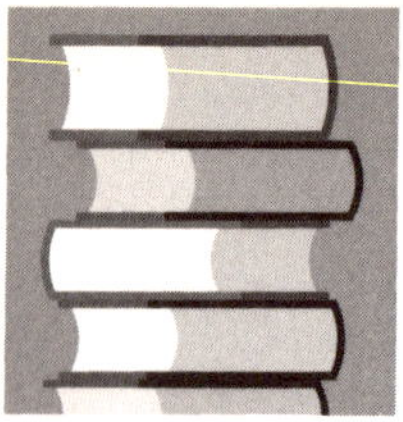

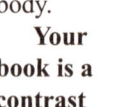

Your book is a contrast to Joan Didion's "The Year of Magical Thinking," where she's almost stuck in amber after her husband's death.
What interested me was the place [Didion] wasn't able to write about, which is the healing process, the real afterwards. Shock wears off, numbness wears off, and there you are. And life goes on.

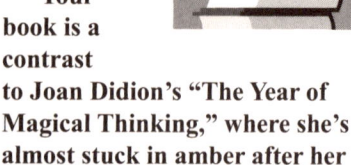

> "I don't accept that I can't have all kinds of girlish, womanish feelings. Why not?"

You began dating again after your daughters placed a singles ad for you in The New York Review of Books. How'd they react to your decision to write about these experiences?
I think it must be very hard for children to see their parents in a state of grief they can't overcome. So I felt it was important, for me and for my family, that they saw I was strong and living and doing well.

You write frankly about the sexuality of older women. Do you think we'll see a change in our society's attitude toward it?

I think the way to deal with this is twofold: I'm not a 24-year-old girl. I'm a 72-year-old woman. And I accept that. But I don't accept that that means I can't have all kinds of girlish, womanish feelings. Why not? I am a grandmother and I love being a grandmother. But if I believed that because I'm a grandmother, I should stay home and knit socks for my grandchildren . . . I'd last another six months in this world.

SPORTS

The Madden Cover Jinx's Next Victim

For the 20th-anniversary edition of its Madden videogame franchise, EA Sports wanted an NFL icon for the cover: Green Bay Packers quarterback Brett Favre. On March 1, EA sent him an offer; the next day he accepted. Two days later he announced he was retiring. The timing, says EA marketing director Chris Erb, "was certainly funny." The notorious Madden "cover jinx"—which

Was EA in on the Favre flip-flop all along?

THE DIGNITY INDEX

Win Nine Golds, Kid, and Then We'll Talk

A mathematical survey of dubious behavior that measures, on a scale of 1 to 100, just how low a person can go.

Asked if she's dating golden boy Michael Phelps, fellow U.S. swimmer (and onetime Playboy model) **Amanda Beard** harpoons the poor guy: "Come on, I have really good taste."
Score: 13

Isn't it ironic that **Rush Limbaugh** called Barack Obama "the little black man-child"? You could describe Rush the same way, if you leave out the words "little," "black" and "man."
Score: 42

It's impossible to know for certain, and MSNBC is denying it . . . but it really, *really* sounded like a noticeably cranky **Tiki Barber** called his female co-host a "c—t" on live television.
Score: 52

stung Michael Vick, Daunte Culpepper and Donovan McNabb, all of whom suffered severe injuries the year they were cover boys—had struck again.

But then in July, Favre unretired, and suddenly the pick looked ingenious—even, dare we say, conspiratorial. Was EA in on the Favre flip-flop all along? "No," Erb says, "but we felt he might come back." They didn't anticipate, though, what happened next: the Packers no longer wanted Favre. Trade rumors ensued. Favre was headed to Minnesota, then Chicago, then Tampa Bay. EA scrambled, releasing screen shots online of Favre in various jerseys. Finally, on Aug. 7, five days before Madden '09 hit the shelves—too late for a recall—he was traded to the New York Jets. So on its Web site, EA posted a new, downloadable Jets roster featuring Favre. Jinx avoided? Only if he gets through the season in one piece.　　　—MATTHEW PHILIPS

A LIFE IN BOOKS

Thomas Frank

The author's witty 2005 book "What's the Matter With Kansas?" examined why people seem to vote against their economic interests. Frank's latest is "The Wrecking Crew: How Conservatives Rule."

MY FIVE MOST IMPORTANT BOOKS

1. **"The Great War and Modern Memory"** by Paul Fussell. Addresses the two great subjects of them all: memory and war.
2. **"The Culture of Narcissism"** by Christopher Lasch. It's guided me on everything from advertising to the rebel right.
3. **"Anti-Intellectualism in American Life"** by Richard Hofstadter. Every battle of our culture wars is just a footnote to this book.
4. **"Which Side Are You On?"** by Thomas Geoghegan. Ironically, the best labor writer ever on labor's decline.
5. **"U.S.A."** by John Dos Passos. Choked with politics and experimentation, a near-forgotten masterpiece.

A BOOK YOU ALWAYS RETURN TO

Edmund Wilson's **"The American Jitters."** Super account of the Great Depression.

A CLASSIC YOU REVISITED WITH DISAPPOINTMENT

F. Scott Fitzgerald's **"This Side of Paradise"** seemed hopelessly juvenile.

WEEK OF SEPTEMBER 8

FAST CHAT

Now He's a Gentle Giant

He was a dead man walking, soon to be fired. Instead, New York Giants coach Tom Coughlin led his team to a stunning Super Bowl win over the New England Patriots, a story he recounts in his new book, "A Team to Believe In." Ever a good sport, NEWSWEEK's Mark Starr, a lifelong Pats fan, spoke with Coughlin as the new NFL season kicks off this week.

You decided to change your style last year, to rein in your temper and be more open. Why?

I had not done a good job of communicating. I would stand in front of our team, feeling like what I was saying was pretty simple. Afterward I might listen in the hallways to three or four different interpretations of what I had said. And if it was gonna be my last year, I was gonna enjoy it.

Why'd that take so many years?

None of the principles changed. Just my approach. Our player-development director said to me, "Let the players see you as you are with your grandchildren." We weren't playing tag, but I understood.

Will you try to "mellow out" even more this season?

Absolutely. It's not easy for me. My mother once said to me, "You're not a backslapper. You are one of the serious ones."

THE DIGNITY INDEX

It's True. I Confess. Women Dig Me.

A mathematical survey of dubious behavior that measures, on a scale of 1 to 100, just how low a person can go.

"Californication" star **David Duchovny's** blunt admission that he's in rehab for sex addiction almost made it seem like a publicity stunt. Did his wife and two kids want him to be that honest? Score: **13**

To MSNBC's bickering political boys, **Chris Matthews, David Shuster, Joe Scarborough** and **Keith Olbermann:** you do realize that the camera is on, right? Score: **29**

On her concert tour, **Madonna** shows a montage with John McCain next to Hitler. We'd give her a higher score but we don't like rewarding pathetic attempts to shock. Score: **60**

WORTH YOUR TIME

'Heat's' Hot Cup of Coffee

Once upon a time, the prospect of Robert De Niro and Al Pacino on screen together, *mano a mano*, would've provoked a wildly different reaction than the one I have whenever I see posters for their new cop flick, "Righteous Kill." Twenty years ago I'd have raced you to the theater. Now? All I see is two bored, scowling men paired up for a movie that sounds as though it's about a surfing competition ("Dude, that was a righteous kill!"), and all I think is, "Oh, no." This isn't the first time De Niro and Pacino have stooped to self-parody in paycheck roles. It's just the first time they've done it as a team. Too harsh? The direc-

---

A LIFE IN BOOKS

Joshua Ferris

The novelist, 34, made a splash in 2007 with his debut novel, "Then We Came to the End," a mordantly funny tale of American office culture during the Internet boom-and-bust of the late 1990s. It was chosen as a finalist for the National Book Award. His picks:

MY FIVE MOST IMPORTANT BOOKS

1. **"Sylvester and the Magic Pebble"** by William Steig. My father read this to me until I was too old, around senior year of college.
2. **"Pale Fire"** by Vladimir Nabokov. Asks: is it such a crime for a lonely bachelor to install two Ping-Pong tables in his basement?
3. **"No Man Knows My History: The Life of Joseph Smith"** by Fawn Brodie. A scrupulously nonjudgmental bio of the founder of Mormonism, no less exciting than the story of the great Gatsby.
4. **"White Noise"** by Don DeLillo. While not his most enduring, complex or seductive, this is his most tender, romantic and funny.
5. **"The Essays and Poems of Ralph Waldo Emerson."** So much more than a high-school chore. Emerson is the first and final American word on everything from nature to power to fate.

A BOOK TO WHICH YOU ALWAYS RETURN

"The Good Soldier" by Ford Madox Ford. The narrator is out to lunch while his wife schemes.

A BOOK YOU HOPE PARENTS READ TO THEIR CHILDREN

"On Death and Dying" by Elisabeth Kübler-Ross. Start them young.

tor is Jon Avnet, the man behind "Fried Green Tomatoes," as well as Pacino's latest, "88 Minutes," which was notable only for being 17 awful minutes longer than the title promised.

My advice: skip "Righteous Kill" and catch De Niro and Pacino together at a moment when "De Niro and Pacino together" actually meant something. It happened only once, in Michael Mann's 1995 crime epic "Heat" and—aside from the climactic, largely wordless shoot-out—only for a single scene: at a roadside diner, the two sit down for the most thrilling cup of coffee in cinema history. (Both actors were in "The Godfather: Part II" but never shared the screen.)

What's great about the diner scene is, ironically, how preposterous it is. In Mann's meticulously constructed saga, there's no earthly reason for the good guy and the bad guy to meet for a chat, except to give the audience this moment of bliss. Once De Niro and Pacino are across the table from each other, the movie drops away, as if Mann pressed "pause," and the two characters discuss who they are and why they do the things they do, like rival samurai trading philosophies during a breather from combat. De Niro's bank robber is wary but calm and guileless; Pacino's cop is a cocksure raconteur, savoring the presence of a worthy adversary. There's no music, no plot, no fancy camera tricks. Just six minutes of pure acting. The men finish their coffee, then return to their separate worlds. If De Niro and Pacino had any sense—any fingertips for the meta-universe of movies, where such collisions are so powerful precisely because they're so rare— they would've left it that way.

—DEVIN GORDON

> **This isn't the first time De Niro and Pacino have stooped to self-parody in paycheck roles. It's just the first time they've done it as a team.**

WEEK OF SEPTEMBER 15

FAST CHAT

Swing and a Miss Woods

If Tiger Woods had to have knee surgery, he picked an ideal time: while he recovers, he gets to spend all day with his 14-month-old daughter, Sam—and his new videogame, Tiger Woods PGA Tour 09. He spoke with NEWSWEEK's Matthew Philips.

How often do you play the game?
A lot more now. A whole lot more now.

It'll be five months before you swing a club again. When was the last time that happened?
Probably since I came out of the womb. I've had injuries here and there, but I've always been able to go hit balls. Now I'm not allowed to do anything.

Does the videogame help keep you sharp?
It is like swinging a club. I've got to watch it, though, because if I'm not careful I'll take a full swing, and I'm not supposed to torque on my leg yet.

Is it tough watching the season unfold without you?
Not really, because I know I can't physically compete with those guys. I couldn't even beat my daughter in a game of golf right now.

She's also just 14 months old.
That's been the best thing ever, getting the chance to see her develop. As golfers, we're always away, so it couldn't have come at a more perfect time.

WEEK OF SEPTEMBER 22

WORTH YOUR TIME

Give HBO Some Credit

Even as American TV has evolved, one of its most charming aspects—the title sequence—has become scarce. To save precious seconds, many shows have jettisoned opening credits in favor of a brief flash of a logo, à la "Lost." It's a shame. A great title sequence is a gilded invitation to join the show's universe.

The credits for the new HBO

series "True Blood" (from Alan Ball of "Six Feet Under") are the perfect *amuse-bouche*. The show is about vampires assimilating into rural Louisiana, and the credits are a flip book of Deep South postcards: images of hungry gators and modest homes, neon crosses and dirt roads. In the final shot, a woman is dunked for a river baptism and appears to emerge in hysterics. Either she's in rapture, or just a hairbreadth from drowning. This is the world of "True Blood," where quaint, romantic notions of the South are recast with dread.

The package was made by Digital Kitchen, the agency behind "Six Feet Under's" Emmy-winning sequence. By hiring it again, Ball proves he understands that the slower the curtain is raised, the more intrigued his audience becomes. —JOSHUA ALSTON

A LIFE IN MOVIES

Neil LaBute

The director and playwright known for provocative social dramas ("In the Company of Men") tackles interracial marriage in his new film, "Lakeview Terrace." His picks:

MY FIVE MOST IMPORTANT MOVIES

1 **"La Dolce Vita."** Every frame is a feast for the senses—profoundly sad and achingly gorgeous.
2 **"Reds."** A truly great American film, made by this country's best actor/director/producer, Warren Beatty. Beautiful and brave.
3 **"Scenes From a Marriage."** Ingmar Bergman's film is an arrow to the heart. Liv Ullmann gives the best female performance. Ever.
4 **"The Magnificent Ambersons."** The greatest film never made. Orson Welles himself claimed it was only a shadow of what might have been. You'll weep with joy.
5 **"Claire's Knee."** Started my love affair with all things Eric Rohmer. It is an absolute feast of simplicity and control.

A FILM PARENTS SHOULD SHOW KIDS

Start with **"The Wizard of Oz."** An American studio picture that gets everything right. Sweet and funny and genuinely scary, there is really only one word for it: magic.

A MOVIE YOU REVISITED WITH DISAPPOINTMENT

Hitchcock's **"Vertigo."** Story conveniences bring it up short, and the fact that a grown man goes by "Scottie" doesn't help.

FAST CHAT

A New Chief in a House of Old Treasures

After a closely watched international search, the trustees of the Metropolitan Museum of Art in New York have chosen a new director—only the ninth in the Met's 138-year history—and they found him right under their noses: tapestries specialist Thomas Campbell, 46. He spoke with NEWSWEEK's Cathleen McGuigan.

With countries demanding back indigenous treasures, are encyclopedic museums at risk?

I think [the Met] is the kind of museum that's more important today than ever. An institution like this can allow visitors to see across geographical and cultural borders, to see all sorts of connections— to see the bigger picture.

You've said you wanted to make the museum experience fresh and relevant. Does technology have a role in that?

Absolutely. Our audience very often doesn't have the history that they might have had in the past. We need to recognize that—we need to tell the stories behind the objects.

Should the Met do more with contemporary art?

We are an encyclopedic museum, and absolutely, judiciously, we should engage in that issue. We all recognize that some of what is contemporary today will be the old masters of the future.

You wrote your thesis on the court of Henry VIII. Did his tapestries depict the dark side of his reign, like the beheading of Anne Boleyn?

[*Laughs*] No, Henry spent phenomenal sums on tapestries showing classical heroes and religious figures from the Old Testament. He was effectively presenting himself as a modern-day patriarch to his own people.

Culture and the Arts-338 | SEPTEMBER

WEEK OF SEPTEMBER 29

COMEDY

The Gentleman From New York Now Has the Floor

Chris Rock stalked onto the stage at Harlem's Apollo Theater late on a Friday night earlier this month and opened his fifth HBO comedy special by explaining why it had been so long since the fourth. He wanted to wait, he told the audience, until the moment was just right. Rock has become the country's smartest, most essential comic by salting his punch lines with blunt social evangelism. And in a prior special, 1999's "Bigger and Blacker," he went on a riff about how the black community desperately needed a new generation of leaders, like Dr. Martin Luther King in his day—a not-uncontroversial stance, given that many of the old leaders were still very much alive. Now here was Rock, less than two months from a historic election, in the

> **Rock wasn't his usual penetrating self. He was plenty funny, but not dangerous.**

cathedral of African-American culture, arriving like a prophet to testify about Barack Obama. Everyone leaned forward: this is what we came for. To laugh, sure, but mostly to hear Rock on Barack. (HBO will air the special, "Kill the Messenger," on Sept. 27.)

Rock cut straight to the chase, opening his set with 10 solid minutes of material about the election. But he stuck mostly to low-hanging fruit, cracking some easy jokes about Obama's funny name and McCain's advanced age. They were good jokes, at least, like his bit about how he'd never in his life met another Barack *or* another Obama, and his dig about McCain picking his nurse to be his running mate. But Rock wasn't his usual provocative, penetrating self. He was plenty funny, but he wasn't dangerous.

Black comics often struggle with their conscience when it comes to joking about black icons, especially when white folks are within earshot. Just ask Dave Chappelle, who never shook the fear that his white fans were laughing at black people, rather than with them, and it caused him to walk away from his TV series at the peak of its popularity. Now that Rock's hoped-for moment of cultural breakthrough had unexpectedly arrived, perhaps the 43-year-old comic—who loves race-baiting his audience with a yelping, defiant "Yeah, I said it!"—was uneasy telling us all what he really, truly thought about Obama and this transfixing campaign.

Rock had other equally squishy reasons to pull his punches. Stand-up comedy is an amoral art. Either you make people laugh or you don't. And if no one's offended, chances are no one's laughing. *"Yeah, I said it!"* But in the 2008 election cycle, comedians have become pawns in the faux-outrage game, their jokes parsed in the service of identity politics. Al Franken's run for the U.S. Senate was nearly capsized this summer by a gag about rape that he floated during a brainstorming session for "Saturday Night Live" in 1995. Poor Bernie Mac, who died in August, made one final headline a month earlier when the Obama campaign was forced to apologize for bawdy jokes Mac told onstage

---

A LIFE IN BOOKS

George Pelecanos

A master of the urban crime novel, Pelecanos was also an Emmy nominee for HBO's "The Wire." His latest novel is "The Turnaround." His picks for the best of his genre:

MY FIVE MOST IMPORTANT CRIME NOVELS

1 **"The Long Goodbye"** by Raymond Chandler. A melancholic ode to loss and the passage of time.
2 **"The Burglar"** by David Goodis. Hypnotic prose and a shocking ending. Call it pulp if you have the need to. It's disturbing art.
3 **"The Last Good Kiss"** by James Crumley. The post-Vietnam stunner that reinvigorated the genre and jacked up a generation of future crime novelists.
4 **"Swag"** by Elmore Leonard. Down-and-dirty, this one smokes front to back, and the voice is one of a kind.
5 **"Clockers"** by Richard Price. My generation's "Grapes of Wrath."

A CLASSIC YOU'VE REVISITED WITH DISAPPOINTMENT

"The Godfather" by Mario Puzo. Except for the page that features Sonny and the bridesmaid. That page never disappoints.

A BOOK YOU HOPE PARENTS READ TO THEIR KIDS

"True Grit" by Charles Portis. A great adult novel with a strong, teenage female protagonist.

at a fund-raiser—in other words, for doing his job. And this month, John McCain adviser Carly Fiorina called Tina Fey "sexist" and "disrespectful" for her Sarah Palin spoof on "SNL"—even though it was Fey, coming to Hillary Clinton's defense, who sparked a debate about sexism during the primaries. If Rock got too raw, would Obama have to apologize for him next?

When Rock did venture into taboo territory, raising the specter of a rigged election—"Sometimes [Obama] acts like he thinks he's gonna win fair and square"—it felt reflexive. His paranoia came off as a habit he was laboring to kick. Tellingly, Rock was at his most lively and inventive during a riff about the day after an Obama victory, as if the most dangerous, most taboo place he could go was believing in an America where the black guy wins. Yeah, he said it.

—Devin Gordon

WEEK OF OCTOBER 13

WORTH YOUR TIME

A Poet for Poet Haters

In Britain, Clive James is known as a Union Jack of all trades: TV presenter, critic, radio host, novelist. He's also been churning out poems for the past 50 years, but by his own admission, the designation of "proper professional poet" has been late in coming.

This oversight will surely be corrected by James's latest poetry collection, "Opal Sunset." Part anthology of his best, part showcase for his new verse, the book displays the same formidable erudition and giddy love of pop culture that infuses James's prose: in his stanzas, Hamlet and Plato get equal play with Elle Macpherson. His early works are reminiscent of his transatlantic counterpart, the former U.S. poet laureate Billy Collins—particularly James's oft-quoted "The Book of My Enemy Has Been Remaindered" ("The book of my enemy has been remaindered/And I am pleased/In vast quantities it has been remaindered/Like a vanload of counterfeit that has been seized") and

THE DIGNITY INDEX

Whoever Hired This Guy Is a Moron

A mathematical survey of dubious behavior that measures, on a scale of 1 to 100, just how low you can go.

A minor offense, to be sure, but PBS's **Gwen Ifill** should've shared her plans for a book about Obama and black politicians prior to hosting the veep debate. Transparency matters. Score: **6**

Raiders owner **Al Davis,** in a wild press conference for the ages, fires the coach he himself hired just 20 months ago and repeatedly calls the guy a "flat-out liar." Score: **38**

Accused of hassling Sydney Pollack on his deathbed about a film release, **Harvey Weinstein** says he'll give $1 million to charity if anyone can prove it. Journo Nikki Finke did. Will he pay? Score: **58**

A LIFE IN MOVIES

Neil Burger

The writer-director of "The Illusionist" returns with a new film, "The Lucky Ones," about three Iraq War vets back at home. His picks:

MY FIVE MOST IMPORTANT MOVIES

1 **"Dr. Strangelove."** Kubrick's hilarious, frightening classic. The ultimate dark comedy about the world on the brink of annihilation.
2 **"La Dolce Vita."** Decadence and social climbing in 1960 Rome. The set pieces and the images are genius.
3 **"The Last Detail."** Two Navy men taking a prisoner up the Eastern Seaboard. A snapshot of 1973 America.
4 **"High Hopes."** In Mike Leigh's movies, every action is so well observed.
5 **"Raging Bull."** A character piece with Scorsese's operatic visual style. Every bit of it is inventive, bravura filmmaking.

A MOVIE PARENTS SHOULD SHARE WITH THEIR KIDS

"Chariots of Fire." A beautiful, lyrical story of two runners passionate about their sport.

A MAJOR MOVIE YOU REVISITED WITH DISAPPOINTMENT

I'll get slammed for this, but . . . **"North by Northwest."** I love Hitchcock, but the plotting feels mechanical and it lacks the real human behavior that grounds his other films.

the Wimbledon-inspired "Bring Me the Sweat of Gabriela Sabatini."

The volume's latter half tilts at Auden in his morally urgent later years, with poems that lambaste suicide bombers and mourn the World War II dead (James's father among them). With wry cultural allusions and his breezy style, James is the ultimate poet for people who hate modern poetry.

—Katie Baker

WEEK OF OCTOBER 20

FAST CHAT

In Zealots We Trust

Historian Sarah Vowell has earned a following with her particular blend of irreverence and patriotism. In her new book, "The Wordy Shipmates," she profiles the Puritans who fought America's original battle between church and state. She spoke with newsweek's Jesse Ellison.

Why should we read a book about Puritans now?

Revisiting the roots of American exceptionalism is always a good idea. And in terms of choosing one's leaders, which we're about to do, the thing I love about the Puritans is the people they put on a pedestal were the best educated, the smartest, the ones they saw as the most good with a capital G. I guess I would like to make a case for that. I don't think a leader should be penalized because he or she knows stuff.

You draw a direct parallel between the Puritans in America and our invasion of Iraq.

The idea that "we're here to help" goes back to the Massachusetts Bay Colony, which had a seal showing an Indian saying, "Come over and help us." That's one of the roots of "We're here to help, whether you want our help or not."

How did you research this book?

Mainly from Puritan primary documents. It's voluminous. I'm looking at just the seven volumes of the writings of Roger Williams. I just got out my tape measure . . . it's eight inches long. That was exciting. I've never gotten out a measuring tape in an interview before.

What did you find that might surprise readers?

I just wrote about the Puritans, so I'm not sure I have my finger

We're not going to agree, so maybe the state shouldn't impose religious practices on people."

You grew up in Oklahoma in a very religious environment.

Yeah, sometimes I feel like a translator to my snotty urban heathen friends. To me, Christianity was about self-loathing. It never would have occurred to me to hate anybody else; I was too busy hating myself.

You write that you identify with the Puritans' "essential questions": Is my country destroying itself? Could I leave? Should I?

Would I leave? No. I'm not one of those people who are moving to Canada depending on which way the election goes. I'll stay and be mad and sad and outraged. And drowned, eventually, probably. But I'll stay.

A LIFE IN BOOKS

Ann Packer

The best-selling author's first novel traced the fallout of a paralyzing dive. In her latest, "Songs Without Words," a family unravels after a 12-year-old's suicide attempt.

MY FIVE MOST IMPORTANT BOOKS

1. **"Howards End"** by E. M. Forster. The repeated phrase "only connect" gave me a goal, and a hint that its realization might not be easy.
2. **"Mrs. Dalloway"** by Virginia Woolf. Taught me, at 19, the irrefutable fact and great mystery of other people's internal lives.
3. **"The Raj Quartet"** by Paul Scott. Scott's breadth of vision of 1940s India bowled me over.
4. **"Disturbances in the Field"** by Lynne Sharon Schwartz. A gorgeously harrowing novel about grief and redemption.
5. **"Matters of Life and Death,"** edited by Tobias Wolff. An anthology by luminaries of the short-story world.

A BOOK YOU ALWAYS RETURN TO

Alice Munro's **"Friend of My Youth."** Hard to pick any one Munro title. Her stories let me see people and begin to understand them.

A BOOK YOU HOPE PARENTS READ TO THEIR CHILDREN

Dr. Seuss's **"The Sneeches and Other Stories."** Star-bellied or plain-bellied, doesn't matter.

OSCARS

No Country for Gold Men

It happens pretty much every year, usually right about now: Hollywood insiders grumble that they haven't seen any Oscar-worthy movies yet and fret that there might not be any to come. The last two best-picture winners—"No Country for Old Men" and "The Departed"—both opened in this pre-Thanksgiving period, but those in the know knew all about those movies long before they hit theaters. This year? Based on an informal newsweek poll of Hollywood experts, the consensus so far is that the field is barren.

One reason for the sluggish start to the Oscar season, insiders say, is the presidential election. Not wanting their films to get overshadowed by a blockbuster vote, some studios pushed their prestige movies into later release dates, creating a December logjam. (One exception is the indie "Slumdog Millionaire," a quiz-show fable that debuted at the Toronto film festival.) By some counts, as many as a dozen Oscar aspirants will be released between Thanksgiving and Christmas, including David Fincher's "The Curious Case of Benjamin Button" and Baz Luhrmann's "Australia."

If enough of the holiday hopefuls flop, Oscar voters might take a second look at some unconventional options. At the top of the list: the box-office monster "The Dark Knight," which will get an ambitious push from Warner Brothers that includes Blu-ray screeners, and Pixar's rapturously reviewed "Wall-E." Then there's "Rachel Getting Married," a small, talky drama now in theaters. Critics love it, and director Jonathan Demme has Oscar pedigree. If this field stays weak, "Rachel" could be getting an Oscar nod, too.

—RAMIN SETOODEH

WEEK OF OCTOBER 27

TELEVISION

They Come From a Land Down Under

Ja'mie King is a spoiled teen princess who calls her friends "skanks" and makes sure to tell poor people, as bluntly as she can, how much she pities them. Jonah Takalua, a monosyllabic Pacific Islander, is a delinquent who bullies his schoolmates, torments his teachers and draws sophomoric graffiti (penises, usually—he's not very good) on every open surface. Mr. G is an egomaniacal drama teacher who has seized control of the school's latest production, which he rechristened "Mr. G—The Musical." Together, they are the stars of the new HBO sitcom "Summer Heights High," a faux documentary in the cringe-comedy tradition of "The Office" set in an Australian high school. If Ja'mie (that's "Jeh-may"), Jonah and Mr. G look eerily similar, it's because they're played by the same actor: Aussie superstar Chris Lilley, a protean comic who is swiftly emerging as his country's Peter Sellers.

Back home, Lilley, 33, is a bit of a cipher. Despite his ballooning fame, he's media shy and soft-spoken. "The press say I'm some reclusive freak," he says. "I get labeled that because I don't like jumping up and down at telethons and walking up every red carpet." He saves his antics for his shows, which he writes and develops himself, sprinkling real people into the cast around him. In his previous series, "The Nominees," which aired on the Sundance Channel in 2006, he played six characters, each vying for the humanitarian title of "Australian of the Year." The sextet included a middle-aged housewife who plans to roll—as in, lie down on the ground and roll—hundreds of miles for charity and an Asian teen hiding his love of theater from his strict parents. "The Nominees" also introduced the deliciously awful Ja'mie, whose snotty digs—at one point, she barks at a phone operator, "I don't know what you look like but you sound so fat"—have made her a cult hero in Australia.

Lilley inhabits each character so thoroughly that within minutes you forget you're watching the same actor. "Once I knew I wanted to do a show about a school," he says, "I spent a lot of time there. Ridiculous amounts of time." It was time well spent, mate.

—Nicki Gostin

RELIGION

Of God and Good Design

How do you create a Bible that entices people who don't read the Bible? Swedish advertising guru Dag Söderberg decided recent versions lacked visual punch, so he made a new one with big, glossy photos, hoping design fans will display it proudly on their coffee tables. It worked in Sweden, where his "Bible Illuminated" sold 30,000 copies last year. Sweden's Archbishop endorsed it and gave a copy to the outgoing prime minister as a parting gift.

When "Bible Illuminated: The New Testament" hits U.S. shelves this month, it might be a harder sell. The book opens with an Andy Warhol poster ("Repent—and Sin No More!") and often juxtaposes modern imagery with ancient scripture. In Matthew, a passage about revenge is paired with a photo of shattered glass from a 1970 shooting of two black students in Mississippi. Mark ("God says, 'I will send my messenger ahead of you to open the way'") runs with photos of Gandhi, Nelson Mandela—OK so far—and Angelina Jolie. "It's a kind of un-Bible approach to presenting the text," says Philip Towner of the American Bible Association, which provided the book's Good News Translation. "The idea is to get the reader to

> **How do you create a Bible that entices people who don't read the Bible?**

A LIFE IN BOOKS

Steven Pinker

The experimental psychologist and Harvard professor has brought big science to the masses with five books since 1994. In his latest, 2007's "The Stuff of Thought," Pinker mines everyday speech for the connections to our basic thoughts and emotions. His picks:

MY FIVE MOST IMPORTANT BOOKS

1. **"The Blind Watchmaker"** by Richard Dawkins. A lucid explanation of natural selection and a model of elegant science writing.
2. **"The Careful Writer"** by Theodore Bernstein. Who would have thought that a style manual could make you laugh?
3. **"Enemies: A Love Story"** by Isaac Bashevis Singer. A novel about a Holocaust survivor with three wives. Every scene is filled with insight about human nature.
4. **"Strategies of Conflict"** by Thomas Schelling. A humane Dr. Strangelove explains why it pays to be an irrational hothead.
5. **"The Mind-Body Problem"** by Rebecca Goldstein. A philosopher grapples with this problem in her doctoral thesis and in her life. I liked it so much, I married the novelist.

A BOOK YOU ALWAYS RETURN TO

"Principles of Psychology" by William James. Like Mark Twain, James has a witty quote on every subject.

A BOOK YOU HOPE PARENTS READ TO THEIR KIDS

"One, Two, Three, Infinity" by George Gamow. A delightful introduction to number theory.

move from the image to the text." Söderberg says he was inspired by the thought that the Bible is frequently referenced but too rarely read. "This is a way to make the text more available," he says. And maybe a bit less holy.

—JESSICA BENNETT

WEEK OF NOVEMBER 3

FASHION

Clothes Make the Ice Man

You might say that Sean Avery is the human equivalent of jock itch. It's his job, as the baddest badass in the National Hockey League, to annoy his opponents, to get under their skin—anything to gain an edge. Like the time he painted his fingernails black. "It was an experiment to see what a guy would do when he saw a fist coming at him and the nails are painted," he says. Or the time he turned his back on a game against New Jersey so he could wave his arms to block goalie Martin Brodeur's view and glare at him like a jackal. "I still remember the look on his face," says Avery. "I think at that point he thought I was officially out of my f——ing mind." The NHL promptly outlawed that kind of diversionary tactic in what is now called "the Avery Rule." "I only got to do it once," he says, "but it was a good once."

If you met Avery on the street, though, you'd never guess he likes to get bloody. Quite the opposite. He may be the most hated guy in the NHL, but he's hands down its best-dressed player, too, with taste that runs to Alexander McQueen, Dries van Noten, Gucci and white patent-leather Saint Laurent shoes. Plenty of athletes are also known for being fashion plates: David Beckham, Roger Federer, Greg Norman. But Avery is cut from a different cloth, and not just because those guys are gentlemen and he's a professional jerk. His real passion is women's fashion—appreciating it, not wearing it. He started as a mini-clotheshorse growing up outside Toronto and gradually developed a taste for couture. With men's fashion, "you do suits and pants and that's about that," he says. "Women's clothes tell a story. That's what's interesting to me." Even though he left the New York Rangers to play for Dallas this year, Avery still makes it back to Manhattan for Fashion Week—he sat between Martha Stewart and Winona Ryder at the fall's Marc Jacobs show. He even spent the summer doing an internship at Vogue. "When you see a guy walking out of a game with a broken nose and a busted lip and two days later you see him at a Vera Wang show, it's probably confusing to some people," he says. "Or intriguing."

So intriguing that New Line has commissioned a screenplay based on his double life. It's sort of "The Devil Wears Prada" with skates and brawls. "I think it's going to be something that guys can take their

---

A LIFE IN BOOKS

Cornel West

Whether writing a treatise on racism or appearing in the "Matrix" trilogy, the Princeton professor enlivens every medium he touches. His latest book, "Hope on a Tightrope," is a "best of" compilation.

MY FIVE MOST IMPORTANT BOOKS

1 **"The Republic"** by Plato. So much of the most profound thought in the West is a serious wrestling with issues raised by this book.
2 **"The Three Sisters"** by Anton Chekhov. In his great-est play, Chekhov makes deep disappointment our constant companion, yet we prevail.
3 **"Beloved"** by Toni Morrison. The author looks unflinchingly at the catastrophic with grace and dignity.
4 **"The Prophets"** by Abraham Joshua Heschel. He lays bare the roles of righteous indignation and indifference in justice.
5 **"In Praise of Folly"** by Erasmus. He shows how we all, particularly Christians, should try to laugh at ourselves and love others.

A CLASSIC THAT, UPON REVISITING, DISAPPOINTED

The poems of Philip Larkin. He's renowned for his comic sensibility, but I found mere wit and iciness.

A BOOK YOU HOPE PARENTS READ TO THEIR CHILDREN

"The Fire Next Time" by James Baldwin. His letter to his nephew is wise advice to love and serve.

girls to," says Avery, who envisions fellow Canadian Ryan Gosling playing him. His internship provided plenty of fish-out-of-ice stories. During one of his first trips to the magazine's cafeteria, he took too much food—making him the first Vogue staffer to do *that*—and promptly spilled beef stroganoff on a horrified woman. The fashion world is with him when he plays, too. On the road he travels with a big bag to hold his favorite magazines: American Vogue, French Vogue, British Vogue, V, V Men. The ribbing from the guys, of course, can get ugly. "They call me a fag, and I laugh," he says. "It's so narrow-minded and stereotypical." And unwise. If you make Sean Avery mad, you might get a fistful of black nail polish.

—MARC PEYSER

China and the Olympics

YEAR IN REVIEW

Looking back, there was never really a question that Beijing would pull off a dazzling Olympics. The joke among the reporters who had covered previous Olympics in Torino and Athens was that it was a little *too* certain—that the heavy-handed Chinese government, with the overwhelming consent of a prideful populace, would do more or less whatever was required to make sure the show came off without a hitch. It did, and then some. The 2008 Beijing Olympics were the most-watched Games in history, a genuinely riveting event, from the breathtaking Opening Ceremonies by Chinese filmmaker Zhang Yimou and fireworks artist Cao Guo-Qiang to the field of play. There, the world witnessed an athletic performance for the ages: American swimmer Michael Phelps winning a record eight gold medals with a rollercoaster ride of Herculean blowouts and heart-stopping finishes. Outside the arena, Beijing was—for better or worse—welcoming and placid. There were no violent clashes between protestors and police. The air quality was endurable. And the host, by almost all accounts, could not have been more accommodating.

But if, before the Olympics, the unpleasant explanations for such smooth sailing would've drawn nothing but scorn from outside observers, 2008 was also the year when the rest of the world began to understand China a little bit better. Thanks in large part to the Beijing Olympics, the West took a longer look at a nation it barely knew and saw a far more complicated picture. The lead-up to the Beijing games featured a delicate balance between a proud country desperate to show how far it had come (socially, economically, culturally and even politically), and a nervous, wary nation bristling at every threat of humiliation on the world stage. To a degree that most outsiders only began to realize in 2008, this sentiment was shared by a wide majority of Chinese, who are as proud and protective of their country as their government is. The dynamic, of course, also presented a golden opportunity for Chinese dissidents throughout the country—but most especially in Tibet, where protests in March led to violent crackdowns and media blackouts. The reaction in the international community was swift but measured; several European leaders announced they would boycott the opening ceremonies, a loss of face that was significant, but slight enough to be tolerable for China's government. President George W. Bush did attend the ceremonies, as did Russian leader Vladimir Putin and France's President Nicholas Sarkozy.

The diplomatic tension, though, all but evaporated in an instant on May 12, when a massive earthquake registering 7.8 on the Richter scale leveled much of China's Sichuan province, killing nearly 70,000 people (including thousands of children whose schools collapsed because of shoddy construction). The epicenter of the quake was a heavily populated region largely untouched by China's rapid economic expansion, and the disaster was both a global human tragedy and a public exposure of corruption and neglect so plain that the government could not possibly ignore it. Tragic though it was, the quake had one positive result: it reframed the world's impression of China, helping outsiders see, perhaps for the first time, into the nation's soul.

WEEK OF JANUARY 28

CHINA

Sex, Lies And Family Planning

Even in the West, the scandal would be juicy. During a Dec. 28 gala launch in Beijing for the Chinese state-run TV network's Olympics coverage, newscaster Hu Ziwei seized the microphone from her husband, celebrity sports anchor Zhang Bin, and publicly denounced him for an alleged affair. The video clip wound up on YouTube, and Chinese blogs exploded with gossip, naming yet another TV personality as Zhang's mistress and the mother of his illegitimate child. But the bloggers further alleged that Zhang's wife was *also* pregnant at the time of her outburst—and that makes the scandal doubly controversial. If true—and Zhang would not confirm or deny the rumor—it makes him one of a number of wealthy Chinese officials, entrepreneurs and celebrities who have flouted the country's family-planning regulations barring most urban couples from having more than a single child. Breaking that ban can result in penalties of up to $100,000, which most Chinese citizens can't afford. But the country's elite can pay it, or wiggle out of it, and do, fueling resentment at a time when the gap between the rich and poor in China has reached alarming proportions. "I feel very angry about it," says Liu Dalin, curator of a Suzhou museum devoted to the history of sex in China.

In fact, the one-child policy is a misnomer. Nine categories of Chinese citizens, including rural couples whose first child is female, can legally have more than one. That allows for loopholes, especially as population mobility has weakened enforcement. Government workers risk getting fired if they break the rules, but other wealthy city dwellers have multiple strategies for "extra births," including paying fees, hiring surrogate mothers and giving birth in Hong Kong or in foreign countries.

The government is especially sensitive about corrupt officials' abusing their ill-gotten wealth for extra kids. Between 2000 and 2005 in Hunan province alone (population: 66 million), 1,968 officials defied family-planning regulations, according to the state-run Xinhua News Agency. One senior parliamentarian had four mistresses and four children. Provincial authorities are now proposing to fine violators up to eight times the average per capita income as punishment. With so much at stake, the Zhang scandal is turning into much more than just another case of sex, lies and videotape. —MELINDA LIU

WEEK OF MARCH 24

CHINA

More Bloodshed in Tibet

As police clashed with Tibetan protesters in Lhasa last week, shops were set on fire, vehicles overturned, ethnic Chinese attacked and crowds turned back by tear gas in the worst civil unrest to seize the remote region in nearly two decades. Although reports are difficult to confirm, Western media estimates of the death toll ranged from two to as many as 20. As in 1989, the last time such violence racked Tibet, relatively modest protests against Chinese rule escalated into wider unrest after authorities cracked down with detentions and brute force. The apparent cause of the turmoil, once again, was the March 10 anniversary of a failed 1959 Tibetan uprising against Chinese rule.

> **Can Chinese officials put the entire roof of the world into lockdown?**

But there's another factor adding to the tension: Beijing will host the 2008 Olympics in less than five months. Obsessed with pulling off a picture-perfect Games, Chinese authorities seem rattled by even minor PR setbacks. After the singer Björk shouted "Tibet! Tibet!" during a recent concert in Shanghai, China's Ministry of Culture declared that she'd broken the law and that it would clamp down on performances by foreign artists. Then at the last minute, authorities halted filming on "Mao's Last Dancer," a movie based on dancer Li Cunxin's memoir about life in Mao's China.

The Olympic torch relay is also mired in controversy. Beijing plans to have runners carry the Olympic flame to the top of Mount

Everest in Tibet—and to ensure no repeat of last year's protests at Everest base camp by pro-Tibet Western activists, officials have barred foreign climbers from summiting the Tibetan side. Now Chinese authorities are leaning on the Nepalese government to impose similar restrictions from their side of the peak. Can Chinese officials put the entire roof of the world into lockdown? According to one foreign analyst involved in monitoring Olympic preparations, who requested anonymity for security reasons, "They're simply just freaking out."

—Melinda Liu

WEEK OF APRIL 7

TIBET

A Race Fight Roils China

With Tibet in turmoil and the 2008 Olympics looming, Beijing is trying to repair its international image. The strategy is a familiar one: control the story. China's state-run Xinhua news agency has packaged official FAQs on the Tibet unrest, while its CCTV released a 15-minute video of "the [March 14] beating, smashing, looting and burning incident." Domestic media paint a graphic scene of Lhasa bloodshed—the blood of ethnic Chinese, that is. Rioters, they report, killed an 8-month-old baby, sliced off a woman's ear and fatally trapped five saleswomen inside a burning store. Chinese TV showed shopkeepers grieving for the dead. "[Tibetans] don't want to work," said one Chinese woman. "They just want to destroy our prosperity."

To justify its crackdown, which according to Tibetan rights groups has claimed some 140 lives altogether, China has portrayed the turmoil as a plot led by the exiled Dalai Lama to foment racist attacks against Han Chinese. This portrayal has triggered anti-Tibetan invective, as well as abusive phone calls and death threats, on the mainland

and abroad. For days, Matt Whitticase of the London-based Free Tibet Campaign received offensive calls between 4 and 6 a.m. "They were highly abusive and anti-Tibetan," he says. "Things like 'F— you! F— you!' and making sexual innuendoes about the Dalai Lama."

The intensity of the racism is partly Beijing's own doing. Many Chinese youths know little about the Dalai Lama, who fled Tibet in 1959, beyond his demonization as an "impudent" separatist. By censoring media, imprisoning cyber-dissidents and employing sophisticated Web policing, Chinese authorities have raised a generation unaccustomed to international criticism of Beijing. "A lot of people [in China] simply aren't aware of the complexities of the Tibet situation," says Rebecca MacKinnon, a Hong Kong-based expert on China's new media. "The backdrop here is rising nationalism."

Tibetans are becoming more aggressive, too. During a tightly managed international media tour of Lhasa last week, 30 distraught monks inside the Jokhang Temple hijacked a press briefing, shouting "Tibet is not free!" Police hustled them off, to an unknown fate, and reporters were forced to move on.

Such polarization jeopardizes the conflict's only solution: dialogue between Beijing and the Dalai Lama. While hotheaded Tibetan youths urge greater militancy, the exiled spiritual leader is saddened by rising anti-Chinese sentiment. Decades ago Tibetans used to refer to Chinese with an affectionate honorific. Now, the Dalai Lama told NEWSWEEK during a March 20 interview, they use the derogatory *gyaro*, meaning "Chinese corpse." For Beijing, the eruption of anti-Tibetan sentiment has at least drowned out any domestic suggestion of government weakness or policy miscalculation. The bad news is that, once unleashed, the rampaging genie of racism may prove impossible to tame—on either side.

—MELINDA LIU

> **Such polarization jeopardizes the conflict's only solution: dialogue between Beijing and the Dalai Lama.**

WEEK OF JUNE 9

CHINA

A Culture Rethinks Psychology

The last time that China suffered a natural disaster approaching the magnitude of the recent earthquake in Sichuan, its Maoist leaders considered psychology a "bourgeois" discipline. Survivors of the 1976 Tangshan quake, which killed at least 255,000 people, were left to cope on their own with post-traumatic stress disorder. On May 12, however, for the first time in its history, China's Communist Party leaders ordered a large-scale mobilization of mental-health workers alongside disaster-relief personnel. The need is great: the calamity killed as many as 80,000, created at least 5,500 orphans and left 5 million homeless. According to one local news report, 600,000 residents may need psychological assistance.

Help was available for 15-year-old Xiang Li, who along with 900 schoolmates was in class when the Juyuan Middle School collapsed. Pinned for three hours in the rubble, Xiang kept shouting encouragement to her friends. Out of her class of 66, she was among only 25 to survive. "I don't have nightmares," she told NEWSWEEK with a bold chirp in her voice. "The earthquake taught me to be brave." But moments later she confided to Dr. Yuan Linfang, head of a psychological-counseling team from Henan, that she actually does suffer flashbacks and nightmares. He gently encouraged her to acknowledge her symptoms. "Some survivors act tough, but they really are having problems," said Yuan, who heads a Henan crisis-intervention hotline organized by the Communist Youth League. Yuan has observed a number of traumatized reactions among Juyuan

> **By the end of 2006 China had just 19,000 trained mental-health professionals.**

students, including one girl who couldn't even bring herself to open a textbook. Many more fear returning to school.

Experts such as Yuan are in short supply. By the end of 2006 China had just 19,000 trained mental-health professionals. Owing to the sheer number of quake survivors and first responders, says Dr.

WEEK OF JUNE 16

CHINA

The Power Of Migrants

For two and a half years, Sichuan native Yu Hongbin has worked in Shenzhen, the Chinese boomtown on the coast opposite Hong Kong, making chips for Nokia cell phones. It's a good life for an 18-year-old. Yu has pulled in nearly $200 a month—more than some Sichuan farmers make in a year—and in the past, he would blow it all on karaoke, hotpot restaurants and his gym membership. But on May 12 he was back in Sichuan washing clothes by a stream when the ground started bucking and houses crumbled. He scrambled to find his mother and came across her, dazed, near the town's "1,000-year-old tree," which locals believe was a talisman.

Now Yu sits in a bus station, on his way back to Shenzhen. The best way to help his family, he says, is to keep on working. "But I'm not going to waste money like I did before," he says. "Now I'm going to send $140 a month back home to my folks. The earthquake made me regret I never sent them money before." Multiply Yu's sense of responsibility by 20 million to 30 million—the estimated number of Sichuanese who, like him, are migrant workers—and you begin to see signs of hope for this western province. Up to a third

> **Yu has pulled in nearly $200 a month—more than some Sichuan farmers make in a year.**

of Sichuan's 85 million natives are thought to be living elsewhere and have, or may find, jobs outside the disaster zone. The money they send home will be critical to helping Sichuanese recover.

China's mobile masses aren't universally welcomed. Migrants

have been blasted as a destabilizing force, blamed for rising crime and urban protests. But they're also recognized as the engine of China's economic boom and, now, a stabilizing force in the quake zone. Entire cities have been buried. Some companies have already gone bankrupt; others plan to rebuild elsewhere. "I'm a farmer and this is my first time to seek work away from home," says Su Zhengjun, at a crowded labor market in Chengdu. "I worry about being cheated by a blackhearted boss, but so long as I get insurance and $143 a month, I'll go anywhere!" And like so many others, he'll send a chunk of that money right back home. —MELINDA LIU

WEEK OF JULY 28

CHINA

Taking Away Olympic Fun

The stage at D22 had fallen silent. Authorities clamped down on the Beijing rock club earlier this month for lacking a performance license. "There was no notice," says owner Michael Pettis. The Chinese capital is full of businesses that have operated for years without a full set of licenses. The rules are often so hard to understand that even city inspectors made little effort to enforce them—until now.

With the Olympics just weeks away, inspectors are dusting off the rulebooks and pouncing on the tiniest of infractions. One pasta restaurant was forced to stop serving salads and desserts—because the license is for "noodles," and enforcers say that's nothing but spaghetti. Some owners have had to close rooftop terraces perfect for summer nights: a falling bottle might hit a passerby. Street-level seating has been banned, too: inspectors recently carted off the ta-

The government's runaway regulators are trampling a once thriving entertainment scene, and threatening to make this the least-fun Olympics ever.

bles, chairs and ornamental hedges from sidewalk restaurants. Now

China and the Olympics-360 | JULY

club owners and patrons worry the next step might be a crackdown on Beijing's previously ignored 2 a.m. closing law. "In the last two months . . . checkups have been harsher and harsher," says Tobi Demke, the Swedish manager of a Thai restaurant.

Entrepreneurs say the government's runaway regulators are trampling a once thriving entertainment scene, and threatening to make this the least-fun Olympics ever. The uncertainties have made clubs nervous about hiring big-name DJs and bands. Nightlife guide Time Out Beijing, which had its own license problem, is planning a double issue for August and September because there's not enough to fill two separate magazines. "They want to make sure everything looks clean and goes smoothly," says editor Tom Pattinson. "They're not so interested in making sure that everyone . . . [learns] what a great, vibrant, exciting city Beijing is."

—MARY HENNOCK *and* MANUELA ZONINSEIN

WEEK OF OCTOBER 6

CHINA

Saving Face Goes Sour

Could a New Zealand dairy trader have done more to prevent China's milk scandal? At press time, Sanlu Group milk products contaminated with the toxic chemical melamine had killed four babies, sickened 53,000 and triggered import bans and recalls worldwide. But 43 percent of Sanlu is owned by New Zealand cooperative Fonterra, the world's biggest dairy trader, and Fonterra has three people on the seven-member Sanlu board. Still, Fonterra executives were in the dark about the mass poisoning until August—eight months after their Sanlu partners found out. Once in the loop, they failed to persuade Sanlu to go public for six weeks. "Fonterra," says Paul French, chief China analyst for the Shanghai-based consultancy Access Asia, "apparently believed all the . . . books in which foreign executives are taught not to let their Chinese partners get offended or 'lose face'."

Indeed, Fonterra took pride in its "trust-based" relationship with Sanlu, which became a joint-venture partner in 2005. That trust, evidently, was misplaced. Fonterra chief executive Andrew Ferrier says his people first learned about the melamine—which was added by independent milk collectors to disguise watered-down product—at a Sanlu board meeting Aug. 2. Instead of going public, Ferrier decided to try working "within the system" and reach a consensus with the Chinese about how to get the most tainted milk possible out of stores and homes. But local Chinese officials fretted that antigovernment anger might endanger "social stability" during the Aug. 8 to 24 Beijing Olympics. Sanlu chairwoman Tian Wenhua was a local Communist Party secretary, meaning she would have known about decrees that sensitive topics—especially food-safety concerns—were taboo during the Games. Fonterra executives told New Zealand Embassy diplomats about the poisoning on Aug. 14, and they informed the Kiwi government in Wellington, which in turn alerted Beijing on Sept. 9. The Chinese central government went public two days later.

Ferrier told NEWSWEEK that Fonterra acted correctly and "it had nothing to do with face." But at the least, its executives were naive not to consider the possibility of a Sanlu cover-up, especially in light of so many recent Chinese export scandals. "We can all be sensitive about not letting Chinese partners feel offended," says French. "But when it's a matter of life and death, you have to draw the line."

—MELINDA LIU

> **Sensitive topics—especially food-safety concerns—were taboo during the Games.**

Society and Living

YEAR IN REVIEW

In 2008, the color of the year was indisputably green. Not the money kind. The ecological kind: green energy, green architecture, green industry, green clothing, green living. Depending on your level of devotion to environmentalism, the use of the word "green" as a catch-all prefix represented an essential breakthrough in America's collective value system—or an irritating (and often sanctimonious) marketing trend aimed at guilting people into paying more for scratchier toilet paper.

In fact, you could reach both conclusions at the same time. Exploding gas prices and an overlong war fought in an oil-rich region—not to mention some truly bizarre, unseasonable weather caused partly by climate change—forced Americans to come to grips with the urgent need to change our consumption habits. And this was the year that evolving dogma collided with capitalism, turning eco-worship into big business, as seemingly everyone tried to turn green living into some serious green. But the wave of every product being labeled "green" got annoying in a hurry—and curmudgeons weren't alone in their dismay. Environmentalists, too, were surprisingly unsettled by the explosion, fearful that an oversaturation of "green" products would turn eco-friendly habits into a fad (like Amy Winehouse or Ugg boots). Eco-warriors also fretted over a glut of products and services pretending to be green when they were actually anything but. Such misleading practices even earned a name: "green-washing." Bombarded with confusing information and adopting complicated habits, well-meaning people learned what Kermit the Frog did long ago: it ain't easy being green.

Green living wasn't the only niche phenomenon to hit the mainstream in 2008; social networking did, too. This was the year your mom joined Facebook, making millions of Millenials scramble to readjust their privacy settings, lest their parents stumble across that photo album of mobile uploads from last Friday night's party. It's already become a cliché to note how sites such as Facebook and MySpace (and the professional version, LinkedIn) have changed everything we do, from event planning to political campaigns—but it bears repeating nonetheless. Barack Obama's success might've still happened even without his three million-plus Facebook friends, but his campaign's prescient grasp of marshalling technology to aid grass-roots organizing set a standard that all movements, not just political ones, will be aping for years to come.

But by the end of 2008, the social story of the year was ultimately a painful one: the economy, fueled for years by an excess of credit and misbegotten loans, hurtled into a brick wall. The prices of basic necessities—gasoline, milk, prescription drugs—shot up, while wages for most American families stayed flat. The ripple effects of newspaper headlines were felt right at the kitchen table, ushering in a rededication to thrift and ending the year with an anxious holiday season.

WEEK OF JANUARY 7

VIRGINIA TECH

How to Prevent a Tragedy

Tucked away in rural southwest Virginia, remote Blacksburg is an unlikely spot for the worst school shooting in U.S. history. Nevertheless, an April 16 rampage by a mentally disturbed student, Seung-Hui Cho, left 32 people dead. In the wake of that tragedy, Virginia Tech has begun to make changes in its campus security, student-privacy policies and mental-health services. But it's not the only one. Here's what some institutions around the country are doing:

CAMPUSWIDE TEXT SYSTEMS

In the aftermath of the shooting, many schools scrambled to devise systems that would allow them to issue campuswide text messages in the event of an emergency—something Virginia Tech was roundly criticized for not doing. Harvard, Penn State and Florida A&M are among the schools that now have such systems; some enable college police to monitor the locations of students on and off campus.

ANONYMOUS HOT LINES

The University of Texas at Austin is among the schools with confidential hot lines for students and staff to report behavior exhibited by campus-community members that they find disturbing. The Austin line can also be used for urgent counseling. It's staffed around the clock.

IDENTIFYING TROUBLE

Washington University in St. Louis and the University of North Carolina at Chapel Hill are among the schools that have focused on training faculty and staff to identify and help troubled students. "The gist of it is, 'Don't worry alone'," says Alan Glass, director of Washington University's student-health services. "We want them to bring anything that concerns them to our attention, so we can determine if we should potentially intervene."

BULKING UP STAFF

Virginia Tech's mental-health center has expanded its staff since the tragedy, and for the first time hired case managers to keep track of challenging situations. It has also joined the ranks of colleges with a standing "threat-assessment team," made up of police, clinicians and school officials, to review cases that present a particularly compelling personal, campus or community threat, says Chris Flynn, who heads the university's mental-health services.

—Pat Wingert

FIRST PERSON

Twice Touched by Fire, This Californian Is Still Dreamin'

Many southern California residents will head into this holiday season still grappling with the ruins of October's wildfires. For NEWSWEEK*'s Jamie Reno, it was an all-too-familiar experience. Our San Diego reporter shares his tale—and explains why his family has decided to stay.*

It's been two months since devastating wildfires swept through southern California, and while more than 2,200 San Diego families lost their homes, the crisis—for now—is over. The fires that chased and terrified us last fall are now just something my wife, daughter and I mention as we sit beside the Christmas tree counting our blessings. But while all is seemingly calm and bright in our home this holiday week, inside me, uneasiness still stirs. Not only because so many people, including good friends, have sadly lost everything, and not only because the threat of a future fire still looms. But also because, for the first time in 25 years, I've actually begun to question my decision to live in this place I've so often called paradise.

Surviving two hellish wildfires in four years will do that to you. It gave us pause to ponder our attachment to home, and what that means. My decision to move here seemed like a good one at the time: I was an Iowa boy with images of golden, endless California summers when I chose San Diego for college and beyond. I thought it was the best place in America to live—and still believe that, most days. But the fires have left me worried, wondering if we should continue to put up with this very dark side of utopia, which you don't see in the brochures or hear about in any of those Beach Boys songs. On Thursday night of what we now refer to as "The Fire Week"—when the winds changed, the temperature dropped, and we finally realized we were probably going to get through this storm—my wife turned to me and smiled, wearily. "I love San Diego," she said, "but I don't want to go through this again."

> **"I love San Diego, but I don't want to go through this again."**

We've talked since about moving. But our deep love for this town, and our respect for those who've lost everything, who rolled up their sleeves and started over in the same spot, have persuaded us to stay, too. I suspect most of you will understand, especially you Kansans with your tornadoes, and you Floridians with your hurricanes, and you Oregonians with your floods. I'm sure I'm not the only one who wondered aloud why anyone in his right mind would live in New Orleans post-Katrina. But how can any of us judge them? Staying is a difficult decision with unknown consequences, but for us, leaving would be harder. In a way, the fires brought me closer to my neighbors than I ever have been. I guess we must be willing to go through these periodic nightmares to keep living out our California dreams. Why? Because it's home.

GAMING

What a Scrabulous Year!

Most journalists who write about videogames compile a list of the year's best games. At NEWSWEEK's Level Up blog, written by yours truly, N'Gai Croal, I'd rather single out the year's most important games. Here's my top five:

1. Scrabulous on Facebook

There's nothing new about Scrabble—which dates to the 1930s—nor was Facebook the first social network. But when you combine a game that most people know with a well-populated community of people with whom users have a real-world connection, the result is perhaps the ultimate time waster. Along with its various quizzes and list comparisons, Facebook is redefining interactive entertainment.

2. Halo 3

No, it wasn't a shoot-'em-up for the thinking gamer, as some claimed. (See entries Nos. 3 and 5, if that's your bag.) But its "saved films" feature, which allows us to record all of our play sessions to the hard drive for subsequent playback, is the equivalent of a TiVo for video-games. For multiplayer, we used it to revel in our pwnage; for single-player, we dropped the camera behind enemy lines to listen to their chatter. The prospect of revisiting previous bursts of play years from now, as if they were home movies, is (for us) strangely intoxicating.

3. Portal

If Halo 3 is a first-person shooter, Portal is a first-person puzzler. You're trying to escape from a research lab, armed only with a gun that fires the titular portals: place one portal against a wall and the other on the ceiling, and when you walk into the wall you'll fall through the ceiling. From this simple, brilliant gameplay concept,

Valve Software has created a minimalist masterpiece, with its twisted narrative serving as the icing on the cake.

4. Wii Play

How do you turn a mediocre collection of mini-games into a yearlong hit? If you're Nintendo, you package it with a Wii Remote and watch as the Wii Play bundle prints money for your company. After all, hardly anyone is buying the highly social Wii to play games by themselves, so those fortunate enough to get their hands on one of the consoles are easy marks for a salesclerk who says, "If you're looking for an extra remote, why not buy Wii Play for just $10 more?" At 3 million copies sold in the United States alone for a gross of $150 million, it's clearly the marketing move of the year.

5. BioShock

Ayn Rand and art deco don't usually serve as inspiration for game designers. Thank goodness the folks at 2K Boston/Australia decided to draw on something besides "Aliens," "Black Hawk Down" and "The Lord of the Rings." At its best, this ambitious story of an undersea utopia gone horribly wrong is both thought-provoking and genuinely moving.

BLUNDERS

Tape Ate My Homework

Like most NEWSWEEK writers, I'm a quick study. Somebody dies whom you know a little about, you take a couple of hours to eke out familiarity with solid fact, and you kick in the piece. But unlike most of my colleagues, I'm a slow learner when it comes to practicalities. I hope this year has finally taught me one thing: when it comes to the tools of your trade, get the best, no matter what the cost.

This past summer I did an interview with Philip Roth; we sat in his agent's office, my Radio Shack cassette recorder on the table between us. We spoke for about 45 minutes, after which I brought the tape to a friend's summer house, and settled in to transcribe it. What I heard was the aural equivalent of a blizzard pelting your windshield, with the noise of the machine's innards grinding away in the foreground and, in the far distance, some voicelike noises. I must have spent six hours going over those 45 minutes of tape, reconstructing what Roth had said, and had to give up

JANUARY | **Society and Living-369**

on some of his best remarks—orphans of the storm.

It made me remember a few other contretemps over the years. The terrific face-to-face interview I did with Rosanne Cash—with the pause button on. A phoner with John Lennon's pathographer—for a cover story—with the headphone and mike wires switched around, resulting in an hour of questions answered by dead air. Luckily for me, he'd recorded the interview, too, in order to protect himself.

So, for 2008, I'm contemplating a digital recorder. I've heard it has no internal grindings to compete with voices—unless bytes or whatever's in there are clattering against each other like billiard balls. If such a mishap is technologically possible, trust me to have it. And this time, for a lot more money.

—DAVID GATES

WEEK OF JANUARY 14

MEDICINE

Are Vaccines the Answer to Addiction?

A vaccine that would teach the immune system to attack and destroy cocaine before the drug reached the brain is poised to enter its first large-scale clinical trial in humans. The shot is still years away from FDA approval, but the underlying concept—inoculating those at risk of addiction—is attracting increased interest.

Besides cocaine, researchers are developing vaccines against such highly addictive substances as nicotine, heroin and methamphetamine. NicVax, a nicotine vaccine by Nabi Biopharmaceuticals, is the furthest along in development. In November, one year into a phase-two clinical trial, the company reported that twice as many people taking the vaccine had quit smoking as those taking a placebo.

Addiction vaccines work the same way as the traditional vaccines used to treat infectious diseases such as measles and meningitis. Basically, they marshal the body's defense system. But instead of targeting bacteria and viruses, these new vaccines zero in on addictive chemicals that people snort, shoot or swallow.

If the new treatments make it to market, experts hope they will overcome one big hurdle that existing anti-addiction medications have failed to clear—widespread resistance to the idea of treating ad-

> **Instead of targeting bacteria and viruses, the new treatments zero in on addictive chemicals.**

dicts with drugs. "Vaccines are nowhere near as stigmatized as giving drug therapy to the addicted," says Baylor College of Medicine psychiatrist Thomas Kosten, who is leading research on the cocaine vaccine. "'Vaccine' sounds more wholesome than 'drug'."

Despite a growing body of evidence that addiction, like so many other diseases, is rooted in a person's genes, it is often seen as a personal weakness, not a medical condition to be treated or cured. That impression, some experts say, has stymied research into potential treatments for the estimated 20 million Americans who struggle with alcohol and drug addiction. "It's easy to interest the scientists, but not so easy to interest the marketing people," says Kosten.

Each of the proposed vaccines employs a similar biochemical strategy. Because the addictive-drug molecules are small enough to evade the body's immune system, they can slip undetected from the lungs and bloodstream into the central nervous system, where they disrupt brain chemistry and turn on addiction pathways that can be difficult to shut off. But when attached to a larger molecule, the addictive substances can't hide. To make the cocaine vaccine, Kosten attached the cocaine molecule to a protein made by cholera-causing bacteria. When injected, the vaccine triggers the immune system to develop antibodies. The next time the drug is ingested, the thinking goes, these antibodies will latch onto it and prevent it from crossing the blood-brain barrier.

Current anti-addiction medications do not prevent addictive drugs from entering the brain. Instead, these treatments block the drugs' neural targets, so that when a drug reaches the brain it has no place to go. Such medications —known as small-molecule therapies—have met with only limited success so far. For example, methadone, a medication used to treat heroin addicts, has itself been associated with addiction and overdose, because in addition to blocking heroin's entrance to brain cells, methadone also mimics the narcotic, producing its own, milder high. Drugs that treat alcohol and nicotine addiction have been effective only in small subsets of patients and have produced severe side effects in some cases. "With these types of drugs, the brain's receptors are still being manipulated, albeit by a replacement drug," explains Nora Volkow, director of the National Institute on Drug Abuse, which funds research on the addiction vaccines. In theory, she says, the vaccines would circumvent some of these problems by neutralizing the addictive substance before it reached the nervous system.

One day, anti-addiction vaccines could be used to prevent substance abuse as well as treat it. "It would be great if we could give kids a vaccine that would make them impervious to the effects of hard drugs," says Volkow. "In reality, we are still many years away from that."

For the cocaine vaccine to succeed, researchers will have to solve several technical problems. In early studies, for example, not all of the subjects developed antibodies against the cocaine-cholera molecule, and some developed much stronger responses than others. "This is not like an antibiotic, which is directed against the invading microbe and has roughly the same effect on everyone," says Volkow. "Here, we are stimulating the immune system, which can react differently depending on the individual."

Another concern is that a serious drug user could overwhelm the immune response by simply ingesting more cocaine than the immune system could handle. He could also switch to another drug, which the vaccine would be powerless to protect against. The determination and desperation of drug addicts notwithstanding, however, vaccines have an extraordinary track record. They could prove to be the solution to one of our most enduring public-health problems.

—JENEEN INTERLANDI

TRANSITION

'He Never Said He Was Innocent'

SALVATORE BONANNO, 75, FORMER CRIME BOSS

Born with Mafia blood and a Mafia name, Bonanno died last week of a heart attack at his home in Arizona. He was profiled in Gay Talese's 1971 bestseller "Honor Thy Father," the first nonfiction book to bring readers inside the family. Last year Talese revisited the Bonannos for a NEWSWEEK *exclusive. He shared these memories:*

I first met Salvatore (Bill) Bonanno inside Manhattan's federal court building in January 1965. He was tall and smartly dressed. He might have been mistaken for a lawyer, not the acting head of a New York crime family.

He was about to face grand-jury questions about his father, Joseph Bonanno, a powerful don who had gone missing the previous year. I was covering the case for The New York Times, and I kept looking at him. We were about the same age, I thought. Our fathers were both from Italy. At one point, he noticed me staring.

And, as if he knew me, he smiled. "I want to write about you," I said later. His lawyer looked at me like I was a lunatic. "Not *now*," I said. "Someday, though." Bill was absolutely silent. But I sensed from his expression that the idea intrigued him.

Some time after that, I was told that we could go out to Johnny Johnson's, a New York steakhouse. From then on, we commenced the art of hanging out. We talked for hours. He seemed to enjoy sharing stories about his school days at the University of Arizona, his double life escorting coeds to parties on football weekends and then driving to the Tucson airport to meet one of his father's friends arriving from the East. It was clear that Bill was reared as a fractured man, cracked over two worlds: the Old World and the New World, the illegitimate world and the legitimate world. But it was never clear which world was his. He wasn't a ruffian, for one thing. He wasn't a "dese, dem, dose" kind of gangster, nothing like Tony Soprano. I never heard Bill Bonanno use the F word. The first time his family came to dinner at my house in New York, he brought a remarkable gift—he always brought gifts—a pie-size metal merry-go-round with a flag on top. When engaged, it played a tune: "Love Makes the World Go Round." I always thought that was funny. I'm not saying he wasn't involved in an ugly world, where ugly, bloody things happened. He was. But he wasn't of it. And he never said he was innocent. I loved that, too.

GADGETS

And Now . . . the eyePhone

Good news for those who think we don't stare enough at screens—soon there will be a way to keep up with e-mail, news feeds and TiVoed movies every waking minute. At the Consumer Electronics Show this week an Israeli company named Lumus will introduce a high-resolution system that beams an image directly to the eye, via glasses barely heavier than normal spectacles. Though Lumus's prototype frames are a bit dorky, the lenses themselves are only 2 millimeters thick, and the see-through image is brighter and less disorienting than previous efforts. Lumus CEO Zvi Lapidot envisions a day when you'll order these "informative glasses" as a routine addition to your usual prescription. Though Lumus is enthusiastic about watching movies with the glasses, more intriguing are the prospects of "Terminator"-style readouts that layer Web-based information onto one's field of vision. Lapidot calls this "augmented reality," and it could include news headlines, GPS navigational directions and possibly, with the addition of tiny cameras and facial-recognition software, a way to ID acquaintances whose names you just can't place.

—STEVEN LEVY

DINING

Gratuitous Technology

Americans are obsessed with saving time, but there are some things we still haven't streamlined. Like sit-down dining. In many restaurants in Europe, a waiter brings the check along with a panini-size wireless device, and customers swipe their own credit cards. It's a rare example of the world's outpacing the land that invented the drive-through. Now American eateries are starting to play catch-up. National chains like Hooters and Legal Sea Foods have been experimenting with wireless credit-card readers for months. Legal Sea Foods aims to be entirely pay-at-table by 2009. B.R. Guest Restaurants, owner of 17 upscale eateries in New York, Chicago and Las Vegas, recently launched its own pilot program. By next year, says Tanya Steele, editor of Epicurious.com, "I think you'll see them at mid- and even high-end restaurants."

Economically, it's a no-brainer. European data show that the scanners actually increase tips by 9 percent, because preset tip buttons ensure that servers aren't shorted by sloppy math. Pay-at-table technology also saves time by eliminating extra trips to the register. Another benefit of scanners: they reduce the risk of identity theft. "The restaurant business is one of the only industries left where a person takes your credit card and disappears," says Roger Berkowitz, president of Legal Sea Foods. There is a lingering etiquette issue, though: when do you tip? In Europe, service is included. But here, deciding on a gratuity while a waiter hovers nearby to take back the scanner could make customers feel rushed. "The key is, no awkward moment," says Grant Drummond, marketing communications director for Toronto-based Ingenico, a leading manufacturer of wireless-pay technology. "Servers should give a little spiel about how the device works, and then walk away." If only those machines could pick up the tab, too.

Economically, it's a no-brainer.

—TONY DOKOUPIL

WEEK OF JANUARY 21

TRANSITION

From Up High, a Noble View

SIR EDMUND HILLARY, 88, EXPLORER
At Camp IV, 20,000 feet above sea level, writer Jan (then James) Morris landed one of the 20th century's great scoops as the first journalist to meet Sir Edmund Hillary on his descent from the summit of Mount Everest in 1953. Morris reflected on the great New Zealand climber upon his death last week:

I vividly remember the moment when, on the way home from Everest in 1953, Ed Hillary, a New Zealand beekeeper, learned that he had become Sir Edmund Percival Hillary. What a laugh—that this least pompous of colonial boys, this most unpretentious of mountaineers, should suddenly become a Knight Commander of the British Empire, by command of Her Majesty the Queen of England. He did not, as I remember, laugh himself. He took the command seriously, but not for a moment allowed it to alter him. This was lucky, because during the next 55 years, he was to become one of the most honored men on earth.

He had been knighted because he was, with his Sherpa colleague Tenzing Norgay, one of the first two men ever to stand on top of the world. But he was to be more deeply respected because of the way he used his fame. His strength was not merely physical. It was spiritual, too, which gave him the higher purpose of devoting his later energies to the welfare of the Sherpas—building schools and clinics, bridges, airfields and monastery reconstructions that were sponsored by his Himalayan Trust. He was the opposite of that contemporary mediocrity, the Celebrity.

"Well," he said when he returned from the summit, "we've knocked the bastard off!" His life was saddened by personal tragedy—his wife and daughter died in a plane crash in 1975—but it is for this bold, breezy, let-'em-all-come assurance, innocently masking the more profound, that I shall always remember Ed Hillary—beekeeper, knight and genuinely heroic non-celeb.

JANUARY | **Society and Living-375**

CRIME

Call Them 'Cat' Burglars

For gearheads, a catalytic converter is an anti-pollution device located on the exhaust system of every car and truck. For small-time thieves, "cat cons" are becoming a quick and easy payday. Cops from Maine to California are reporting a surge in cat-con thefts, because each one contains a few grams of platinum, which has skyrocketed in price from $500 an ounce in 2000 to more than $1,500 today. In Stockton, Calif., thieves took off with more than 400 cat cons last year; Akron, Ohio, police report about 100 such thefts from used-car lots just since Dec. 20. Criminals need only a minute to slip under a vehicle, remove the bulky part with wrenches or saws and disappear. Police officials say the crooks then sell the cat cons to salvage yards for between $25 and $200. The bill to replace them can run to up $2,000, says John Nielsen, director

---

CLOSURE

A Prosecutor Run Amok

In the mass-media age, major news stories captivate us for a moment and then vanish. We revisit those stories to bring you the next chapter.

STARTING POINT

In spring 2006, after an African-American stripper claims she was gang-raped at a Duke lacrosse party, Durham (N.C.) County District Attorney **Mike Nifong** charges three white players with rape and kidnapping. He calls them "hooligans" and says he has "no doubt" that a crime occurred.

FEVER PITCH

The case consumes the national media, winding up on NEWSWEEK's cover—but then it falls apart: the victim recants, and the D.A. becomes an icon of prosecutorial abuse. All charges are dropped.

PRESENT DAY

Disbarred after 28 years of practice, Nifong, 57, still lives in the Durham area, passing his time writing poetry and performing as a soloist in his church choir, according to an ex-colleague who didn't want to be named discussing a friend. "All he ever wanted to be was a prosecutor," this person says. "It was part of his identity. What's he going to do now?" For a while, at least, he'll be facing the tide of lawsuits against him. —TONY DOKOUPIL

of the AAA's national Auto Repair Network. No one keeps national statistics on cat-con theft, Nielsen says, so the full scope isn't clear. But "as long as someone's willing to pay for it, someone will steal it," says Nielsen. One prevention tip: "cat" burglars tend to target SUVs and other high-clearance vehicles for the ease of theft and higher platinum yields—so maybe it's time to trade in the big pickup for a low-rider. —ANDREW MURR

RELIGION

Sex and the Synagogue

The rise of interfaith marriage is a sensitive issue among American Jews, and now two powerful forces in the religion are teaming up to do something about it: rabbis and JDate, the top matchmaking Web site for Jewish singles. For the first time in its 10-year history, the site is offering a bulk rate to rabbis who want to buy membership accounts for their congregants. According to Gail Laguna, JDate's vice president of communications, singles who sign up through their congregation get a slight discount on the site's $149 six-month subscription fee. "This is a way for us to break down the walls of the synagogue," said Rabbi Michael Cahana, who leads the Congregation Beth Israel in Portland, Ore. "We should use all the technological tools that are available to us."

The rabbis who negotiated the bulk rate are also picking up the tab. Since September, Rabbi Donald Weber of Temple Rodeph

---

THE DIGNITY INDEX

Sorry, I Meant to Say Something *Not* Offensive

A weekly mathematical survey of dubious behavior that measures, on a scale of 1 to 100, just how low a person can go.

First **Mitt Romney** swipes Obama's "change" buzzword. Then, after wet eyes help out Hillary, Mitt goes weepy, too. Whatever works, huh? Score: **19**

Britney Spears is about as undignified as they come right now, but you know what's even worse, Dr. **Phil McGraw**? Leeching off Britney Spears. Score: **62**

Clintonite **Andrew Cuomo** calls Obama's political style "shuck and jive." Says he meant "bob and weave"—same idea, only without the slur. Score: **79**

JANUARY | Society and Living-377

Torah in Marlboro, N.J., has paid out of his own pocket for 24 six-month subscriptions. Cahana and Rabbi Kenneth Emert of Temple Beth Rishon in Wyckoff, N.J., who purchased a dozen three-month memberships, anted up for single congregants using money from their synagogues' discretionary budget. "When I heard that another rabbi was putting his money where his mouth is, I did too," says Emert, whose offer includes just one stipulation: "No mothers, no grandmothers." Singles, in other words, have to sign up themselves. The financial aid is appreciated. If not for Emert, says 29-year-old public-interest lawyer Noah Mamber, "I would have had to choose between JDate and food."

The rabbis say they felt compelled to act because of the gradual dilution of the faith through marriage. Almost half of American Jews marry non-Jews, a rate of exodus that has more than tripled since 1970. "This is about creating an opportunity," says Cahana. Sometimes even Cupid needs a nudge. —TONY DOKOUPIL

WEEK OF JANUARY 28

TRANSITION

For Him, the Game Was Everything

BOBBY FISCHER, 64, CHESS MASTER

He became a chess grand master at age 15 and a cold-war hero at 29, when he dethroned the Soviet world champion Boris Spassky in a storied 1972 match. Soon after, though, Fischer, a tempestuous personality, withdrew from the public eye. Following two decades of seclusion, he emerged briefly in 1992, defying an executive order by President George H.W. Bush forbidding him from participating in a rematch against Spassky in the former Yugoslavia, then under U.N. sanctions. (Fischer won easily.) Later, he was jailed in Japan, accused of a passport violation, and made headlines more than once for anti-Semitic comments. He eventually settled in Iceland. When he died last week of kidney failure, his longtime friend Larry Evans, a chess prodigy and writer, noted a fitting irony: Fischer died at 64, which is also the number of squares on a chessboard. Evans shared these memories of his late friend:

I was with Bobby from the beginning. I met him when he was 13, on the drive home from a Canadian tournament in 1956. Later, I became his collaborator on "My 60 Memorable Games," his masterpiece. Bobby remembered each game like it was a short story: he memorized opponents' facial gestures, their precise moves, the way in which they interacted. But getting those details out of him was like pulling teeth—he didn't want to give away his secrets. I'd say, "Well, if he makes this move, then what do you do?" I scribbled it all down and tried to be as faithful to his words as I could. Those calculations were key to understanding Bobby's thinking. His sanity seemed to desert him beyond the confines of those 64 squares.

As a human being, Bobby left much to be desired. He was stubborn, difficult, and those qualities got worse and worse as time went on. I think he was bitter because he felt the American government didn't give him the credit he deserved; he felt he'd helped win the cold war, in a small way. And the great tragedy of his life was not defending his world title in 1975 against Russia's Anatoly Karpov.

But his redeeming quality was his sense of humor. We started on his book in 1967, but after months of work, Bobby withdrew the manuscript. A year or so later, we got a note from the publishers, Simon & Schuster. They wanted to know what to do with the lead plates we used in those days to print books. Bobby was living in a Brooklyn flat at the time, and he said, "Larry, do you think I should store the plates in my apartment?" I looked at him like he was crazy. "Bobby, do you realize how many tons that stuff weighs?" I asked. "It'll come crashing through the floor and kill the tenants below." Apparently it was the push he needed: "Well, the world's coming to an end anyway," he said. "I guess I should publish the book."

A Quiet Hero in The Cancer War

DR. JUDAH FOLKMAN, 74, CANCER RESEARCHER

Folkman, who died last week of a heart attack, pioneered the theory of angiogenesis: that tumors grow by recruiting blood vessels for nourishment. Senior Writer Claudia Kalb, coauthor of a NEWSWEEK *cover story about his research, shared these memories of Folkman:*

It's hard to believe that Judah Folkman couldn't ward off death. He had long ago survived the most brutal of battles: scientific skepticism. In the 1970s, when he first proposed his radical theory of angiogenesis, he was mocked. Folkman told me he often heard researchers "laughing in the corner" or excusing themselves to go to the bathroom when he got up to speak at scientific meetings. Today angiogenesis has spawned an entire field of research and led to more than 10 cancer drugs now on the market.

The son of a rabbi, Moses Judah Folkman spent a lifetime trying to answer the prayers of his patients. He shared photographs of them as if he were showing off family albums; he told me about their hobbies and their dreams. He was a healer, a visionary with a probing intellect and a grandfatherly spirit. During our first interview, Folkman spent hours poring over the science, offered me cookies, then walked me out the front door of Children's Hospital Boston in his white lab coat to be sure I'd get home safely in a cab. Folkman wasn't interested in being a celebrity—he refused to be photographed alone for our cover story because he didn't want to be singled out for research he insisted was collaborative. His followers believe he should have been awarded the Nobel Prize. He believed he just had to keep asking questions. "You have to think ahead," Folkman told me. "Science goes where you imagine it."

FAST CHAT

Drawing a Conclusion

There are more than 200 syndicated comic strips in U.S. newspapers, but only 15 feature regular black characters drawn by African-Americans. So Darrin Bell ("Candorville") and eight other minority cartoonists have devised a "demonstration" of sorts: on Feb. 10, they will each draw a version of the same strip—a jab at readers and editors who think all their work is alike. Bell spoke with NEWSWEEK's Tony Dokoupil.

You're not calling this a protest?
It's more of a reminder that our strips are not interchangeable just because the characters are the same color.

Can you explain the timing?
I just thought, enough is enough. When one of my cartoons gets added to a page, I dread asking my syndicate what I replaced because it's too often one of the other 15 "black" strips, even though they have nothing to do with mine thematically. Many of us have even been told: adding one means cutting another.

And you sense racism at work?
The comics page just seems to be one of those areas of life where bigotry creeps in. If the first thing someone thinks when they see "Watch Your Head" [a comic about black pals in college] is "black strip" instead of "college strip," that's racism creeping in.

How big of a problem is this?
The industry forecast is mostly sunny with patches of racism. We just want everyone in and out of the rain.

WEEK OF FEBRUARY 18

PETS

In the Yard, Taking Care Of Business

The green economy is targeting a new color: brown. Each year the United States' 72 million dogs produce about 274 pounds of poo per pooch. Most of it ends up in landfills, where it oozes methane, a greenhouse gas. So eco-preneurs are offering biodegradable bags and compost services as well as new technologies that turn doggie dreck into energy. "Everybody's done it on a grandiose scale with 5,000-head cattle operations," says William Brinton, president of Woods End Laboratories, an environmental-testing lab. "[This is] the same technology, just simplified."

Lori Riegel of Tucson, Ariz., calls a local franchise called Doo Care to compost her greyhound and terrier-schnauzer droppings, and Mark Klaiman, co-owner of San Francisco's Pet Camp kennel, donates its dog waste to an off-site plant that converts it into electricity. (Eventually he hopes to use such energy to help fuel Pet Camp.) Others are trying to go green by flushing dog doo down the toilet. Sheryl Eisenberg, author of the Natural Resource Defense Council's "This Green Life" column, warns that leaving it in your yard can taint storm water and beaches. "The animals are part of our footprint," she says. Or paw print.

> "The animals are part of our footprint," she says. Or paw print.

—KAREN SPRINGEN

WEEK OF FEBRUARY 25

KIDS

Say 'Cheese!' And Now Say 'Airbrush!'

The grade-school class portrait is a time capsule of sorts—a bittersweet reminder of forgotten cowlicks, blemishes and buckteeth. Awkward, at least in retrospect, is awfully cute. So it's sad to think that those mortifying snapshots might soon be a thing of the past. Photo agencies and a horde of Web sites now offer retouching services that allow students to wipe out their every imperfection—and parents are signing up their children at younger and younger ages. "It surprises me so much when a mom comes in and asks for retouching on a second grader," says Danielle Stephens, a production manager for Prestige Portraits, which has studios in most states and offers retouching for as little as $6. "I have a 12-year-old, and I'd be afraid that if I asked for retouching she'd think she wasn't good enough."

Not all parents are as worried about the message they'll send. The rise in airbrushing is a byproduct of a culture consumed with the idea "that the body is perfectible," says psychoanalyst Susie Orbach. Stephens says that nearly every middle- and high-school order comes with a retouching request. At Legacy Photo outside Philadelphia, the tally is about half. "People want their kids to look perfect rather than teach them to appreciate their flaws," says Kelly Price, a Legacy photographer whose youngest clients are sixth graders.

There is no specific data on photo alteration for kids, but all the agencies contacted by NEWSWEEK agreed that the clients are getting younger. Most limit the service—they won't change body shape or facial structure—but all offer at least the basics. One, called Natural Beauties, touts a "total makeover" package for tots that includes new hair, skin, makeup, eyebrows and even facial expressions. (The site's owner, Alycia Collins, declined to comment.) "Retouching was meant for problems like a bump or scrape, but it's gotten to be a vanity," says Stephens. "Kids don't need to look like a model in a magazine." Sure, but do they know that? —JESSICA BENNETT

> "Retouching was meant for problems like a bump or scrape, but it's gotten to be a vanity," says Stephens. "Kids don't need to look like a model in a magazine."

SHOPPING

Price Check In Aisle Sex

The next time you hit Walgreens with your 8-year-old in tow, know this: you may end up explaining what that oval-shaped sex product sitting next to the shampoo is for. A growing "sexual health" sales drive is bringing risqué products— including lubricants, massage oils and, well, *vibrators*—into your local drugstore. Chains such as Wal-Mart, CVS and Rite Aid have begun carrying Wet, a sexual lubricant that's been a staple at the Hustler store for more than a decade, and many carry Durex's Little Gem "personal massager," which hit stores in August. Since 2003, big chains like CVS say they've more than quadrupled their shelf space for the sex-product category. "Now a soccer mom can be comfortable buying these types of products right along with her toothpaste and shampoo," says Tim Cleary, Durex's sales vice president. Not surprisingly, the retailers themselves aren't too eager to discuss the products. A Walgreens spokeswoman demurred, saying only that the offerings reflected "changing customer interest." What changed it? Widespread access to the Internet and shows like "Sex and the City," says New Jersey sex therapist Sandra Leiblum. "We're much more open now to experimenting sexually," Leiblum says. But what's next, warming gel at the supermarket? Now, there's a way to spice up your grocery list.

> "Now a soccer mom can be comfortable buying these types of products right along with her toothpaste and shampoo."

—SUSANNA SCHROBSDORFF

WEEK OF MARCH 3

COMMERCIALS

This Is Your Brain on Scary Ads

The image is meant to shock: a little girl's face atop a woman's body, cleavage spilling over a low-cut cocktail dress. Behind it, the explanation: "When you look at a young girl as something more, you need help." The ads are disturbing, to put it mildly. But more disturbing, its creators say, is what they're trying to combat: 71 percent of teen pregnancies in inner-city Milwaukee are the result of statutory rape. The ads never made it into print—United Way pulled them after they leaked online and led to a minor tempest. But industry experts say the campaign represents a genre of public-service advertising that's becoming more lurid than ever.

Shock advertising is an age-old gimmick. But compared with milder fare from years past ("This is your brain on drugs"), today's imagery is "like a sledgehammer to the face," says Steve Hall, founder of the industry blog AdRants. For instance: the ad displayed above—an anti-drunk-driving spot for Arrive Alive—featuring a scantily clad girl collapsed in a men's bathroom. Experts have called it muddled and pointlessly provocative.

Still, deterrence by disgust can work. In 2006, a series of Volkswagen safety ads drew attention for showing its cars in heart-stopping traffic accidents; within weeks, sales inquiries were up. A more recent ad for Canadian workplace safety features a glowing young chef describing her fiancé, whom she'll never marry, she says, because she's about to be in a "terrible accident." She then slips and scorches her face with a cauldron of boiling water. The series of ads, all based on real accidents, has collected 1.7 million YouTube views. "Some small amount of discomfort is worth it if it creates positive change," says Gary Mueller, founder of Serve, the agency behind the statutory-rape ads. The small discomfort, though, is getting bigger. —JESSICA BENNETT

CLOSURE

When Tonya Met Nancy

In the mass-media age, news captivates us for a moment and then vanishes. We revisit those stories to bring you the next chapter.

STARTING POINT

Olympic figure skater Tonya Harding's ex-husband **Jeff Gillooly** masterminds the 1994 plot in which a hired thug clubs the knee of Harding's rival Nancy Kerrigan, forcing her out of the U.S. championships. Harding (below, left) goes on to win, securing an Olympic spot.

FEVER PITCH

Gillooly pleads guilty to racketeering and serves six months in prison. The phrase "getting Gillooly'd" enters the vernacular as a synonym for a sneak attack.

PRESENT DAY

Gillooly, who could not be reached for comment, returns home to Oregon and changes his name to Jeff Stone. He remarries, has two kids and opens a tanning salon. Between 2000 and 2003, he's arrested twice on domestic-violence charges; both are dropped. By 2006, he is selling used cars, though one of his employers has its license revoked. Now 40, he's divorced again and dating a Portland exotic dancer, according to the woman's sister.

—J.B.

WEEK OF MARCH 10

MILITARY

What's That on Your Arm?

The mysterious world of covert military operations has always had a kind of sex appeal—the illicit tease of the unknowable. But enthusiasts are piercing that secrecy with an unconventional weapon: the uniform patch. In a new book, "I Could Tell You But Then You Would Have to Be Destroyed by Me," military buff Trevor Paglen gives readers a peek into the shadows, linking dozens of colorful patches to the missions they represent, among them flight-test squadrons, space agencies, even Area 51 research. Macabre imagery dominates: skeletons and grim reapers, ghosts and dragons. One patch, believed to be from a top-secret aircraft unit, shows a bare-chested boxer, three dogs, a pig, a guitar and a beer. It reads, WORLD'S OLDEST KNOWN FLYING PIG.

Uniform patches are a military tradition, symbolic down to the last detail. Paglen found many of the book's examples at the homes of vets he knew. With the help of journalists, historians and hundreds of Freedom of Information Act requests, he rounded up 75. "I wanted to create a window into that black world," Paglen says. The Pentagon

ENOUGH ALREADY

Your Profile Is Not Cool

Every subject wears out its welcome eventually. In this new feature, we say when.

The appeal of Facebook is simple: it's a revolutionary way to stay in touch, network, build shrines to yourself and procrastinate on the job. It is, without a doubt, a social phenomenon. But it's also nearly five years old. Every media outlet has covered every angle of its rise. There is nothing left to say, *so can we please stop talking about it?* By all means, use Facebook till your face melts. I sure do. But I don't want to hear another word about your status updates, or who wrote what on your wall, or how you dealt with that ex-boyfriend who SuperPoked you with a sheep. Now if you'll excuse me, I've just been nudged—it's my turn on Scrabulous. —JESSICA BENNETT

MARCH | **Society and Living-385**

isn't letting any more light in. Department of Defense spokesman Bob Mehal told NEWSWEEK that it "would not be prudent to comment on what patches did or did not represent classified units." That's OK. Some mysteries are more fun when they stay unsolved.

—KAREN PINCHIN

WEEK OF MARCH 17

FOOD

The Carbon Cost From Farm to Fork

It's the golden rule of the local-food movement: the fewer miles that food travels, the better for the environment. The only problem is, it may not be true. "Very few studies support the idea that local-food systems are greener," says Rich Pirog of Iowa State University's Leopold Center for Sustainable Agriculture. When it comes to calculating the carbon cost of a certain dish, the method of transport matters as much as the distance from farm to fork. Sea-freight emissions are less than half of those associated with airplanes, trains are cleaner than trucks and a tractor-trailer can be a green machine compared with an old pickup. If you live east of Columbus, Ohio, it's actually greener to drink French Bordeaux than wine from California, which is trucked over the Rockies, according to one study. How food is grown and harvested is also key, says Gail Feenstra, a food-systems analyst at the University of California, Davis. New York state apples, for instance, can be less ecofriendly than those imported from New Zealand, where, among other things, growing conditions produce greater yields with less energy. We need a complete picture of carbon emissions, Feenstra says—not just a mile marker.

—TONY DOKOUPIL

WEEK OF MARCH 24

CHARITY

Oprah's Big Enough Give

When the Oprah Store debuted in Chicago last month, shoppers snapped up affordable cosmetic cases, dog leashes and other items emblazoned with the mogul's signature "O." But the best bargains were in "Oprah's Closet," a small, unadvertised section of the store that sells her previously worn designer clothes at cut-rate prices to raise money for her charity, the Angel Network. Oprah's red Manolo Blahnik heels, for instance, are just $300, about half the retail price for similar shoes at Neiman Marcus and a fraction of what other Oprah-touched items have fetched at open auctions. Nice—but the gambit does raise a tiny ethical

CLOSURE

He's Up In Arm

In the mass-media age, major news stories captivate us for a moment, then vanish. We revisit those stories to bring you the next chapter.

STARTING POINT

In spring 2003, climber **Aron Ralston**, then 27, was pinned for four days against a rock wall in Utah's isolated Blue John Canyon when an 800-pound boulder crushed his right hand. To escape, he cut off his lower arm with pliers and a pocket blade, then rappelled down a 60-foot cliff and hiked six miles to safety.

FEVER PITCH

The story blankets the national press, winding up as a two-hour documentary on NBC. GQ and Vanity Fair named Ralston "Man of the Year," and Miller Lite cast him in its "Man Laws" ad campaign.

PRESENT DAY

Ralston, now an Aspen-based celebrity mountaineer, climbs or skis 80 days a year, dividing the rest of his time between charity work and the lecture circuit, with clients such as Goldman Sachs and Hewlett-Packard. (Speaking fee: at least $25,000, according to the Nationwide Speakers Bureau.) A movie of his life is in the works. "If I was transported back in time," Ralston told NEWSWEEK, "I wouldn't change a thing. I wouldn't bring a different knife. I wouldn't bring a jacket. I'd want it to happen exactly as it did." —TONY DOKOUPIL

quandary: if she's doing it for charity, is she obliged to maximize the return? Or is it OK for her to engage in charity-lite if it helps less-affluent fans get a piece of the action? Don Halcombe, a spokesman for Winfrey's Harpo Inc., says it was "important to Oprah" that her castoffs be accessibly priced. And according to Noah Pickus, director of Duke's Kenan Institute for Ethics, Oprah's in the clear. "She's seeking a balance between two things she sees as valuable: charity and a form of democratic experience," he says. "There isn't a contradiction here." Good to know. Still, it's too bad. At a 2004 charity auction, Oprah's Fendi sunglasses alone netted $2,000. —KURT SOLLER

> If she's doing it for charity, is she obliged to maximize the return?

WEEK OF MARCH 31

LIBRARIES

Too at Home in the Stacks

It's a core value of public libraries that their doors are open to everyone. But patience is running thin with one group: the homeless. With nowhere else to go, society's down-and-out flock to libraries for clean restrooms, comfortable chairs and a safe haven. More than 100 homeless people a day hang out in the Martin Luther King Jr. Memorial Library in Washington, D.C., while librarians in Las Vegas, Detroit and Portland, Ore., estimate similar crowds. According to Loriene Roy, president of the American Library Association, it's a matter of principle versus reality—"the philosophy of serving all people," she says, "and the reality of what happens when we do." Given the prevalence of addiction and mental illness among the homeless, what happens can be unsettling: drug use in the stacks, masturbating at the computers, fouling the grounds. The strain on staff, and other visitors, has become so acute that city library leaders will meet during a conference this week in Minneapolis to discuss new approaches, says Pamela Stovall, associate director

> Some libraries have already instituted an exclusion system to penalize bad behavior.

of D.C.'s MLK library. Some libraries, including Portland's downtown branch, have already instituted an exclusion system to penalize bad behavior: one day for shaving in the bathroom, three years for fighting. But the Philadelphia Free Library has a more enterprising program. It pays homeless patrons to monitor the restrooms, and it plans to employ them at a new café. Participation in the program, like the library, is open to all. —TONY DOKOUPIL

ADVERTISING

You're Fine As You Are!

The new ad campaign for Weight Watchers wants us to know that it's on our side. "Diets are mean," reads one slogan; "Go on a diet diet," urges another. Tylenol is now distributing free tips on preventing

---

CLOSURE

Memories of a 'Miracle'

In the mass-media age, news stories captivate us for a moment and then vanish. We revisit those stories to bring you the next chapter.

STARTING POINT

June 2002: **Elizabeth Smart,** 14, is abducted from her home in Salt Lake City. Her father goes on TV to plead for her return, prompting a nationwide search.

FEVER PITCH

Nine months later, Smart is found just 20 miles from home, disguised in a veil, wig and glasses and in the company of her captors, Wanda Barzee and Brian David Mitchell, a polygamist who claimed to be a Mormon prophet. He'd forced Smart to be his "wife."

PRESENT DAY

Now a 20-year-old sophomore at Utah's Brigham Young University, Smart is living in an apartment in Provo with friends, majoring in music and playing the harp in the university orchestra. She says she does whatever she can to help other victims of kidnapping; she recently helped write a Department of Justice Survivor Guide. "I'm doing wonderfully," Smart told newsweek. "Miracles happen." Mitchell and Barzee have repeatedly been deemed mentally unfit to stand trial. They are being held in Utah. —JESSE ELLISON

common aches and pains—only without the help of Tylenol or any other pill. Spokespeople for the companies say their campaigns are "honest" or "educational."

It's an odd strategy: trying to win over consumers by suggesting that we don't need what they're selling. Have companies forgotten about the bottom line? No, they've just learned that shoppers are susceptible to flattery. If customers believe a company "has what's good for me in mind, that's a big, big plus," says C. B. Bhattacharya, a marketing professor at Boston University. The approach has worked for Dove, whose Campaign for Real Beauty, which debuted in 2004, urges women to love their bodies just as they are. It's helped Dove vault from a soap brand into a $1 billion company with new lines of lotions and self-tanners.

> **It's an odd strategy: trying to win over consumers by suggesting that we don't need what they're selling.**

Such ads also stand out in a market cluttered with unrealistic promises. The risk is that you'll decide you're doing fine, no purchase necessary. And no company wants to make that sale.

—SARAH KLIFF

WEEK OF APRIL 7

HEALTH

Plight of The Teenage Insomniacs

Rachel Estrella, a high-school senior in Barrington, R.I., gets into bed every night before 10, hoping to beat her insomnia. One frustrating hour later, she gets up. She reads. She writes. She waits. Finally, at 1 or 2 a.m., Estrella's mind and body give in. On average, she gets four to five hours of sleep a night—nowhere near the nine recommended for teens. "I'm exhausted," she says. "There are times when I feel like I want to be knocked out because there would be some relief."

Plenty of kids have trouble getting up for early-morning school bells. Teen insomniacs have it much worse. Night after night,

Society and Living-390 | APRIL

they struggle to sleep; day after day, they suffer. In a new study published in March in the Journal of Adolescent Health, researchers report that insomnia in adolescents is as prevalent as substance abuse and other disorders, like depression and ADHD. "That was a surprise," says lead author Robert Roberts of the University of Texas School of Public Health. One quarter of the 3,134 participants said they had one or more symptoms of insomnia, such as trouble falling asleep or staying asleep, every night. And 5 percent fit the classic definition, meaning their nighttime sleep problems interfered with their ability to function during the day.

The study is unique because it evaluated the effect of sleeplessness in adolescents over time. Researchers interviewed participants, ages 11 to 17, at the beginning and end of a 12-month period. Over the course of the year, insomnia symptoms and hard-core insomnia persisted for many, and the impact was significant. Those with chronic insomnia were five times more likely to think their mental health was poor, three times as likely to have health problems and trouble at school, and twice as likely to use alcohol and drugs like marijuana and cocaine. A previous study found that the use of prescription sleep medications spiked by 45 percent in children under 19 between 2001 and 2006. It is also possible, says Roberts, that adolescents are turning to drink and drugs in an effort to self-medicate.

The biology of the tired teenage brain is still emerging. Mary Carskadon of Brown University kicked things off when she identified a shift in the internal clock of teens that made them feel sleepy later at night. Now she's launching a study to pinpoint exactly how that happens. In the meantime, teens like Estrella, whose insomnia is compounded by sleep apnea and restless-leg syndrome, can be treated. Good "sleep hygiene" starts with a routine bedtime and awakening time and a ban on cell phones and other tech at night. And cognitive-behavioral therapy helps by restructuring negative thought patterns ("I can't sleep"), says Estrella's doctor and Brown researcher Judith Owens. The goal: I can sleep, and I will.

—CLAUDIA KALB

> "There are times when I feel like I want to be knocked out because there would be some relief."

APRIL | Society and Living-391

WINE

Tastes Great, Less Billing

In a world without price tags or labels, which wines would rule? Food writer Robin Goldstein offers an answer in "The Wine Trials," a new book based on a blind taste test of 540 wines, priced between $1.50 and $150. Goldstein's 500 volunteer tasters, a group that included experts and everyday drinkers, sipped more than 6,000 glasses of wine and recorded their impressions on a simple scale of bad, OK, good and great. Their results might rattle a few wine snobs, but the average oenophile can rejoice: 100 wines under $15 consistently outperformed their upscale cousins. For instance, after the initial ratings were turned into numbers (1 for "bad," 4 for "great"), a $9.99 bottle of Domaine Ste. Michelle Brut outscored a $150 bottle of Dom Perignon, while Charles Shaw Cabernet Sauvignon, known as "Two-Buck Chuck," bested the $55 version from Stags' Leap Artemis. Several box wines, much derided in some circles, also cracked the top 100. This is what happens when you "get past the jargon and pomposity of wine writing," says Goldstein. "People shouldn't have to apologize for serving cheap wine."

His motto—"If you hide the label, the truth comes out"—is beginning to sound like more than a pet theory. In January, scientists from Caltech and Stanford

Selected Blind-Tasting Results

Oyster Bay Sauvignon Blanc
New Zealand
price $13
rating* 2.75

Quinta da Aveleda Vinho Verde
Portugal
price $6
rating 2.61

Feudi di San Gregorio Falanghina
Italy
price $15
rating 2.57

Marqués de Cáceres White Rioja
Spain
price $9
rating 2.43

Cakebread Cellars Chardonnay
U.S.A.
price $40
rating 2.13

Beringer Private Reserve Chardonnay
U.S.A.
price $35
rating 2.06

*RAW AVERAGES

upended traditional measures of taste with the results of a mischievous study in which volunteers were invited to try Cabernet Sauvignon priced at $5, $10, $45 and $90. The twist? There were actually only two kinds of wine offered, marked with different prices. The $90 wine was presented at its real price as well as marked down to $10, while the $5 bottle was also marked up to $45. The results were surprising: price appeared to dictate pleasure. The wine drinkers liked the $90 bottle best, the $5 bottle least. When the same volunteers were offered sips without price data, though, they preferred the $5 option. According to Paul Glimcher, director of New York University's Center for Neuroeconomics, if the price is different, the brain's perception of the experience will be, too. The lesson? Don't overthink it.

—ROXANA POPESCU

FAST CHAT

A Cure for Common B.S.

In "Beyond Bullsh*t," Samuel Culbert, a professor at UCLA's Anderson School of Management, tries to cure the scourge of cubicle culture: excessive b.s. He spoke with NEWSWEEK's Tony Dokoupil:

"If you hide the label, the truth comes out."

Why did you write this book?

I wanted to explain why bulls—t has become the etiquette of choice in office life.

How do you define b.s.?

It's telling people what you think they need to hear. It may involve finessing the truth or outright lying, but the purpose is always self-serving. And while I appreciate the role of some b.s. in keeping the corporate peace, it makes people feel beaten up, deceived—even dirty. When people talk straight at work, companies make out better because the best idea usually wins. In contrast, when people are bulls—tting, they hide their mistakes and the company suffers.

What's required to create a culture of straight talk at work?

Straight talk is the product of relationships built on trust. No one advocates something that's good for the company that's not also good for them. By the same logic, no one has ever washed a rental car. The trick is to create a work environment where people feel sure that they'll be rewarded for their ideas.

What does your b.s. detector tell you about the current economy?

Whenever there's a recession, there's a boom in bulls—t.

APRIL | Society and Living-393

WEEK OF APRIL 14

CRIME

A Child Stripper's Saga

It wasn't the first time the 12-year-old Dallas girl had disappeared. In 2006, after flunking the fifth grade, she ran away out of fear she'd get in trouble, says her grandmother. Eventually, her family found her on the street in a downtown entertainment district. Then last November, the girl went missing again. Her family searched for three weeks until her father spotted her in the same neighborhood, wearing a skimpy outfit and stiletto heels, says her grandmother, who declined to be named to protect the child's identity. The girl said she'd been working as a stripper at Dallas's Diamonds Cabaret. According to her police statement, she'd been taken there by a couple with whom she'd sought refuge and who made her earn her keep by stripping.

The case, which became public last month, has shocked the Dallas area. Many residents are outraged that the club remains open. (Its owners didn't return calls seeking comment.) Officials are now working on new provisions that would make it easier to revoke a cabaret's license if it employs minors. Authorities have also moved against the couple who allegedly housed the girl. In February, they indicted David Bell, 22, and Demonica Abron, 28, on charges of felony sexual performance of a child, among other counts. The defendants could not be reached for comment.

The girl, says her grandmother, is "a 12-year-old trapped in an 18-year-old's body." She told police she tried to leave the couple's home at one point, but was blocked by Bell, who she said also forced her to perform oral sex on him. One night, she escaped while he slept. Now, says her grandmother, "she's doing fine. I just hope this is the last of it."

—GRETEL C. KOVACH *and* ARIAN CAMPO-FLORES

COLLEGES

For Seniors, The Waiting Game Is On

High-school students just survived what experts say was the most brutal college-admissions season ever—but now it's the colleges' turn to sweat. A record number of applications, a wobbly economy and changes to financial-aid and early-decision programs have made it difficult for many of the most selective colleges to gauge how many of their accepted students will actually enroll. To hedge their bets, some schools accepted more students than usual and also assembled longer wait lists (graphic).

Institutions rely on historical models to determine their acceptance totals, says Barmak Nassirian, associate executive director of the American Association of Collegiate Registrars and Admissions Officers, and "most of the time [the models] are amazingly good. But we run into problems during periods of turmoil." This year's dilemma was generated by a record number of high-school seniors—the classes of 2008 and 2009 represent the tip of the baby boom's baby boomlet—who are all competing for roughly the same number of freshmen slots. Many students concluded that they could improve their odds by applying to a greater number of schools, says Maria Laskaris, Dartmouth's dean of admissions. A few years ago, most students applied to five or six schools; this year, college counselors at some of the more competitive high schools had to impose caps of 10 to 12 per student.

The problem for colleges, says Nassirian, is that they don't know how many of their accepted students have also been accepted elsewhere—or "if they're the student's first choice, or their 10th. Students always think the colleges hold all the cards, but they don't." As a result, some college administrators are working the phones, lobbying their best candidates for a commitment. "That," Nassirian says, "was unheard of 20 years ago."

> "Students always think the colleges hold all the cards, but they don't."

—PAT WINGERT *and* DANIEL STONE

WEEK OF APRIL 21

EDUCATION

Color Blind At Schools That Aren't

Like most university recruiters who target Hispanic students, Christina Diaz crisscrosses the country, attending college fairs and chatting up potential applicants. Except in her case, there's a twist: she represents Grambling State University, a 107-year-old historically black college in Louisiana. And she's no anomaly. Other traditionally black institutions such as North Carolina A&T and Central State University in Ohio have also ramped up their Latino outreach. According to National Hispanic College Fairs, which organizes events at 50 locations nationwide, historically black colleges and universities, or HBCUs, now represent about 13 percent of participants, compared with virtually zero 10 years ago. Though Latinos account for only 2 percent of students at HBCUs, they're the fastest-growing group at some institutions.

What explains the increase? HBCUs are increasingly losing African-American students to mainstream universities. And outside the top tier of black higher education—places like Howard University and Spelman College—many HBCUs find themselves in dire financial straits. To survive, some are reaching out beyond their traditional base. "Schools that once had as their mission a need to educate the newly free [are] now expanding their mission into the 21st century," says Robert Dixon, Grambling's provost and vice president for academic affairs. Already, the school, whose enrollment is 4,700, has sought to broaden its appeal to white students by expanding its nursing and mass-communications departments. Now, with an eye on the fast-growing Hispanic population, it's considering Latino studies.

Some HBCU alumni worry that such changes dilute the heritage of black colleges. "They believe

> **To survive, some black colleges have started recruiting Latinos.**

the school should look the same as when they were students," says Dixon. But "the way one begins doesn't have to determine the future." At Grambling, where the number of Hispanic applicants has increased from 33 in 2006 to 53 and counting this year, the Latino students seem to be blending in fine. "I had some butterflies" at first, says sophomore Brian Bustos. But he says he gets along well with his black suitemates; he exposes them to Colombian *cumbia* tunes, while they turn him on to the latest tracks in underground hip-hop. David Myers Jr., a black freshman, welcomes the new influx. "I believe it will make Grambling stronger," he says. For some historically black schools, it could make them survivors.

—Catharine Skipp *and* Arian Campo-Flores

HEALTH

Jared's Way Is Subpar

For a decade, Jared Fogle has been "the Subway guy." Now he's trying to fit into a new role: the childhood-obesity guy. Fogle is touring the nation on what he calls a "Tour de Pants," promoting his plan to fix how kids eat. He hopes to build "the ultimate not-for-profit group to really fight childhood obesity," he says. While experts say they're pleased with his initiative, they're not so convinced by his strategy.

Fogle's plan funds school wellness programs and educates parents about healthy decisions and "at risk" signs. Researchers take issue with the latter goal, which "blames the family for problems that are only partially their fault," says Adam Drewnowski, director of the University of Washington's nutritional-science program. Repeating familiar messages—water is better than soda, fruit is better than fries—also runs the risk of tuning parents out. "We don't want to beat them over the head with how to read a label or not to eat fried foods," says Karrie Kalich, a health-science professor at Keene

> "We don't want to beat them over the head with how to read a label or not to eat fried foods," says Karrie Kalich.

State College. "Education alone usually doesn't adjust behavior in a significant way." But Fogle says he's undeterred, citing the many parents he's met who "just don't know what's truly healthy for their kids."   —Sarah Kliff

WEEK OF APRIL 28

ADVERTISING

White Milk In His Veins

Like most glam-rock gods, White Gold loves the white stuff. No, not the Bolivian marching powder—this guy gets high on milk. The dude drinks it mid-shred, right out of his transparent guitar.

If you've never heard of White Gold, it's probably because he doesn't really exist: he's the star of a new advertising campaign from the Cali- fornia Milk Processor Board. Imagine mock-rockers Spinal Tap shilling for Big Dairy in a naked bid to reach spin-savvy teenagers while they reach for sodas. "This struck us as the perfect way and the perfect tone," says CMPB

CLOSURE

Of Subways and Squirrels

In the mass-media age, news captivates us briefly, then vanishes. We revisit those stories to bring you the next chapter.

STARTING POINT

On Dec. 22, 1984, Manhattan electrical engineer Bernie Goetz opens fire on four black teens who hassle him for $5 on a city subway. All four are wounded, and one is left paralyzed.

FEVER PITCH

Goetz is hailed as a hero "subway vigilante" by New Yorkers fed up with raging crime. He's acquitted of attempted murder and spends eight months in jail.

PRESENT DAY

In 1996, Goetz is found guilty in civil court of acting recklessly, and the teen he paralyzed is awarded $43 million—forcing Goetz into bankruptcy. In 2001, he runs unsuccessfully for mayor, then in 2005 for the city's public-advocate office. (He lost.) Now 60, Goetz is a vegetarian activist and operates a makeshift squirrel hospital out of his apartment. (Squirrels, he tells NEWSWEEK, are "sociable, playful, affectionate and loving.") As for the past, Goetz—and New York—have moved on. "It's inconceivable New York City crime would go back to the way it was," he says.

—Chris Flavelle

executive director Steve James. "We're a bunch of middle-aged dairy guys. One guy said, 'I don't get it, and that's probably a good thing'." The question is whether White Gold can stop people from souring on milk. According to the Department of Agriculture, consumption slumped 14 percent between 1981 and 2006; in California, the price of whole milk has climbed 44 percent since 2003.

Already, White Gold has his own MySpace page courtesy of his creator, the ad firm Goodby, Silverstein. (Top friend: Foo Fighter Dave Grohl.) Two full-length videos of White Gold's oddly excellent songs "Tame the White Tiger" and "One Gallon Axe"—co-written by the real-life Detroit rock outfit Electric Six—are up on YouTube and will soon be available on iTunes. "Behind the Music"-style TV spots began airing two weeks ago, including one in which he reminisces about the time he replaced a broken guitar string midsolo with a lock of his nutrient-enriched tresses.

White Gold is a viral hit for the moment, but it may not have the timeless, malleable appeal of the iconic "Got Milk?" mustache campaign (which, by the way, isn't going away). No matter. To borrow his lyric, White Gold is "milk magical." —BRIAN BRAIKER

> **"This struck us as the perfect way and the perfect tone," says CMPB executive director Steve James.**

WEEK OF MAY 5

SCIENCE

This Is Your Brain on a Videogame

If proponents of video and computer games are right, the generation that grew up honing its hand-eye coordination by shooting aliens in Halo should be starting to nail real-life aircraft-carrier landings right about . . . now. But while studies show that the games can improve visual and spatial skills—and that playing violent ones makes it harder to control anger, especially when someone goads or disses you—only now are scientists studying the games' overall effects on players' hearts and minds. Next week, at the Games for Health Conference in Baltimore, Carmen Russoniello of East Carolina University will report that three nonviolent puzzle and word computer games affect heart rates and brain waves in a way that suggests they might be used therapeutically, such as for treating high blood pressure or depression.

Russoniello assigned volunteers, ages 19 to 57, to either search the Web for articles or to play one of three games: Bejeweled 2, which taps visual and spatial skills; Bookworm Adventures, in which players make words out of Boggle-like arrays, and Peggle, a Pachinko-like aim-and-shoot game. After 15 minutes he wired them up to EEGs, which measure brain waves, and a heart monitor, and then he asked them to fill out questionnaires about their mood.

Compared with the group that searched for articles, the heart monitors showed, only Bejeweled (an untimed version) reduced physiological stress. But with all three, the players felt less fatigued than before the games, less "mentally confused," more vigorous, less angry, less depressed and less mentally tense. The different games affected each of these to varying degrees—Bejeweled increased vigor the most, for instance, while Peggle reduced mental tension the most. EEGs hint at what caused these feelings: Peggle upped brain waves linked to a desire to engage with life, while Bejeweled reduced brain waves associated with avoiding and withdrawing, and Bookworm got brain waves in sync, a state associated with relaxation.

Now for the caveats, starting with the fact that the games' maker, PopCap, paid for the study (though Russoniello says it had no say in the design or data analysis). More problematic, the data are silent on whether the mood and brain changes last more than a few minutes; in contrast, mental

Players felt less fatigued than before the games, less angry and less depressed.

training such as meditation seems to bring permanent beneficial brain changes. The challenge now for videogame manufacturers itching to make what are essentially health claims: showing that the games reduce stress and improve mood better than a good book, a stroll in a garden, a movie or any other activity that tickles your brain waves.
—Sharon Begley

WEEK OF MAY 12

ENERGY

At MIT, the Greening of Young Minds

It's a Monday night at MIT, just a few weeks before final exams. Grad students Tegin Teich and Todd Schenk could be studying or relaxing. Instead, they're hustling through a maze of basement hallways in search of notorious energy hogs: vending machines. The average soda dispenser consumes 3,500 kilowatts a year—more than four times the juice for a home refrigerator.

To conserve electricity, MIT's administrators have been installing devices called Vending Misers, which use motion detectors to turn off a machine's lights and cooling systems when people aren't nearby, cutting energy consumption by 50 percent. Trouble is, MIT isn't exactly sure where all its vending machines are located, or which ones already have the devices installed. So tonight it's enlisted

---

TRANSITION

On His Long, Strange Trip

ALBERT HOFMANN, 102
Creator of LSD

The Swiss chemist discovered the drug by accident in 1938 and raved about its power to generate "wonderful visions," which he defended after LSD was widely banned for safety reasons in the 1960s. Hofmann died last week at his home in Basel, Switzerland. John Perry Barlow, a former lyricist for the Grateful Dead, met Hofmann on a 1990 "pilgrimage" to his home, and he shared these memories with NEWSWEEK's *Jessica Bennett:*

Albert Hofmann was an accidental prophet. But his casual revelation likely introduced more people to the spiritual dimension than any other discovery of the last 500 years. Around 1966, enough of my generation had taken LSD to just cut loose. We had a sudden feeling of permission: we felt it was OK to look critically at the world, to ask serious questions about the war, about how this country was governed and what to do with our lives. LSD did that. It made authority look funny. There were many things conspiring to make that moment in history a little crazy, but our reaction would have been very different without LSD. It set us free in a way we'd never been before—maybe in a way that nobody had been. Hofmann was, and is, our patron saint.

the MIT Energy Club to help figure it out.

It's just one event on the club's very busy calendar. With 750 students, the four-year-old group is MIT's fastest-growing extracurricular organization. Many of its members aim to build careers in "green tech" fields, and club events offer a chance to network and learn about the challenges and opportunities in emerging energy fields. In recent weeks, members had lunch with the U.S. Energy secretary and toured a nuclear reactor. Others discussed national biofuel policy as part of a wonky biweekly discussion held over beer and pizza at a local pub. Club members say the group exposes them to people and ideas from other disciplines; as a result, M.B.A. types become better versed in the science of climate change, while science geeks get comfortable reading business plans and understanding concepts like return on investment. In contrast to left-leaning campus environmentalists of a decade ago, who might have joined Greenpeace after school, "most of our [members] really believe in the power of the tools of capitalism to solve the problem," says founder Dave Danielson, who earned a Ph.D. in material sciences last fall.

Down in the basement at MIT, the club is getting some early results. Teich and Schenk have found a group of eight vending machines. Four of them are hooked up to Vending Misers, but only one is functioning. "This is like wiring a stereo," Schenk says, untangling wires to make the devices work. Later, Teich climbs on top of a different machine to pick off layers of masking tape left over from a paint job that had rendered the gizmo's sensor inoperable. "We probably just saved [MIT] $100" in reduced electricity bills, Teich says. It won't save the planet—but every bit counts.

—DANIEL MCGINN

At 750 members, MIT's Energy Club is the university's fastest-growing student group.

WEEK OF MAY 19

ARCHITECTURE

This Old Modernist House

The subprime mortgage crisis hasn't bruised one chunk of the real-estate market: top vintage modern houses. This week, two midcentury classics hit the auction block. The stunning Kaufmann House in Palm Springs, Calif., designed by Richard Neutra in 1946, is selling at Christie's on May 13 as part of an auction of postwar art. Impeccably restored, the glass-and-sandstone modernist icon is estimated to fetch $15 million to $25 million. The more modest 1960 Esherick House—one of the few private residences designed by the influential Louis Kahn—is part of a contemporary-design auction on May 18 at Richard Wright in Chicago. Estimated to bring $2 million to $3 million, the stucco house in Chestnut Hill, Pa., is a small jewel full of Kahn's big ideas, with its heavy walls in counterpoint to the rich wood details and the beautiful play of light.

Preservationists lose sleep when great modern houses go on the market. Many Neutra houses, for example, have been radically altered or even bulldozed after they were sold. Such midcentury dwellings often don't fit contemporary family life; the Esherick House has only one bedroom and the kitchen, with its sculptural copper details, is "challenging," says Wright. But that may not matter to the potential buyers who are targeted by these auctions: they treat these houses as works of art. And just in case, the Kaufmann House comes with strings attached, barring its new owner from making structural changes. Christy MacLear, director of Philip Johnson's Glass House, now a museum, believes art auctions "are a wonderful way to put these modernist homes into the hands of those who will treasure them." Maybe preservationists can rest a little easier.

—CATHLEEN MCGUIGAN

HIGHER ED

The Laptop Gets Booted

The tech revolution at the nation's top law and business schools, where students now routinely use laptops and wireless connections in class, has created an insurgent population: professors, who believe they're losing the fight against wandering minds. In retaliation, at schools such as Harvard, Yale and Columbia, some profs have banned laptops from class altogether. In a more measured approach, the University of Chicago Law School cut its classroom Wi-Fi signal this spring, citing an "epidemic" of Web browsing during lectures, while at UCLA law, profs can activate a "kill switch" to disable Wi-Fi if they sense an attention deficit. The results, they say, are striking. "I'm getting much better eye contact," says Michigan law professor Richard Friedman, who installed a no-laptop policy in January. "It's been like renewing an acquaintance with an old friend." To others, though, the crackdown lets the real culprits off the hook. "If you're so boring that students are zoning out, you ought to rethink if you should be teaching," says UCLA law professor Stephen Bainbridge—though he admits that he's flipped the kill switch in his own classroom more than once. Tetris, anyone?

> "I'm getting much better eye contact," says Michigan law professor Richard Friedman.

—MATTHEW PHILIPS

WEEK OF JUNE 2

DRINK

Boxed *Vino* Goes Primo

Fans of boxed wine have always taken the good with the bad, the good being the price; the bad, of course, being the quality. But for those who've outgrown cheap hangovers but not cheap prices, a new breed of "premium" boxed wines has arrived. Made from pure wine varietals that don't carry additives or extra sugar, these wines have long been popular in Europe and Australia (where they make up 50 percent of sales, say industry experts), and are now the fastest-growing sector of the American market. Sales were up 50 percent in 2007, according to AC Nielsen.

Brands such as Black Box, Bota Box and the Wine Cube by—get ready—Target use California grapes, and are stored with bags that collapse to keep out oxygen so the wines last longer—some up to six weeks. They're still cheap: a three-liter carton (that's four bottles) goes for about $20.

That's still unlikely to attract connoisseurs. "My patrons would laugh me right out of the restaurant if I brought a box over to their table," says James Endicott, a Manhattan sommelier. But the wines should be a hit for less discerning drinkers. "Wine should taste good. It's that simple," says Steph Waller, a California wine lover who is working on a book called "Box of Wine: A Cultural Icon." Waking up without a headache can't hurt, either. —JESSICA BENNETT

> "My patrons would laugh me right out of the restaurant if I brought a box over to their table."

WEEK OF JUNE 9

PSYCHOLOGY

They'd Give Their Right Leg

When Josh amputated his own hand with a power tool a few years ago, he says he was fully prepared. He had tried before, once by crushing it beneath a truck (the jack didn't collapse right), another time by almost hacking it off with a table saw (he lost his nerve). Sometimes he would drive around for miles with his hand dangling out the window, hoping to get sideswiped. But this time he was determined. He had practiced on animal legs bought from a butcher. He kept a supply of bandages nearby to stop the bleeding, and a cell phone in case he got dizzy. Today Josh—who insists on using a pseudonym because his family thinks he lost his hand in an accident—says he feels wonderful, that his self-amputation ended a "torment" that had plagued him since middle school. "It is a tremendous relief," he tells NEWSWEEK. "I feel like my body is right."

On the scale of bizarre ailments, Josh's case surely ranks near the top. But his condition has a name: scientists call it body-integrity identity disorder, or BIID,

> **Victims of body-integrity identity disorder have a relentless desire to amputate healthy limbs.**

a rare diagnosis characterized by a relentless desire to amputate healthy limbs. In the past decade, small BIID communities have coalesced on the Web, where they lobby for surgery as a safe and legal option. "You almost have to see it to believe it," says Dr. Michael First, a professor of clinical psychiatry at Columbia University. "These people say, 'Every minute of my life I feel like something is wrong.' But it doesn't impair their ability to relate to other people. They are completely in touch with reality."

Their macabre stories are irresistible fodder for Hollywood. Opening next week is a new film, "Quid Pro Quo," about a journalist looking for a man who has offered a doctor $250,000 to amputate

---

ENOUGH ALREADY

Our Summer Wish List

Every subject eventually wears out its welcome. In this recurring feature, we say when.

Summer is almost here, and if history is a guide we've got only about three months to enjoy it. So to maximize our bliss, what follows is a list of words and concepts we don't want to hear—and people we don't want to hear from—until autumn at the earliest:

Flag pins. Torch protests. The Reverend Wright and the Reverend Hagee. Jose Canseco. Roger Clemens. Barry Bonds. "The Republican brand." "Cougars." Newly crowned American Idol David Cook. Cougars who lust after newly crowned American Idol David Cook. The Smart Car. The entire Lohan family. The entire Simpson family. Reality TV about hairdressers and lumberjacks. President Bush's overuse of the word "awesome." "Hello, I'm a Mac." "And I'm a PC." Florida. Michigan. Ringing phones at 3 a.m. Products labeled "green." Obama Girl. "LOL." "OMFG." "L8R."

his leg. But BIID is also attracting attention from researchers who compare it to phantom-limb syndrome, in which amputees still feel pain in their lost limb, and to gender-identity disorder, which causes people to feel they were born into the wrong sex. The key questions: Is BIID a mental illness or an ironclad aspect of one's identity? How should it be treated? "Clearly, surgery has helped some people more than anything else. That's a fact," says First. Sufferers agree. "Nothing touches it other than surgery," says Sean O'Conner, who runs the Web site BIID-info.org. "Psychiatry doesn't work. Medication doesn't work."

Neurologists at the University of California, San Diego, have found in BIID patients some variation in the right parietal lobe, the area of the brain responsible for creating a "map" of where one's body exists in space. "Because of this dysfunction . . . this sense of unified body image isn't formed," says Dr. Paul McGeoch. "They can feel that [their limb] is there, but it doesn't feel like it should be. It feels surplus. Something's gone wrong." But they don't know why. And for BIID sufferers, only the most drastic measures seem to put it right. —JESSE ELLISON

WEEK OF JUNE 16

TECHNOLOGY

See You at Reunion. Or Maybe Not.

Before he graduated from Tulane in 2003, Ardalen Minokadeh spent most of his waking hours in one of two places: P.J.'s Coffee on Maple Street and the late-night carrels at the University Center. But he didn't revisit any of his old New Orleans haunts during his five-year college reunion last month, because he didn't go. He already sees plenty of his closest Tulane pals, and as for the dozens of more distant friends from school, why does he need a reunion when he's got Facebook? Social networking has largely been a force for good, reconnecting grade-school classmates, creating a whole new approach to dating and enabling employers to check up on new hires. But it might just kill the college reunion.

Historically, reunions have

used voyeurism as a lure. Who lives where, who got hitched, who got fat—you had to show up to find out. But now the answers are all online. "Facebook has turned the idea of college reunions from an expensive necessity to just expensive," says Kevin Pang, who skipped his five-year reunion at the University of Southern California last week.

That's bad news for colleges: reunions are the most reliable fund-raising tool in their arsenal. "It works, there's no question," says Derek Wittner, Columbia University's deputy vice president for development, adding that reunions often account for a third of overall giving. "[They are] used, by design, to encourage more aggressive philanthropy every five years." Reunions work, says Alison Traub, a development officer at the University of Virginia, because they make people feel involved and provide a "natural timetable" for donations. "Fund-raising is all about creating artificial deadlines—'Won't you make a gift before reunion?'" Colleges know from their own research that if you get graduates to start donating young, they'll keep it up late into life. The danger is that an attendance falloff at reunions now could have a ripple effect for decades. "If reunions were to go away," says Tim Caboni, a scholar at Vanderbilt's Peabody College of Education, schools will "have to figure out other ways to tap into loyalty."

So far, college administrators report no such decline. But they have reason to be nervous. Anyone attending a five-year reunion in 2008 was part of the last class for which Facebook was not an integral part of campus life; it began catching on in mid-2003. The class of 2004—next summer's reunion crop—will be the first real test.
—ADAM B. KUSHNER

> **Historically, reunions have used voyeurism as a lure.**

WORKPLACE

Call for Fido On Line Two

The dog days of summer are coming early this year: June 20 is Take Your Dog to Work Day, and thousands of companies are rolling out the welcome mat. FirstComp insurance in Omaha will offer pets a bone-shaped cake and a wading pool, while the conference room at Village Green, a property-management company in Michigan, will host a doggie masseuse. (That's massages for dogs, not *by* dogs.) Pets in the workplace increase "morale, productivity and camaraderie," says Andrew Field of the Montana-based company Printing ForLess.com, where every day is Take Your Dog to Work Day. Such lenient policies are surprisingly common: 17 percent of Americans say that their companies are Fido-friendly, according to a new survey.

If you're among the estimated 5 percent of the population with dog allergies, though, Take Your Dog to Work Day may be a misery— a good time to Take a Personal Day. "I hate to sound negative," says Dr. Andy Nish of the American Academy of Allergy, Asthma & Immunology, "but I do have concerns." There's a reason that most hospitals and schools don't permit dogs. Companies typically require visiting pooches to be gentle and housebroken—or else the pets get "fired." Even dogs, it seems, aren't safe from downsizing.

—Karen Springen

WEEK OF JUNE 23

RELIGION

God's Word, According to Wikipedia

A few times a week, Alastair Haines, a grad student at the Presbyterian Theological Centre in Sydney, sits down with a Greek version of the New Testament and translates a bit of Paul's first letter to the Corinthians. Haines doesn't speak Greek, but he can read it. When he's done, he loads his work onto a Wikipedia page as part of the Wiki Bible Project, a take-all-comers effort launched in January to create "an original, open content translation of the Bible's source texts," which by most counts includes about 30,000 manuscripts. Along with Haines, who admits to signing up for duty as a way to put off finishing his dissertation, 21 others have answered Wikipedia's call to "claim a chapter!" The eclectic group includes a liberal Christian living in the United Arab Emirates and a Methodist financial counselor in Texas. Some claim to be formally trained in Biblical Hebrew and classical Greek; others, such as user John Kloosterman, admit to being "without qualifications of any kind." The project will take a few years to complete and require constant refinement, says John Vandenberg, one of project's main administrators. But "that is part of the beauty," he writes. "It's a laissez-faire translation."

But Biblical scholars see the potential for an inaccurate, bias-filled mess. "Democratization isn't necessarily good for scholarship," says Bart Ehrman, a professor of religious studies at the University of North Carolina at Chapel Hill, who worked on the most recent translation of the New Revised Standard Version in 1988. "Those were the best Greek and Hebrew scholars in the country, and it took them 20 years." Repercussions of mistranslations are great. (Old Testament scholar Richard Friedman says he's already found errors in Wiki's Genesis translation.) In the Middle Ages, Ehrman notes, someone added 12 verses to the Gospel of Mark where Jesus says believers will "pick up serpents"; it now forms the textual basis for Pentecostal snake handlers.

Advocates say the discussion pages will be a microcosm of a theological debate that has been raging for centuries. Of course, those debates had winners and losers. "We're lucky," says Barnard College Biblical scholar Alan Segal, "that we no longer live in a period where they burn the scholars."
—MATTHEW PHILIPS

MILITARY

No Glass Ceiling Here

For 25 years, Lory Manning lived in a universe foreign to many women she knew. She participated in international negotiations and oversaw $3 million budgets. Her path to power: the Navy. Manning, who now works for a nonprofit, says she "never would have gotten these opportunities elsewhere."

Women and minorities often express dissatisfaction with barriers in the civil work force, but, according to a new University of Massachusetts study of 30,000 active-duty personnel, they are the most satisfied military employees.

> "Democratization isn't necessarily good for scholarship," says Bart Ehrman.

> "They figure it's part of being a woman in the military," says University of Maryland sociologist Mady Wechsler Segal.

(White men are the least.) The service's racial diversity and rank-based hierarchy "level the playing field," says the study's author, sociologist Jennifer Hickes Lundquist. If the satisfaction among enlisted women seems surprising—especially given that a third reported experiencing sexual harassment in a recent Pentagon survey—there is a possible explanation: "They figure it's part of being a woman in the military," says University of Maryland sociologist Mady Wechsler Segal, who is unaffiliated with the survey. It may not sound like progress, but for a level playing field, it's a risk that some military women seem willing to take. —SARAH KLIFF

WEEK OF JUNE 30

IDEAS

The Best Brand? No Brand.

"I'm not much of a consumer." It's a refrain that New York Times columnist Rob Walker heard a lot while researching "Buying In," his fascinating new book about the dialogue between who we are and what we buy. His salient point: while none of us likes to think of himself as a brandobsessed zombie who uses his credit cards to purchase an identity, our behavior often tells a different story.

The Big Idea: According to Walker, we have entered an era of "murketing," a hybrid of the words "murky" and "marketing." It has two levels of meaning. "The first," he writes, "refers to the increasingly sophisticated tactics of marketers who blur the line between branding channels and everyday life." The other refers to "the modern relationship between consumer and consumed," which is "defined not by rejection at all, but rather by frank complicity."

Evidence: Dunkin' Donuts recruited teenagers to wear temporary tattoos of the company's logo on their foreheads. Turner Broadcasting paid ex-art students to build mysterious flashing signs around several cities. Savvy marketers have also found ways to cozy up to consumers who resent being walking advertisements. American Apparel built brand loyalty out of selling logo-free clothes. Pabst Blue Ribbon made itself into a hit beer by cultivating an ordinary image. Adbusters Blackspot sneakers—which look like Chucks with a circular black smudge—are a protest brand that says, "I'm not into brands at all."

Conclusion: Millennial consumers—whom Walker calls "the least rebellious generation since the youth concept was invented"—have been billed as resistant to branding. But like the rest of us they still reach for brands to express their cultural selves. The point? Buying in is fine, as long as we know who's pulling the wool over our eyes—and most of the time we're doing it to ourselves.

—TONY DOKOUPIL

THERAPY

My Shrink Says . . . Blog!

Why do people write confessional blogs? It's a creative outlet. It's a forum to vent. It's an exercise in exhibitionism. To mental-health experts, though, it's more than that: a blog is medicine. Psychiatrists are starting to tout the therapeutic power of blogging, and many have begun incorporating it into patient treatment. A forthcoming study in the journal CyberPsychology & Behavior even suggests that bloggers might be happier than nonbloggers.

Mental-health experts say blogs are a step up from plain old diaries, chiefly because of the built-in

CARS

A Whole New Layer of Skin

Who needs an auto show when you've got your own skin flick? BMW just went viral with a YouTube posting of GINA, a curvaceous concept car with plastic skin instead of metal. In a week, it generated 2 million hits. In the languid vid, GINA stretches her gull-wing doors and blinks her cat-eye headlights. Chief designer Chris Bangle explains that her jumpsuit can be zipped on in two hours. The message: A car's steel skeleton protects you, so why not wrap your ride in something more lifelike? Sadly, BMW has no plans to bring GINA to life. But it's building plenty of Bimmer buzz.

—KEITH NAUGHTON

audience. As kids, we learn that if we air our problems, we get help. We associate communication with consolation, particularly when the going gets tough. Blogging fulfills that primal need for sympathy. "Writing is an effort of the brain to communicate for comfort," says Harvard neurologist Alice Flaherty. "Diaries are a form of that communication, but removed. Blogging gets you closer to that sympathetic audience, and that's what makes it therapeutic." According to psychologist John Suler, the anonymity of blogging provides another therapeutic boost: it's high intimacy with low vulnerability.

But blogger beware. "Revealing too much," says Suler, "can cause

> **"Writing is an effort of the brain to communicate for comfort," says Harvard neurologist Alice Flaherty.**

shame or guilt." So blog to your heart's content, but leave some things to the imagination.

—JESSICA BENNETT

WEEK OF JULY 21

RELIGION

The Amma Will Hug You Now

Last week a Manhattan convention center was the scene of a literal love-in when an estimated 15,000 people lined up to get free hugs from Mata Amritanandamayi, better known as "Amma" or the "Hugging Saint." The 54-year-old native of India has hugged 27 million people worldwide, say her followers, and has gained a fan base in the West, where she's wrapping up a 10-city North American tour. Accompanied by white-robed groupies who caravan behind her tour bus, Amma, considered a saint by her acolytes, spends upwards of 18 hours a day giving hugs. "I am not like a battery that needs to be recharged, I am eternally connected to the power source," she says through a translator. (Amma speaks only Malayalam.) Hindu by birth, she does not affiliate with a specific religion—"My religion is love"—and encourages people to find faith through service. Amma is a trademarked brand with nonprofit status and volunteer projects that include a hospital in India and soup kitchens in the United States. She's funded by donations and proceeds from DVDs of her chanting, swimsuits and saris sold at events.

But despite the mysticism and the mobile gift shop, most just come for the good vibes. "I believe in God and I'm religious," says Mike Daniels, a city employee. "But I just wanted to get my hug."

—Grace Wyler

> **Despite the mysticism and the mobile gift shop, most just come for the good vibes.**

sity engineering student. So he's come up with a simple (and Kramer-esque) solution: his Easy PB&J jar has straight interior walls and twist-off lids at both ends. He spent eight years perfecting his invention and hopes to begin production later this year. "It's a really novel concept," says Lee Zalben, founder of Peanut Butter & Co., a Manhattan sandwich store. The peanut-butter industry, however, is hurting from an uncertain supply of peanuts and soaring fuel costs, and may be slow to embrace a packaging change. "It would seem much more expensive to manufacture," says Leslie Wagner of the Peanut Advisory Board. In that case, we'll just have to keep using our fingers.

—Caitlin McDevitt

INVENTIONS

Here's a Nutty Idea

Each year, Americans buy 700 million pounds of peanut butter. But about 3.5 million pounds of it ends up unused, stuck at the bottom of the jar, according to Sherwood Forlee, a former Princeton Univer-

Society and Living-414 | JULY

WEEK OF JULY 28

RELIGION

Working Out With Jesus

When Dawn Harvey leans back on her elbows, legs outstretched, rapidly pedaling, she's not just toning her abs—she's kicking Satan in the head. And when she and her Camp Springs, Md., aerobics class of 12 women stretch their palms to the sky, pumping them upward in cadence, it's not just for their triceps' benefit—it's a come-hither to their celestial inheritance. "Don't think about the pain—think about how much you love him!" screams instructor Melanie Kelly, over organ-trilling gospel music. "Y'all better praise!" This is gospel aerobics, the answer

This is gospel aerobics.

to your prayers if you're feeling feeble in body or flimsy in soul. It's hymn-singing, shoulder-bobbing, one heck of a workout—and it's happening in a musty church basement near you.

Praise with push-ups has been possible at boutique gyms like Crunch for some time. But the point is mostly kitsch, not message. So churchgoers are bringing gospel back home, to the fellowship halls of at least 100 parishes in largely minority communities nationwide. Participants say the classes are important for black women, a group that struggles with obesity. They can't hurt the soul, either: studies show a correlation between prayer and good mental health. At Gospelcize Kick, a Uniondale, N.Y., "exercise ministry" run out of a local parish, members even get a little extra: Scripture, a faithfitness newsletter and recipes. "Nothing to me inspires like gospel music," says Kelly, a 35-year-old systems analyst who holds class on the carpeted floor of a one-room church. Amen—now where's the water fountain? —SARAH BALL

WEEK OF AUGUST 11

CARS

Honda Gets It Right, All Over Again

How do you know your ride is hot? When it's not only the most popular car on the road, but also the favorite boost among thieves. That's the case with the Honda Civic. In 2007, Americans bought 331,000 of them, and stole 51,000—more than any other model. This year, Civic sales are up 16 percent, and in May, the 36-mpg car supplanted Ford's hulking F-series pickup truck as America's favorite ride. In this summer of Detroit's discontent, the Civic has become Honda's engine. With GM losing $15.5 billion in the second quarter and even Toyota slashing pickup and SUV production, Honda is in high gear, reporting record profits and sales up 3 percent this year, while overall U.S. auto sales are down by 11 percent.

Fueling Honda's joyride is the same $4-a-gallon gas that's sent other major automakers skidding. Since its humble beginnings during the oil embargoes of the 1970s, Honda has been all about the mileage. Even during the SUV boom and the $1-a-gallon era of the 1990s, Honda stuck to its guns and refused to build anything with a V-8 engine. When Detroit was minting money on Hummers and Explorers, the automotive establishment ridiculed Honda's gas sippers. "They said that we

> **Fueling Honda's joyride is the same $4-a-gallon gas that's sent other major automakers skidding.**

didn't understand the market," says Honda executive VP Dick Colliver. "They didn't think I was too smart; it didn't bother me."

Now it's like "That '70s Show" all over again. Honda dealers are putting buyers on waiting lists, and the company is building a Civic factory in Indiana to keep up. Gas prices drove Moravia, N.Y., farmer Herrick Kimball to ditch his pickup for a Honda Accord, which he uses to haul chicken feed from a trailer hitched to the bumper. "I can load an Accord up like a pickup truck," he says.

Next April, Honda will release a small hybrid priced around $20,000 that it says will get better mileage than a Prius. That should attract even more fuel-conscious consumers, but analysts wonder if Honda, which derives most of its sales from the U.S. and Japan, has deep-enough pockets to develop the high-tech electric cars of tomorrow. "Honda lacks the global scale of other automakers," says veteran auto analyst Dave Cole. For now, though, Honda is giving new meaning to "hot car"—just ask Ohio dealer Don Smith. He sent a woman on a test drive, and she never came back. "A Honda is not easy to steal without the keys," he says. "And we gave her the keys." In this panic at the pump, those are the keys drivers covet.

—Caitlin McDevitt *and* Keith Naughton

IDEAS

Hey, Man, Learn to Drive!

The best way to enjoy Tom Vanderbilt's new book, "Traffic: Why We Drive the Way We Do (and What It Says About Us)," is to forget the psychobabble title and merge like a commuter into the text itself. Like real traffic, it's sometimes slow going. But it's also a delightful tour through the mysteries and manners of driving. Think you do it well? Vanderbilt thinks not.

The big idea: "Driving," Vanderbilt writes, "is probably the most complex everyday thing we do in our lives." Yet most people zip around without ever realizing that their driving is based on faulty perceptions and folksy "superstitions" about life on the road.

Examples: Women can't drive? Actually, men are the terrors: they speed more, honk more, drink more, wear seat belts less and are more likely to be involved in fatal accidents. Nice people merge early? Waiting until the last second to change lanes when traffic bottlenecks actually helps things flow more smoothly. The other lane is moving faster? On the contrary, manic lane changers make up only four minutes of lost time—while the stress of cutting all those people off, Vanderbilt notes, probably takes more time off their lives.

Conclusion: Don't expect traffic nirvana any time soon. Confronted with bad driving all around them, most people give their own wheel-work two thumbs up—and don't see a need to change. Even if they did, they'd still be human. And that, says Vanderbilt, is exactly the problem.

—Tony Dokoupil

PSYCHOLOGY

When Life Is Like a TV Show

As a Director of Psychiatrics at New York's Bellevue Hospital Center, Joel Gold has seen thousands of delusional patients. But a few years ago, he began noticing a different sort of paranoia: young white men who believed they were the subjects of their own reality-TV shows. Some, says Gold, who with his brother has written a preliminary paper and hopes to author a larger study, seemed pleased by their roles—excited by the anticipated million-dollar payout. Others were tormented. One came to New York to check whether the World Trade Center had actually fallen—believing 9/11 to be an elaborate plot twist in his personal storyline. Another came to climb the Statue of Liberty, believing that he'd be reunited with his high-school girlfriend at the top, and finally be released from the "show."

Grandiose, paranoid delusions are a staple among schizophrenics and psychopaths. Typically, they apply to one aspect of a patient's life—say, irrationally believing a spouse is cheating. But these patients, much like Jim Carrey's character in the 1998 film "The Truman Show," believe their entire lives are being broadcast, and that everyone is in on the joke. The numbers are small—Gold has observed only five firsthand and has heard from or about more than a dozen since—but he and others think "The Truman Show Delusion," as Gold now calls it, is the pathological product of our insatiable appetite for self-exposure. Delusions are often related to the larger cultural and political climate: during the cold war some people thought they were being monitored by the KGB. Today, some might think Al Qaeda is after them. When all it takes is a Webcam and the click of a mouse to be seen and heard by millions, and with hundreds of surveillance cameras capturing our movements each day, it's not necessary to go on "Big Brother" to feel like you're in the public eye. "If you have a predisposition to paranoia, going on YouTube and seeing some guy doing something can really shake you up," says Gold. You could think, "Is the world watching *me*?" Perhaps the key to sanity is knowing that while the whole world isn't watching, someone probably is.

—JESSE ELLISON

> **"Is the world watching *me*?"**

HEALTH

Jump-Start That Heart

Call it the "Russert effect." The death of the 58-year-old newsman, of sudden cardiac arrest, has sparked a surge in defibrillator sales—in hopes that the device could save others from a similar fate. Big manufacturers such as Philips and Defibtech say their phones have been ringing nonstop since Russert's passing on June 13. It's too soon to tally sales, but Philips estimates a 30 percent increase in inquiries, and Defibtech CEO Glenn Laub, a cardiac surgeon, says he's being "deluged" by calls. "It's human nature to take stock of our own lives after someone we feel close to passes away," says Philips spokesman Ian Race.

There's no telling whether a defibrillator could have saved Russert's life. There was one available at his NBC office, but it was used only after the arrival of the paramedics. Still, defibrillation is the most effective emergency

> **Defibrillation is the most effective emergency treatment for cardiac arrest.**

treatment for cardiac arrest—the No. 1 killer in America—and can increase survival odds from 2 to 50 percent (higher if it's used within three to four minutes). Easy-to-use devices designed for the home and office cost about $1,200, and an American Heart Association study determined that even an untrained sixth grader can operate one. It might not be the happiest thing to plan for, but it could just save your life.   —CAITLIN MCDEVITT

WEEK OF SEPTEMBER 8

BUSINESS

The Next Big Thing Is ... The Bus?

If all you did was follow the headlines, you'd think it's been a lousy summer for the bus industry. In July, Greyhound made news when a Canadian man was decapitated by a fellow passenger on a bus trip to Winnipeg. A week later a bus in Texas drove off a bridge, killing 17 people. And, of course, swollen gas prices must be ruining the industry's bottom line, right?

In fact, the bus biz is enjoying a renaissance. Ridership is up for the first time since 1960, thanks to

The bus biz is enjoying a renaissance.

the rise of discount carriers such as Megabus, and Greyhound's Bolt-Bus. With cheap fares and slick new buses equipped with Wi-Fi and electrical outlets, companies have lured travelers looking for a dependable ride on someone else's gas dime. And no dingy bus stations: the new carriers offer strictly curbside pickup.

"We're remaking the image of the bus," says Megabus president Dale Moser, whose company offers Web fares as cheap as $1. In May it expanded from the Midwest into the jampacked Northeast corridor, which already has 12 passenger-bus lines. "I don't think they'll all survive," says DePaul University transportation professor Joe Schwieterman. "It's never been this competitive." Or this cozy.

—MATTHEW PHILIPS

WEEK OF SEPTEMBER 15

GOOGLE

The Cloud's Chrome Lining

With the formal beta launch of Chrome, google is trying to redraw the browser-war battlelines. But with Microsoft's Internet Explorer dominating 72 percent of the market share, why take them on—especially considering IE's home-team advantage of being built into every Windows machine? Because Google wants your browser to do more than surf the Web. It already offers a free suite of software applications (e-mail, a word processor, spreadsheets, etc.) online—or in the "cloud," untethered from your hard drive. Chrome serves them all up in one neat package, like an online operating system. A breakdown:

TABS: Ever lose an e-mail you were typing because another open Web page froze up? Frustrating. Chrome's individual tabs (unlike Mozilla's Firefox) run on their own dedicated chunk of memory, meaning that if one page crashes, it doesn't take the whole browser with it. You can even put a shortcut to one of Google's many applications—Gmail, Docs, Maps—onto your desktop. It opens in its own window even when you're not online, further blurring the line between browser and operating system.

THE 'OMNIBOX': In keeping with Google's ascetic esthetic, Chrome's design is clean and simple. The tabs have been moved to the top of the screen, the menu and status bars removed entirely. The address bar has been rechristened the "Omnibox," doubling as a search field—a menu of suggested pages appears as you begin to type your search term or URL. Chrome's only toolbar is dedicated to bookmarks.

START-UP PAGE: There is no default home page on Chrome. As a starting point you get an array of thumbnails of the sites you've visited most often and most recently—unless, that is, you visited those sites via "incognito mode," which has already been dubbed "porn mode" by bloggers who know of such things. Incognito mode doesn't record on your hard drive the sites you've visited. (But your employer's server still does, so behave.)

DRAWBACKS: For now, Chrome is available for free download only on Windows XP/Vista. There's no way to e-mail a page or organize your bookmarks. A bigger concern is a vulnerability in WebKit, the engine used to design Chrome, which could expose users to malicious "carpet-bombing" attacks. Expect a fix before too long; in the meantime, surf safely.

—BRIAN BRAIKER

> "The reports of my death are greatly exaggerated."
> —*Vice Apple CEO Steve Jobs, September 2008*
> *Perspectives*

WEEK OF SEPTEMBER 22

EDUCATION

It Makes Teachers Touchy

Teachers are conditioned to tolerate a lot of abuse—it's a professional hazard—but what faculty members at Sir G. E. Cartier Elementary School in London, Ontario, went through last spring seems beyond the call of duty: a few of them agreed to be duct-taped to a gym wall while students hit them in the face with pies. Why on earth would they do that? To raise $3,000—enough cash for an interactive whiteboard, the most coveted piece of educational technology on the market right now. These Internet-age chalkboards are essentially giant computer touchscreens, and they're all the rage among teachers. But with little room for them in school budgets, many educators are doing whatever it takes to raise the money themselves. "We're a desperate breed, aren't we?" says Sharon Zinn, one of three teachers who volunteered for Cartier Elementary's whipped-cream-flavored firing squad.

At schools fortunate enough to have them, interactive whiteboards are a blessing for educators struggling to engage a generation of students weaned on the Web. In the U.K.—where 70 percent of all primary and secondary classrooms have interactive whiteboards, compared with just 16 percent in the United States—

> **Interactive whiteboards are a blessing for educators struggling to engage a generation of students weaned on the Web.**

students in those classrooms made the equivalent of five months' additional progress in math. So far, the data on the efficacy of touchscreens in U.S. classrooms is inconclusive, but promising. Multiple recent studies suggest that the devices boost attendance rates and classroom participation. Ever since Dorchester School District 2 in Summerville, S.C., installed 1,200 interactive boards in its classrooms, disciplinary incidents are way down. "Students were bored" before the touchscreens arrived, says Superintendent Joe Pye. "Trips to the principal's office are almost nonexistent now."

But for some teachers, the learning curve with the device is steep, and a generation gap has opened with teachers who are still accustomed to writing lesson plans with a pen and paper. Many older educators are "petrified" of the boards, says Peter Kornicker, a media specialist at P.S. 161 in Harlem, where despite a student poverty rate of 98 percent, all 35 classrooms are equipped with touch-screens. "As always, it comes back to the ability of teachers to leverage this technology," says Andy Rotherham of Education Sector, a Washington, D.C.-based think tank. "We have to train them to use it. Otherwise, it's just another underused, expensive gizmo."

—MATTHEW PHILIPS

WEEK OF OCTOBER 6

PAGE TURNER

A Nation, Glazed and Confused

"Doughnuts," Homer Simpson once marveled. "Is there anything they can't do?" From one expert to another: In "Glazed America: A History of the Doughnut," anthropologist Paul Mullins traces the pastry from sweet-tooth snack to shining symbol of national gluttony.

THE IDEA: In the 1920s, automation helped doughnut makers surpass the union-controlled bagel industry, turning doughnuts into the breakfast king. As obesity rates increased, doughnuts became central to what Mullins calls the "moral battleground" to get lazy, overweight Americans off the couch.

THE EVIDENCE: The Salvation Army got soldiers hooked on doughnuts during World War I, then chains such as Krispy Kreme and Dunkin Donuts, launched in 1937 and 1950 respectively, prompted an explosion. Consumption transcends class and background: cops love 'em, criminals love 'em. They're staples in poor neighborhoods, and in wealthier, gentrified enclaves, they've survived the Starbucks boom.

THE CONCLUSION: Doughnuts are the forbidden dough. But we've caved into our craving, against our better judgment. In other words, Homer won. —OSCAR RAYMUNDO

WEEK OF OCTOBER 13

RELIGION

A Battle Over Billy Graham

The evangelist Billy Graham turns 90 next month, and in this final chapter of his life, a number of laudatory books and movies are scheduled for release. One of these, a biopic called "Billy: The Early Years," arrives in theaters this week, and if the present family skirmish triggered by the movie is any sign of things to come, Graham's grown children still need to fine-tune their public-relations strategy.

Gigi, who at 63 is the eldest of Billy and Ruth Graham's five children, endorsed the movie and wrote a positive blurb for its Web site. "The Early Years," which shows young Billy finding Jesus at a tent revival and meeting his beloved Ruth in college, is "very sweet," she told NEWSWEEK. "I've

---

CLOSURE

An Aviator's Final Flight

In the mass-media age, news stories captivate us, then vanish. We revisit those stories to bring you the next chapter.

STARTING POINT

On Sept. 3, 2007, record-setting adventurer Steve Fossett, 63, takes off from a Nevada ranch for a short pleasure trip in a single-engine plane and never returns. A frantic search for wreckage begins.

FEVER PITCH

Fossett is declared legally dead in February 2008 after the search, covering 20,000 miles and costing $1.6 million, turns up nothing. The absence of evidence prompts conspiracy theories that the millionaire faked his own death.

PRESENT DAY

On Sept. 29, a hiker stumbles across some of Fossett's belongings in a steep section of the Sierra Nevadas. Searchers find plane fragments and possible human remains strewn across a field of debris. "It's a tragic ending," Paul Ciolino, a private investigator involved in the case, told NEWSWEEK. "But he went out doing something he loved. How many people can say that?" —JESSE ELLISON

seen it 14 times, and I've learned something new each time." She likes the film because it presents her parents in a positive light and promotes a gospel message.

But Franklin, the fourth child, who is president of the Billy Graham Evangelistic Association, does not agree. In August he made a statement saying as much in an effort to distance the BGEA from the project. "Though Gigi has signed on to work with the producers in promotion of this project, no one else in the family supports or has endorsed the film—including [Billy] Graham, who has no personal inclination to view it," a BGEA spokesman explained in an email to NEWSWEEK. Further, the spokesman wrote, the movie contains inaccuracies about the family history. For example, Billy did not faint at Gigi's birth as the movie depicts; in fact, he was out of town. And Billy and Ruth never would have played catch, because Ruth was not athletic. Gigi disputes this. "If she never threw a baseball, she could play a mean game of croquet in her wheelchair at night," she says. "As his big sister, I would have suggested that Franklin not say anything."

Franklin's spokesman says that Franklin and Gigi maintain "a great relationship," but in this matter they "have had to agree to disagree." Ruth Graham's journal describes bitter (but probably normal) rivalry among the Graham siblings as early as 1955. "Anne [the second child] and Franklin," she wrote, "fought during the time I have with the Lord alone … grumbling, interrupting, slurring each other." Still, the question of how the children will handle their competing pet projects in Billy's name remains very much alive. "If you find out, will you let me know?" asks Gigi. Her voice, like her father's, is as sweet as sugar.

—LISA MILLER

PAGE TURNER

One Smart Book About Number Two

It may not be fodder for dinner discussion. Or book clubs. Or, come to think of it, polite conversation of any kind. But journalist Rose George, author of "The Big Necessity: The Unmentionable World of Human Waste and Why It Matters," was undaunted, delving deep into the history and implications of a daily act that dare not speak its name. Warning: what follows is, in a word, gross.

THE IDEA: The poop paradox, George writes, is that "it can be both food and poison. It can contaminate and cultivate." Fecal matter plays a role in 80 percent of illnesses worldwide, but it can also be used as an energy resource, fertilizer—even medicine.

THE EVIDENCE: Martin Luther reportedly ate a spoonful of his own waste daily, and ladies of the French court used a powdered version as snuff. Today excrement helps power 15.4 million homes in China, where it also increases crop yields by an estimated 50 to 60 percent. But harnessing the power of waste takes infrastructure—something lacking for the 2.6 billion people without toilets.

THE CONCLUSION: Potty humor may make you giggle, but world sanitation standards should make you cringe. We can put our waste to work for us, but not until we get over the taboo of discussing it.

—SAMANTHA HENIG

WEEK OF OCTOBER 20

GENEALOGY

The Man Who Would Be Our King

The children of Paul Emery Washington think of their father as an unpretentious guy who climbed the corporate ladder to become regional manager at CertainTeed manufacturing. Now 82, the Texas native takes care of his wife, who suffers from Alzheimer's disease, and spends time with his children. "I think he would've been a great king," says son Bill Washington. That may sound odd—except that Paul Emery Washington is a descendant of George Washington, America's first president and perhaps the only man in history who turned down the position of monarch.

Had George Washington ascended to the throne, Paul Emery Washington might now be King Paul I. Lore has it that President Washington was so adored after the Revolutionary War that a group of citizens frustrated with the Continental Congress floated the idea of

> "We've done so well as a country without a king. I think George made the best decision."

a coup d'état and the installation of King George. But Washington squelched the idea. Since then, historians and genealogy buffs have pondered what might've happened if he'd been a bit more power hungry. Without the Web, though,

Society and Living-426 | OCTOBER

they could follow the Washington family tree only so far before getting stumped.

This year, however, Ancestry.com's chief family historian, Megan Smolenyak, got on the case. She concluded that the men who led the country would've had names like Lee, Felix or Frank—not Abraham or Teddy. "We would have had a King named Spot," Smolenyak says of the son who would've reigned between King Bushrod I and Bushrod II. "How cool is that?" King Larry, meanwhile, would have been in power from 1935 to 1997. And now? There are nearly 8,000 living descendants of Washington, and of the 200 men who carry his name, Paul is at the end of two genealogical lines. That makes him the likely heir—America's ninth or 10th king, depending on which line you follow.

That's a concept that Paul would rather not think about. "I doubt if I'd be a very good king," he says. "We've done so well as a country without a king. I think George made the best decision." Paul's middle son, for his part, is somewhat relieved he isn't the crown prince, especially considering he's an Obama Democrat in a family of Republicans. "I don't think I'd be a very good subject," Bill says. "I would have had my head chopped off a long time ago." So for his sake, God save the president. —KURT SOLLER

PAGE TURNER

Your Brain Will Never Be the Same

Is the internet changing the way our brains work? That's the provocative question raised by UCLA neuroscientist Gary Small in his new book, "iBRAIN: Surviving the Technological Alteration of the Modern Mind." His equally provocative answer: yes, it is.

THE IDEA: All the multitasking, Internet searching and text messaging has made millennial brains

> **"Digital natives" are less capable of reading faces or picking up subtle gestures.**

particularly adept at filtering information and making snap decisions. At the same time, the tech-savvy people Small calls "digital natives" are less capable of reading faces or picking up subtle gestures. The reverse is true of their grandparents, whom Small dubs "digital immigrants." As technology spreads, Small suggests, natural selection will favor these newly wired brains, and older neural pathways will disappear, taking traditional communication skills with them.

THE EVIDENCE: fMRI studies are starting to show what we've long suspected: the persistent use of technology strengthens certain brain-activity patterns. In some users, Web surfing triggers reward pathways that have been linked to addiction. But proof that such changes weaken other brain regions, or that these changes can be inherited, is lacking.

THE CONCLUSION: The elasticity of the human brain means that you can have it all: reap the cognitive benefits offered by modern technology, avoid becoming an Internet junkie and preserve traditional social skills. The key, says Small, is to manage your time wisely. —JENEEN INTERLANDI

WEEK OF OCTOBER 27

PAGE TURNER

Forgive Me, Pepsi, for I Have Sinned

Why do you choose Coke over Pepsi, Corona over Bud, Crest over Colgate? You don't think much about these choices, you say; your gut decides. Marketing guru Martin Lindstrom says otherwise. Your preference for Macs over PCs is embedded in your brain circuitry. In "Buyology," he shares the results of a three-year, $7 million study, in which he submitted 2,000 people to fMRI scans to explore what, exactly, happens in your brain to make you stand in line all night for an iPhone.

THE IDEA: People lie; brain images don't. To create successful brands, companies need to learn what people *really* want, not what they say they want.

THE EVIDENCE: Lindstrom tested smokers, some of whom said they heeded the health warnings on cigarette packages. According to fMRI tests, the warnings did not dampen cravings; in fact, they stimulated them. There's a religious aspect to these brain connections, too. The same areas of the brain "lit up" when people looked at religious symbols—the Virgin Mary, for example—as when they looked at strong brands, like the iPod. Weak brands generated less brain activity.

THE CONCLUSION: The most successful brands (Nike, Harley-Davidson) stimulate the brain's emotional centers in a positive way—a lot like religion. They create community, rituals and a common adversary. Coke Zero, says Lindstrom, succeeds because it poses as an enemy to its sugary sibling, Coke. —LISA MILLER

WEEK OF NOVEMBER 3

FAST CHAT

Gossip Girls, With God in Their Hearts

In the hyperrich and hyperreligious Dallas enclave known as the Park Cities, Bible study is a contact sport. Author Kim Gatlin, a wealthy, gorgeous divorcée, was inspired to write "Good Christian Bitches" about the backbiting women in her orbit. She spoke with NEWSWEEK's Gretel C. Kovach.

Is this phenomenon of catty, devout women specific to Dallas?
This is a universal subject. In every affluent neighborhood and every trailer park you have people who are going to gossip and disappoint each other and betray one another. That's just an ugly part of human nature.

Have you ever been a good Christian bitch?
Absolutely. We're all guilty of it to a degree. It's already gotten to be a term with my girlfriends. They'll call me and say, "I was the biggest G.C.B. today," or, "I just got G.C.B.'d so bad!" All Southern girls are taught to love Jesus, but just because we're Christians doesn't mean we're perfect.

Will your pastor get past the title of the book?
The title is not mocking God. It's mocking those of us who love God and don't always make the best choices to honor him.

Do any Dallasites think you're a big sinner for writing this novel?
Yeah, they think I'm going to hell. [Laughs] But I'm not! There's been so much gossip about my book about the evils of gossip that I have enough material for a second book. The biggest problem is going to be from the people who will be disappointed when they realize it's not about them.

Appendix: Best of 2008

2008 PRESIDENTIAL PRIMARY TIME LINE

JANUARY 3

Iowa (caucus)

Democrats
Barack Obama 38%
John Edwards 30%
Hillary Clinton 29%
Bill Richardson 2%
Joe Biden 1%

Republicans
Mike Huckabee 35%
Mitt Romney 25%
John McCain 13%
Fred Thompson 13%
Rudy Giuliani 3%
Ron Paul 10%

Democratic candidates Joe Biden and Chris Dodd withdrew from the race on January 3.

JANUARY 5

Wyoming (Republican caucus)

Democrats
n/a

Republicans
Mitt Romney 67%
Fred Thompson 25%
Duncan Hunter 8%

JANUARY 8

New Hampshire (primary)

Democrats
Hillary Clinton 39%
Barack Obama 36%
John Edwards 17%
Bill Richardson 5%

Republicans
John McCain 38%
Mitt Romney 32%
Mike Huckabee 11%
Rudy Giuliani 9%
Ron Paul 8%
Duncan Hunter 1%
Fred Thompson 1%

JANUARY 15

Michigan (primary)

Democrats
Hillary Clinton 55%
Dennis Kucinich 4%
Chris Dodd 1%
Uncommitted 40%

Republicans
Mitt Romney 39%
John McCain 30%
Mike Huckabee 16%
Ron Paul 6%
Fred Thompson 4%
Rudy Giuliani 3%
Uncommitted 2%

JANUARY 19

Nevada (caucus)

Democrats
Hillary Clinton 51%
Barack Obama 45%
John Edwards 4%

Republicans
Mitt Romney 51%
Ron Paul 14%
John McCain 13%
Mike Huckabee 8%
Fred Thompson 8%
Rudy Giuliani 4%
Uncommitted 3%
Duncan Hunter 2%

Republican candidate Duncan Hunter withdrew from the race.

South Carolina (Republican primary)

Democrats
n/a

Republicans
John McCain 33%
Mike Huckabee 30%
Fred Thompson 16%
Mitt Romney 15%
Ron Paul 4%

JANUARY 20

Democratic candidate Bill Richardson withdrew from the race.

JANUARY 22

Republican candidate Fred Thompson withdrew from the race.

JANUARY 26

South Carolina (Democratic primary)

Democrats
Barack Obama 55%
Hillary Clinton 27%
John Edwards 18%

Republicans
n/a

JANUARY 29

Florida (primary)

Democrats
Hillary Clinton 50%
Barack Obama 33%
John Edwards 14%
Dennis Kucinich 1%
Bill Richardson 1%
Joe Biden 1%

Republicans
John McCain 36%
Mitt Romney 31%
Rudy Giuliani 15%
Mike Huckabee 13%
Ron Paul 3%
Fred Thompson 1%

JANUARY 30

Democratic candidate John Edwards suspended his campaign. Republican candidate Rudy Giuliani withdrew from the race.

FEBRUARY 1–3

Maine (Republican caucus)

Democrats
n/a

Republicans
Mitt Romney 52%
John McCain 21%
Ron Paul 18%
Mike Huckabee 6%
Uncommitted 2%

FEBRUARY 5 ("SUPER TUESDAY")

Alabama (primary)

Democrats
Barack Obama 56%
Hillary Clinton 42%
John Edwards 1%

Republicans
Mike Huckabee 41%
John McCain 37%
Mitt Romney 18%

Alaska (caucus)
Democrats
Barack Obama 75%
Hillary Clinton 25%

Republicans
Mitt Romney 44%
Mike Huckabee 22%
Ron Paul 17%
John McCain 16%
Uncommitted 2%

American Samoa (Democratic caucus)
Democrats
Hillary Clinton 57%
Barack Obama 42%

Republicans
n/a

Arizona (primary)
Democrats
Hillary Clinton 50%
Barack Obama 42%
John Edwards 5%

Republicans
Mike Huckabee 47%
John McCain 47%
Mitt Romney 35%
Mike Huckabee 9%
Rudy Giuliani 3%
Fred Thompson 2%

Arkansas (primary)
Democrats
Hillary Clinton 70%
Barack Obama 26%
John Edwards 2%

Republicans
Mike Huckabee 60%
John McCain 20%
Mitt Romney 15%
Ron Paul 5%

California (primary)
Democrats
Hillary Clinton 51%
Barack Obama 43%
John Edwards 4%

Republicans
John McCain 42%
Mitt Romney 25%
Mike Huckabee 12%
Rudy Giuliani 4%
Fred Thompson 2%

Colorado (caucus)
Democrats
Barack Obama 67%
Hillary Clinton 32%
Uncommitted 1%

Republicans
Mitt Romney 60%
John McCain 19%
Mike Huckabee 13%
Ron Paul 8%

Connecticut (primary)
Democrats
Barack Obama 51%
Hillary Clinton 47%
John Edwards 1%
Uncommitted 1%

Republicans
John McCain 52%
Mitt Romney 33%
Mike Huckabee 7%
Ron Paul 4%
Rudy Giuliani 2%
Uncommitted 0%

Delaware (primary)
Democrats
Barack Obama 53%
Hillary Clinton 42%
Joe Biden 3%
John Edwards 1%

Republicans
John McCain 45%
Mitt Romney 33%
Mike Huckabee 15%
Ron Paul 4%

Georgia (primary)
Democrats
Barack Obama 66%
Hillary Clinton 31%
John Edwards 2%

Republicans
Mike Huckabee 34%
John McCain 32%
Mitt Romney 30%
Ron Paul 3%
Rudy Giuliani 1%

Idaho (Democratic caucus)
Democrats
Barack Obama 80%
Hillary Clinton 17%
John Edwards 1%
Uncommitted 3%

Republicans
n/a

Illinois (primary)

Democrats
Barack Obama 65%
Hillary Clinton 33%
John Edwards 2%

Republicans
John McCain 47%
Mitt Romney 29%
Mike Huckabee 17%
Ron Paul 5%
Rudy Giuliani 1%
Fred Thompson 1%

Kansas (Democratic caucus)

Democrats
Barack Obama 74%
Hillary Clinton 26%

Republicans
n/a

Massachusetts (primary)

Democrats
Hillary Clinton 56%
Barack Obama 41%
John Edwards 2%

Republicans
Mitt Romney 51%
John McCain 41%
Mike Huckabee 4%
Ron Paul 3%
Rudy Giuliani 1%

Minnesota (caucus)

Democrats
Barack Obama 66%
Hillary Clinton 32%
Uncommitted 1%

Republicans
Mitt Romney 41%
John McCain 22%
Mike Huckabee 20%
Ron Paul 16%

Missouri (primary)

Democrats
Barack Obama 49%
Hillary Clinton 48%
John Edwards 2%

Republicans
John McCain 33%
Mike Huckabee 32%
Mitt Romney 29%
Ron Paul 5%
Rudy Giuliani 1%
Fred Thompson 1%

Montana (Repubican primary)
Democrats
n/a

Republicans
Mitt Romney 38%
Ron Paul 25%
John McCain 22%
Mike Huckabee 15%

New Jersey (primary)
Democrats
Hillary Clinton 54%
Barack Obama 44%
John Edwards 1%

Republicans
John McCain 55%
Mitt Romney 28%
Mike Huckabee 8%
Ron Paul 5%
Rudy Giuliani 3%
Fred Thompson 1%

New Mexico (Democratic caucus)
Democrats
Hillary Clinton 49%
Barack Obama 48%
John Edwards 1%
Bill Richardson 1%

Republicans
n/a

New York (primary)
Democrats
Hillary Clinton 57%
Barack Obama 40%
John Edwards 1%

Republicans
John McCain 50%
Mitt Romney 27%
Mike Huckabee 10%
Ron Paul 6%
Rudy Giuliani 3%

North Dakota (caucus)
Democrats
Barack Obama 61%
Hillary Clinton 37%
John Edwards 1%

Republicans
Mitt Romney 36%
John McCain 23%
Ron Paul 21%
Mike Huckabee 20%

Oklahoma (primary)

Democrats
Hillary Clinton 55%
Barack Obama 31%
John Edwards 10%
Chris Dodd 1%
Dennis Kucinich 1%
Bill Richardson 1%

Republicans
John McCain 37%
Mike Huckabee 33%
Mitt Romney 25%
Ron Paul 3%
Rudy Giuliani 1%
Fred Thompson 1%
Duncan Hunter <1%

Tennessee (primary)

Democrats
Hillary Clinton 54%
Barack Obama 40%
John Edwards 4%

Republicans
Mike Huckabee 34%
John McCain 32%
Mitt Romney 24%
Ron Paul 6%
Rudy Giuliani 1%
Fred Thompson 3%

Utah (primary)

Democrats
Barack Obama 57%
Hillary Clinton 39%
John Edwards 3%

Republicans
Mitt Romney 89%
John McCain 5%
Mike Huckabee 1%

West Virginia (Republican caucus)

Democrats
n/a

Republicans
Mike Huckabee 52%
Mitt Romney 47%
Ron Paul 1%

FEBRUARY 7

Republican candidate Mitt Romney suspended his campaign.

FEBRUARY 9

Kansas (Republican caucus)

Democrats
n/a

Republicans
Mike Huckabee 60%
John McCain 24%
Ron Paul 11%
Mitt Romney 3%

Louisiana (primary)

Democrats
Barack Obama 57%
Hillary Clinton 36%
John Edwards 3%
Joe Biden 2%
Chris Dodd 1%
Uncommitted 1%

Republicans
Mike Huckabee 43%
John McCain 42%
Mitt Romney 6%
Ron Paul 5%
Rudy Giuliani 1%
Fred Thompson 1%

Nebraska (Democratic caucus)

Democrats
Barack Obama 68%
Hillary Clinton 32%

Republicans
n/a

U.S. Virgin Islands (Democratic caucus)

Democrats
Barack Obama 90%
Hillary Clinton 7%
Uncommitted 3%

Republicans
n/a

Washington (caucus)

Democrats
Barack Obama 68%
Hillary Clinton 31%
Uncommitted 1%

Republicans
John McCain 25%
Mike Huckabee 23%
Ron Paul 22%
Mitt Romney 16%
Uncommitted 14%

Maine (Democratic caucus)

Democrats
Barack Obama 60%
Hillary Clinton 40%

Republicans
n/a

FEBRUARY 12

Washington, D.C. (primary)

Democrats
Barack Obama 75%
Hillary Clinton 24%

Republicans
John McCain 68%
Mike Huckabee 16%
Ron Paul 8%
Mitt Romney 6%
Rudy Giuliani 1%

Maryland (primary)

Democrats
Barack Obama 61%
Hillary Clinton 36%
John Edwards 1%
Uncommitted 1%

Republicans
John McCain 55%
Mike Huckabee 29%
Mitt Romney 7%
Ron Paul 6%
Rudy Giuliani 1%
Fred Thompson 1%

Virginia (primary)

Democrats
Barack Obama 64%
Hillary Clinton 35%
John Edwards 1%

Republicans
John McCain 50%
Mike Huckabee 41%
Ron Paul 5%
Mitt Romney 4%
Fred Thompson 1%

FEBRUARY 19

Hawaii (Democratic caucus)

Democrats
Barack Obama 76%
Hillary Clinton 24%

Republicans
n/a

Washington (Republican primary)

Democrats
n/a

Republicans
John McCain 50%
Mike Huckabee 37%
Ron Paul 5%
Mitt Romney 2%
Fred Thompson 1%

Wisconsin (primary)

Democrats
Barack Obama 58%
Hillary Clinton 41%
John Edwards 1%

Republicans
John McCain 55%
Mike Huckabee 37%
Ron Paul 5%
Mitt Romney 2%
Fred Thompson 1%

FEBRUARY 23

Northern Mariana Islands (Republican caucus)

Democrats
n/a

Republicans
John McCain 91%
Mike Huckabee 4%
Ron Paul 4%

FEBRUARY 24

Puerto Rico (Republican caucus)

Democrats
n/a

Republicans
John McCain 91%
Mike Huckabee 5%
Ron Paul 4%

MARCH 4

Ohio (primary)

Democrats
Hillary Clinton 53%
Barack Obama 45%
John Edwards 2%

Republicans
John McCain 60%
Mike Huckabee 31%
Ron Paul 5%

Republican candidate Mike Huckabee withdrew from the race.

Rhode Island (primary)

Democrats
Hillary Clinton 58%
Barack Obama 40%
John Edwards 1%
Uncommitted 1%

Republicans
John McCain 65%
Mike Huckabee 22%
Ron Paul 7%
Mitt Romney 4%
Uncommitted 2%

Texas (primary)

Democrats
Hillary Clinton 51%
Barack Obama 47%
John Edwards 1%

Republicans
John McCain 51%
Mike Huckabee 38%
Ron Paul 5%
Mitt Romney 2%
Uncommitted 1%

Texas (Democratic caucus)

Democrats
Barack Obama 56%
Hillary Clinton 44%

Republicans
n/a

Vermont (Democratic primary)

Democrats
Barack Obama 59%
Hillary Clinton 39%
John Edwards 1%
Dennis Kucinich 1%

Republicans
n/a

MARCH 8

Wyoming (Democratic caucus)

Democrats
Barack Obama 61%
Hillary Clinton 38%
Uncommitted 1%

Republicans
n/a

MARCH 11

Mississippi (primary)

Democrats
Barack Obama 61%
Hillary Clinton 37%
John Edwards 1%

Republicans
John McCain 79%
Mike Huckabee 13%
Ron Paul 4%
Mitt Romney 2%
Fred Thompson 2%
Rudy Giuliani 1%

APRIL 5

U.S. Virgin Islands (Republican caucus)

Democrats
n/a

Republicans
Uncommitted 47%
John McCain 31%
Mitt Romney 19%
Ron Paul 2%

APRIL 22

Pennsylvania (primary)

Democrats
Hillary Clinton 55%
Barack Obama 45%

Republicans
John McCain 73%
Ron Paul 16%
Mike Huckabee 11%

MAY 3

Guam (Democratic caucus)

Democrats
Hillary Clinton 50%
Barack Obama 50%

Republicans
n/a

MAY 6

Indiana (primary)

Democrats
Hillary Clinton 51%
Barack Obama 49%

Republicans
John McCain 78%
Mike Huckabee 10%
Ron Paul 8%
Mitt Romney 5%

North Carolina (primary)

Democrats
Barack Obama 56%
Hillary Clinton 42%
John Edwards 1%
Uncommitted 1%

Republicans
John McCain 74%
Mike Huckabee 12%
Ron Paul 7%
Uncommitted 4%

MAY 13

Nebraska (Republican primary)

Democrats
n/a

Republicans
John McCain 87%
Ron Paul 13%

West Virginia (primary)

Democrats
Hillary Clinton 67%
Barack Obama 26%
John Edwards 7%

Republicans
John McCain 76%
Mike Huckabee 10%
Ron Paul 5%
Mitt Romney 4%
Rudy Giuliani 2%

MAY 20

Kentucky (primary)

Democrats
Hillary Clinton 66%
Barack Obama 30%
John Edwards 2%
Uncommitted 2%

Republicans
John McCain 72%
Mike Huckabee 8%
Ron Paul 7%
Mitt Romney 5%
Rudy Giuliani 2%
Uncommitted 5%

Oregon (primary)

Democrats
Barack Obama 59%
Hillary Clinton 41%

Republicans
John McCain 81%
Ron Paul 15%

MAY 27

Idaho (Republican primary)

Democrats
n/a

Republicans
John McCain 70%
Ron Paul 24%

JUNE 1

Puerto Rico (primary)

Democrats
Hillary Clinton 68%
Barack Obama 32%

Republicans
n/a

JUNE 3

Montana (primary)

Democrats
Barack Obama 56%
Hillary Clinton 41%
Uncommitted 2%

Republicans
n/a

South Dakota (primary)

Democrats
Hillary Clinton 55%
Barack Obama 45%

Republicans
n/a

JUNE 7

Democratic candidate Hillary Clinton suspended her campaign.

JUNE 12

Republican candidate Ron Paul suspended his campaign.

AUGUST 28

Barack Obama accepted the Democratic nomination at the Democratic National Convention in Denver, Colorado.

SEPTEMBER 4

John McCain accepts the Republican nomination at the Republican National Convention in Minneapolis, Minnesota.

2008 BEIJING SUMMER OLYMPICS

Medals Awarded (by country)
August 8 – August 24, 2008

Rank	Nation	Gold	Silver	Bronze	Total
1	China (CHN)	51	21	28	100
2	United States (USA)	36	38	36	110
3	Russia (RUS)	23	21	28	72
4	Great Britain (GBR)	19	13	15	47
5	Germany (GER)	16	10	15	41
6	Australia (AUS)	14	15	17	46
7	South Korea (KOR)	13	10	8	31
8	Japan (JPN)	9	6	10	25
9	Italy (ITA)	8	10	10	28
10	France (FRA)	7	16	17	40
11	Ukraine (UKR)	7	5	15	27
12	Netherlands (NED)	7	5	4	16
13	Jamaica (JAM)	6	3	2	11
14	Spain (ESP)	5	10	3	18
15	Kenya (KEN)	5	5	4	14
16	Belarus (BLR)	4	5	10	19
17	Romania (ROU)	4	1	3	8
18	Ethiopia (ETH)	4	1	2	7
19	Canada (CAN)	3	9	6	18
20	Poland (POL)	3	6	1	10
21	Hungary (HUN)	3	5	2	10
21	Norway (NOR)	3	5	2	10
23	Brazil (BRA)	3	4	8	15
24	Czech Republic (CZE)	3	3	0	6
25	Slovakia (SVK)	3	2	1	6
26	New Zealand (NZL)	3	1	5	9
27	Georgia (GEO)	3	0	3	6
28	Cuba (CUB)	2	11	11	24
29	Kazakhstan (KAZ)	2	4	7	13

Rank	Nation	Gold	Silver	Bronze	Total
30	Denmark (DEN)	2	2	3	7
31	Mongolia (MGL)	2	2	0	4
31	Thailand (THA)	2	2	0	4
33	North Korea (PRK)	2	1	3	6
34	Argentina (ARG)	2	0	4	6
34	Switzerland (SUI)	2	0	4	6
36	Mexico (MEX)	2	0	1	3
37	Turkey (TUR)	1	4	3	8
38	Zimbabwe (ZIM)	1	3	0	4
39	Azerbaijan (AZE)	1	2	4	7
40	Uzbekistan (UZB)	1	2	3	6
41	Slovenia (SLO)	1	2	2	5
42	Bulgaria (BUL)	1	1	3	5
42	Indonesia (INA)	1	1	3	5
44	Finland (FIN)	1	1	2	4
45	Latvia (LAT)	1	1	1	3
46	Belgium (BEL)	1	1	0	2
46	Dominican Republic (DOM)	1	1	0	2
46	Estonia (EST)	1	1	0	2
46	Portugal (POR)	1	1	0	2
50	India (IND)	1	0	2	3
51	Iran (IRI)	1	0	1	2
52	Bahrain (BRN)	1	0	0	1
52	Cameroon (CMR)	1	0	0	1
52	Panama (PAN)	1	0	0	1
52	Tunisia (TUN)	1	0	0	1
56	Sweden (SWE)	0	4	1	5
57	Croatia (CRO)	0	2	3	5
57	Lithuania (LTU)	0	2	3	5
59	Greece (GRE)	0	2	2	4
60	Trinidad and Tobago (TRI)	0	2	0	2
61	Nigeria (NGR)	0	1	3	4
62	Austria (AUT)	0	1	2	3
62	Ireland (IRL)	0	1	2	3
62	Serbia (SRB)	0	1	2	3
65	Algeria (ALG)	0	1	1	2
65	Bahamas (BAH)	0	1	1	2

Rank	Nation	Gold	Silver	Bronze	Total
65	Colombia (COL)	0	1	1	2
65	Kyrgyzstan (KGZ)	0	1	1	2
65	Morocco (MAR)	0	1	1	2
65	Tajikistan (TJK)	0	1	1	2
71	Chile (CHI)	0	1	0	1
71	Ecuador (ECU)	0	1	0	1
71	Iceland (ISL)	0	1	0	1
71	Malaysia (MAS)	0	1	0	1
71	South Africa (RSA)	0	1	0	1
71	Singapore (SIN)	0	1	0	1
71	Sudan (SUD)	0	1	0	1
71	Vietnam (VIE)	0	1	0	1
79	Armenia (ARM)	0	0	6	6
80	Chinese Taipei (TPE)	0	0	4	4
81	Afghanistan (AFG)	0	0	1	1
81	Egypt (EGY)	0	0	1	1
81	Israel (ISR)	0	0	1	1
81	Moldova (MDA)	0	0	1	1
81	Mauritius (MRI)	0	0	1	1
81	Togo (TOG)	0	0	1	1
81	Venezuela (VEN)	0	0	1	1
	Total	**302**	**303**	**353**	**958**

2008 NOBEL LAUREATES

**Awarded by the Nobel Foundation
December 2008**

Chemistry
Osamu Shimomura (Japan)
Martin Chalfie (USA)
Roger Y. Tsien (USA)

Economics
Paul Krugman (USA)

Literature
Jean-Marie Gustave Le Clézio (France)

Peace
Martti Ahtisaari (Finland)

Physics
Yoichiro Nambu (USA)
Makoto Kobayashi (Japan)
Toshihide Maskawa (Japan)

Physiology/Medicine
Harald zur Hausen (Germany)
Françoise Barré-Sinoussi (France)
Luc Montagnier (France)

2008 PULITZER PRIZES

Presented by the Pulitzer Prize Board
May 29, 2008

Journalism

Public Service
The Washington Post

Breaking News Reporting
Staff of *The Washington Post*

Investigative Reporting
Walt Bogdanich and Jake Hooker of *The New York Times*
Staff of *Chicago Tribune*

Explanatory Reporting
Amy Harmon of *The New York Times*

Local Reporting
David Umhoefer of *Milwaukee Journal Sentinel*

National Reporting
Jo Becker and Barton Gellman of *The Washington Post*

International Reporting
Steve Fainaru of *The Washington Post*

Feature Writing
Gene Weingarten of *The Washington Post*

Commentary
Steven Pearlstein of *The Washington Post*

Criticism
Mark Feeney of *The Boston Globe*

Editorial Writing
No award

Editorial Cartooning
Michael Ramirez of *Investor's Business Daily*

Breaking News Photography
Adrees Latif of Reuters

Feature Photography
Preston Gannaway of Concord (NH) *Monitor*

Letters, Drama, and Music

Fiction
The Brief Wondrous Life of Oscar Wao by Junot Diaz

Drama
August: Osage County by Tracy Letts

History
What Hath God Wrought: The Transformation of America, 1815–1848 by Daniel Walker Howe

Biography or Autobiography
Eden's Outcasts: The Story of Louisa May Alcott and Her Father by John Matteson

Poetry
Time and Materials by Robert Hass
Failure by Philip Schultz

General Nonfiction
The Years of Extermination: Nazi Germany and the Jews, 1939–1945 by Saul Friedländer

Music
"The Little Match Girl Passion" by David Lang

Special Citation
Bob Dylan

2008 ACADEMY AWARDS

Presented by the Academy of Motion Picture Arts & Science
February 24, 2008

Best Picture
Atonement
Juno
Michael Clayton
No Country for Old Men
There Will Be Blood

Director
Paul Thomas Anderson, *There Will Be Blood*
Joel Coen and Ethan Coen, *No Country for Old Men*
Tony Gilroy, *Michael Clayton*
Jason Reitman, *Juno*
Julian Schnabel, *The Diving Bell and the Butterfly*

Actor in a Leading Role
George Clooney, *Michael Clayton*
Daniel Day-Lewis, *There Will Be Blood*
Johnny Depp, *Sweeney Todd*
Tommy Lee Jones, *In the Valley of Elah*
Viggo Mortensen, *Eastern Promises*

Actor in a Supporting Role
Casey Affleck, *The Assassination of Jesse James by the Coward Robert Ford*
Javier Bardem, *No Country for Old Men*
Philip Seymour Hoffman, *Charlie Wilson's War*
Hal Holbrook, *Into the Wild*
Tom Wilkinson, *Michael Clayton*

Actress in a Leading Role
Cate Blanchett, *Elizabeth: The Golden Age*
Julie Christie, *Away from Her*
Marion Cotillard, *La Vie en Rose*
Laura Linney, *The Savages*
Ellen Page, *Juno*

Appendix-453

Actress in a Supporting Role
Cate Blanchett, *I'm Not There*
Ruby Dee, *American Gangster*
Saoirse Ronan, *Atonement*
Amy Ryan, *Gone Baby Gone*
Tilda Swinton, *Michael Clayton*

Animated Feature
Persepolis
Ratatouille
Surf's Up

Art Direction
American Gangster
Atonement
The Golden Compass
Sweeney Todd
There Will Be Blood

Cinematography
The Assassination of Jesse James by the Coward Robert Ford
Atonement: Seamus McGarvey
The Diving Bell and the Butterfly
No Country for Old Men
There Will Be Blood

Costume Design
Across the Universe
Atonement
Elizabeth: The Golden Age
La Vie en Rose
Sweeney Todd

Documentary Feature
No End in Sight
Operation Homecoming: Writing the Wartime Experience
Sicko
Taxi to the Dark Side
War/Dance

Documentary Short Subject
Freeheld
La Corona (The Crown)
Salim Baba
Sari's Mother

Film Editing
The Bourne Ultimatum
The Diving Bell and the Butterfly
Into the Wild
No Country for Old Men
There Will Be Blood

Foreign-Language Film
Beaufort (Israel)
The Counterfeiters (Austria)
Katyn (Poland)
Mongol (Kazakhstan)
12 (Russia)

Makeup
La Vie en Rose
Norbit
Pirates of the Caribbean: At World's End

Original Score
Atonement
The Kite Runner
Michael Clayton
Ratatouille
3:10 to Yuma

Original Song
"Falling Slowly," *Once*
"Happy Working Song," *Enchanted*
"Raise It Up," *August Rush*
"So Close," *Enchanted*
"That's How You Know," *Enchanted*

Screenplay—Adapted

Christopher Hampton, *Atonement*
Sarah Polley, *Away from Her*
Ronald Harwood, *The Diving Bell and the Butterfly*
Joel Coen & Ethan Coen, ***No Country for Old Men***
Paul Thomas Anderson, *There Will Be Blood*

Screenplay—Original

Diablo Cody, Juno
Nancy Oliver, *Lars and the Real Girl*
Tony Gilroy, *Michael Clayton*
Brad Bird, *Ratatouille*
Tamara Jenkins, *The Savages*

Short Film—Animated

I Met the Walrus
Madame Tutli-Putli
Même les Pigeons Vont Au Paradis
My Love (Moya Lyubov)
Peter & the Wolf

Short Film—Live Action

At Night
Il Supplente (The Substitute)
Le Mozart des Pickpockets (The Mozart of Pickpockets)
Tanghi Argentini
The Tonto Woman

Sound Editing

The Bourne Ultimatum
No Country for Old Men
Ratatouille
There Will Be Blood
Transformers

Appendix-456

Sound Mixing
The Bourne Ultimatum
No Country for Old Men
Ratatouille
3:10 to Yuma
Transformers

Honorary Oscar: *Robert Boyle*

2008'S TOP MOVIES*

	Movie	Released	Total Gross
1.	The Dark Knight	7/18/08	$527,822,000
2.	Iron Man	5/2/08	$318,298,000
3.	Indiana Jones and the Kingdom of the Crystal Skull	5/23/08	$317,011,000
4.	Hancock	7/4/08	$227,946,000
5.	WALL-E	6/27/08	$222,449,000
6.	Kung Fu Panda	6/6/08	$215,395,000
7.	Dr. Seuss' Horton Hears a Who!	3/14/08	$154,444,000
8.	Sex and the City	5/30/08	$152,596,000
9.	Mamma Mia!	7/18/08	$143,536,000
10.	The Chronicles of Narnia: Prince Caspian	5/16/08	$141,596,000
11.	The Incredible Hulk	6/13/08	$134,500,000
12.	Wanted	6/27/08	$134,294,000
13.	Get Smart	6/20/08	$130,246,000
14.	Tropic Thunder	8/15/08	$110,080,000
15.	The Mummy: Tomb of the Dragon Emperor	8/1/08	$102,176,000
16.	Journey to the Center of the Earth	7/11/08	$101,110,000
17.	Step Brothers	7/25/08	$100,469,000
18.	You Don't Mess with the Zohan	6/6/08	$100,019,000
19.	10,000 B.C.	3/7/08	$94,771,000
20	Eagle Eye	9/26/08	$87,903,000
21.	Pineapple Express	8/8/08	$87,341,000
22.	21	3/28/08	$81,159,000
23.	What Happens in Vegas	5/9/08	$80,200,000
24.	Jumper	2/15/08	$80,163,000
25.	Cloverfield	1/18/08	$80,034,000

*as of November 1, 2008

2008 TONY AWARDS

Presented by the American Theatre Wing
June 15, 2008

Best Play
August: Osage County
Rock 'n' Roll
The Seafarer
The 39 Steps

Best Musical
Cry-Baby
In The Heights
Passing Strange
Xanadu

Best Book of a Musical
Cry-Baby, Mark O'Donnell and Thomas Meehan
In The Heights, Quiara Alegra Hudes
***Passing Strange**, Stew*
Xanadu, Douglas Carter Beane

Best Original Score (Music and/or Lyrics)
Written for the Theatre
Cry-Baby, music & lyrics: David Javerbaum & Adam Schlesinger
In The Heights, music & lyrics by Lin-Manuel Miranda
The Little Mermaid, music by Alan Menken,
   lyrics by Howard Ashman and Glenn Slater
Passing Strange, music by Stew and Heidi Rodewald, lyrics by Stew

Best Revival of a Play
Boeing-Boeing
The Homecoming
Les Liaisons Dangereuses
Macbeth

Best Play
August: Osage County
Rock 'n' Roll
The Seafarer
The 39 Steps

Best Musical
Cry-Baby
In The Heights
Passing Strange
Xanadu

Best Book of a Musical
Cry-Baby, Mark O'Donnell and Thomas Meehan
In The Heights, Quiara Alegra Hudes
***Passing Strange*, Stew**
Xanadu, Douglas Carter Beane

Best Original Score (Music and/or Lyrics) Written for the Theatre
Cry-Baby, music & lyrics: David Javerbaum & Adam Schlesinger
In The Heights, music & lyrics by Lin-Manuel Miranda
The Little Mermaid, music by Alan Menken,
   lyrics by Howard Ashman and Glenn Slater
Passing Strange, music by Stew and Heidi Rodewald, lyrics by Stew

Best Revival of a Play
Boeing-Boeing
The Homecoming
Les Liaisons Dangereuses
Macbeth

Best Revival of a Musical
Grease
Gypsy
Rodgers & Hammerstein's South Pacific
Sunday in the Park with George

Best Performance by a Leading Actor in a Play
Ben Daniels, *Les Liaisons Dangereuses*
Laurence Fishburne, *Thurgood*
Mark Rylance, *Boeing-Boeing*
Rufus Sewell, *Rock 'n' Roll*
Patrick Stewart, *Macbeth*

Best Performance by a Leading Actress in a Play
Eve Best, *The Homecoming*
Deanna Dunagan, August: *Osage County*
Kate Fleetwood, *Macbeth*
S. Epatha Merkerson, *Come Back, Little Sheba*
Amy Morton, August: *Osage County*

Best Performance by a Leading Actor in a Musical
Daniel Evans, *Sunday in the Park with George*
Lin-Manuel Miranda, *In The Heights*
Stew, *Passing Strange*
Paulo Szot, *Rodgers & Hammerstein's South Pacific*
Tom Wopat, *A Catered Affair*

Best Performance by a Leading Actress in a Musical
Kerry Butler, *Xanadu*
Patti LuPone, *Gypsy*
Kelli O'Hara, *Rodgers & Hammerstein's South Pacific*
Faith Prince, *A Catered Affair*
Jenna Russell, *Sunday in the Park with George*

Best Performance by a Featured Actor in a Play
Bobby Cannavale, *Mauritius*
Raul Esparza, *The Homecoming*
Conleth Hill, *The Seafarer*
Jim Norton, *The Seafarer*
David Pittu, *Is He Dead?*

Best Performance by a Featured Actress in a Play
Sinead Cusack, *Rock 'n' Roll*
Mary McCormack, *Boeing-Boeing*
Laurie Metcalf, *November*
Martha Plimpton, *Top Girls*
Rondi Reed, *August: Osage County*

Best Performance by a Featured Actor in a Musical
Daniel Breaker, *Passing Strange*
Danny Burstein, *Rodgers & Hammerstein's South Pacific*
Robin De Jesus, *In The Heights*
Christopher Fitzgerald, *Young Frankenstein*
Boyd Gaines, *Gypsy*

Best Performance by a Featured Actress in a Musical
de'Adre Aziza, *Passing Strange*
Laura Benanti, *Gypsy*
Andrea Martin, *Young Frankenstein*
Olga Merediz, *In The Heights*
Loretta Ables Sayre, *Rodgers & Hammerstein's South Pacific*

Best Scenic Design of a Play
Peter McKintosh, *The 39 Steps*
Scott Pask, *Les Liaisons Dangereuses*
Todd Rosenthal, *August: Osage County*
Anthony Ward, *Macbeth*

Best Scenic Design of a Musical
David Farley and Timothy Bird &
 The Knifedge Creative Network, *Sunday in the Park with George*
Anna Louizos, *In The Heights*
Robin Wagner, *Young Frankenstein*
Michael Yeargan, *Rodgers & Hammerstein's South Pacific*

Best Costume Design of a Play
Gregory Gale, *Cyrano de Bergerac*
Rob Howell, *Boeing-Boeing*
Katrina Lindsay, *Les Liaisons Dangereuses*
Peter McKintosh, *The 39 Steps*

Best Costume Design of a Musical
David Farley, *Sunday in the Park with George*
Martin Pakledinaz, *Gypsy*
Paul Tazewell, *In The Heights*
Catherine Zuber, *Rodgers & Hammerstein's South Pacific*

Best Lighting Design of a Play
Kevin Adams, *The 39 Steps*
Howard Harrison, *Macbeth*
Donald Holder, *Les Liaisons Dangereuses*
Ann G. Wrightson, *August: Osage County*

Best Lighting Design of a Musical
Ken Billington, *Sunday in the Park with George*
Howell Binkley, *In The Heights*
Donald Holder, *Rodgers & Hammerstein's South Pacific*
Natasha Katz, *The Little Mermaid*

Best Sound Design of a Play
Simon Baker, *Boeing-Boeing*
Adam Cork, *Macbeth*
Ian Dickinson, *Rock 'n' Roll*
Mic Pool, *The 39 Steps*

Best Sound Design of a Musical
Acme Sound Partners, *In The Heights*
Sebastian Frost, *Sunday in the Park with George*
Scott Lehrer, *Rodgers & Hammerstein's South Pacific*
Dan Moses Schreier, *Gypsy*

Best Direction of a Play
Maria Aitken, *The 39 Steps*
Conor McPherson, *The Seafarer*
Anna D. Shapiro, *August: Osage County*
Matthew Warchus, *Boeing-Boeing*

Best Direction of a Musical
Sam Buntrock, *Sunday in the Park with George*
Thomas Kail, *In The Heights*
Arthur Laurents, *Gypsy*
Bartlett Sher, *Rodgers & Hammerstein's South Pacific*

Best Choreography
Rob Ashford, *Cry-Baby*
Andy Blankenbuehler, *In The Heights*
Christopher Gattelli, *Rodgers & Hammerstein's South Pacific*
Dan Knechtges, *Xanadu*

Best Orchestrations
Jason Carr, *Sunday in the Park with George*
Alex Lacamoire & Bill Sherman, *In The Heights*
Stew & Heidi Rodewald, *Passing Strange*
Jonathan Tunick, *A Catered Affair*

Special Tony Award
Robert Russell Bennett (1894–1981)

Special Tony Award for Lifetime Achievement in the Theatre
Stephen Sondheim

Regional Theatre Tony Award
Chicago Shakespeare Theater

Newsweek, published continuously for more than seven decades, has the most extensive global network of all newsweeklies, with a total of 12 editions in more than 190 countries, and a worldwide audience of over 23 million. The magazine holds more prestigious National Magazine Awards, given by the American Society of Magazine Editors (ASME), than any other newsweekly. *Newsweek* offers comprehensive coverage of world events with a global network of correspondents, reporters, and editors covering national and international affairs, business, science and technology, society, and arts and entertainment. In addition to popular regular departments like "Periscope," *Newsweek* also features respected commentators such as Jonathan Alter, Ellis Cose, Anna Quindlen, Jane Bryant Quinn, Robert J. Samuelson, Stuart Taylor Jr., and George Will. Newsweek.com offers the weekly magazine online, daily news updates, Web-only columns from *Newsweek*'s top writers, photo galleries, audio and video reports from correspondents, podcasts, mobile content, and archives.

Devin Gordon is a Senior Editor in Newsweek's "Periscope" department. In 2006, he was named Deputy Editor of the Arts and Entertainment department as well as the magazine's television critic. Previously, he was a senior writer covering film, sports, and pop culture. He was part of the Newsweek reporting team for three recent Olympics, including the Salt Lake City winter games in 2002, the Athens summer games in 2004, and the Turin winter games in 2006. Gordon joined the magazine in 1998 after graduating from Duke University, and since then has written extensively about movies, music, sports, and pop culture trends. Gordon lives in New York City.

Get Newsweek for up to 86% off the Cover Price!

Subscribe Now for Just $25
To order visit
www.nwsub.com/periscope